Understanding Central America

Understanding Central America

Global Forces, Rebellion, and Change

FOURTH EDITION

John A. Booth
University of North Texas

Christine J. Wade
Washington College

Thomas W. Walker
Ohio University

Westview Press

A Member of the Perseus Books Group

Published in the United States of America by Westview Press, A Member of the Perseus Books Group, 5500 Central Avenue, Boulder, Colorado 80301–2877.

Find us on the World Wide Web at www.westviewpress.com

Westview Press books are available at special discounts for bulk purchases in the United States by corporations, institutions, and other organizations. For more information, please contact the Special Markets Department at the Perseus Books Group, 11 Cambridge Center, Cambridge, MA 02142, or call (617) 252-5298 or (800) 255-1514, or email special.markets@perseusbooks.com.

Library of Congress Cataloging-in-Publication Data

Booth, John A.

Understanding Central America : global forces, rebellion, and change / John A. Booth, Christine J. Wade, Thomas W. Walker. — 4th ed.

p. cm.

Includes bibliographical references and index.

ISBN-13 978-0-8133-4195-8

ISBN 0-8133-4195-7 (pbk. : alk. paper) 1. Central America—History—1951–1979. 2. Central America—History—1979– . 3. Political stability—Central America—History—20th century. 4. Democratization—Central America. 5. Social conflict—Central America—History—20th century. 6. Revolutions—Central America—History—20th century. I. Wade, Christine J. II. Walker, Thomas W., 1940– . III. Title.

F1439.B66 2006

972.805—dc22

2005004456

The paper used in this publication meets the requirements of the American National Standard for Permanence of Paper for Printed Library Materials Z39.48–1984.

10 9 8 7 6 5 4 3 2 1

To Patti,
to Greg, and
to Anne

Contents

Tables and Illustrations

Tables

Photographs

Map

Preface to the Fourth Edition

We have completely revised and reorganized this edition of *Understanding Central America* from the third edition, and a new co-author, Christine J. Wade, has joined us. Multiple transformations of the region—the formal democratization of several countries, the end of several civil wars, and the adoption of new neoliberal economic development models—required a major rearrangement of the book. We have moved the theoretical materials on dependency and regime change into a new Chapter 2. Our framework now more explicitly ties both economic development and political transformation to the evolution of Central America's role in the changing international economic system. Country Chapters 4 through 8 have expanded to incorporate more historical background (from prior editions' Chapter 4). There are now separate chapters on each country, each updated through 2004. We have added a completely new chapter on the public opinion and political participation of Central Americans and how these affect political support and may thus affect the prospects for democratic consolidation.

Acknowledgments

We owe many people and institutions in the United States and Central America our sincerest thanks for their time, support, encouragement, and patience. For support that has gotten us into the field during the years when our book was written and updated, we thank the Latin American Studies Association; the Advisory Council on Church and Society of the United Presbyterian Church, USA; the Inter-American Dialogue; the International Human Rights Law Group; the Washington Office on Latin America; Hemispheric Initiatives; Alice McGrath; the University of North Texas; the Heinz Foundation, University of Pittsburgh; Ohio University; Washington College; and The Carter Center. For collaboration in Central America we gratefully acknowledge the assistance of the Facultad Latinoamericana de Ciencias Sociales (FLACSO) and the Centro Superior Universitaria Centroamericana (CSUCA) in Costa Rica, the Asociación y Estudios Sociales (ASIES) in Guatemala, and the Confederación Nacional de Profesionales (CONAPRO) Héroes y Mártires in Nicaragua. For generously granting Thomas Walker the right to reuse some material he had originally written for a Presbyterian Church publication (incorporated into Chapters 1 through 3 and Chapter 10), we are indebted to the United Presbyterian Church, USA. We gratefully acknowledge the cooperation of the U.S. Agency for International Development and Mitch Seligson, then of the University of Pittsburgh, now at Vanderbilt, for providing us the public domain survey research data employed in Chapter 9.

Several dozen kind folks in Central America have granted us interviews and helped us collect data on their countries, without which this book would have been completely impossible to write. E. Bradford Burns, Richard E. Clinton, Jr., Sung Ho Kim, Harold Molineu, Mitch Seligson, and some anonymous reviewers read portions of the manuscript at different stages in its evolution and made valuable suggestions. Our thanks to Cece Hannah for typing the first edition manuscript, to Steve Lohse for research assistance on the second edition, and to Mehmet Gurses and Nikolai Petrovsky for research assistance on the fourth edition. Over time several editors at Westview Press both encouraged us and remained patient as we labored on successive editions. We especially thank Miriam Gilbert and Barbara Ellington for their assistance and guidance during work on the first two editions, Karl Yambert and Jennifer Chen for their efforts on the third, and Steve Catalano and Kay Mariea for their help with the fourth.

John A. Booth
Christine J. Wade
Thomas W. Walker

Understanding Central America

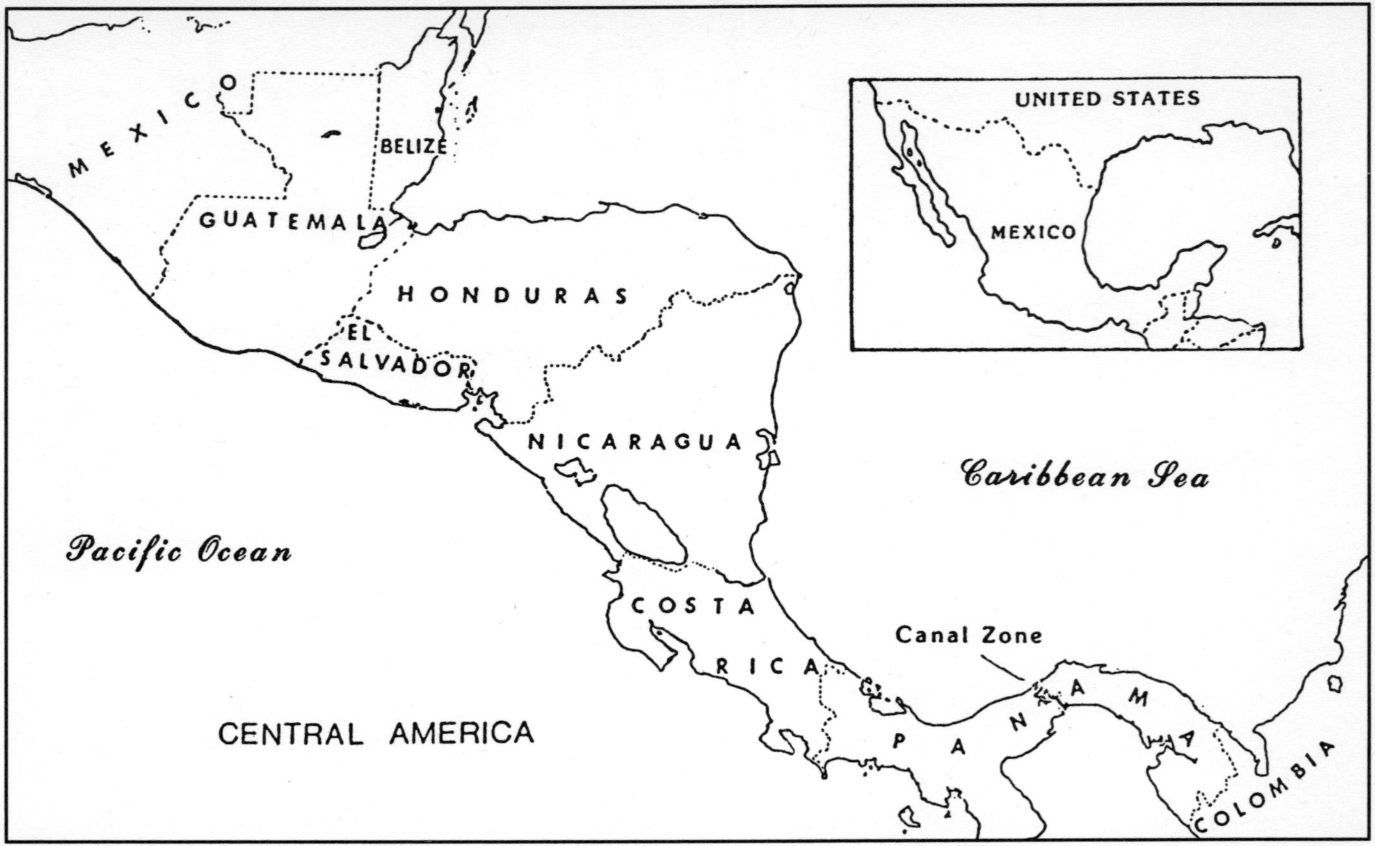

Reprinted from Harold Molineu, *U.S. Policy Toward Latin America: From Regionalism to Globalism*, 2nd ed. (Boulder: Westview Press, 1990, p. 4), Copyright © Westview Press, 1990.

1

Crisis and Transformation

Central America lies so close to the United States that from Miami or Houston one can fly to Managua or Guatemala City more quickly than to Chicago or Boston. The region's five countries, each profoundly shaped by proximity and trade with the United States, had roughly 20 million people in 1975 and attracted little of the world's attention, but that was about to change. For two decades after World War II, the area had seemed a placid geopolitical backwater of the United States. Despite its mostly despotic regimes, Central America was poor but friendly to U.S. interests. The region was making moderate progress under an economic strategy that gave development planning roles to its governments and the regional common market. Yet in the early 1960s revolutionary groups appeared, followed by economic crises and political unrest in the 1970s. Central America then surged into world headlines as its governments, aided by the United States, cracked down on rapidly multiplying opposition. By the late 1970s waves of state terror, revolutionary insurrection, counterrevolution, and external meddling engulfed the region, taking over 300,000 lives, turning millions into refugees, and devastating economies and infrastructures.

The first two editions of *Understanding Central America* focused on the tidal wave of violence during the 1970s and 1980s and tried to explain why great revolutionary movements wracked three Central American countries while the other two remained relatively politically stable.[1] We argued, based on scholarly theories of revolution, that grievances arose from regionwide economic problems and from the political repression of mobilized demands for reform. When regimes in Nicaragua, Guatemala, and El Salvador violently refused to accommodate these demands, their opponents and would-be reformers coalesced and radicalized into revolutionary political opposition. In Nicaragua insurrection culminated in a rebel victory and eleven years of social revolution under the Sandinistas. In El Salvador and Guatemala civil war resulted in protracted stalemates eventually followed by negotiated peace and a significant alteration of the status quo. In striking contrast, political stability—while threatened—prevailed in Honduras and Costa Rica. Their governments undertook modest economic and political reforms and kept repression at moderate levels.

External actors, especially the United States, struggled to shape these events by providing political and material resources to the political actors. The United States worked hard, devoting enormous diplomatic and political energy and spending several billion dollars trying to determine winners and losers locally and affect institutions and policy. This outside manipulation of Central American politics profoundly affected all five countries and became most visible in the countries at war, where it intensified and prolonged their conflicts.

In the third edition of this book we expanded our focus to explain regime changes in the region—whether arising from revolutionary impulses or those managed by elites to prevent revolution. It struck us that by the late 1990s each Central American nation, starting from different regime types and following sharply divergent paths, had arrived at one common regime type—a sort of minimalist electoral democracy. While hardly ideal democracies in execution, these civilian-led, constitutional, electoral regimes were sharply different from and less abusive than most governments in place in the 1970s.[2] This convergence on the same type of governance in five adjacent countries could hardly have been coincidental. We concluded that the regime change process regionwide resulted from the interaction of global economic and political forces with the politicoeconomic realities and actions of internal political actors.[3] Certain contextual forces and actors, we argued, pushed Central America's key players to settle on formal electoral democracy as their new preferred regime type, rather than returning to their traditions of military or personalistic authoritarianism.

By 2004 as we were writing this fourth edition, Central America's political violence and repression were well below their civil war levels, human rights performance was somewhat better than in prior decades, and the region's five major nations practiced at least a minimalist formal electoral democracy. The Cold War had ended and U.S. fears of Communist expansion in the hemisphere had thus subsided to non-crisis levels. This had persuaded the United States to live with leftist parties participating openly in governance in the isthmus, as long as the left did not win actual control anywhere. Again there was moderate economic progress in at least part of the region, which now employed a new strategy of economic development, neoliberalism, that much more openly than ever exposed Central America to the larger world economy. With its political systems thus moved toward electoral democracy, its economies liberalized, and the anticommunist geopolitical imperative of prior decades receding, Central America had gradually faded from the world's headlines.

But had the region in the early 2000s resumed its prior status of a placid geopolitical backwater of the United States, or had it merely slipped from the sight of the media? Now that the region's epochal spasm of violence had receded and democracy, even in a limited form, had developed, should one at this juncture even pay much attention to Central America? The answer, we believe, is very definitely yes. One reason why Central America remains important lies in that very wave of extreme violence and its diminution, and in the common adoption of formal electoral democracy throughout the region. These large waves of shared turmoil and change across several nations allow us to understand certain great forces beyond the nation-state. These forces have compelled diverse sets of such apparently independent actors as the local elites of five Central American nations to reach common outcomes by following shared plans not entirely of their own devising. While there is much worth knowing about Central America in its own right, the region's experience with these greater meta-national forces may tell us much about how individual nations and groups of nations interact with the world environment.

Another reason why Central America should retain our attention resides in its ongoing poverty. An estimate for 1999 put the number of direly poor Central Americans at around 20 million—two-thirds of the region's populace.[4] Despite decades of turmoil, change, and realignment, the misery and dismal prospects of millions of its citizens had thus remained remarkably stable. Old sources of poverty were persisting and new ones had developed as Central America's economies opened themselves up to the world through neoliberalism. Examining how both global and local forces had affected Central America's poor will tell us something about how capitalism had evolved and functions in Latin America and the developing world.

A third reason to study Central America is that, as if persistent poverty were not problem enough, its societies and political systems must cope with daunting new and old social and political pathologies. The end of civil wars and military and police reforms, paradoxically, failed to improve the security of many citizens. Police reform in Guatemala and El Salvador caused crime waves as cashiered, corrupt former policemen became well-organized gangsters while the reformed new police lacked the resources to counter them effectively. Youths repatriated to Central America from U.S. inner cities brought with them criminal gangs that were soon the scourge of several countries. Security forces responded to youth gangs and to impoverished street children alike with draconian violence. Assassinations of political figures remained disconcertingly common in several countries. Newspapers regionwide reported a stream of political corruption scandals, one of which landed a former Nicaraguan president, Arnoldo Alemán, in prison. Examining these problems can illumine the local and global forces behind them and the raft of difficulties that the region's civilian political leaders must overcome for democracy to consolidate and for economic development to ameliorate poverty.

A shorthand term for the big forces that act on Central America is *globalization*. Globalization refers to compelling systemic forces that act above and beyond the level of the nation-state, and above and through international institutions, bypassing national borders to affect local actors. Global forces have pressed on the political and economic actors of Central America and pushed them in similar directions and at the same times. What are these global forces? World-scale economic forces generate markets, commodity price cycles, and market crises that shape domestic economies and determine the success or misery of nations and of the rich and poor within nations. Changes in the structure of the global economy, trade, and class systems force realignments of domestic economic organization and classes. New ways of organizing the world economic and political arenas produce new ideologies to justify institutions and new operating policies for institutions. These globalized belief systems and policies constrain local actors by favoring some, weakening others, and reshaping national institutions to fit global needs and preferences. We believe Central America's revolutions, regime changes, economic development strategies, evolving classes, worsening social problems, and persistent poverty in recent decades all reveal the impact of the global upon the local.

The "Central America" upon which we focus in this book consists of Guatemala, El Salvador, Honduras, Nicaragua, and Costa Rica.[5] We will not address Belize and Panama individually. Although Belize is technically Central American, that English-speaking microstate only became independent from Great Britain in 1981 and has a history fairly distinct from the region's other states. Panama, though often lumped with the other countries of the region, is technically outside Central America. Its pre-Columbian indigenous cultures were South American, and from the beginning of the national period until 1903, Panama was an integral (though poor) part of the South American republic of Colombia. "The five," however, share a common political heritage from the colonial period, during which Spain administered them as a unit. During the early national period (1823–1838) they formed a single state called the United Provinces of Central America. In the late nineteenth century, several ill-fated attempts at reunification occurred. In the 1960s the five joined to form a common market. More recent unification efforts include a common regional parliament and shared trade agreements with the United States. Out of this history comes a sense of Central American national identity and, among a surprisingly large segment of the region's educated elite, a hope that someday the larger homeland might be reunited.

Central America, as defined above, is small. Its combined land mass of 431,812 square kilometers is barely larger than that of California (404,975 square kilometers). Moreover, its estimated total 2004 population of around 36.3 million was similar to California's. The country with the smallest surface area, El Salvador, is smaller even than Maryland, whereas the largest, Nicaragua, is barely larger than Iowa. In population, the five varied in 2004 between a low of 4.1 million in Costa Rica (similar to South Carolina) and a high of 12.6 million in Guatemala (similar to Ohio).[6] Central America's population has doubled since the 1970s, but the rates of population growth have diminished (Table 1.1) due to rapid urban growth and outmigration to the United States and elsewhere (Appendix Table A.2). Central America's natural resources are modest. However, had different political systems and economic models prevailed across Central America during the nineteenth and twentieth centuries, there certainly would have been enough arable land to provide adequate sustenance for the present population, while at the same time producing some primary products for export. Yet responses to international market demands by the region's elite led to land ownership concentration, an overemphasis on export, and inadequate production of consumer food staples. Instead of growing beans, corn, rice, plantain, and cassava for local consumption, big landholders normally concentrated on lucrative exports such as coffee, cotton, sugar, and beef. Central America also has a variety of, but not abundant, mineral resources. One possible recent exception is Guatemala, with its nickel and its modest oil reserves. Historically, Nicaragua was once viewed as the logical site for a future trans-isthmian waterway. However, the building of the Panama Canal and the development of modern air and surface communication have rendered that potential unlikely to be developed.

Central America's main resource is clearly its people. Contrary to the ethnic stereotypes often held by North Americans, Central Americans are as hardworking as most other humans on this planet. To verify that statement, one need only observe the bustle of most Central American cities at daybreak, or follow the activity of a typical Central American through the long hours of his or her daily routine. Central Americans are also remarkably resilient. The strength with which they have faced more than their share of hardship—including intense repression, occasional civil war, foreign occupation, and such frequent natural disasters as volcanic eruptions, earthquakes, hurricanes, mudslides, and floods—impresses outside observers, especially those used to fairly safe natural and human-made environments.

Despite their similarities of geography and juxtaposition to the world outside the isthmus, there are some sharp differences among the Central American nations (Table 1.1). For example, in economic development, Costa Rica in 2000 had a gross domestic product (GDP) per capita (a comparative measure of overall economic activity per citizen) of $5,870. (For comparison, U.S. GDP per capita then was around seven to eight times higher than Costa Rica's.) Costa Rica's GDP per capita was almost a third higher than its nearest rival in the region, El Salvador. And with 3.3 times more GDP per capita, Costa Rica's economy in 2000 far outperformed those of Honduras and Nicaragua, the region's poorest countries.

Are such stark economic differences inevitable in the region? Not at all. Five decades ago, the countries of Central America had much more similar levels of economic activity than they do today. But as Table 1.1 reveals, overall national economic activity changes from 1950 to 2000 differed enormously. While Costa Rica's GDP per capita rose 236 percent over this period and Guatemala's rose 181 percent, Nicaragua's actually declined by 16 percent. Masked by the data's fifty-year span is something that makes this startling fact even worse: Nicaragua's GDP per capita actually doubled from 1950 to the early 1970s but was subsequently beaten back to pre-1950s levels by war, revolution, deliberate international strangulation, and disinvestment by its elites. During these same five decades Costa Rica's government, a politically stable democracy, pursued a development strategy that invested in its citizens' human development (especially education and health care) more than any other country in the isthmus. Thus Costa Ricans weathered the half-century's storms much better and emerged in better shape than their neighbors, enjoying higher prosperity, literacy, and life expectancy and much lower rates of working children and infant mortality than their neighbors. Recent economic growth rates somewhat mirror the five-decade history of economic development, with the more prosperous countries growing faster and the poorer ones doing worse (Table 1.1).

These comparisons of economic change strongly argue against the inevitability of poverty, at least within Central America itself. Even starting out poor and with scarce resources, Costa Rica's development strategy and democratic government produced great success. And Honduras, the poorest country in the region in 1950 and governed largely by its armed forces until 1985, achieved the region's second highest levels of overall investment and government spending on social programs. Thus by 2000 Honduras managed to more than double its average economic activity level and to do so despite a fourfold population increase.[7] In dismaying contrast, Nicaragua, the nation most torn by political violence, first boomed economically but then regressed through the ravages of insurrection, revolution, economic embargo, and a second civil war. Choices made by Guatemala's leaders over five decades have kept a third of its population illiterate, left life expectancy the lowest and infant mortality the highest in the region, and created the circumstances in which over a quarter of children ten to 14 years old work—all this despite a 181 percent increase in GDP per capita. These contrasting facts reveal that local political and economic elites, even though constrained by

TABLE 1.1 BASIC SOCIOECONOMIC DATA ON CENTRAL AMERICAN COUNTRIES, *C.* 2000

	Costa Rica	*El Salvador*	*Guatemala*	*Honduras*	*Nicaragua*
Gross domestic product per capita GDP/capita, 2000 (in constant 1996 U.S. $)					
	5,870	4,435	3,914	2,049	1,767
Percent growth rate of GDP/capita, 2002					
	1.0	0.4	–.06	.06	–1.5
Percent change in GDP/capita (constant US dollars), from 1950 to 2000					
	236	114	181	113	–16
Percent of indigenous population					
	0.8	7.0	66.0	15.0	5.0
Percent of Afro-origin population					
	2.0	–	–	5.0	13.0
Percent self-reported adult literacy, *c.* 2000					
	89	80	65	82	77
Percent of children ages 10–14 who work					
	3.5	8.4	27.7	15.5	12.2
Life expectancy, 2002					
	78	70	66	66	69
Infant mortality per 1,000 live births, 2002					
	9	33	36	32	32

SOURCES: David E. Ferranti, et al., *Inequality in Latin America and the Caribbean: Breaking with History?* Advance Conference Edition (Washington, DC: International Bank for Reconstruction and Development/The World Bank, October 2003), Tables 3.1, A.26, B.3; Alan Heston, Robert Summers, and Bettina Aten, *Penn World Table Version 6.1*, Center for International Comparisons at the University of Pennsylvania (CICUP), October 2002; Interamerican Development Bank, Departamento Regional de Operaciones Región II, *Situación económica y perspectivas, Istmo Centroamericano y República Dominicana* (Washington, DC: May 2004), pp. i–v; Interamerican Development Bank, country notes, www.iadb.org/exr/country/, accessed June 14, 2004.

global forces and their own resources, had much to say about economic development and human welfare outcomes.

Even well-intentioned Central America elites, however, now face tough domestic and global obstacles. Table 1.1 highlights other characteristics of the population of some Central American countries that pose problems. Guatemala, for instance, would long have to struggle with the question of how to integrate the approximately two-thirds of the population that is indigenous and much of which speaks no Spanish. Similarly, El Salvador would continue to confront an enormous social headache posed by the country's high density of population.

By the late twentieth century, a powerful global constraint known as *neoliberalism* was confronting all Central American governments with important new rules and policy preferences promoted by powerful international economic actors. Under pressure from abroad in the 1980s and 1990s, all isthmian nations adopted neoliberal development strategies. No country in the region could deviate much from this austere capitalist development model that stingily discourages governmental social spending and human capital investment. In this neoliberal international environment, international trade and aid agreements blocked useful local policies that might improve the lot of the poor. At the beginning of the twenty-first century, no isthmian country could embrace even the social democratic development model that Costa Rica followed from 1950 to 1985, much less a revolutionary development model like Nicaragua's in the early 1980s.

It is true that, despite institutional barriers to human development that we will detail in later chapters, the human resources of the region are a very positive factor. The dignity, determination, and remarkable humor of the Central American people must be taken as a cause for hope. Poverty in Central America has not always been inevitable. But we believe it is increasingly difficult these days for isthmian governments to reduce poverty—even assuming national leaders and other elites might acquire a new determination to move in that direction.

In sum, Central America is small in size and population, poor in resources, and beset by problems. As the twenty-first century began, these problems affected mostly the region's own people, but held little threat for the region's Latin American neighbors and for the United States. Its small nation-states had been riven by severe internal strains that had quieted as the twenty-first century began. Isthmian countries were and are pushed and pulled by international pressures, both economic and political, that have as often intensified domestic strains as reduced them. The deepening U.S. involvement there in the 1980s and the efforts that numerous Latin American and European nations made to promote negotiated settlements to the various open and latent conflicts in the region at that time made these strains and conflicts worthy of serious study. Globalization and its contemporary effects on the region deepen our need to understand Central America and its place in the world.

U.S. interests and involvement in the isthmus have fluctuated widely over the past century and a half. A period of protracted U.S. inattention to Central America after World War II contrasted with intense U.S. concern in the late 1970s when Nicaraguans rebelled against the Somoza regime. Although they lavished attention on Central America, the Carter and Reagan administrations treated and described the region so differently as to bewilder many observers—including academic and policy experts, and especially Central Americans themselves. The first Bush administration remained powerfully involved in Central America but gave the region much less noisy public attention than had its predecessors.[8] With the Cold War clearly over and with problems in the Balkans and Middle East looming, the Clinton and second Bush administrations paid much less visible attention to Central America. But not having forgotten the isthmus entirely, they labored assiduously to keep neoliberal economic policies on track and block leftist parties from winning national elections in El Salvador and Nicaragua.

The waning of front-line U.S. attention as geopolitical winds have changed has not eliminated Central America's endemic poverty, its problems with development strategies and political order, or its constant need to adjust to evolving global forces. In our effort to help the reader understand Central America, we will examine these pressures and problems and consider the relative importance of evolving domestic and external influences on the region.

CENTRAL AMERICANS
(photo of baby in hammock by John Booth; other photos by Steve Cagan)

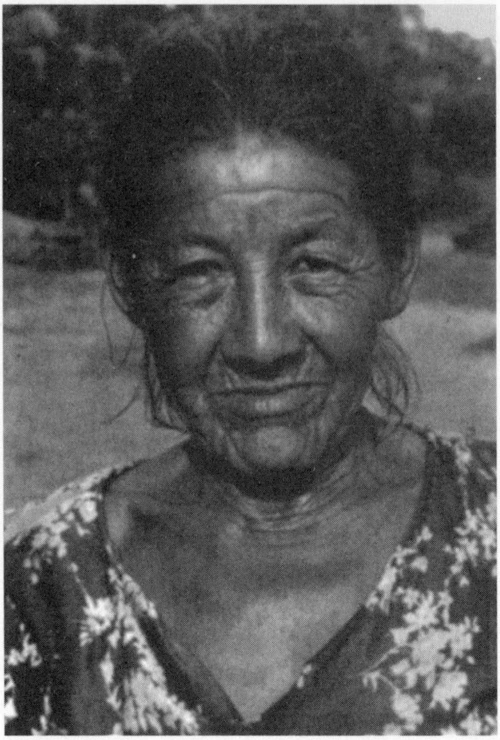

2

Global Forces and System Change in Central America

This chapter focuses on explanations for Central America's two principal problems of the recent past and likely future—political and economic system change. We believe these are interrelated, driven by common forces which we sketch out below and illustrate in subsequent chapters. Despite certain differences among them, Central American nations have marked commonalities of history, global context, and political and economic development. These similarities strongly suggest that much that affects Central America is part of a larger world dynamic. We contend that common forces led to Central America's rebellions, and that many of the same forces shaped the overall process of regime change that eventually led from authoritarianism toward electoral democracy and economic development strategies.[1]

The main thrust of our theory about system change in Central America comes from some fairly simple premises. First, the economic and the political arenas of human activity are very entangled. Much of what occurs in what we think of as the political world stems from economic forces, and political decisions affect economic outcomes. Second, nations—their governments, their economies, and thus their citizens—exist within an evolving international or global environment. Thus local problems can quickly become global problems and cycle back to the local. For example, a pipeline explosion in Iraq (a local problem) can quickly elevate world market oil price futures (a world problem), which in turn can raise fuel costs for consumers from Ohioans heating their homes in winter to bus and taxi owners in Honduras.

A third premise is that inequality exists within and between societies and that outcomes usually follow power. Within nations there exist hierarchies of minorities of elites (those who control resources and institutions) and non-elites (ordinary citizens who are less well off and less powerful). In the world of nations there are hierarchies of more powerful and weaker states. Elites from different societies often cooperate across national boundaries for mutual benefit, while non-elites find this more difficult. Elites from large nations often successfully cooperate with each other as individuals, through organizations, or through governments and multilateral institutions to promote their interests and those of their nations. The elites of small nations sometimes promote small-nation cooperation, but tend not to be as successful getting what they desire as those of powerful nations. Small nations' elites often find it very advantageous to cooperate with external elites, especially those representing large and powerful interests whether governmental or private. Increasingly, private global economic elites operating above the level of the nation-state have forged a world economy with new rules that favor global capital above the interest of even powerful nation-states.

Small nations such as those of Central America tend to be very sensitive to powerful global forces and actors. Their sensitivity to the political and economic world outside their borders derives from the very limits of their wealth, resources, populations, and military capacities. Central Americans, elites and non-elites alike, depend very heavily on what their countries export (commodities) and import (manufactured goods and energy), and have large, powerful, and often pushy neighbors. In this globalized world, problems move across borders quickly, and powerful actors—whether bigger states, international organizations, or even global non-state elites—can usually (not always) compel the compliance or cooperation of others.

After World War II, Central American economies faced economic stagnation and deep poverty that led the region's leaders to fear possible leftist revolutions. Isthmian governments thus collaborated on a regional economic integration scheme to promote capitalist economic growth and to preserve their regimes. Although successful for a while, that system crashed in world economic and domestic political crises during the 1970s and 1980s. Struggling to recover, Central American states—under heavy pressure from outside political and economic actors—eventually adopted a new, common economic development model. We seek to understand the region's persistent poverty, what governments have done and are doing about it, and how the region's economies fit into and move with the world economy.

The region has also experienced great political transformations directly related to the economic changes just mentioned. The political regimes prevalent until the 1970s, all but one authoritarian coalitions, passed through a long spasm of violence to become by the late 1980s and 1990s today's electoral democracies. Ironically, the very economic development programs designed to prevent leftist rebellions and preserve regimes actually promoted the violence that helped forge several new electoral democracies and change their ruling coalitions. Thus we also want to understand the region's political turmoil and its roots in economic change. We seek to explain the emergence of electoral democracy, and to explore its quality and prospects for the future.

We begin with a section examining Central America's poverty and its causes, with special attention to the economic situation of Central Americans at the beginning of the twenty-first century. We then inventory Central America's political regimes changes from 1970 onward and put forward a theory to explain them.

Poverty and Its Causes

Common sense interpretations of the causes of Central America's 1970s and 1980s turmoil often stress poverty. Indeed, poverty has always been a serious problem in the region. Even in relatively prosperous Costa Rica severe economic difficulties afflict many. Most experts and observers of the region recognize that poverty constitutes a persistent crisis of great human cost and cries out for social and economic reforms.

Common sense betrays us, however, if we attempt to explain Central America's 1970s–1980s rebellions as simply the product of poverty. Most of the world's population lives in poverty, yet rebellion by those worst off is rare. Poverty alone cannot account for the revolts in Nicaragua, El Salvador, or Guatemala. Indeed, if poverty alone were sufficient to cause rebellions, Honduras should have exploded with popular fury long before Nicaragua or El Salvador. We thus encounter the paradox that among Central America's five nations, the poorest historically (Honduras) and the richest (Costa Rica) have been the most stable, while those that had the most rapid industrialization and economic growth in the 1960s and 1970s have been the most unsettled.

To affirm that poverty alone did not cause Central America's rebellions, however, is not to say that poverty did not contribute. In fact, there is an important link between *becoming* impoverished and popular unrest. Large segments of Central America's poor and middle classes *became* much worse off during the 1970s and early 1980s. It was not the grinding, long-term deprivation of persistent poverty, but this change—impoverishment, declining living conditions—that motivated much of the region's unrest. In this section we focus on the nature of Central American poverty—the long-standing, grinding deprivation that affects large segments of the population. We summarize some of what this severe poverty means for the lives of contemporary Central Americans. In the following country chapters we will examine how impoverishment contributed to popular unrest and rebellion in the 1970s–1980s, and the prospects for its eventual abatement.

Poverty Measured

The human condition in Latin America generally lies somewhere between the extreme deprivation and despair of parts of Africa and the relative prosperity of North America, Europe, and Japan. Within Latin America, the economic indicators for Central America as a whole fall well below the median for the entire region. Latin America in 2000 had a gross domestic product (GDP) per capita of roughly $8,000, but not even relatively wealthy Costa Rica, with a GDP per capita of $5,870 approached that figure. The other four ranged from El Salvador, with a per capita GDP of $4,435 down to Nicaragua with $1,767.[2]

GDP per capita figures must be explained and put into context. First, for comparison, overall economic activity in the United States in 2000 (GDP per capita) was roughly nine times that of the average for Central America. Second, remember that the "average" indicated GDP in per capita figures is a statistic that distorts reality. GDP per capita divides annual total value of goods and services produced in a given country by the total population. In Central America, where a small minority controls most of the resources and earns most of the income, averaging the income of the wealthy with that of the rest of the population gives per capita GDP values that grossly overstate the real condition of most people. Indeed, the real income per capita of the poorer half of the population in most of Central America probably runs between $500 and $1,000 per year. Finally, while "average" Salvadorans thus struggled to make do on roughly one-twentieth of what the average U.S. citizen had to work with, they and other Central Americans faced prices for many consumer products—food, clothing, health care—almost as high as those in the United States.

Table 2.1 presents dramatic data about poverty's dynamics. Severe income inequality characterizes most of Central America. In four countries in the late 1990s almost two-thirds of the population lived on less than US$2 a day. Nine percent of Costa Ricans had incomes below the regional poverty line in the late 1990s, and from 17 to 47 percent of the rest of Central Americans' incomes were below the poverty line. More tellingly, in Costa Rica, Guatemala, and El Salvador in the 1990s the percent in poverty shrank during the 1990s, but in Honduras and Nicaragua it actually grew. Thus, in the region's two poorest countries, more rather than fewer people had become impoverished. Moreover, these data provide no assurance that those who remain trapped below the $2 per person per day poverty standard (constituting truly deep poverty) have not become poorer still.

Table 2.1 illustrates the importance of income distribution to poverty. Even in Costa Rica, with the region's highest national average income, the wealthiest tenth (decile) of the people on average earned 25 times more income than the poorest tenth. Compared to the rest of the region, however, Costa Rica's income ratio between the richest and poorest deciles appears modest. In sharp contrast, the next highest rich-to-poor income ratio was El Salvador's at 47, and the other countries'

TABLE 2.1 RECENT DYNAMICS OF POVERTY IN CENTRAL AMERICA

	Costa Rica	*El Salvador*	*Guatemala*	*Honduras*	*Nicaragua*
EDUCATIONAL INEQUALITY					
Percent of population attending school of					
ages 6–12	96	86	77	85	85
ages 13–17	66	70	53	52	62
ages 18–23	34	27	21	20	28
Mean years schooling (population over 25),					
In 1960	3.9	1.7	1.4	1.7	2.1
In 2000	6.0	4.5	3.1	4.1	4.4
Percent of population over 25 with no schooling, *c.* 2000	9.4	35.0	47.1	25.9	18.0
INCOME INEQUALITY					
Percent below poverty line, early 1990s	11.2	21.6	28.5	36.7	28.8
Percent below poverty line, late 1990s	9.2	16.8	25.1	47.2	47.3
Percent of children ages 10–14 who work	3.5	8.4	27.7	15.5	12.2
Share of individuals living on less than $2.00 US per day, late 1990s	30	63	68[a]	75	72
Ratio of incomes of wealthiest 10% to poorest 10% of population, *c.* 2000	25.1	47.4	63.3	49.1	56.2

SOURCES: David E. Ferranti, et al., *Inequality in Latin America and the Caribbean: Breaking with History?* Advance Conference Edition (Washington, DC: International Bank for Reconstruction and Development/The World Bank, October 2003), Tables A.42, A.23, A.12, A.26, 4.1; Alan Heston, Robert Summers, and Bettina Aten, *Penn World Table Version 6.1*, Center for International Comparisons at the University of Pennsylvania (CICUP), October 2002; Interamerican Development Bank, Departamento Regional de Operaciones Región II, *Situación económica y perspectivas, Istmo Centroamericano y República Dominicana* (Washington, DC, May 2004), pp. i–v; Interamerican Development Bank, country notes, www.iadb.org/exr/country/, accessed June 14, 2004.

[a]Authors' estimate based on percent below poverty line and GDP per capita from Ferranti et al.

ratios ranged upward to 63 in Guatemala. Thus the wealthiest decile of Guatemalans earned, on average, 63 times more income per person than those among the poorest decile. Put concretely, if we estimate not unreasonably that the poorest Guatemalans each eked out a living on $500 per year, the wealthiest tenth of Guatemalans would have enjoyed a comfortable $31,500 apiece.

Education can provide one way out of poverty, but data reveal the difficulties Central Americans confront. Self-reported illiteracy rates for 2000 ran from a low of 11 percent in Costa Rica to a high of 35 percent in Guatemala. Honduras, El Salvador, and Nicaragua registered 18 percent, 20 percent, and 23 percent illiteracy, respectively (Table 1.1). In addition, many who can read have only basic education because elite-dominated systems have long placed scant emphasis on public education. Table 2.1 illustrates this with data for 2000: Except for Costa Rica's 96 percent attendance rate, from a sixth to a fourth of Central Americans aged from six to twelve did not attend school. Secondary age attendance rates are worse. Attendance rates for higher education (ages 18 to 23) ranged from only one in five Guatemalans and Hondurans to a regional high of one in three Costa Ricans. The average total schooling of adults (over 25) was highest in Costa Rica at six years, and then ranged downward from 4.5 years in El Salvador to only 3.1 in Guatemala. Almost half of Guatemala's adult population and a third of El Salvador's had no schooling.

For the region as a whole, therefore, one may fairly say that the typical Central American is poor—meaning poorly fed, housed, and educated, and has little or no access to medical care or cultural and recreational opportunities.[3]

Basic food production illustrates the point. Land in the region is very inequitably distributed. Typically, the rich and powerful control the best land and on it grow export products rather than food staples. In a capitalist economy, this makes good sense to landowners because export products earn greater profits than domestically marketed staples. But this has over time allowed export producers to progressively buy up and concentrate land in fewer hands, and so countries produce fewer staples in relation to population. Meanwhile the prices of these scarcer staples rose inexorably with population growth and thus forced the common citizen to make do on less and cheaper food. At present, Central Americans generally eat very little animal protein, deriving their essential amino acids, instead, from corn and beans. But even these foods are expensive because costly imported staples have replaced insufficient domestic production.

Conditions and trends are somewhat better in public health. Especially since World War II, improved techniques against several communicable diseases have allowed international health organizations and Central American governments to reduce the frequency of certain killer diseases. This has lowered death rates and raised life expectancies, which in 2002 ranged from a regional mean of around 69–66 years in Guatemala and Honduras, 70 in El Salvador, and 69 in Nicaragua—to a respectable high of 78 in Costa Rica (Table 1.1). Costa Rica, whose governments excelled for decades in providing decent, low-cost health care to much of the populace, widely beat out its neighbors in reducing infant mortality. Costa Rica in 2002 reported 9 infant deaths per 1,000 live births (similar to advanced industrial countries) compared to the other four countries which reported around 33 infant deaths per 1,000.

Improved preventive medicine has extended the life span of Central Americans, but most still faced serious health problems as the twenty-first century began. Local hygiene normally remained poor. Most rural and many urban houses lacked interior plumbing, and many lacked even backyard latrines. Except for Costa Rica, the curative medical system was grossly inadequate. Private medical care—nearly as expensive in Central America as in the United States—lay mostly beyond the reach of many. Hospitals, doctors, and pharmaceuticals in most countries remained scarce, expensive, and usually consistently available only to the wealthy and a minority of the urban middle class. As a result, good health was largely a matter of privilege or luck.

High natural population growth rates exacerbate poverty. In 2000, annual population growth rates were 2.0 percent in El Salvador, 2.1 percent in Costa Rica, 2.5 percent in Honduras, and 2.6 percent in Guatemala and Nicaragua (Table 1.1). If Central America's current rates of population growth persist, the countries of the region will double in population every 30 to 40 years. The population grows rapidly for several reasons. Advances in public health have reduced death rates. Second, the median age has fallen into the mid teens (as opposed to around 30 in the United States) and placed more of the female population in childbearing age. Finally, high fertility is normally related to poverty and low levels of urbanization. While poverty persists, much of Central America has significantly urbanized in recent decades with around half the population living in cities and towns (more in Nicaragua) by the late 1990s.[4] Urbanization makes education more widely available to women and encourages wider use of birth control. The longer high growth rates persist, the more urgent and difficult they will make efforts to reduce social inequities and improve living conditions. However, the much higher population growth rates of previous decades have begun to tail off across the region.

The Causes of Poverty

Poverty in Central America is neither completely natural nor inevitable. Foreigners once argued that Central Americans were poor because they were racially inferior. For instance, one geography text used widely in U.S. primary schools a half century ago claimed that "except where white men have established plantations, the resources [of Central America] are poorly developed. Most of the Indians, mestizos, and negroes are poor and ignorant . . . few care to work hard. More white men are needed to start plantations and to fight tropical diseases."[5] Today we recognize such statements, also found in prominent encyclopedias of the same era, to be racist nonsense. Likewise, one cannot maintain that the region lacks sufficient resources to support its human population. El Salvador *is* overpopulated.

But Central America as a whole has enough good land not only to produce some primary products for export and foreign exchange but also to grow sufficient staples to feed its people. And though not exceptionally blessed in this regard, the region also has significant energy and mineral resources.

In fact, much of Central America's poverty is largely a human artifact—produced by exploitation of the many by the region's powerful upper classes as they operate within the larger world economic system. Powerful foreign interests often joined and supported Central America's local elites in this exploitative behavior. Evidence that it need not have been so—that human volition caused much of the region's poverty—leaps out of some of the data in Table 2.1 and Table 1.1. In this data, one repeatedly finds that Costa Rica has done better than its neighbors in economic growth, economic equality, poverty reduction, providing education and literacy, and promoting its citizens' health. Moreover, Costa Rica accomplished these things while also exporting agricultural commodities and having only modest resources. It also did so despite ranking only third in GDP per capita behind El Salvador and Guatemala in 1950. How did Costa Rica do so much better by its citizens than its four northern neighbors? The answer, we contend, stems from the political will of Costa Rican leaders. Even though operating in a disadvantageous economic context like the rest of Central American elites, Costa Rica's leaders decided to adopt and keep democracy, abolish the armed forces, moderate income inequality, and invest in education and health over the long haul. The leaders of the other nations did not make these choices, at least not consistently enough to do the job.

Dependency. What developed over time and accounts for much of the Central American economic system, was what many scholars call *dependency*.[6] Though there is some disagreement on specifics, most experts view dependency as a complex political, economic, and social phenomenon that retards the human development of the majority in certain privilege-dominated Third World countries with heavily externally oriented economies. In such countries, even during periods of rapid economic growth, the benefits of growth normally do not meaningfully "trickle down" to the majority of the people. The *dependentistas* (dependency theorists) argue that the social stagnation of dependent countries derives from the combination of an income-concentrating, externally oriented, and externally conditioned form of capitalism with political systems controlled by privileged minorities who benefit from such poorly distributed growth.

We hasten to emphasize that in order for the *dependency syndrome*—with all of its negative human consequences—to exist, a country must have *both* an externally oriented economy (specializing in commodity exporting) *and* a socially irresponsible political elite. External economic orientation, though essential, is not enough alone to cause the socially regressive dependency syndrome. The Korean and Japanese economies are both heavily externally oriented, but their elites seem to have a greater sense of social responsibility than Latin America's and have allowed growth to promote generally improved living standards. Cuba from 1959 to the collapse of the Socialist bloc and Soviet Union in 1989 provides another example of dependence without the poverty-generating dependency syndrome. Critics of Cuba argue that the island republic's revolutionary government simply replaced dependence on the United States with dependence on the Socialist bloc. Quite so. However, a crucial difference was that the Cuban political elite distributed the income from its externally dependent economy so as to significantly improve general levels of public health, education, housing, and nutrition. Thus while dependent on the Soviet bloc for aid, Cuba avoided the dependency syndrome per se.

Capitalist development in dependent countries such as those of Central America differs sharply from what occurred in the industrialized countries. In the Western industrial nations the common citizen became crucially important to the economy as a consumer. In the United States, for instance, domestic consumers absorb most industrial production. So for at least a century it was not in the U.S. ruling class's interest to exploit common citizens to the extent that they could no longer consume. So, in an internally oriented economic system like that of the United States, income redistribution through the graduated income tax, social welfare programs, and a free labor movement actually served the interest of the moneyed elite as well as that of the common citizen. However, in dependent Third World countries the tiny upper and middle classes that control the political system derive most of their income directly or indirectly from exports or from the local manufacture by multinational corporations of products that the upper and middle classes—but not the masses—consume. In such a system the common citizen becomes important not as a consumer but as a vulnerable source of cheap labor.

Under this type of system, average citizens have little opportunity to lift themselves up by the bootstraps because they have little access either to the means of production or to the riches that flow therefrom. By its nature, the elite-run dependency system produces an inexorable concentration of both property and income. In rural areas, stimulated by the growing lure of high profits through export, the rich and the powerful simply buy out or drive poor peasants from the land. In the cities, local elites and foreign enterprises dominate incipient industrialization. Foreign firms enjoy huge advantages in technology and brand recognition and often retard the formation of locally based industry. Nevertheless, the local elites benefit from contracts, services, and employment for the educated few, as well as occasional payoffs and bribes. Meanwhile only limited advantages accrue to a host country from the presence of foreign firms that export both profits and earnings from licenses, patents, and materials sold at inflated prices by parent companies. They tend to use capital-intensive rather than labor-intensive technology, thus draining foreign exchange for the purchase of costly industrial equipment and providing limited "trickle down" in the form of wages. And finally, by obtaining much of their capital locally they dry up domestic capital that might otherwise be available to native entrepreneurs.

This system favors a privileged local elite and its foreign associates while ignoring the interests of the vast majority. Elites face powerful economic disincentives to improve the miserable condition of the masses. Any switch to a more socially responsible, mixed economic system could involve much economic dislocation and personal sacrifice that many among Central America's dominant elites simply will not accept without a fight. Indeed, the two main Central America experiments with such a more socially responsible, state-led development model only arose from violent political conflicts—the Costa Rican civil war of 1948 and the Nicaragua revolution of 1979.

At this point, one might reasonably ask why the dependency system developed in Central America while a consumer-driven economy arose in North America. And why has the great bulk of the Central American people not been able to alter a system that is so contrary to their interests? Much of the answer to the first question lies in the distinct ways in which North America and Central America were colonized. European nonconformists originally settled North America seeking a new life and greater freedom. These people tamed the land with their own labor and eventually developed into a large class of freeholders. North America did develop an aristocracy of sorts, but it never completely dominated the common citizen.

In Central America, the *conquistadores* sought quick riches. They superimposed their administration over that of the indigenous peoples and immediately began exacting tribute in gold and slaves. Within decades, the Spaniards plundered the region's gold and decimated much of its native population by slavery and contagion with Old World diseases. The Spanish mercantile system steadily drained resources from the region. Subjugated masses of indigenous *peones,* mestizos, and eventually, black slaves and mulattoes supplied most of the physical labor. Only in Costa Rica, with few easily exploitable resources and not many native peoples, did even a few Spaniards come to till the soil. Costa Rican economic and political elites, absent a coercible indigenous workforce, learned to co-opt and cajole their working classes.

Small wonder, then, that nearly five centuries later, the four northern countries of Central America had severe mass poverty and huge class disparities, whereas Costa Rica had developed a relatively more democratic, egalitarian, and socially just system. Evidence that elite decisions underlie these within-region differences stands out in certain facts: After 1950 Costa Rica's governments directed far more of their national budgets to social spending (health, education, and welfare) than other Central American governments. Costa Rica consistently dedicated more of its budget to social welfare partly because, after 1949, it had no armed forces to support. The Costa Rican governments' overall spending and social spending as a percent of GDP were nearly always greater than those in other isthmian countries.[7] Even after sharp curtailment under international pressure in the 1990s, Costa Rica's 1998 social welfare spending was 16.8 percent of GDP, compared to the next-best effort (Nicaragua at 12.7 percent) (Table 2.2). In contrast, the Salvadoran government's social spending—a crude measure of elite commitment to reducing poverty—was at 4.3 percent of GDP, the region's worst, but exceeded little by Guatemala (6.2 percent) or Honduras (7.4 percent).

This also leads us to the answer to the second question as to why the mass of citizens have not changed these systems for the better: Rather than docilely accept their imposed and sorry lot, numerous groups have revolted when things got rapidly worse: indigenous peoples resisted the conquistadores; peasants revolted against land concentration caused by the late-nineteenth-century Liberal reforms and the spread of coffee cultivation; peasants and workers under Nicaraguan nationalist Augusto C. Sandino resisted U.S. occupation from 1927 to 1933; workers led by El Salvador's homegrown Communist Agustín Farabundo Martí revolted in 1932; Nicaraguans en masse successfully rebelled against the Somoza regime in 1978–1979, and mass-based insurrections took place in El Salvador and Guatemala beginning in the late 1970s.

Such struggles between popular-based movements and those in power, however, have usually been very unequal. The entrenched elite has typically enjoyed huge advantages in military, economic, and propaganda resources. And the privileged elites have normally also counted on the support of foreign powers, be they

TABLE 2.2 RECENT ECONOMIC DATA ON CENTRAL AMERICAN GOVERNMENTS

	Costa Rica	*El Salvador*	*Guatemala*	*Honduras*	*Nicaragua*
Government spending overall as percent of GDP, 1998					
	20.8	16.1	14.9	15.7	28.6
Government social spending as percent of GDP, *c.* 1998					
	16.8	4.3	6.2	7.4	12.7
External debt as percent of GDP in					
1982	110.3	42.0	17.6	69.4	121.5
1991	73.0	36.7	29.8	118.9	649.1
2003	21.1	30.1	13.9	66.4	85.9

SOURCES: Alan Heston, Robert Summers, and Bettina Aten, *Penn World Table Version 6.1*, Center for International Comparisons at the University of Pennsylvania (CICUP), October 2002; Interamerican Development Bank, *Economic and Social Progress in Latin America, 1983 Report* (Washington, DC, 1983), country profiles; Interamerican Development Bank, *Economic and Social Progress in Latin America, 1992 Report* (Washington, DC, 1992), country profiles; and Interamerican Development Bank, country notes, www.iadb.org/exr/country/, accessed June 14, 2004.

Spain in the colonial period or the United States in the twentieth century. During the Cold War Central America's ruling classes learned that merely by labeling their opposition as "Bolshevik" or "Communist" they could usually win U.S. support ranging from direct armed intervention to economic and military aid. From 1946 through 1992 the United States provided US$1.8 billion in military assistance to the region (98 percent of it to Guatemala, El Salvador, Honduras, and to prerevolutionary Nicaragua) to shore up authoritarian regimes against challenges from the left (see Appendix Table A.3).

During the 1960s the United States assisted Central American governments economically via the Alliance for Progress. From 1962 through 1972 the Alliance provided US$617 million (Appendix Table A.3) in aid to help build Central America's roads, ports, schools, and service infrastructures. This complemented the five-nation Central American Common Market's (CACM) effort to promote a jointly state-directed, import-substitution industrialization program and customs union. Intended to advance both economic development and security objectives, the CACM stimulated rapid economic growth, but national elites mismanaged the distribution of its benefits. Following a very distinct strategy from that of Costa Rican leaders, the regimes of Guatemala, El Salvador, and Nicaragua resisted sharing the benefits of growth with most citizens.

Afflicted by rising oil prices and falling commodity prices in the mid-1970s, the Common Market development model eventually failed spectacularly. For every isthmian country this crisis brought high inflation, unemployment, and foreign debt while sharply lowering productivity and real wages. Worsening circumstances mobilized many citizens in protest, and some to violence, destabilizing several governments. Despite US$5.6 billion in economic aid from 1977 to 1988 (Appendix Table A.3) plus assistance from other nations, turmoil blocked Central America's economic recovery. Eventually under pressure from the United States and the major world multilaterial lending organizations such as the International Monetary Fund, all five countries embraced a new economic model known as *neoliberalism* and embarked on programs of *structural adjustment.*

The new strategy of neoliberalism went hand-in-hand with regional and international political efforts to end the civil wars and promote electoral democracy. That outside elites and Central American leaders pushed together for peace, democratization, and neoliberal economic reform is no accident. Robinson summarizes:

> As the transnational ruling bloc emerged in the 1980s and 1990s it carried out a "revolution from above," involving modifications in global social and economic structures through the agency of [transnational system] apparatuses aimed at promoting the most propitious conditions around the world for . . . the new global capitalist production system. This global restructuring, the so-called "Washington consensus," [or] neo-liberalism, is a doctrine . . . [that calls for]

> worldwide market liberalization, . . . the internal restructuring and global integration of each national economy . . . [and] an explicitly political component . . . [that] revolved around the promotion of "democracy."[8]

The transnational apparatuses pushing the neoliberal model in Central America included the U.S. Agency for International Development (USAID) and several multilaterial lending entities such as the International Monetary Fund and Inter-american Development Bank. Together they exacted internal political and economic "reforms" from debt-ridden Central American nations in exchange for critically needed loans to keep their economies functioning.

Pushed energetically by international lenders, the United States, and Europe, this neoliberal development model advocated certain basic changes: (1) downsizing government by laying off public employees; (2) balancing public budgets by cutting programs and subsidies to food, transport, and public services; (3) privatization of state-owned enterprises; (4) deregulation of private enterprise; (5) currency devaluations to discourage imports and encourage investment; and (6) sharp reduction of tariff barriers to foreign trade. Neoliberalism's external and domestic advocates believed such measures would eliminate inflation, increase productivity, stimulate international trade (especially exports), and lay a foundation for future economic growth. Although many would be dislocated and suffer in the short run, long-term economic growth would eventually "trickle down" to everyone.

For Central Americans with a sense of history, neoliberalism—which shares many characteristics with the raw liberalism of the late nineteenth and early twentieth centuries—portended mixed blessings. In the short term peace and democracy plus monetary and price stability brought parts of the region economic recovery through improved growth, investment, and trade. Operating under the new, austere rules, Central American governments substantially reduced the heavy foreign debt they had accumulated by the early 1990s (Table 2.2). On the other hand, because these policies, including debt repayment, reduced governments' capacity to protect and assist their citizens, they also had great potential to worsen the disparities between the rich and poor and to hurt the small middle class. Ironically, then, after achieving hard-fought political reforms, Central Americans found their governments still pursuing (or in Costa Rica's case newly pursuing) economic policies that might aggravate economic and social inequality—one of the central problems that contributed to the violence of the 1970s and 1980s.

Whether the newly democratic institutions born of those struggles will allow Central American nations to prevent impoverishment remains to be seen. Will their elites somehow balance growth with equity, as Costa Rica did for five decades, or will old elites' greedy habits take hold again? In short, will neoliberalism accommodate socially conscious government policies, or will it provide an excuse to stifle them?

Regime Change in Central America

We turn now to the recent transformations of the political systems of Central America, and specifically of their political regimes. Observers concur that much changed in the isthmus since 1970 but disagree about the meaning of these changes overall and in individual cases. We believe regional political transformations and the economic processes just discussed are related and largely driven by common forces.

Regimes are coherent systems of rule over mass publics normally established among a coalition of a nation's dominant political actors. The coherence of a system of rule refers to a persistent and identifiable set of political rules determining access to power and decisionmaking.[9] Political regimes thus stand distinct from the particular governments or administrations that operate under the same general rules. For instance, Costa Rica has had a single civilian democratic regime since the 1950s, consisting of a series of constitutionally elected presidential administrations. Likewise, Guatemala in the 1970s had a military authoritarian regime, subdivided into governments headed by various president-generals.

A new regime differentiates itself from its precursor when change occurs in *both the fundamental rules of politics and the makeup of its ruling coalition* (a regime shift). We propose seven basic regime types that roughly cover the Central American experience between 1970 and 2004: *military authoritarian,* dominated by a corporate military establishment in coalition with a narrow range of civilian sectors; *personalistic military,* the only case of which was Nicaragua, dominated by the Somoza family and military in coalition with segments of the Liberal and Conservative parties and key financial sectors; *reformist military,* dominated by reformist military elements and willing to liberalize or democratize the political system; *civilian transitional,* with elected civilian rulers backed by a strong military and mainly incorporating center and rightist parties. There are also a *revolutionary regime* (dominated by a weakly restrained revolutionary party with a center-left coalition) and a *revolutionary transitional regime* (civilian-dominated and moving toward accommodating the revolutionary party and toward constitutional restraints), which only occurred in Nicaragua. Finally, *civilian democratic regimes* have elected, civilian, constitutionally restrained governments, broad ruling coalitions, and political competition open to parties from left to right.

Table 2.3 displays Central America's political regimes since 1970 according to this scheme. Over three decades only Costa Rica remained politically stable. Among the other four countries we count twelve regime shifts (changes between categories).[10] Nicaragua's 1978–1979 insurrection culminated in a four-and-a-half-year period of revolutionary rule until internationally observed elections took place in 1984. With new members in the ruling coalition and National Assembly and top public officials separated from the revolutionary armed forces, the

TABLE 2.3 CENTRAL AMERICAN REGIME TYPES, 1970–2004

Costa Rica	*El Salvador*	*Guatemala*	*Honduras*	*Nicaragua*
CD[a]	MA	MA	MA	PM
	RM (1979)	RM (1982)	RM (1980)	Rev (1979)
	CT (1984)	CT (1985)	CT (1982)	RevT (1984)
	CD (1992)	CD (1996)	CD (1996)	CD (1987)

NOTE: Explanation of regime types notation: CD = civilian democratic, CT = civilian transitional, MA = military authoritarian, PM = personalistic military, RM = reformist military, Rev = revolutionary, and RevT. See text for fuller explanation of types. Date of inception of new regimes is in parentheses.

[a]Uninterrupted from 1949 to the present.

new revolutionary transitional regime's National Assembly drafted a new constitution (1985–1987), the promulgation of which instituted constitutional civilian democracy in 1987. Honduras's military regime, anxiously eyeing neighboring Nicaragua's revolutionary turmoil at the end of the 1970s, moved quickly toward transitional civilian democratic rule. Full civilian democracy came only in 1996. El Salvador and Guatemala traversed three similar stages after military authoritarian rule: In both, a military-led reformist regime during civil war engineered changes that led to a civilian transitional regime; the settlement of each war eventually ushered in a much more inclusive civilian democratic government.

How and why did these regime shifts occur? We examine both what caused the changes and the mechanisms or processes of change.

Causes. Several factors, interacting in complex ways, drove most regime change: Rapid economic growth in the 1960s followed by severe reversals in the 1970s impoverished many and generated widespread mobilization and demands for political and economic reform. Grave economic problems and mass unrest also undermined authoritarian coalitions. Violent resistance to and repression of those demanding reform by some governments drove opposition unification, radicalization, and revolutionary insurrection. Fear of a revolution like Nicaragua's prompted the militaries of other nations, some with U.S. aid, to initiate very gradual political reforms and eventually to accept transitional civilian regimes with liberalized rules. During the wars themselves, the failure of the armed forces to defeat the insurgents added impetus to calls from international actors (neighboring Latin American states, Europe, and the Catholic Church) to accept negotiated regime change. Finally, the end of the Cold War convinced the United States in the early 1990s that it was now in its interest to promote rather than resist the negotiated settlements all Central American regimes had agreed to in principle in 1987.

Processes. If these were the likely causes, how did the changes occur? A widely based mass insurrection initiated the revolutionary regime in Nicaragua by defeating the authoritarian Somoza regime in 1979. The Nicaraguan revolutionary government enacted party and electoral laws similar to those of Western Europe and Costa Rica in 1983 and won internationally observed elections in 1984. In the ensuing revolutionary transitional period the National Assembly wrote a new constitution that took effect in 1987, ushering in the civilian democratic regime.

The overthrow of Somoza and beginning of the Nicaraguan revolution in 1979 were political earthquakes that motivated regime change elsewhere in the isthmus. Despite certain differences among them, military coups d'état ushered in reformist military episodes in El Salvador, Guatemala, and Honduras. The new military regimes in El Salvador and Guatemala at first continued high levels of repression. Their critics rightly remained quite skeptical that meaningful changes in political rules might have taken place. But gradually the military reformers produced new constitutions (some exculpating the military for their crimes while in power) and then allowed elections that brought civilians to nominal power while allowing at least some formerly excluded centrist and center-left civilian groups back into the political arena.

Isthmian nations have much of their history, global contexts, and political and economic development in common. As noted, these common attributes demonstrate that Central America exists within a larger world dynamic that constrains its component states in similar ways. Just as common forces caused Central America's three great national revolts in the 1970s, the same forces influenced the overall process of regime change leading from authoritarianism toward electoral democracy. In fact, the revolutionary movements were key steps in the process of regime change that led to the region's formal democratization.

A Theory of Regime Change in Central America

Our explanatory argument integrating Central America's insurrections and other regime changes employs elements of regime change theory and the dependency and world-system theories already discussed. We will briefly review the political science literatures on regime change, revolution, and democratization and show the considerable extent to which the three overlap and inform each other. These common features lead us toward a more general explanation of the recent remarkable transformation of Central American politics.

Students of regime change examine the causes, processes, and outcomes of regime change. Barrington Moore explored how the characteristics of several established regimes and the interaction of their various social classes shaped the particular characteristics of new regimes.[11] Guillermo O'Donnell examined the role of military–middle-class coalitions as bureaucratic authoritarianism replaced civilian governments in Argentina and Brazil.[12] The contributors to Juan Linz et al.'s *The*

Breakdown of Democratic Regimes examined the nature of democratic regimes and both the causes of and processes involved in their collapse and replacement by authoritarian rule. Some decades later, O'Donnell et al.'s *The Transitions from Authoritarian Rule* performed a similar exercise on the breakdown of authoritarian governments of southern Europe and Latin America.[13] Mark Gasiorowski has employed quantitative analysis to account for factors that contribute to regime change.[14]

In sum, the regime change literature makes clear that regimes are systems of rule over mass publics established among a coalition of a nation's dominant political actors. Regime coalition members benefit from inclusion in the regime. Social and especially economic change can generate and mobilize new political actors who may seek inclusion into the ruling coalition and its benefits. They may or may not be admitted by those within the regime. Contented, indifferent, unorganized, or effectively repressed populations and groups do not seek inclusion in the regime, nor do they violently rebel. Strong, flexible regimes with satisfied allies rarely collapse or wage war against their populations.

Charles Anderson's classic work explains that Latin American regimes have corporatistic tendencies, meaning that new actors usually win admission to the regime coalition only when they prove themselves capable, if excluded, of destabilizing the existing regime. Regime transformations in the region therefore often involve conflict because excluded forces must fight for inclusion.[15] This view accounts for the well-documented case of Costa Rica's last regime shift. The narrowly based coffee-grower–dominated quasi-democracy of the 1930s was disrupted by emergent working- and middle-class actors who forged a new regime after winning a brief but violent civil war in 1948.[16]

The second relevant literature concerns political violence and revolution, part of which involves regime change. We have extensively reviewed this literature in earlier editions, so we merely highlight key portions here.[17] First, for a rebellion to occur a fundamental basis of conflict must exist that defines groups or categories of affected persons that provide "recruiting grounds for organizations."[18] What bases of conflict are most likely to lead citizens to widespread rebellion, a phenomenon that John Walton usefully designates the *national revolt?*[19] Walton, Theda Skocpol, Jeffrey Paige, Mancur Olson, Mason, and many others argue that rapid economic change and evolving class relations typically drive the mobilization required for a violent challenge to a regime.[20] For agrarian societies, inclusion into the world capitalist economy through heavy reliance upon export agriculture may harm huge sectors of the peasantry, urban poor, and middle sectors and thus provide large numbers of aggrieved citizens.

Once motivated, groups must organize and focus their struggle for change upon some target, most likely the regime in power. Rod Aya and Charles Tilly have shown that effective organization for opposition requires the mobilization of resources. They emphasize the key role of the state in shaping rebellion. The state is not only the target of the rebels, but it also reciprocally affects the revolt as it both represses rebels and promotes change.[21] Walton, Skocpol, Jack Goldstone, and Ted Gurr concur that once a contest over sovereignty begins, political factors such as organization and resource mobilization by both sides eventually determine the outcome.[22] Goldstone, James DeFronzo, and Bill Robinson particularly emphasize the contribution to successful revolutionary movements of both external actors and interelite competition, elite alienation, and factors that may weaken the state's capacity to act.[23] Perhaps the most satisfactory explanation is that offered by Timothy Wickham-Crowley.[24] Rejecting single-factor theories, he argues that Latin American history in recent decades demonstrates that successful insurrection requires a combination of four factors: the right social conditions in the countryside; an intelligent and flexible guerrilla movement; a despicable target regime ("mafiacracy"); and the right international conditions. The last of these can include economic forces (e.g., falling international commodity prices that impoverish and thus mobilize local actors) and political ones (e.g., something that distracts a hegemonic actor from its normal clients, or overt decisions not to intervene on behalf of a regime).

The third literature is the growing body of scholarship on democratization. What domestic forces lead to democratization, the process of moving from an authoritarian to a democratic regime? The four main explanations focus on political culture, political processes, social structures and forces (both domestic and external), and elites. The cultural approach argues that the ideal of political democracy can evolve within a society or spread among nations by cultural diffusion among elite and mass political actors.[25] Elite and mass preference for democracy promote its adoption and help sustain it. Process approaches examine the mechanics of and paths toward democratic transition.[26] In these emphases they resemble and overlap the regime change literature.

Structural theories emphasize how shifts in the distribution of critical material and organizational resources among political actors can lead to democracy.[27] Democratic regimes emerge when the distribution of political and economic resources and the mobilization of actors permit formerly excluded actors to disrupt the extant authoritarian coalition. Another structural approach examines the imposition of democracy by external actors.[28] The fourth approach examines the roles of leaders.[29] Key societal elites must engineer specific democratic arrangements (elite settlements) and agree to operate by them. The broader the coalition of political forces involved, the more stable and consolidated a democratic regime will be. Robinson's explanation of the emergence of what he calls "polyarchy," a minimalist variant of formal electoral democracy, encompasses aspects of structural democratization theory (global economic and political forces and institutions impinge on the local) and elite democratization theory (external, international, and global elites cooperate with and impose democratic rules of the game on local elites).[30]

While different in emphasis, these three literatures have much in common. All three concern regime change or efforts to promote it, although the democratization literature emphasizes transition in one particular direction. Elements of all three envision a polity as having numerous actors, whose makeup and roles can evolve, and they all treat political regimes as coalitions of key actors that survive through successful mobilization of resources in and around the state or governmental apparatus. All three recognize that regimes can experience crisis, whether through challenge from without, deterioration from within, or the erosion of state capacity. All have causal explanations for change, although there are divergent emphases and outright disagreements both within and between fields over the importance of such factors as psychology, political culture, leaders and elites, masses, and social structures. However, the more sophisticated treatments in the revolution/violence and democratization literatures tend to treat causality as both complex and multiple.

Finally, in each of these fields and from a substantial literature on foreign policy, there is a recognition that international constraints can shape regime change.[31]

Foreign governments, international institutions and other actors from outside a nation can act as players in domestic economics and politics. They can strengthen a prevailing regime by supporting it or weaken it through opposition or withheld support. External actors can supply resources to domestic actors, altering their capacity to act and relative strength. Key external actors can pressure domestic actors to adopt certain policies or regime types, employing as inducements such vital resources as money, trade, arms, and political cooperation. The international context can also constrain a nation's regime type by demonstration effect—having mostly democratic neighbors makes it easier to adopt or retain a democratic regime.

Though these bodies of literature do not explicitly address this matter, we believe that drawing from these elements we may advance the following outline of a theory of regime change: Political systems are, for our purposes, nation-states with defined populations and territorial boundaries. Political systems exist within an international context consisting of various types of actors, including nation-states, formal and informal alliances among nations, corporations, the world political economy, international organizations, and political and ideological groupings. Political regimes are coherent systems of rule over mass publics established among a coalition of the nation's dominant political actors. Political actors within nations include individuals but, more importantly, encompass organized groups, factions, ideological groupings, parties, interest sectors, or institutions, each pursuing objectives within the political system and each with resources to bring to bear. Actors may or may not constitute part of the regime coalition, the group of actors who dominate and benefit most from the state, its resources, and its policymaking capacity.

Political regimes persist based upon two things: They must constantly manage the state and economy well enough to keep coalition members' loyalty. And they must continuously keep actual and potential outside-the-regime actors (both domestic and external) content or indifferent or, if neither of these, keep them disorganized, uninterested, distracted, immobilized, or otherwise effectively repressed. Many factors can potentially destabilize a regime. International or domestic economic forces may disrupt the political economy (harm a nation's established economic system or the security of regime coalition's members or other actors). Such forces may include rapid economic growth followed by a sharp downturn, or a sharp recessive episode by itself. Powerful external actors (a major regional power or hegemon, for instance) may withdraw support and resources from a regime or may shift from tacit support to active opposition, thus creating a permissive external environment for opponents. Ideologies or different real-world polities may suggest alternative political and economic rules (republicanism instead of monarchy, socialism instead of capitalism, or civilian democracy instead of military authoritarianism) to key actors within or outside the regime coalition.

A regime experiences a crisis when such forces (1) undermine the loyalty and cooperation of some or all of the coalition members, (2) undermine the resource base and capacity of the regime to respond to challengers, or (3) mobilize external actors against the regime. Regime crises can take various forms based upon the severity of the challenge and distribution of resources among actors. Regime coalition members may renegotiate the regime's political rules and benefits and deny significant adjustments to outside actors. Regimes may make policy changes to mollify aggrieved outside actors. Regimes may initiate co-optative incorporation of new coalition members to quell a disruptive challenge; this will typically involve reforming extant political rules and payoffs. Outside-the-regime actors may initiate a violent challenge to the regime's sovereignty via a coup d'état, insurrection, or even an external invasion. Inside-the-regime actors may also employ a coup to displace incumbents or, more interestingly, to initiate a new regime. It is also possible for leaders of a regime voluntarily to institute regime change on their own terms, even in the absence of a regime crisis, although one might reasonably expect such transformations to take place in response to anticipated challenges to the regime or polity. (Whatever the motivation, we consider this combination of alterations—change in the coalition membership plus an adjustment of the rules—to constitute the minimum adjustments necessary to be classified as a regime change.)

The evolution and outcome of a regime crisis will depend upon the ability of the regime and its challengers to mobilize and deploy their respective resources. The closer the regime and its challengers are to resource parity and the stronger both are, the longer and more violently they will struggle over power. A dominant actor (such as the military) in a weak to moderately strong regime confronted with a significant but potentially growing opposition might initiate a regime change (co-optative reform, including new actors) to minimize expected damage to its interests. Other things equal, a strong, flexible, resource-rich regime will be likely to reform and/or successfully repress or continue to exclude its opponents and to survive. A weak regime confronting a strong opposition coalition may be overthrown and replaced by a revolutionary regime likely to then exclude some of the old regime's coalition. A protracted crisis, especially a lengthy civil war, eventually increases the likelihood of a negotiated settlement and regime transformation with new political and economic rules, redistributed benefits, and the inclusion into the political game of both former challengers and old-regime actors.

The settlement upon a new regime will derive from the eventual resolution of forces among the various political actors, and may, in turn, depend heavily upon the role of external actors. A single regime shift may not bring enough change to permit political stability. Military reformism, for instance, although intended to pacify a polity by including certain new actors and by enacting policy reforms, may utterly fail to satisfy violent, ideologically antagonistic opponents. Despite establishing a new coalition, new rules, and new policies, a revolutionary regime may quickly attract direct or indirect external opposition. If important actors (internal or external) remain unsatisfied or unsuccessfully repressed, the new regime may be unstable. Protracted instability for a newly constituted regime, we believe, increases the likelihood of its failure and further regime shifts.

Explaining Regime Change in Central America

From the common elements of the theories examined above we offer the following propositions to account for the origin and development of regime change in Central America since the 1970s. The argument emphasizes the world economic and geopolitical and ideological context and its evolution, the regimes present in the 1970s and the causes of the crises that undermined them, regimes' and actors' responses to crisis, and the interplay of resources and external forces that shaped the ultimate outcome.

The Evolving Context from the U.S. Viewpoint. The geopolitics of the Cold War predominated on the world scene in the 1970s and set the context for Central American geopolitics. U.S. policy was preoccupied with the threat of the Soviet Union and its perceived desire to expand its influence within the Western Hemisphere. The United States therefore tended to regard most of the region's political and economic reformists and the opponents of Central America's friendly, anticommunist, authoritarian regimes as unacceptable potential allies of pro-Soviet/pro-Cuban communism. Civilian democracy, though an ideological preference of the United States, remained secondary to security concerns in this tense world environment. U.S. promotion of civilian democracy was therefore seen as too risky because it might encourage leftists.

Central America's authoritarian regimes thus usually enjoyed the political, military, and economic support of the United States. Indeed, U.S. military personnel trained Latin American officers during the Cold War using special manuals that explicitly advocated the use of illegal detention, torture, and murder (state-sponsored terror) against a wide spectrum of groups opposed to pro-U.S. regimes.[32] This behavior created a profound contradiction between the proclaimed values of the United States and the reality of U.S. policy in the region. It also caused Central Americans in the center and on the left to be highly skeptical of the virtues of formal electoral "democracy" as practiced against a backdrop of unprecedented levels of state terror under pro-U.S. regimes.

U.S. thinking regarding the ideological geopolitics of Central America took several twists and turns from the late 1970s through the early 2000s. In the latter half of the 1970s, Congress and the Carter administration came to view the inhumane anticommunist authoritarian regimes of Nicaragua, Guatemala, and El Salvador as unacceptable. This policy change encouraged Central America's reformists and revolutionaries and briefly created a more favorable international environment for regime change. After the Sandinistas' victory in 1979, however, U.S. human rights policy in Central America was "put on the back burner,"[33] and Washington once again began advising Central American regimes to clamp down on "subversives." When that posture ran up against congressional opposition in the first few years of the Reagan administration, U.S. diplomats once again began stressing democracy by insisting on formal elections in pro-U.S. countries, albeit against a background of state terror. This policy was continued under the first President Bush until the end of the Cold War, when Washington's second-order preference for civilian democracy could come to the fore, thus allowing support for the peace process and the emergence of cleaner, more inclusive elections in El Salvador and Guatemala. Under the second President Bush U.S. commitment to formal democracy slipped. The White House applauded the unsuccessful 2002 attempted coup against constitutionally elected Venezuelan president Hugo Chávez. The United States also interfered in elections in Brazil, Bolivia, El Salvador, and Nicaragua by telling voters there that to elect leftist candidates would be viewed negatively and could lead to unspecified U.S. sanctions.

The Evolving Context from Central American Viewpoints. Prior to 1979 many leftists in Central America shared Fidel Castro's profound distrust of U.S.-sponsored electoral democracy. (Most moderate reformers likely preferred real electoral democracy but were repressed by U.S.-sponsored regimes.) However, from the time of their victory in 1979, many Sandinistas viewed electoral democracy as compatible with the economic/participatory democracy it sought to construct. The FSLN (Frente Sandinista de Liberación Nacional—Sandinista National Liberation Front) also viewed electoral democracy as a stratagem that might enhance the acceptability of their revolution to the openly hostile United States and their Central American neighbors. Thus in 1983–1984 they enacted a well-designed electoral system for selecting the government.

Whatever they initially envisioned as their ideal post-victory government, the insurgents in El Salvador (by 1982) and Guatemala (by 1986) had decided not to fight for all-out victory but rather for a negotiated settlement including demilitarization and civilian rule in which they would be able to take part. Much later, with the Cold War waning and the U.S. opposition to negotiated settlements ended, the armed forces of each nation—exhausted by the long civil wars—decided they could accept electoral rules of the game, with the leftists included, in exchange for peace and institutional survival.

Certain emergent capitalist sectors sympathetic to trade liberalization, involved in nontraditional exporting and linked to transnational capital, emerged to challenge traditional economic elites for control of private-sector organizations and rightist parties. These groups embraced electoral democracy as a key to peace, neoliberal economic reforms, and revitalized economies. Operating both through business-dominated organizations and political parties and supported by powerful external actors like USAID and the IMF, these transnationally oriented groups would eventually become dominant ruling coalition members across the region, and play major roles in negotiating peace and running transitional governments, post-settlement governments, and managing economic policy.

The Views of Other Actors. European nations, other Latin American nations, and such international organizations as the United Nations and Organization of American States once largely deferred to U.S. influence in the region. However, during the 1980s they became increasingly fearful that the isthmian civil wars and U.S. intervention could escalate further. These external actors therefore embraced and promoted electoral democracy as the mechanism for promoting their interest in the pacification of Central America. The preference for formal democratization at first put Europe at odds with the strenuous U.S. military and diplomatic efforts to contain Central American leftist movements. Eventually, especially with the Cold War's waning, the shared concern of major industrial powers for a healthy global capitalist environment operating along neoliberal lines contributed to the emergence of the Washington consensus favoring formal democracy.

The Catholic Church in the isthmus was influenced by liberation theology in the 1960s and 1970s, a phenomenon that encouraged social mobilization which in some cases contributed to insurrection. By the 1980s, however, the institutional Church reined in and downplayed liberation theology while emphasizing formal democratization and improved human rights as a means toward achieving social justice. Catholic hierarchs on balance became more politically conservative. Some variation in practice and policy remained, as indicated by the performance differences among Church human rights offices in the region. With the main exception of Nicaragua in the 1970s, evangelical Protestants (growing rapidly in number since the 1960s) tended to either eschew politics or identify during elections with conservative and sometimes antidemocratic forces.

The 1970s Regimes. In the early 1970s only Costa Rica among the region's nations had a broadly inclusive, constitutional, civilian-led democratic regime. It had evolved from that country's 1948 civil war and 1948–1949 revolution.

The other four nations had military-dominated authoritarian regimes: Nicaragua's was a personalistic military regime dominated by the Somoza clan, a narrow coalition of key business interests and parts of the two major parties. Guatemala and El Salvador had corporately run military authoritarian regimes, allied with some business and large-scale agricultural interests and with the collaboration of weak political parties. Honduras had a military authoritarian regime that incorporated one of the two strong traditional political parties and tolerated a very strong but anticommunist labor sector.

Causes of Regime Crises. A wave of economic problems afflicted all Central American countries in the late 1970s and early 1980s. Rapidly escalating oil prices and resultant inflation, the deterioration of the Central American Common Market (in the mid- and late 1970s), and natural or economic catastrophes (e.g., the 1972 Managua earthquake, 1978–1979 Common Market trade disruptions) greatly reduced real income and employment among working-class and some white-collar sectors.

The grievances caused by increasing inequalities, declining real income, economic/natural catastrophes, and the political dissatisfactions of would-be competing elites led in the mid- and late 1970s to various events: the development of opposition parties; the rapid growth of agrarian, labor, neighborhood, and community self-help organization; and reformist demands upon the state and protests of public policy. Regime coalitions experienced some defections, and the economic resources of all five regimes eroded.

Regime Responses to Crisis. In both the short and long term, Central American regimes responded quite differently to unrest, mobilization, and demands for change. In the short term, the divergences were most striking. Where regimes responded to demands with ameliorative policies to ease poverty and permit the recovery of real wages, with political reform, and with low or modest levels of force or repression, protests failed to escalate further or subsided.

Costa Rica's regime did not shift. Honduras's military authoritarian regime voluntarily returned nominal control to civilians and the armed forces gradually reduced military tutelage of national politics. In contrast, regimes in Nicaragua, El Salvador, and Guatemala in the short run rejected ameliorative policies and with U.S. assistance sharply escalated repression by public security forces. They then experienced increased protests and opposition organization and resource mobilization. In the longer run, the regimes that responded with violent repression and refusal to ameliorate the effects of economic crisis found themselves facing violent, broadly based insurrections. They struggled to mobilize the economic and political resources to resist the revolts, including seeking external assistance, especially from the United States. They also eventually undertook extensive policy changes in their struggles to manage, repress, divide, and isolate their violent challengers. Nicaragua under Somoza was the least flexible. Military authoritarian regimes in El Salvador and Guatemala were overthrown from within by military reformers who gradually adopted more flexible policies that eventually moved toward civilian transitional regimes.

Outcomes. The outcomes of Central America's regime crises depended upon the relative success of each regime in mobilizing and maintaining domestic and external material support and organization. Failure to stabilize the situation (to placate or repress enough outside-the-regime actors) led to regime shifts.

In Nicaragua, Somoza lost direct U.S. and regional support and vital economic resources, helping the Sandinistas oust him and establish the revolutionary regime. The Somoza wing of the old Liberal Party was discredited and Somoza's National Guard was defeated and disbanded. The Sandinistas formed a center-left coalition and governed by revolutionary rules for several years. Under the revolutionary regime, top FSLN leaders dominated the executive, the Sandinista armed forces replaced all security forces, and center and right political forces grew increasingly unhappy with the regime. There was some division within the FSLN between a more "vanguardist," less democratic faction on the one hand and more genuine democrats on the other. Perhaps because the revolutionary regime knew it was in the world media spotlight and needed to retain as much international support as possible, the democratic faction prevailed. Somocista Liberals and an increasing number of other disaffected economic and political elements formed various outside-the-regime forces, including the U.S.-backed Contra rebels. The revolutionary regime's response to this challenge and the counterrevolutionary war included nearly continuous economic and political reform, including adopting democratic electoral rules and holding the 1984 election. The resulting elected revolutionary transitional regime's National Assembly began drafting a new constitution. We consider the adoption of the constitution in early 1987 the beginning of civilian democratic rule in Nicaragua because it formalized the rules of the political game along traditional liberal-democratic lines, with clear division of powers and checks on executive authority.[34]

The Honduran military regime, faced in 1979 with domestic turmoil and the Nicaraguan revolution next door, preemptively initiated transition to civilian democracy. The traditional Liberal and National parties dominated the fairly inclusive transitional civilian regime. However, flush with massive political, economic, and military resources, earned by cooperating with U.S. efforts to defeat the revolutionary left in Nicaragua and El Salvador, the armed forces retained great power and influence. This delayed transition to civilian democracy until after the military's power was eventually trimmed by further reforms in the mid-1990s.

A 1979 coup d'état in El Salvador and another in Guatemala in 1982 instituted ostensibly reformist military regimes (although their reformist intent early on was questionable). These governments at first repressed moderates and centrists who remained outside the regime coalitions while they attempted but failed to defeat leftist rebel coalitions. The failure of this strategy, plus pressure from the United States (a major resource supplier to the Salvadoran regime), led to the adoption of civilian transitional governments that, although weak, governed with broader coalitions and liberalized rules. This behavior won over some of the political center in each country, depriving the rebel coalitions of important allies and resources and contributing to the stagnation of both civil wars. The Central American Peace Accord of 1987 provided a mechanism for eventual negotiations between the parties to the stalemated civil conflicts. Military exhaustion, U.S. exasperation with the Central American quagmires, the rise of new domestic transnational elites, and the Cold War's end moved all actors' positions. The United States, other outside actors, national militaries, the civilian reformist regimes, and the rebels all eventually embraced more inclusive civilian democracy and some economic reforms, position changes that helped settle both wars.

Discussion

What has regime change actually meant? Many observers have expressed doubts about the quality of the new regimes in Central America, deriding them as "democracy light" or "low-intensity democracy" to emphasize their shortcomings. Robinson uses the term "polyarchy" to describe these civilian electoral regimes that remain dominated by elites and unresponsive to the interests of mass publics despite the rupture with open authoritarianism.

We share many of these misgivings, but nevertheless reject the idea that regime change lacks political meaning for the ordinary citizen. Impressionistic evidence that democracy, however flawed, has made life less dangerous and fearsome has been seen by the authors in the bearing of Central Americans on recent trips to the region. Citizens express more support for their governments than they did a decade ago (see Chapter 9). Evaluations by outside observers in Table 2.3 also reveal improving political climates, but also flawed performance. Over the twenty years between 1981–1983 and 2001–2003, the authors of the Political Terror Scale registered declines in repression levels in El Salvador, Guatemala, and Nicaragua. Honduras's score rose slightly, a discouraging sign. Freedom House's scores for political rights for 1981 and 2003 mark real progress in four countries (no change in Costa Rica's good score). On civil liberties Costa Rica lost a point over the same period for restrictions on press freedom, and Honduras did not improve. In contrast, the most violent and repressive cases in the early 1980s, El Salvador, Guatemala, and Nicaragua, all improved.[35]

These dry statistics have real meaning for real people. Repression scores and rights and liberties indexes are not mere numbers. They stand for political murders and rights abuses by government. Improved scores mean that fewer Central Americans are being murdered and repressed by their governments than two decades ago. Many flaws remain in these performances. Even Costa Rica could do better on civil liberties, according to Freedom House, and the rest have considerable room to improve. The repression and rights situations in Honduras, middling in the 1980s, have changed little with democratization. But regime change to even low-intensity democracy in several countries has filled the glass of freedom at least part way up, if not to the brim.

Since the 1970s Central American polities have undergone dramatic transformations: Rapid, inequitable economic development drove mass mobilization and protest that shattered several seemingly stable, U.S.-backed authoritarian regimes, which variously gave rise to military-led reformism, violent insurrection, and revolutionary transition. From such disparate initial outcomes, however, a new and coherent pattern emerged in the late 1980s and 1990s—all of Central America's governments became civilian electoral democracies. The outcome has brought measurable improvements in the security, freedom, and political lives of citizens of at least three of the region's five countries, opportunities for further progress notwithstanding.

TABLE 2.4 SOME EFFECTS OF REGIME CHANGE IN CENTRAL AMERICA

	Costa Rica	*El Salvador*	*Guatemala*	*Honduras*	*Nicaragua*
Political Terror Scale Score (1 = very low repression, 5 = very high repression)					
Mean for 1981–1983	1.0	4.0	4.0	2.3	3.3
Mean for 2001–2003	1.0	2.3	3.0	3.0	2.7
Freedom House Rankings for 2003 (1 = most free, 7 = least free)					
Political Rights 1981	1	6	6	4	5
Political Rights 2003	1	2	4	3	3
Civil Liberties 1981	1	4	6	3	5
Civil Liberties 2003	2	3	4	3	3

SOURCES: Mark Gibney, *Political Terror Scale 1980–2003*, accessed June 17, 2004 at www.unca.edu/politicalscience/faculty-staff/gibney.html; and Freedom House, *Freedom in the World 2004*, www.freedomhouse.org/research/freeworld/2004/table2004.pdf, accessed June 24, 2004.

3

The Common History

One great truth about Central America is that, while there exist many similarities among the five countries, there are also significant differences. Both similarities and differences arose largely from the early history of the region as it experienced conquest, the colonial period, independence, union with Mexico, and fifteen years of common political identity as part of the United Provinces of Central America.[1]

Conquest to 1838

Spanish conquest profoundly affected the nature of Central America's present-day societies. Spain conquered the territories that are today Nicaragua, Honduras, El Salvador, and Guatemala in the two decades following the first Spanish penetration in 1522. Spain imposed its rule upon those indigenous peoples lucky enough to survive the tremendous depopulation of the region caused by enslavement and exposure to Old World diseases. Costa Rica's experience immediately set it apart from the other four countries. Spaniards did not settle there until the 1560s because, unlike the other areas, it offered no easily exploitable resources in either gold or native slaves. Indeed, the hostile indigenous inhabitants resisted European penetration. In the end, the Spanish neither pacified nor conquered Costa Rica's original inhabitants, but either exterminated them or pushed them into remote areas. Thus the population of the Central Valley of Costa Rica became heavily Iberian and a racially distinct and exploited underclass never developed.

In the rest of Central America, however, the Spaniards imposed their dominion despite passive and active resistance by the native people. Though this period meant annihilation for many, some original populations survived. When the

Spaniards arrived, they encountered millions of indigenous people in what are today the four northernmost countries of Central America. By coopting and controlling native *caciques* (chiefs), the bearded foreigners proved very effective in extracting local riches in the form of gold and native slaves. In addition, the conquistadores unwittingly brought with them a variety of diseases to which Old World populations had become essentially immune. The native peoples, having no natural immunity, perished in large numbers.

It is estimated that in western Nicaragua alone, a population of over one million declined to a few tens of thousands by the end of the conquest. It is unlikely that the Spaniards killed very many natives outright. Rather, careful historical research indicates that they exported as many as half a million indigenous Nicaraguans to Panama and Peru as slaves. Most subsequently died either in passage to their destination or in slavery within a year or two thereafter. The bulk of the rest of the populace apparently succumbed to disease.[2] Only in Guatemala did large numbers of indigenous peoples survive, perhaps partly because the conquistadores found it harder to completely subjugate the relatively more advanced society they encountered in that area. Perhaps, too, the cooler climates of the mountainous parts of Guatemala presented a less congenial environment for the spread of disease.

The drastic reduction in the native population was not the only change wrought by the conquest in the region of northern Central America. Prior to the conquest, labor-intensive agriculture typified this area. The common people grew corn, beans, peppers, and squash on land consigned to them by their caciques. Although obliged to turn over to the chief as tribute part of the crop, the rest they controlled for home consumption, barter, or sale in local markets. By the end of the conquest, depopulation had converted most of the indigenous farmlands back to jungle. The economy had become externally oriented, with the Spaniards controlling the region's human and natural resources to produce articles for trade among the colonies and with the mother country. The remaining indigenous population (still more numerous than their white masters) supplied the labor that produced the gold, silver, timber, and cattle products (hides, tallow, and dried beef) for export. Most of the wealth that this economy produced went to the white elite. The culture and process of dependent underdevelopment had begun.

Many aspects of culture changed practically overnight as the conquistadores sought to impose their religion, language, and ways on the conquered. Of course, nowhere was native culture *completely* obliterated. In Guatemala, where hispanicization was least effective, the indigenous peoples retained their languages and hid many aspects of their old religion under a patina of Catholicism. Even in El Salvador, Honduras, Nicaragua, and Costa Rica, where the native populations were most decimated, some indigenous traits remained. For instance, to this day, everywhere in the region, corn and beans (native staples) constitute the heart of local cuisine. Moreover, many indigenous place names remain, as do the names of hundreds of common objects, from peppers and turkeys to grindstones. Yet, by and large, Central America was hispanicized. Spanish became the lingua franca except in rural Guatemala and certain remote regions elsewhere. A mystical, elite-supporting, pre-Reformation version of Catholicism became the nearly universal religion. Even the cities, often built on or next to the sites of pre-Columbian centers of habitation, eventually took on Spanish characteristics, with the typical Iberian arrangement of plazas, cathedrals, and public buildings.

The conquest established new class patterns. The larger pre-Columbian societies of Central America had been hierarchically ordered, with chiefs and associated elites dominating the masses. That may have allowed the Spaniards so easily to superimpose themselves on the system. But what became most different after the conquest was a new racial configuration of class. With the exception of Costa Rica, what emerged was a highly unequal, two-class society, with people of Spanish birth or descent constituting the ruling class and everyone else comprising a downtrodden lower class. Within the lower class, there eventually evolved a subsystem of stratification as the biological union between Spaniards and native women produced *mestizos,* who though never considered equals by the Spaniards, nonetheless held higher social status than persons of pure indigenous stock.

During the rest of the colonial period, from the late sixteenth century to 1821, the Viceroyalty of New Spain (Mexico) nominally ruled over the Kingdom of Guatemala, which today constitutes the five countries of Central America (plus Chiapas in present-day Mexico). In fact, however, the viceroyalty had little control over the kingdom, which in practice was administered directly by Spain. In turn, the nominal capital Guatemala only loosely controlled the other provinces of Central America. Underpopulated, geographically isolated, and economically insignificant, the tiny Costa Rican colony became a neglected backwater, helping to account for its distinctive evolution. Elsewhere, resentment grew between the provinces and the central administration in Guatemala as the newly emerging system of dependency inevitably caused the greatest development to take place in that administrative center. Even within individual provinces, such as Nicaragua, regional differences and rivalries developed and festered. Therefore, while Central Americans shared a common experience on the one hand, the seeds of division and disintegration were germinating on the other.

Besides these political factors, other important economic and social patterns that emerged during the conquest persisted into the colonial era. Costa Rica's relative backwardness and isolation led to a more self-contained economy. A persistent labor shortage, relatively equal land distribution, access to unclaimed crown lands for poor farmers, and the lack of an easily exploitable indigenous population produced a large class of free farmers unused to subjugation by the colony's leading families. Though such factors can easily be given too much importance, they appear to have helped Costa Rica to develop a fairly successful liberal, democratic political system by the mid twentieth century.

In contrast, in the rest of Central America, an externally oriented, elite-controlled, dependent pattern of economic activity became ever more entrenched. The Spanish first exploited the region's human and material resources to produce cacao, silver, gold, timber, and cattle products for export. Later, export production expanded to include indigo and cochineal for the blue and red dyes needed by a growing European textile industry. As in present-day Central America, fluctuations in external demand produced periods of boom and bust in the local dependent economies. New groups joined the population. The colonies imported slaves to replace some of the labor supply lost with the decimated indigenous population, and later there arose mulatto offspring of white-black unions. The social and economic gap between the European and *criollo*[3] elite and the non-European majority remained wide. With the premium placed on export and maximizing profits for the elites, the masses were generally allowed to consume only at a subsistence level. It is small wonder that the four republics of northern Central America are typified to this day by wide social and economic disparities and by a socially irresponsible economic elite.

Central America passed from colonial rule to formal independence with almost no violence. When Mexico broke from Spain in mid-1821, Central America also declared its independence. In January 1822, it joined the Mexican empire of Agustín de Iturbide. El Salvador resisted union with Mexico but was incorporated by force of arms. However, by mid-1823, soon after the abdication of "Agustín the First," Central America tired of its association with Mexico and declared its independence. Only the former Central American province of Chiapas chose to remain a part of the larger country to the north. From then until 1838, the region was fused—legally, at least—into a federation called the United Provinces of Central America or the Central American Republic.

At first Central Americans felt enthusiasm about the union. The idea made good sense. Clearly, a federated republic could be stronger politically and economically than would five tiny independent nations. Yet from the start, several factors undermined the success of the United Provinces. First was the long history of resentment of Guatemala by the outlying provinces. This resentment grew as Guatemala, the largest of the five states, received eighteen of the forty-one seats in the congress (according to the principle of proportional representation) and therefore dominated policymaking. Second, although the constitution of 1824 declared the states to be "free and independent" in their internal affairs, it also contained nationalist and centrist features that undermined the provinces' autonomy. Finally, rivalry between emerging Liberal and Conservative factions of the ruling elite generated conflict both within each province and across provincial boundaries. Meddling in their neighbors' affairs became a common practice of Central

American leaders. These factors saddled the union with constant tension and recurrent civil war. The experiment finally came unglued in 1838, as first Nicaragua and later the other countries split from the federation. Despite several reunification efforts later in the nineteenth century, the bitterness and national rivalries that had destroyed the United Provinces in the first place sufficed to block its resurrection.

1838 to the Present

Continuing poverty and hardship for most of the region's people have marked the era since the disintegration of the Central American federation. The patterns of dependency and elite rule that took firm root in each of the republics except Costa Rica during the colonial period continued through the nineteenth century and into the twentieth century. Costa Rica, too, soon developed debilitating external economic dependencies. Overall, although the region as a whole experienced occasional surges of development, that development seldom benefited the majority of Central Americans. After independence, Central America's tiny, privileged elites—those who had inherited economic power and social standing—continued to use their control of government to repress popular demands. They perpetuated for their own benefit an essentially unregulated, externally oriented, "liberal" economic system. Except in Costa Rica, the continued existence of Liberal-Conservative factionalism, relatively large indigenous communities to supply forced labor, and the emergent *hacienda* system all helped strengthen the military's political role. Armies (at first belonging to individual *caudillos*) fought civil wars, subdued peasants who had been forcibly deprived of their land, and implemented forced labor laws against these new "vagrants." This heavy military involvement in economic and political life retarded the development of civil political institutions and spawned both military rule and considerable political violence. Central American nations spent most of the period from 1838 until 1945 under either civilian or military dictatorships. Even Costa Rica showed little democratic promise. Although less turbulent than its neighbors, it experienced elite rule, militarism, dictatorship, and political instability well into the twentieth century.

Politics

In the nineteenth century, the basic conflict within the elite was between those people who came to call themselves Conservatives and those who described themselves as Liberals. Before independence and in the first decades afterward, the Conservatives advocated authoritarian, centralized government (sometimes even monarchy), greater economic regulation, and a continuation of special privileges for the Catholic Church. Liberals espoused limited representative democracy, decentralized government, free trade and reduced economic regulation, and a separation of church and state. Conservatives tended to come from more traditional large-scale landholders who had benefited from Crown licenses and export monopolies. Liberals were more likely to be the disgruntled large landowners who lacked Crown licenses to export their crops or urban elites concerned with commerce.

One important difference was that whereas Conservatives generally remained wedded to more traditional economic practices, the Liberals—who by the late nineteenth century had come to dominate all the Central American nations—advocated "modernization" within an externally oriented, laissez-faire economic framework. Specifically, Liberals championed new export products—such as coffee and bananas—and development of government institutions and material infrastructure (highways, railroads, and ports) to facilitate growth in the export economy. Liberals also strove to reduce the role of the Catholic Church in some countries. And, to promote exports, they enacted legislation that stripped most indigenous communities of lands once reserved for them by the Spanish Crown. Despite such early contrasts and after considerable warfare between the two factions, by the late nineteenth century ideological and policy differences between Liberals and Conservatives had largely vanished. Liberals, when in power, ruled in an authoritarian manner and eventually reached accommodations with the Church, thus eliminating a longstanding difference between the parties. Conservatives eventually supported laissez-faire economics and the expansion of coffee production.

The Liberal and Conservative parties degenerated over time into ideologically indistinguishable clan-based political factions. Conservatives generally ruled in the mid-nineteenth century but Liberal regimes eventually supplanted them. Liberal hegemony in Central America thereafter lasted well into the twentieth century and, as it died, spawned an extreme right-wing form of militarism that plagued Guatemala, El Salvador, and Honduras until the 1990s. One should not confuse the Central American meaning of the term "Liberal" with the vernacular meaning of that word in the United States. Central American Liberals were exponents of classical Liberal economic policies (capitalism) and republican government. They held elitist attitudes, advocated essentially unregulated free enterprise, and generally believed the proposition that "government is best which governs least." Indeed, in the U.S. political system today, modern conservatives would likely find themselves very much at home with the economic policies of nineteenth-century Central American Liberals. The modernization that liberalism brought simply tended, in most countries, to accelerate the concentration of wealth and income in the hands of the elite and to increase the dependency of local economies on the international economic system.

Eventually, however, Central American liberalism drew fire from more popularly oriented political movements motivated by the Great Depression and World

War II's economic dislocations. In Costa Rica, challenges to Liberal dominance and political reforms began in the late nineteenth century and a labor movement developed in the early decades of the twentieth. In the mid-1940s, the government of Rafael Calderón Guardia allied with Communist-dominated labor and the Catholic Church to curtail liberalism with labor and social security legislation. In 1948–1949 a social democratic revolution went even further by retaining Calderón's reforms, abolishing the army, and giving the state significant new economic regulation and planning roles. In El Salvador during the 1930s, local Liberals responded to depression-driven labor and peasant discontent by ruling through the military. An abortive labor and leftist uprising in 1932 gave the army and landowners leave to massacre thirty thousand peasants. The military kept control of the presidency for the next five decades, and by the 1970s sometimes acted independently on economic policy and ignored the wishes of its former Liberal masters.

In Guatemala in 1944, social democrats overthrew a "modernizing" dictator, Jorge Ubico, and began a mild form of democratic revolution that accommodated indigenous groups and organized labor. Although a successful CIA-sponsored counterrevolution took place in 1954, the military, not civilian Liberals, took power and ruled the country into the 1980s. In Nicaragua, U.S. armed intervention favored Conservatives between 1909 and 1927. The United States then switched sides and help reinstall the Liberals to power, but this led to the establishment of the Somoza family dictatorship. The Somozas ruled Nicaragua from 1936 until a mass-based insurrection brought the social-revolutionary Sandinista National Liberation Front (Frente Sandinista de Liberación Nacional—FSLN) to power in 1979. Many Nicaraguan Liberals exiled themselves in the United States and waited for the Sandinista revolution to end in 1990 to return to national politics. In traditional Honduras, Liberals and Conservatives (the National Party) alternately held formal office under the watchful eye of an overweening military throughout the 1980s and into the 1990s. It was only in the mid-1990s that Honduras's civilian leaders began to come to power in a real sense.

Interestingly, the "neoliberalism" which would come to dominate the region in the late twentieth and early twenty-first centuries would, in many ways, harken back to the crude liberalism prevalent at the turn of and into the twentieth century. Like its forerunner, neoliberalism would promote free trade, largely unregulated capitalism, and a role for government limited mainly to "housekeeping" activities and promotion of trade. And, like nineteenth-century liberalism, it would tend to accentuate inequitable distribution of income and property even as it achieved sometimes impressive growth in GDP.

External Involvement

International pressures battered Central America after 1850. Great powers (particularly Britain and the United States) pursued economic, political, and security interests in the region. Britain carved the colony of British Honduras from the Guatemalan territory of Belize and the Miskito Protectorate from eastern Nicaragua to promote and protect British mining, timber, and geopolitical interests. British influence was greatest during the first half of the nineteenth century but thereafter U.S. influence increasingly supplanted the British. Foreign intervention exacerbated the Central American nations' well-established penchant for interfering in each others' internal affairs and led to international disputes within the region and overt and covert military and political intervention by outside powers. Tennessean William Walker undertook the most flagrant (but not only) intervention into Nicaragua. Contracted by business partners of Cornelius Vanderbilt in an effort to take over of Vanderbilt's transit route across the isthmus, Walker brought mercenaries to Nicaragua in 1855. In league with out-of-power Liberals, he formed an army and toppled the Conservative government. The United States quickly recognized the fledgling Liberal government of Walker, who announced his intention to reinstitute slavery, make English Nicaragua's official language, and seek U.S. statehood.

Conservatives in power in the other four Central American nations agreed to send troops to oust Walker. War ensued in 1856, with Conservative forces partly financed by the British and by Vanderbilt. Walker capitulated in 1857 and fled Nicaragua under U.S. protection. He soon attempted another filibuster, but Honduras captured and executed him in 1860. This 1856–1857 struggle against William Walker's takeover of Nicaragua, known as the National War, briefly rekindled interests in reunification of Central America, reinforced Conservative political hegemony in Nicaragua for many years, and contributed to anti-U.S. nationalism among Central Americans.[4]

By 1900 the dominant outside power in the isthmus, the United States, energetically promoted its economic and security interests. U.S. diplomats served U.S. banks by peddling loans to the region's governments. U.S. customs agents seized Central American customs houses to repay the loans, and U.S. marines intervened in domestic political problems in Honduras, Nicaragua, and Panama. Transit across the narrow isthmus, especially a ship canal, especially motivated Washington. When President Theodore Roosevelt could not win agreement from either Colombia or Nicaragua for a proposed canal lease agreement, he sent U.S. troops in 1903 to ensure that local and foreign insurgents could "liberate" Colombia's province of Panama. This intervention secured for the United States the right to build a canal through what then became the Republic of Panama. When Nicaragua's president José Santos Zelaya contemplated making a canal deal with Germany in 1909, the United States helped foment a Conservative rebellion against him and landed U.S. troops to back it up. Zelaya resigned and the new government gave the United States a canal-rights treaty that effectively guaranteed that

Nicaragua would never have a canal. U.S. marines returned to Nicaragua in 1912 and remained there most of the period until 1933.

The United States under Franklin Roosevelt flirted with good neighborliness toward Central America during the 1930s. During World War II security interests led to heavy U.S. assistance to train and modernize Central America's armies. After 1945 the United States emphasized containment of communism by backing anticommunist regimes. It enlisted other Central American governments to help oust the reformist civilian government of Guatemala in 1954 and to reinforce the Somoza regime after the Managua earthquake in 1972.

Fidel Castro's overthrow of the Batista regime in Cuba in 1959 reinforced the U.S. tendency to concentrate its Central American policy upon the containment of communism. U.S. economic and military assistance strengthened the region's armies, pursued counterinsurgency against leftist rebels, promoted regional economic integration and development, worked to divide organized labor, and undermined political reformers of the left and center. The Carter administration's novel emphasis on human rights (1977–1979) led to aid cutoffs for abusive military governments in Guatemala and El Salvador and to the ebbing of U.S. support of Nicaragua's Somoza regime. When the FSLN-led popular rebellion toppled Anastasio Somoza Debayle in 1979, however, U.S. policy in Central America shifted sharply back toward the 30-year tradition of containment of communism. Washington lifted its military aid ban for El Salvador and involved itself deeply in trying to block the growing rebellion there. Always pursuing containment, the U.S. tactic of allying openly with military despots was modified slightly under the Reagan and subsequent administrations, which found it useful, in dealing with a very reluctant Congress, to at least appear to be promoting electoral democracy as the best model for the isthmus. The United States policy had two prongs: On one hand, it encouraged elections and nominal transition to civilian rule. On the other, it promoted and financed a large counterrevolutionary force to fight Nicaragua's Sandinista government, devoted massive economic, military, and political aid to bolster nominally civilian governments (under military tutelage) in El Salvador and Honduras, and invaded Panama to overthrow its military government in 1989. Even after the Cold War ended in 1989, the Sandinistas lost power, and the Salvadoran and Guatemalan insurgents signed peace accords, U.S. diplomats repeatedly interfered in Central American elections to discourage voting for leftist parties.

Economic and Social Change

In the economic arena, Central America has specialized in exporting agricultural commodities since 1838. After 1850 coffee gradually became a major export throughout the region (except Honduras). During the twentieth century, other commodity export production developed (bananas, cacao, cotton, sugar, and beef), and, like coffee, each of these products was subject to great world market price swings. Cyclical recessions and depressions in the international economy hit Central America hard. Industrialization was slow, the extreme inequalities in the class systems intensified, and dependency upon imported food and manufactures grew.

Coffee production wrought major socioeconomic changes in the late nineteenth century: It concentrated landownership in the hands of major coffee growers, millers and exporters, who constituted new national economic elites that promoted and protected their interests by controlling (or sharing control of) the state.[5] Other export crops had regional importance with similar effects on the distribution of wealth and political power.

The agro-export elites eventually had to enlist the national armed forces to suppress popular discontent. Together they opposed socioeconomic reform so tenaciously that their rule has been labeled "reactionary despotism."[6] Baloyra described the reactionary coalitions of Central America as

> bent on the preservation of privilege [and their] monopoly of public roles and of the entrepreneurial function. . . . The dominant actors of the reactionary coalitions of Central America do not believe in suffrage, do not believe in paying taxes, and do not believe in acting through responsible institutions. Their basic ideological premise is that the government exists to protect them from other social groups in order to continue to accumulate capital without the restraints created by labor unions, competition, and government regulation.[7]

During the 1950s and 1960s Central American investors began the extensive cultivation of grains for the regional market and cotton for the international market. Except for Honduras,[8] each Central American nation by the mid-1970s had greatly reduced its smallholding and subsistence agricultural sector (small farmers) and greatly expanded migrant wage-labor forces. A large rural labor surplus developed, cityward migration by unemployable campesinos swelled, domestic food production shrank, and landownership and agricultural production became still more concentrated in fewer hands. National dependency upon imported foodstuffs rose throughout the region, as did the number of citizens directly affected by imported inflation.

Following the 1959 overthrow of Fulgencio Batista in Cuba,[9] Central American governments despaired of the region's slow growth rates. In 1960 they formed the Central American Common Market (CACM) to spur regional economic integration, foreign investment, intraregional trade, and industrialization. A stated rationale was to diversify and increase production so that wealth might "trickle down" to the poor and undercut the potential appeal of socialism. The CACM's objectives converged in 1961 with those of the U.S. Alliance for Progress, which sought to bolster the capitalist development model. The Alliance sought to undercut the left by greatly increasing public development aid to Central America and thus encouraging private investment. During the 1960s, to varying degrees in each nation, the CACM and Alliance brought a surge in domestic and foreign investment. It concentrated in the capital-intensive production of consumer goods, manufactured mainly with imported raw materials and fuel. Gross domestic products and GDPs per capita grew rapidly well into the 1970s, mainly because of a rapid increase in industrial production and productivity while input prices remained stable.[10]

Students of the CACM agree, however, that its industrial boom failed to absorb the rapidly growing labor supply and in some nations shifted wealth and income away from working-class groups. The number of factory and middle-class jobs grew because of industrialization until the early 1970s, but rural and urban unemployment simultaneously rose throughout the region. Moreover, the CACM's development model began to exhaust its potential for growth in the 1970s. Imported industrial raw materials suffered upwardly spiraling prices after 1967—input costs rose 150 percent from 1968 to 1976. These higher costs reduced investment rates, productivity, output growth, and the competitiveness of Central American products.[11] In Nicaragua, El Salvador, and Guatemala, the industrial sector's share of exports declined markedly (averaging roughly 6 percent overall) from the 1970–1974 to the 1975–1979 period. Balance-of-payments pressures afflicted all the Central American economies in the 1970s because of declining terms of trade (the relative costs of imports versus exports), a recession in the world economy, and higher foreign interest rates. According to Weeks, "each government in effect decided to pursue a separate strategy to weather the crisis, rather than a collective one."[12] By the end of the 1970s the CACM accord began to break down, and in the 1980s the breakdown was complete.

After World War II socioeconomic change accelerated in Central America. Population almost doubled between 1960 and 1980 and high growth rates persisted. The expanding commercial agricultural sector and the increasing concentration of landownership forced peasants off the land and thus swelled both agricultural labor migration and the region's urban populations. Enhanced educational programs increased school attendance, literacy, and raised participation in higher education everywhere in the isthmus. Ownership of radio and television receivers and of broadcast facilities spread, and roads were improved and means of transportation developed. Such changes made communication easier and faster and spread awareness of national problems. Economic activity shifted away from agriculture and toward manufacturing and services. Overall economic activity (measured as GDP per capita) more than doubled between 1960 and 1980. However, this growth was unevenly distributed, and as noted, a sharp recession reduced production regionwide in the late 1970s and the 1980s.

The wrenching economic strains of the 1970s caused cascading political and economic difficulties, detailed in the country chapters. At the macrosocial level,

Central American nations tried to borrow their way through recession and political crisis. All multiplied their foreign debt severalfold while their economies eroded. Interest payments on this debt undermined economic recovery efforts, made governments more dependent on foreign lenders, and eventually forced them to undergo neoliberal structural adjustment programs in the late 1980s and 1990s. By 2000, under neoliberal policies, Costa Rica, El Salvador, and Guatemala had found new sources of growth in assembly plant production, nontraditional exports, and tourism so that their economic growth resumed and their foreign debt had declined. Sadly, by 2000 only El Salvador and Costa Rica had recovered enough to surpass their 1980 levels of gross domestic product (GDP) per capita. Neither Honduras nor Nicaragua experienced real economic growth between 1980 and 2000. Tragically, Nicaragua's 2000 per capita GDP was only 44 percent of that of 1970. Still reeling from a decade of externally financed civil war and economic destabilization, Nicaragua had become one of the hemisphere's historically most dramatic cases of economic collapse.[13]

The second great consequence was both macro- and microsocial—enormous political turmoil. At the system level, it aggravated economic crisis throughout the 1980s by disrupting production and frightening away capital. At the microsocial level, the living conditions of rural and urban lower-class citizens deteriorated while they witnessed the rapid enrichment of economic elites. This impoverishment and growing inequality stimulated class conflict in the form of regionwide mobilization of protest, opposition, and demands for economic and political reform. Some governments violently repressed such mobilization, which brought about revolution in Nicaragua and lengthy civil wars in El Salvador and Guatemala. These, combined with deepening economic crisis and escalating foreign intervention in Central American affairs, sparked a series of regime changes in the region's governments between 1979 and 1996. Only Costa Rica—the sole democracy in the region in the 1970s—escaped regime change during this tumultuous era.

In summary, the rapid but inequitable economic growth of the 1960s and 1970s caused economic policies and class conflict that transformed Central America both politically and economically in the 1980s and 1990s. Political change was generally toward electoral democracy and lessened repression and violence. The economic results varied widely, however. All countries suffered in the 1970s–1980s crisis, and all eventually adopted the neoliberal economic model as their best hope for development. It worked best in Costa Rica and El Salvador, whose economies recovered and began to grow again. But the other three nations remained either stagnant (Guatemala) or shrank further into misery. As we wrote this in 2004, Central Americans enjoyed more freedom and democracy than in the 1970s, but many of them were also poorer and their economic prospects remained bleak.

4

Costa Rica

A slogan on a popular T-shirt sold to tourists in Costa Rica proclaims "*¡Costa Rica es diferente!*" (Costa Rica is different). Evoking the country's stable democracy and high levels of social development, the expression makes the national tourism agency's pitch but also states the myth of Costa Rican exceptionalism. Schools, the media, and popular tradition still inculcate Costa Ricans with the notion that their country stands apart from the rest of Central America's dictatorships, political violence, and underdevelopment.[1] The truth of the Costa Rica's distinctiveness is manifest, yet as the twenty-first century began there was less to the myth than met the eye. For most of the nineteenth and twentieth centuries Costa Rica clearly differed from its neighbors in important and visible ways. In its economy, however, Costa Rica always experienced the same international commodity price swings and dependent development as its neighbors. From the 1950s on, however, Costa Rica's governments simply managed these economic problems better, easing their impact on citizens and masking underlying similarities to neighbors.

But as the twentieth century ended, Costa Rica was gradually becoming more like its neighbors in both politics and economics. As formal electoral democracy and improved human rights spread region-wide, Costa Rica became less politically distinctive because other isthmian regimes adopted systems more like Costa Rica's. But in the economic arena, it was Costa Rica that evolved toward a model common across Central and Latin America. Global economic system changes compelled Costa Rica to abandon a post–civil war development strategy that served its people well for decades. Forced like its neighbors to adopt a neoliberal economic development model, Costa Rica reconfigured its links to the world economy and changed domestic welfare policies. Neoliberalism may have begun pushing Costa Rica gradually toward the human development levels of other

Central American nations as the policies and services that once distinguished it were steadily eroded.[2]

As we argued in Chapter 2, Central American nations have experienced shifting global political and economic forces from the establishment of Spanish colonialism to the present. At key junctures global forces have imposed dramatic alterations in isthmian economies and political arrangements. Local conditions, resources, and actors have shaped and channeled these common external pressures to produce divergent local effects. Costa Rica's evolution through these forces has been the most distinctive almost from the outset, but one should not lose track of the similarities in pressures driving change.

Historical Background

Deviant from certain key patterns set in the rest of Central America during the colonial period, Costa Rica remained an exception to many isthmian social, economic, and political norms until the 1990s. Rather isolated from the rest of Central America because of distance and rugged terrain, Costa Rica remained more racially and economically homogeneous than its neighbors. This does not mean that Costa Rica lacked social disparities or that it remained economically self-contained. Rather, Costa Rica's social inequities were never great enough to let one class or race completely dominate others to the detriment of the majority as elsewhere in the isthmus. Despite embracing export agriculture, Costa Rica never fully developed the dependency system prevalent elsewhere in the isthmus, with its tremendous human costs.

The roots of eventual Costa Rican democracy were planted in the nineteenth century, although true democratic rule would not consolidate until the mid-twentieth century. From 1824 to 1899, one Costa Rican government in five ended by coup d'état and the military ruled the country 44 percent of the time.[3] During most of that epoch, moneyed rural families governed the country. Such elections as did occur were indirect, confined to a tiny, literate elite, and often rigged. However, certain economic trends and political reforms prevented a total domination of Costa Rican national politics by a landed oligarchy. The first dictator-president, Braulio Carrillo (1835–1842), for instance, increased the already fairly large number of small farmers by distributing municipal lands to the inhabitants. He also promoted coffee cultivation and included small farmers, in contrast to elsewhere in Central America. This helped form a class of smallholding yeoman farmers that continuously renewed itself by expanding the agricultural frontiers.

The incipient landed elite continued to rule the country until its control was broken by the military, which greatly expanded after the 1857 Central American war. The military's leader, Liberal dictator Tomás Guardia (1870–1882), took power and attacked the wealthy by confiscating some of their properties and exiling a number of their leaders. Guardia contracted foreigners to construct new roads and railways needed to move coffee to market. In the late nineteenth century, a labor shortage kept rural wages high as coffee production spread. By then market forces in the rapidly growing coffee industry had begun to concentrate land ownership and thus had pushed many smallholders off the land. In order to secure the labor essential to the nation's wealth, large coffee farmers had to pay decent wages and the government had to pass reformist public policies. Costa Rican peasants and workers therefore generally experienced less exploitation and repression than found elsewhere in Central America.

Despite the militarization of politics during the Guardia dictatorship, precursors of democracy developed in the second half of the nineteenth century. Elections, though indirect, elite-dominated, and often fraudulent, became important by the 1840s. The growth of commerce, government, transport, immigration, and urban centers swelled the number of people available for and interested in political activity. The modernizing Liberals (Guardia and his civilian successors) greatly increased education spending and thus literacy by 1900. Because the ability to read was a key criterion for voter eligibility, increasing literacy also expanded suffrage.[4]

By 1889 an economic slowdown and the Liberals' anticlericalism generated support for an opposition Catholic Union Party and its presidential candidate José J. Rodríguez. Backed by the Catholic Church, Rodríguez won the vote among the electors, but the army tried to block him from taking office. Incited by the Church, angry citizens took to the streets and forced the army to back down. This election, often incorrectly cited as the birth of Costa Rican democracy, was nevertheless significant because it forced the military to respect an opposition victory and because ordinary citizens mobilized to defend an election. After Rodríguez, however, authoritarian elite rulers and election fraud returned.[5]

From 1905 to 1914, presidents Cleto González Víquez and Ricardo Jiménez Oreamuno further broadened suffrage, established direct popular election of public officials, and permitted free and open opposition campaigns for office. A military regime led by the Tinoco brothers seized power in 1917 during the hard times associated with World War I. In 1919 popular protest and an invasion by exiled elites toppled the Tinoco regime, Costa Rica's last military government. Civilian, constitutional rule continued thereafter, and the Costa Rican electorate expanded continuously.

The completion of the Atlantic railroad led to the development of an additional export crop, bananas. The foreign-owned banana industry, concentrated in the sparsely populated Atlantic coastal lowlands, had little effect on Costa Rican politics in the early twentieth century. Later, as hard times developed, labor organizers led by Communists organized the banana plantations, and union influence and political power grew. By the 1940s, the deep economic slump caused by the

Great Depression and World War II had caused great social dislocations. This pitted against one another factions of the political-economic elite, working classes and unions, and an emerging middle class. In the early 1940s, President Rafael Calderón Guardia, a popular medical doctor and reformist coffee aristocrat, broke with the rest of the coffee-growing political class. Bidding to dominate the government, he allied with the Communist labor unions and the Catholic Church. Assisted by Communist legislators, Calderón enacted and began implementing Costa Rica's first labor and social security laws.

Calderón's alliance with the Communists and, in 1948, electoral fraud and legislative tampering with the presidential election results provided pretexts for a brief but violent civil war. A coalition between elite politicos angry at Calderón and middle-class elements, dominated by a junta of social democrats led by José "Pepe" Figueres Ferrer, rebelled. The rebels defeated the government within a few months. From that time to the 1990s, the country's social democrats—the National Liberation Party (Partido de Liberación Nacional—PLN), led for three decades by Figueres—set the tone of Costa Rican political life. In keeping with a well-established tradition of political accommodation, the victorious National Liberation junta retained Calderón's social reforms for workers. The junta went even further by nationalizing the banking and insurance industries. A constituent assembly rewrote the constitution in 1949. The new constitution enfranchised women and blacks and abolished the army, the latter an act that would ensure future political stability. In late 1949, the junta turned the presidency over to the rightful winner of the 1948 election, Otilio Ulate, who was not a part of the National Liberation movement.

When the PLN and Figueres first won the presidency in 1954, they began expanding the social legislation initiated under Calderón. Increasingly broad segments of the populace received health and social security coverage. Even the conservative coalition governments that periodically replaced the PLN in power preserved and expanded such social welfare policies. After 1949, successive governments held scrupulously honest elections at regular intervals under the auspices of a powerful and independent Supreme Electoral Tribunal. When defeated at the polls, the PLN willingly gave over control of the presidency and Legislative Assembly to an amorphous conservative opposition coalition. The PLN won the presidency seven times and the opposition won it six times between 1949 and 1998. Opinion surveys showed that Costa Rican citizens strongly supported democratic civil liberties and alternation in power by the competing parties.

In sum, Costa Rica's center-left social democratic PLN governments took power and consolidated a new political and economic regime in the 1940s and 1950s despite the prevailing trends elsewhere in the isthmus. Similar post–World War II movements favoring democracy appeared in Guatemala, Honduras, Nicaragua and El Salvador, but eventually all failed. Instrumental in the failure of prodemocracy mobilization around Central America were U.S. anticommunist policies that aided and encouraged national armed forces and rightist elites to block the left as it fought for reform. In contrast, in Costa Rica the prodemocracy reformers had defeated the Communists in the 1948 civil war and thereafter contained their influence. This put Costa Rica's new regime on the good side of the United States and helped it survive where others nearby would not.

Despite developing a model constitutional democracy and the consolidation of electoral democracy, not all remained well in Costa Rica. From the 1970s forward commodity price shifts, great-power geopolitics, civil war in neighboring nations, and an evolving international economy repeatedly disturbed Costa Rica's political and economic systems, challenged its institutions, and forced frequent adjustment to ever-changing realities.

Weathering Global Forces

Costa Rica experienced the same global economic forces as its neighbors during the 1970s and 1980s, which generated some internal unrest. Nevertheless it escaped without regime change the violent strife that afflicted much of the isthmus. Costa Rica's relative stability was no accident—it resulted from elites' decisions in the 1970s and 1980s to alleviate some of the erosion of popular living standards and to avoid brutal political repression. These decisions stemmed partly from late-nineteenth-century rulers and landowners accommodating peasants to secure a labor supply. At mid-twentieth century both Calderón Guardia and his PLN successors employed political and economic reforms to placate and stabilize mobilized working and middle classes. This tradition of elite accommodation of mobilized lower sectors, we believe, provided Costa Rica's leaders a model that allowed them to preserve stable electoral democracy in the 1970s–1980s despite grave challenges.

The government's task proved difficult over the longer term. Costa Rica's post–civil war social democratic development model relied on state-led development projects and Central American Common Market (CACM)-coordinated import substitution industrialization that enlarged the government's payroll and economic role. Costa Rica also had social welfare programs, ambitious for a developing country, that dated from the 1940s and grew during the 1950s and 1960s. Industrialization aside, Costa Rica's economy and the government's budget in the 1970s still depended heavily on international market prices for its exports (coffee, bananas, and goods sold to the CACM) and its imports (especially vital petroleum). Problems arose, however, when skyrocketing oil costs after 1973 and simultaneously falling export prices caused inflation, layoffs, and a public revenue crunch.

Sources of Class Conflict. How did the Costa Rican variant of the Central American crisis of the 1970s arise? The Central American Common Market brought accelerated economic growth and industrialization in the 1960s and early 1970s. Costa Rican per capita gross domestic product rose at an average annual rate of 3.4 percent from 1962 through 1971, and at an average of 2.6 percent from 1972 through 1979. Per capita GDP in constant 1986 dollars almost doubled from 1960 to 1980. Among Central American nations, Costa Rica had the largest share of its workforce (16 percent) in manufacturing by 1983. By 1987, Costa Rica (at 23 percent) ranked second in the isthmus in terms of manufacturing's contribution to domestic production. The agricultural sector workforce shrank from 51 percent to 29 percent between 1960 and 1980.[6] Commerce, services, and government all expanded in Costa Rica as the nation rapidly modernized and urbanized.

The prevailing theory about the onset of rebellion in Central America in the 1970s contends that severe declines in real working-class wages and living conditions mobilized many people into labor, political, and protest organization and activity.[7] Because many urban and rural wage earners in Central America had little or no margin of safety, a drop in their real earnings (wages corrected for inflation) could catastrophically reduce their ability to survive. Such a rapid erosion of life chances provided a powerful impetus to join political or labor groups seeking redress of such problems.

Data on Costa Rica reveal that wage workers lost ground relative to other income earners in the mid-1970s, but recovered much of their purchasing power by 1978–1979. An index of working-class wages shows that Costa Rican workers' real pay rates fell in 1975 and 1976, but recovered and then began to exceed earlier levels by the late 1970s. Wages fell again in 1982 but began an immediate recovery in 1983–1984 and remained relatively high through the rest of the 1980s.[8] While working-class earnings and living standards declined in Costa Rica during the mid-1970s, the losses were less severe and sustained than those in Guatemala, Nicaragua, and El Salvador, because the Costa Rican government found ways to let real wages recover much of their earlier purchasing power.[9] From 1982 until the late 1990s Costa Rican workers gained ground against inflation fairly steadily.

Income Distribution. Another insight into economic class disparity in Costa Rica comes from shifts in the distribution of income among classes. One measure of changing income inequality during the 1970s is the share of national income paid out as employee compensation; decreasing employee compensation would suggest a shift of income away from salaried and wage-earning workers and toward investors and entrepreneurs. Data reveal that between 1970 and 1975, the employee-compensation share of all national income fluctuated somewhat, but tended to increase.[10] During the 1960s and early 1970s, Costa Rican public policy redistributed income toward the middle three-fifths of the populace, mainly at the expense of the richest fifth.[11] In both relative and absolute income trends, Costa Rica clearly contrasts with what the evidence will later show for Nicaragua, El Salvador, and Guatemala. In Costa Rica, wages fluctuated during the 1970s and early

1980s, but generally recovered after short-term declines. In the three other countries, wages declined but did not recover, increasingly aggrieving those losing out.

Wealth. During the 1970s Costa Rica also avoided sharp increases in class inequality observed to have occurred in Nicaragua, El Salvador, and Guatemala. Although Costa Rica was a member of the CACM and was also hit by rapid energy-driven consumer price increases of the mid-1970s, data reveal that in Costa Rica these factors affected wealth distribution less than elsewhere in the isthmus.

Costa Rica's social democratic economic development model and low military expenditures brought that nation into the 1970s with a social welfare system and economy that attenuated inflation's impact on popular living conditions. Data comparing Costa Rican spending on social programs to other isthmian nations' appear in Table A.5 (Appendix). In the 1970s and early 1980s Costa Rica's ratio of spending for social services versus defense was between four and five times greater than that of its nearest competitor in Central America. The benefits of these policies became manifest in Costa Rica's higher literacy, greater longevity, and lower mortality rates.[12] As noted above, income distribution in Costa Rica actually became modestly more egalitarian during the 1960s and 1970s, helping to prevent the rapid movement of wealth toward the upper classes observed in Nicaragua, Guatemala, and El Salvador.

In Costa Rican agriculture, concentration of land ownership grew steadily in the 1960s and early 1970s, but the availability of some land that could still be colonized until the late 1960s and the still-growing banana industry absorbed much of the surplus agricultural work force. Moreover, during the 1974–1978 period, Costa Rica developed an aggressive and successful land reform program that distributed land to numerous peasants and staved off the deterioration of living standards for many.[13] Additionally, the growth of employment in urban services and manufacturing absorbed much of the surplus agricultural population and prevented the sharp growth of rural unemployment and poverty through the late 1980s.[14]

Popular Mobilization. The Costa Rican government carefully managed citizen mobilization in one critical arena—labor—but encouraged it in others. On the one hand, following the 1948 civil war the government worked to fragment the national union movement (including industrial workers, service workers, and white-collar public employees) among competing, party-affiliated confederations in order to curtail union power.[15] On the other hand and in notable contrast, during the 1960s and early 1970s the government itself used social promoters to help organize communal self-help organizations. Hundreds of community development associations, largely uncoordinated among themselves, worked on local projects and made small demands to legislators for funds for local improvements. The community development movement, promoted by the state itself, was at first fairly docile and easier to coopt than leftist-led unions had been in the 1930s and 1940s.

By the 1970s, however, union membership began to expand.[16] Then the oil-price and inflation shocks from the global economy stirred popular mobilization.[17] Unions became more militant. Industrial disputes rose sharply during 1975–1976 when real wages declined but subsided when wages recovered in the late 1970s. Wage disputes rose again in 1982 after real wages fell again, then leveled off in 1983 and 1984 when earnings once again recovered purchasing power. Economic austerity measures included public employee layoffs, service cuts, and sharp consumer price increases in the late 1980s and early 1990s.[18] Civil society, including government-promoted community organizations, became more restive in response. Hard times brought numerous strikes and demonstrations, but wage and policy concessions eventually quelled them.[19]

The political party system of Costa Rica remained stable in the 1960s and 1970s; the social democratic National Liberation Party (PLN) alternated in power with a coalition of moderately conservative parties under the Unity banner. The traditional Unity coalition of conservative parties reorganized and institutionalized itself into the Social Christian Unity Party (Partido de Unidad Social Cristiano—PUSC) in 1985. Radical left parties won a few seats to the Legislative Assembly during the 1970s, but were weak outside the union movement. As living standards of most Costa Ricans declined during the 1980s, mobilization of demands by a broad array of interest groups increased and public approval of the government declined. Organized labor attempted but failed to forge a militant general labor confederation. Voting for leftist parties—long considered a bellwether of protest—declined in the 1982 and 1986 national elections. Costa Rica's more radical parties and labor became increasingly estranged and divided in the early and mid–1980s. Polls revealed that even in the midst of a severe recession, most citizens remained loyal to the regime.

In sum, although Costa Rica experienced increased organization and protest, no dramatic increase in antiregime organization or coalition formation developed from the late 1970s through the early 1990s.[20] Unlike Nicaragua, Guatemala, and El Salvador, Costa Rica experienced no significant challenge to the sovereignty of the state.

Government Response to Popular Mobilization. Central American regimes all experienced popular mobilization during the 1970s and 1980s, but they responded to it very differently. In contrast to Costa Rica, the Salvadoran, Guatemalan, and prerevolutionary Nicaraguan regimes reacted violently to popular organization and protest. Although their regimes were quite different in the late 1970s and early 1980s, Costa Rica (a democracy) and Honduras (a military government) each addressed popular mobilization relatively moderately. This prevented the mobilization of new opponents to the government angered by repression, and thus avoided escalating conflict.

Costa Rica kept an open, constitutional regime with clean elections and considerable popular access to public officials. Costa Rican officials typically responded to mobilized demands by accommodating rather than repressing them. Even when demands escalated into civil disobedience, demonstrations, strikes, and riots, the government usually responded with moderate force and used study and compromise to defuse conflict. For instance, Costa Rican rulers met violent civil disturbances—land invasions in the early 1970s, the Limón riot of 1979, banana workers' strikes in 1980, 1981, and 1982, and street vendors' strikes in 1991—with moderate official force so that deaths among protesters were rare.[21] Different administrations from both PLN and PUSC sought to accommodate diverse demand-makers by negotiating with them, forming panels of inquiry or making conciliatory policy gestures.

As later chapters will spell out, Central America's major national revolts of the 1970s and 1980s (Nicaragua, El Salvador, Guatemala) arose from sharp increases in inequality and decreases in popular living standards during the mid-1970s. These grievances drove popular mobilization that demanded redress of the working majorities' wages and living standards. Costa Rica also experienced this mobilization but responded to it by allowing workers' wages to recover, with other ameliorative policies and with typically low repression. This combination of amelioration of grievances and low repression defused popular anger, demobilized much protest, and prevented an upward spiral of conflict that in three neighboring nations caused open rebellions against the regime. Thus Costa Rica's political regime survived the onslaught of globally driven economic uncertainty and turmoil by following the national political and economic elite's longstanding accommodative traditions. But the global strains of the 1970s and 1980s nonetheless left marks on Costa Rica—not of political regime change but transformations in its economic development model and in the political party system.

The Economic Development Model Transformed

As noted above, simultaneously declining export revenues and upwardly spiraling energy costs pushed Costa Rica into a severe economic crisis. Rapid inflation drove down demand and real wages, which further reduced consumer demand. The governments of the mid-and late 1970s and early 1980s, rather than curtail public spending to address shrinking state revenues, borrowed abroad to finance the growing public deficit. In the short term this lightened the impact of the economic crisis on the Costa Rican public, but in the middle term it disastrously affected the government's financial health. Foreign debt as a share of GDP rose from 12 percent in 1970 to 147 percent in 1982. Foreign interest payments consumed a third of export earnings and further weakened the public and private sectors. Similar difficulties and escalating civil wars elsewhere in Central America combined to collapse Costa Rica's regional markets and to drive away tourists and foreign capital. In 1981 the administration of Rodrigo Carazo Odio found its foreign reserve coffers empty and defaulted on Costa Rica's foreign debt. This pushed the currency (the colón) into a ten-year slide that eroded 90 percent of its value.[22]

When the PLN's Luis Alberto Monge became president in 1982 these dire economic predicaments forced him to seek international assistance that would come with high costs. One source of help sprang from U.S. wishes to secure a southern base for its efforts to unseat Nicaragua's Sandinista revolution. The Reagan administration pressured Costa Rica and Monge agreed to collaborate with the Nicaraguan counterrevolutionaries and their American helpers. In exchange the United States compensated Costa Rica with over US$1.1 billion in aid during the mid-1980s, much of it in the unusual form of outright grants instead of loans. These funds effectively delayed Costa Rica's reckoning with its sick economy while addicting it ever more to external aid. By 1985 a second source of international aid had to be invoked.

The flow of U.S. grants for pro-Contra activities ended when Monge's successor, PLN president Oscar Arias Sánchez, in 1987 successfully advanced the Central American Peace Accord and sharply reduced Costa Rica's cooperation with the Contras. Although Costa Rican peace initiatives would soon win Arias the Nobel Peace Prize, the Reagan administration opposed them and retaliated with sharp aid cuts that reduced economic output and increased inflation.

Costa Rica's second source of external aid, borrowing from intergovernmental lenders and individual nations, also came heavily conditioned. As Robinson details, the emergence of "global" capitalism in the late twentieth century had begun to draw Central America into the evolving global economy and society.[23] This would involve replacing the previous epoch's traditional agro-exports and import-substitution industrialization (ISI) development orientation with a neoliberal economic model emphasizing free-market capitalism, a smaller public sector, liberalization of markets, privatization of public-sector enterprises, and reorientation of production toward nontraditional exports. The principal promoters of the new style of global capitalism included the U.S. government and other major capitalist countries plus several international lenders (the Interamerican Development Bank, International Monetary Fund, Paris Club). These institutions, their policies heavily influenced by the United States' heavy voting weight on their policy boards, shared and promoted a neoliberal agenda for economic reform in developing countries.

These states and organizations combined to effectively force Costa Rica into three structural adjustment agreements (SAAs) in 1985, 1989, and 1995, with the Monge, Arias, and Figueres Olsen administrations, respectively. In exchange for the credit essential to restructure Costa Rica's foreign debt and keep the deeply indebted, foreign reserve-starved state and economy afloat, the United States, International Monetary Fund, Paris Club, and Interamerican Development Bank forced Costa Rica to enact neoliberal economic policies that revolutionized its development model. Supported by conservative domestic economic interests and by the neoliberal PUSC (which fortuitously avoided having to sign any of the SAAs), Costa Rica trimmed its public-sector payroll, social service programs (education, health), and infrastructure investment, privatized most of the nation's many publicly owned enterprises and banking, and cut subsidies to agricultural commodity producers, public utility consumers, and housing. The government began energetically promoting nontraditional exports, reducing trade barriers, and substantially integrating Costa Rica into the global economy.[24]

Successive governments in San José, through both legislation and executive decrees, adopted the neoliberal economic model (public-sector wage cuts and layoffs, privatization, and reductions in public services) that deviated from the social democratic development model in place since the 1950s.[25] These policy changes generated citizen mobilization and protest, but, as in the 1970s, again the government responded with amelioration. Repression remained low, real wages were kept up and social assistance and housing subsidy programs rose sharply. Income distribution among classes remained fairly stable into the 1990s despite the economic turmoil. Voting for leftist parties remained low. Outside of protest mobilization, there appeared three significant signs that economic difficulties and the economic model change angered Costa Ricans: Voters ousted the governing party in successive elections in 1990, 1994, and 1998. Voter turnout in the 1998 election dropped from the usual level of 82 percent to only 71 percent and then failed to recover in the 2002 national election. The two-party system in place since the rise of the PUSC began to change, marked especially by a crisis in the long-dominant National Liberation Party.[26]

In contrast to these political discontents, the new development model's short- and middle-run economic successes made Costa Rica a poster child for neoliberalism. Its emphasis on nontraditional exports and liberalization of the economy, the settlement of the region's civil conflicts in the 1990s, and Costa Rica's significant human capital advantages together stimulated a period of rapid economic growth that continues at this writing. During the 1990s Costa Rica's combined rate of investment between government and private sector sources was high for the region in relative terms, but had contracted somewhat by 2000. Government spending on social services far exceeded any other country in the area. GDP per capita grew by nearly 25 percent between 1990 and the early 2000s, driven by a tourism boom, domestic and foreign investment, new computer assembly plant and on-line services industries, and expanded textile manufacturing.[27]

As this was being written, problems arising under the new Costa Rican development model were still developing. According to Robinson, they include some of the following: Deregulation had allowed a new private banking system increasingly dominated by international capital and promoting integration into the world capitalist economy. Investment in traditional agriculture and agricultural extension services had declined, as had production of domestically consumed agricultural commodities. These changes had pushed rural populations to urban areas in search of employment. Investment in industry, however, had lost ground to investment in the commercial sector and services. The informal sectors (petty commerce and services—often street vendors, unlicensed taxis, etc.) had grown rapidly among those unable to find formal-sector employment. Female participation in the workforce had risen sharply without a proportionate accompanying public investment in family social services and childcare. Large numbers of Nicaraguan immigrants had flooded Costa Rica to assume lower-skilled jobs in nontraditional agriculture, construction, and domestic service. Nicaraguan immigrant workers, vulnerable to police and immigration authorities, experienced employer victimization while exerting downward pressure on wages and undermining Costa Rican worker organization and mobilization efforts.[28]

In sum, external forces assisted by the debt crisis of the 1980s forced Costa Rica to adopt a neoliberal development model. Yet even when forced to adopt this set of distributively stingy policies, Costa Rican governments found ways to cushion some of the economic blows to citizens and managed a short-term macroeconomic turnaround. Other less advantageous macro- and microeconomic consequences would continue to play themselves out later. Throughout this difficult period, the overarching framework of the constitutional democratic regime established in the late 1940s and early 1950s remained solidly in place.

Changes in Politics and Parties

Despite the survival of the constitutional democratic regime, the revolution in the Costa Rican economic system began to affect the Costa Rican party system.[29] Scholars believe globalization and neoliberalism have had two main impacts on Latin American political parties: At the macro level, the structural constraints they impose have undermined ruling social democratic parties by undercutting their preferred redistributive and protectionist public policies, alienating working- and middle-class supporters of social democratic parties and boosting other parties more amenable to neoliberal reforms. At the micro level, social democratic parties have divided ideologically and lost programmatic focus as they became unable to campaign on either their traditional programs or required neoliberal reforms. Campaigns have thus turned to personalistic or populist electoral appeals to distract voters' attention from unpalatable economic options.[30] Similar effects have been observed for Costa Rica and its parties, undermining the long-dominant social democratic PLN and benefiting the newer PUSC.

The PLN. Neoliberalism harmed the social democratic National Liberation Party because PLN presidents had to sign and implement all three structural adjustments accords. As Costa Rica's leftist parties declined in the 1970s and early 1980s, popular-sector interests within the PLN lost importance while the party's own emerging advocates of neoliberalism gained ground. The neoliberal imperative drove wedges between traditionalist social democrats and the PLN's neoliberal reformers. Having to govern while implementing structural adjustment also alienated the party's neoliberal technocrats in office from those Liberacionistas contemplating future presidential candidacies.[31]

By the late 1980s the PLN's message to voters, longtime supporters, and activists became muddled as its actions in power undermined traditional Liberación ideology and policies. The PLN lost its perennial control of the Legislative Assembly from 1990 on and won the presidency only once during the 1990s. The PLN presidential vote share shrank steadily after 1986, when Arias captured 52.3 percent. The struggling party in 1994 nominated for president José Maria Figueres Olsen, son of PLN founder and two-time president José Figueres Ferrer. The family name helped the party win the presidency in 1994 but not a Legislative Assembly majority. Figueres Olsen had to implement the unpopular 1995 structural adjustment agreement and his administration experienced several scandals. This record further eroded Liberación's support in elections, including the defection of some of its core voters. Turnout in the 1997 PLN presidential primary election fell sharply because of "the negative weight of an unpopular Liberación administration, . . . [and] a very fragmented party."[32]

Other factors—not all related to neoliberalism, to be sure—divided the party and reduced its discipline and appeal to voters and insider-activists. These include the adoption of presidential primaries completely open to non-PLN members, the domination of presidential campaign organizations over the traditional party apparatus, and growing preeminence of technocrats over long-term party loyalists and activists. The rapid shift to retail campaigning (dominated by television) in the 1980s and the adoption of a primary nominating election for the presidency by the PLN combined to break down the PLN's tradition of face-to-face and grassroots organization and support. By the twenty-first century Liberación seemed in dire straits. In the 2002 election the party split and many of its voters and top leaders defected to the new Partido de Acción Ciudadana (Citizen Action Party—PAC). As a result the PLN's presidential vote was only 31 percent, and it captured only 30 percent of the Legislative Assembly seats, its worst performance in five decades.[33]

In 2003 Costa Rica's Supreme Court amended the constitution to permit former presidents to run for second terms. This change opened the door for former

PLN president Oscar Arias to enter the 2006 presidential race. Whether Arias could revive the hopes or fortunes of the PLN remained to be seen.

PUSC. As much as globalist pressures for neoliberalism harmed the PLN, they favored the formation and growth of the Social Christian Party. Rafael Angel Calderón Fournier's administration (1990–1994) in principle embraced structural adjustment, which had seriously lowered the short-term economic well-being of most Costa Ricans. By good luck, however, the party escaped any PUSC government having to actually sign a structural adjustment agreement. Thus the PLN got most of the blame for the resulting austerity policies. When the PUSC took power it worked to offset the widespread decline of living standards in the 1980s and early 1990s and avoid the political fallout by diverting public infrastructure and health and education spending into palliative social programs in housing and temporary welfare assistance.[34] As this was being written in late 2004, twin corruption scandals broke in Costa Rica implicating both immediately former PUSC presidents Calderón and Rodríguez and members of their administrations in various acts of bribe taking and campaign finance violations. Foreign firms appeared to be implicated in both cases.

Party System Legitimacy. We must ask whether party government could remain legitimate in Costa Rica under the onslaught of such difficulties. Would the vaunted democratic political system threatened by these trends? Some indicators suggest a developing problem: The PLN suffered its multiple woes. Voter turnout declined in the 1998 and 2002 elections from the usual 80 percent to 70 percent. Trust in parties in general declined between the early 1990s and 2002. Third-party votes in 1998 roughly doubled their level of the previous three elections and then trebled again in 2002. Because neither the PLN nor PUSC could garner sufficient votes in 2002 to win the presidential election outright, the country had its first-ever runoff presidential election in 2002. Surveys after 1990 expressed citizens' declining satisfaction with parties and other national institutions and a waning interest in politics.[35]

Costa Rica's political malaise, partly due to the shortcomings of the major parties, had not, as we wrote, spread into a more worrying larger disaffection of its citizens with the constitutional regime and democracy. At twenty-first century's beginning it therefore remained an open question whether the party system would restabilize as a two-party system, or whether the PLN's decline and PUSC's embarrassment might lead to further realignment.

Contemporary Costa Rican Politics

The political and economic impact of the neoliberal model was palpable. Throughout the 1980s real wages and public investment, most notably in the areas of health and education, declined.[36] Between 1990 and 2000 Costa Rica fell 20 places to 48th in the Index of Human Development.[37] While overall poverty declined, there was evidence that the poorer segments of the population had grown increasingly vulnerable.[38] Thus even Costa Rica could not blunt the effects of neoliberal policies.

While Costa Rica largely escaped the crime wave experienced by the rest of the region, it did not avoid an economic slowdown that was evident by 2000. During the late 1990s, the Costa Rican economy enjoyed considerable growth attributable to the plant construction and sales of Intel, a leading producer of microchips.[39] But declining prices for coffee and bananas and a drop in sales by Intel further exposed weakness of the country's reliance on a few key exports.[40] Although remaining significantly better than the rest of the region, unemployment and inflation increased. To manage its mounting deficit, the government cut back spending and investment. Additionally, successive administrations experienced tremendous pressure from domestic elites and the international community to privatize several key state-owned enterprises—especially telecommunications—in an effort to forestall a potential fiscal crisis and meet IMF conditionality.[41]

Economic stagnation and neoliberal policies resulted in an ever more volatile mix. The administrations of both Rodríguez and Abel Pacheco de la Espriella pursued privatization amidst both legislative and popular opposition to such policies. Rodríguez oversaw legislation that made it possible for foreign investors to provide public services. In 2000 the legislature approved the privatization of the Costa Rican Electrical Institute (ICE). Following some of the largest demonstrations in the country's history, the measure was ruled unconstitutional by the Constitutional Tribunal.[42] Public-sector employees were increasingly at odds with government policy. In 1999 some 15,000 striking teachers protested wages and disinvestment.[43] Large strikes by public workers, including those from the energy and telecommunications sectors and teachers, continued through the Pacheco administration. Pacheco, who pledged to address poverty during his campaign, instead announced numerous austerity measures to further cut government spending. The Pacheco administration was plagued by public protest, legislative stagnation and internal division, including the resignation of several cabinet members. By July 2003 the president's approval rating fell to 10 percent, further conveying the increased dissatisfaction with politics as usual.[44]

Conclusions

During the 1970s, Costa Rica at least partly ameliorated the growing difficulties afflicting working-class victims of rapid economic change and carried it off with low repression. Second, policy permitted working-class wages to recover or retain purchasing power, and shifted some wealth and income to certain lower-class groups. This combination of moderate repression and some accommodation of working-class interests, contrasted with high repression and no accommodation in Somoza's Nicaragua, Guatemala and El Salvador, kept Costa Rica relatively politically stable.

Costa Rica's consolidated democratic regime weathered the 1970s and 1980s intact, but the country nevertheless experienced two major middle-term effects from its shifting role in the international political economy. External pressures both structural and political forced Costa Rica to abandon its longstanding social democratic economic model and embrace neoliberalism. This transformation undermined the traditional platform of the National Liberation Party and began to diminish its electoral success and erode its position as the system's dominant party. The new Social Christian Unity Party, more amenable to neoliberalism, formed and grew into a formidable competitor for the PLN. The PUSC appeared to have replaced the PLN as the dominant party in the political system.

By the early 2000s Costa Rica's erstwhile social democratic development model of the 1950s through the 1980s had vanished, and under the new development model the state reduced its promotion of equality-enhancing economic policies and human development. Such policies and their effects had once distinguished Costa Rica from its Central American neighbors and for decades validated the country's exceptionalist myth. Not only had this economic transformation begun to affect citizens' well-being, but it had surprisingly rapid effects on a once-stable political party system. This leads us to close this chapter not with a conclusion but with two great questions: Would Costa Rica now tend to converge with the rest of Central America as its policy outputs weakened future social development? And should convergence mean a relative or absolute decline in Costa Ricans' well-being, would this destabilize the Costa Rican polity and undermine its consolidated democracy?

5

Nicaragua

Nicaragua is potentially one of the richest countries in Central America, with abundant arable land, considerable hydroelectric, thermal, and (possibly) fossil energy reserves, and significant timber and mineral resources. It also has access to two oceans and a lake and river system that could make it an ideal site for an interoceanic waterway. Yet Nicaraguans today are among the poorest Central Americans and Latin Americans. The paradox arises from the extreme degree to which patterns of dependency established in the colonial period became institutionalized, and in the twentieth century were then deepened by war and geopolitics. Despite paroxysms of war, revolution, and counterrevolution, Nicaragua's perennially fractured political and economic elites continue to fail to advance the country's development.

Historical Background

Nineteenth-century Nicaragua was plagued by civil wars and foreign interference. During the first several decades, the Liberal and Conservative elites, based in the cities of León and Granada, respectively, struggled with each other to control the national government. At the same time, Britain and the United States—both actively interested in building a transoceanic waterway—maneuvered against each other in an attempt to insert themselves into the power vacuum left by Spain.

At midcentury, foreign interference and the Liberal-Conservative conflict both came to a head in a war. In the late 1840s the British and Americans had almost come to blows over a British attempt to seize the mouth of the San Juan River. In the resulting Clayton-Bulwer Treaty (1850), the United States and Britain mutually renounced the right to embark on any unilateral exploitation of the region. However, the California gold rush of the 1850s deepened U.S. interest in Central America as a shortcut between the eastern and western coasts of North America. In 1855 one of two competing transit companies in Nicaragua and Panama became embroiled in Nicaragua's Liberal-Conservative clash. That year the Liberals, in exchange for help in the business dispute, imported a small mercenary army of North Americans commanded by adventurer William Walker to help them defeat the Conservatives. As we noted, the plan backfired when the flamboyant Tennessean seized power for himself. This left Nicaragua's Liberals so discredited by association with the "gringo" interloper that the Conservatives ruled virtually unchallenged until 1893.

In the nineteenth century, globalization in the guise of spreading coffee cultivation brought Nicaragua profound social and economic changes. Before 1870, intra-elite turmoil and relatively low foreign economic control had permitted Nicaragua to develop an internal market and a surprisingly large free peasantry. One foreign observer stated: "Peonage such as is seen in Mexico and various parts of Spanish America does not exist in Nicaragua. . . . Any citizen whatever can set himself up on a piece of open land . . . to cultivate plantain and corn."[1] This pattern changed radically when growing international demand for coffee brought its widespread cultivation to Nicaragua. Coffee production required new lands and cheap labor. Accordingly, in the 1870s the elite began to dispossess the peasant and Indian farmers in much of the northern highlands, using chicanery, self-serving legislation, and violence. No longer self-sufficient, former peasants had few options except peonage on coffee plantations. When some of the victims of the process rebelled in the War of the Comuneros of 1881, the elite-run government contained the uprising by killing thousands of the poorly armed insurgents.

Coffee production at the expense of peasant smallholding accelerated under a modernizing Liberal dictator, José Santos Zelaya (1893–1909). Zelaya also built educational and governmental infrastructure (censuses, archives, a more modern army) and defended the interests of Nicaragua and Central America against a burgeoning imperialist urge in the United States. After the United States decided to build a transisthmian canal in Panama, Zelaya began to seek a canal deal with U.S. rival naval powers Germany and Japan. To protect its canal monopoly, in 1909 the United States encouraged Zelaya's Conservative opposition to rebel against him and then landed marines to protect the rebels. In 1909, Zelaya resigned and in 1910 the Liberals relinquished power to the minority Conservative Party. By 1912, however, the Conservatives had made such a mess of public affairs that a combined Liberal-Conservative rebellion occurred. That revolt was put down only after U.S. marines physically occupied Nicaragua.

From 1912 to 1933, with the exception of a short period in the mid-1920s, the United States maintained an occupation force in Nicaragua. U.S.-dominated governments in this era generally followed Washington's dictates, even when clearly contrary to Nicaraguan interests. The Chamorro-Bryan Treaty of 1916, for example, gave the United States rights to build a canal in Nicaragua. The Americans had no intention of constructing such a canal; they simply wanted to block possible competition for the U.S.-built waterway just completed in Panama. In 1928, another puppet government under U.S. pressure gave Colombia several important Nicaraguan islands, including San Andrés, to mollify Colombian resentment of the U.S. role in taking Panama from Colombia in 1903.

And finally, during the latter part of this period, the United States forced Nicaragua to create a modern constabulary combining army and police. A movement to resist U.S. occupation of Nicaragua sprang up in 1927, led by the charismatic local guerrilla-patriot Augusto C. Sandino. U.S. marines could not put down Sandino's resistance, so the constabulary—the Nicaraguan National Guard (Guardia Nacional)—was significantly enlarged to assist in the struggle. The war was a standoff, and the United States eventually withdrew its troops at the turn of the year 1932–1933. The National Guard then became the vehicle by which its first Nicaraguan commander, Anastasio Somoza García, created and consolidated the Somoza family dictatorship, which subsequently brutalized and oppressed Nicaragua for over four decades.

As the first Nicaraguan commander of the National Guard, Anastasio Somoza García had Sandino assassinated in 1934 and used the guard to seize political power in 1936. Thereafter, three Somozas held power from 1936 until 1979. Somoza García was either president or the power behind puppets until his assassination in 1956. His son, Luis Somoza Debayle, ruled directly or through surrogates until 1967. Luis's younger brother, Anastasio Somoza Debayle, was "elected" to the presidency in 1967 and held power from then until 1979. Throughout this period, the Somoza dynasty rested on two primary pillars of support: the United States and the Nicaraguan National Guard. A Somoza always commanded the Guard and purposely isolated it from the people. They allowed the Guard to become thoroughly corrupt to ensure its loyalty to the Somozas. The Guard became a sort of Mafia in uniform, running prostitution, gambling, and protection rackets, taking bribes and extorting kickbacks for various legal and illegal activities.

U.S. support for the Somozas was secured in two ways: personal ingratiation and political subservience. The Somozas were masters at cultivating Americans. Each was educated in the United States, spoke fluent vernacular English, and knew how to be a "good old boy" among ethnocentric, often homesick North American diplomats and visitors. On the political plane, the Somozas always supported U.S. policy, be it anti-Axis during World War II or anti-Communist thereafter. They allowed Nicaragua to serve as staging grounds for the CIA-organized exile invasions of Guatemala (1954) and Cuba (1961), contributed a small force to participate in the U.S. occupation of the Dominican Republic in 1965, and offered to send Nicaraguan troops to fight in both Korea and Vietnam.

As a result, U.S. support for the Somozas usually remained strong and visible. Especially after the beginning of the Alliance for Progress in 1961, the United States gave Nicaragua many millions of dollars in aid for social and economic projects (despite ample evidence that the Somozas and their accomplices stole much of the aid). U.S. ambassadors were normally unabashedly pro-Somoza. What is more, during the 1960s and 1970s, the dictatorship received U.S. military support far out of proportion to that of other Central American countries (Appendix, Table A.3). By the time the Somozas were finally overthrown, their National Guard was the most heavily U.S.-trained military establishment in Latin America.

Global Forces and Insurrection

Effects of Rapid Economic Growth. Under the direction of the Somozas and the stimulus of the Central American Common Market and Alliance for Progress, Nicaragua underwent rapid industrialization and expansion of commercial export agriculture during the 1960s and early 1970s. Overall economic growth statistics were impressive; per capita gross domestic product rose an average of almost 3.9 percent each year for the decade 1962–1971, and an average of 2.3 percent annually between 1972 and 1976, by far the fastest increase in the region.[2] This brought other social change: Between 1960 and 1980 Nicaragua had Central America's biggest surge in urban population and manufacturing output and its biggest decline in the agricultural workforce (Appendix, Tables A.1 and A.2).

Despite impressive growth, government policies prevented the benefits from this new economic activity from reaching poorer Nicaraguans. The regime repressed unions and kept wages—normally set by the regime—low. Consumer prices rose moderately between 1963 and 1972. But after the 1973 Organization of Petroleum Exporting Countries (OPEC) oil embargo, escalating oil prices drove inflation up to almost 11 percent a year from 1973 through 1977. Real earnings of ordinary Nicaraguans (wages corrected for inflation) peaked in 1967, then began a long slide that by the late 1970s ate away a third of their 1967 purchasing power. Another measure of workers' welfare, employees' share of national income, increased during the 1960s but fell sharply in 1974 and 1975.[3] Thus wage-earning Nicaraguans suffered a palpable drop in their ability to feed and shelter their families.

Income inequality between rich and poor Nicaraguans had become very great by 1977, when the wealthiest fifth of the people earned 59.9 percent of the national income, while the poorer half were left with only 15.0 percent.[4] The devastating Managua earthquake of December 24, 1972 probably triggered this income shift away from wage earners when it put tens of thousands of white- and blue-collar workers out of work.

Nicaragua's middle class experienced a decade of improving living standards during the 1960s but suffered a sharp reversal as of 1973. Middle-class employment shrank markedly in the mid-1970s when the earthquake destroyed many small businesses and commercial jobs. Nine thousand manufacturing jobs (about 13 percent of the total) disappeared from 1972 to 1973, as did 15,000 service sector jobs (over 7 percent of the total). New jobs shifted to the poorer-paid construction sector, which nearly doubled in size by 1974, and to the informal sector.[5] The government levied a stiff surtax to finance reconstruction on those still employed, but corrupt officials stole much of its proceeds. The workweek was increased by as much as 25 percent without increasing pay.[6]

During the CACM boom employment failed to keep up with rapid growth in the workforce. Underemployment—an inability to find full-time work or acceptance of agricultural wage labor because of insufficient farmland for family subsistence farming—affected up to five times as many as were unemployed. Unemployment rose from below 4 percent in 1970 to 13 percent by 1978 despite rapid economic growth.[7] Hardest hit were workers the earthquake left jobless and peasants forced off the land by the rapid expansion of agricultural production for export.

In agriculture, concentration of land ownership increased from the 1950s through the 1970s, especially in the fertile and populous Pacific zone. High cotton prices permitted speculating largeholders to squeeze subsistence cultivators off the land and into the oversupplied wage labor market.[8] "The process of agricultural development was a concentrator of both land and income."[9] In the 1950s and 1960s the government gave progressively preferential treatment in trade, credit, and financial policies and material-technical support to agroindustries belonging to the Somozas' and their cohorts.

During the 1960s and 1970s, Nicaragua's three major capitalist factions, which centered around the Banco de América, the Banco Nicaragüense, and the Somoza family interests, began to converge.[10] Once separated from each other by regional, clan, and political party differences, these investor factions increasingly prospered and intertwined their interests under the CACM. Following the Managua earthquake, however, the Somoza faction became aggressively greedy, undermining other investor groups. Growing political and labor unrest caused many Nicaraguan capitalists to doubt whether the regime could sustain growth. Anastasio Somoza Debayle's upper-class support began to erode in the mid-1970s, which prevented the unification of the bourgeoisie.

By both relative and absolute measures of income and wealth, poor and middle-class Nicaraguans lost some of their share of overall national income and wealth, and suffered a sharp drop in their real earning power during the 1970s. Even some wealthy Nicaraguans lost ground in the 1970s. Such losses doubtless gave many Nicaraguans strong economic grievances.

Popular Mobilization. The decline of working-class wages in the late 1960s and early 1970s revitalized the nation's long suppressed industrial labor movement,[11] which stepped up organization, work stoppages, and strikes in pursuit of wage gains in 1973–1975.[12] The erosion of middle-class living standards also expanded union membership and organization and brought strikes by such public sector workers as teachers and health personnel. Catholic social workers, missionaries, and priests began organizing unions among Pacific-zone peasant wage laborers in the 1960s. As a tool for teaching the gospel, Catholic social promoters also organized hundreds of small Christian base communities (*comunidades eclesiales de base,* CEBs) among urban and rural poor people. CEBs, joined by Protestant-organized groups after the Managua quake, encouraged community self-help activism and demanded better urban services and housing.[13] Peasant unions increasingly pressed for wage gains, especially after 1975.[14]

As the economy deteriorated, especially after 1974, Nicaraguan private sector pressure organizations grew and more boldly criticized the government. Such private-sector groups as the business leader-dominated Democratic Liberation Union (Unión Democrática de Liberación—UDEL) called for political and economic reform.

New opposition political parties (particularly, the Social Christian Party) became active in Nicaragua in the 1960s and 1970s.[15] New anti-Somoza factions of the old Conservative and Liberal parties developed during the 1970s. Elements from the Conservative Party united with the Social Christian Party and the anti-Somoza Independent Liberal Party in the National Opposition Union (Unión Nacional Opositora—UNO) to contest the 1967 national election. Student opposition to the regime grew rapidly during the 1970s. The Sandinista National Liberation Front (Frente Sandinista de Liberación Nacional—FSLN), the only surviving rebel group of some 20 guerrilla bands that had appeared between 1959 and 1962, greatly expanded its links to and support from university student groups during the 1970s.[16]

Government Repression and Its Effect on Opposition. President Anastasio Somoza Debayle declared a state of siege and began a program of demobilization in late December 1974 after an embarrassing FSLN hostage-taking incident. During the resultant three-year reign of terror in rural areas, the National Guard murdered several thousand mostly innocent people suspected as subversives or possible FSLN sympathizers.[17] During a brief lifting of the state of siege because of Carter administration pressure, public protests against the regime rose rapidly. The government reacted by redoubling repression, especially in urban areas. The National Guard targeted and murdered hundreds of youths suspected of pro-Sandinista sympathies. From 1977 on, the guard conducted an intensifying war against the citizenry that drove thousands, especially young people, to join the FSLN.

Following the January 1978 assassination of Pedro Joaquín Chamorro, editor of the opposition newspaper *La Prensa,* bourgeois elements redoubled their efforts against the Somoza regime. Key business interests such as the Superior Council of Private Initiative (Consejo Superior de la Iniciativa Privada—COSIP) joined with unions and moderate parties to support general strikes, and to form the Broad Opposition Front (Frente Amplio Opositor—FAO). Strongly backed by the United States and Nicaragua's Catholic hierarchy, the FAO strove unsuccessfully to negotiate an end to the Somoza regime lest the FSLN overthrow it.[18]

Popular uprisings spread across urban Nicaragua between August and October 1978. On August 23, 1978, a small Sandinista unit seized the National Palace, taking more than 2,000 hostages, including most members of the Chamber of Deputies. They negotiated the release of 60 Sandinistas from prison, a ransom, and safe passage out of the country. Days afterward, opposition leaders called a successful general strike. In September, thousands spontaneously attacked National Guard posts and drove the regime's troops out of several communities. These revolts in Masaya, Rivas, Jinotega, Matagalpa, Estelí, and Managua typically occurred without much FSLN coordination. The National Guard crushed each uprising, slaughtering civilians and damaging property and public services.

The FSLN, split for several years over tactics, realized that popular outrage had rendered its internal debate sterile. The three Sandinista factions quickly reunified in 1979 under the Joint National Directorate (Dirección Nacional Conjunta—DNC) and built a network of wealthy and prominent supporters embodied by the Group of Twelve (Grupo de los Doce). When the FAO-regime negotiations collapsed in early 1979, moderate and even conservative anti-Somocistas turned to the Sandinistas as the last option to defeat the regime. In 1979 the FSLN forged the United People's Movement (Movimiento Pueblo Unido—MPU) and National Patriotic Front (Frente Patriótico Nacional—FPN) coalitions, confederations that united virtually the entire opposition. Under the military leadership of the FSLN, the MPU and FPN were committed to the defeat of the Somoza regime. In May 1979 an FSLN-led provisional government formed in San José, Costa Rica, to formally embody the opposition's revolutionary claim to sovereignty.

By opening its military ranks to all regime opponents and by forging broad alliances, the FSLN won extensive resources for the final offensive against the regime. Its military ranks ballooned from fewer than 500 troops under arms in mid-1978 to between 2,500 and 5,000 by June 1979. The revolutionary coalition in 1979 enjoyed effective control over parts of northern Nicaragua, sanctuary for bases and political operations in Costa Rica, diplomatic support from France and various Latin American regimes. FSLN agents purchased weapons from private dealers in the United States and took delivery at a base camp in Honduras. Cuba, Venezuela, Panama, and Costa Rica assisted arms shipments to the FSLN for the final offensive. Whenever FSLN forces entered a community in combat, many local residents would spontaneously fight alongside them or otherwise assist, vastly enhancing the guerrillas' strength and capabilities.

The Outcome. The FSLN-led coalition's unity, material resources, popular support, military capacity, and external backing all grew rapidly in late 1978 and 1979. The coalition's revolutionary government in exile in 1979 took advantage of enthusiastic support from Costa Rica, where it enjoyed political sanctuary and popular sympathy and where the FSLN had secure bases. Within Nicaragua, FSLN troops enjoyed massive voluntary popular support in combat against the National Guard.

The Somoza regime's strength faded in 1978 and 1979 while its opposition grew. Numerous spontaneous popular uprisings against the government took place in late 1978. The regime lost the support of virtually all social classes and interest sectors, save portions of Somoza's Liberal Nationalist Party (Partido Liberal Nacionalista—PLN) and the National Guard. PLN and regime supporters—many corrupt and anxious to escape with their wealth—began leaving Nicaragua. The flow of deserting Somocistas became a flood after National Guard troops casually murdered ABC reporter Bill Stewart before the network's cameras on June 20, 1979. The tyrant's associates sensed that this horrible deed had stripped away their remaining legitimacy outside Nicaragua.

The Carter administration had announced its opposition to Somoza's continued rule, a big loss for the regime. The United States struck new aid to Nicaragua from the 1979 budget and blocked pending deliveries by some of Somoza's arms suppliers. Although the U.S. government wanted Somoza out, it also tried ineffectually to keep the Sandinistas from power. The Organization of American States and numerous Latin American regimes had openly sided with the opposition by 1979. The National Guard fought tenaciously against the Sandinistas and Nicaraguan people, but was progressively encircled and pushed back toward Managua during the seven-week final offensive. Having looted the national treasury of dollars, Somoza ultimately gave up and left Nicaragua for Miami on July 17, 1979. When the guard collapsed two days later, the Sandinista-led rebel coalition took power. These dramatic events mark the first great regime change we examine in Central America in the 1970s and 1980s, Nicaragua's passage from personalistic military rule to revolution. This regime change started both a long process of transformation and violent resistance in Nicaragua, and prompted much change elsewhere in the isthmus (Chapters 6–8).

THE TRIUMPH. FSLN militia guard checkpoint in Northern Nicaragua and jubilant citizens destroy the horse from Anastasio Somoza's statue in Managua, July 1979 (photo by Thomas Walker)

The Revolution

The revolutionary government faced many problems. The war had killed 50,000 people—almost 2 percent of the populace. (An equivalent loss to the United States today would be nearly 5 million—some 125 times the U.S. death toll in the Vietnam War.) There were also an estimated \$1.5 billion in property losses, plus all-important export and domestic crops unplanted. The new government had inherited \$1.6 billion in international debts from the old regime. To its chagrin, the new government realized that it would have to assume and pay Somoza's debt to remain creditworthy in international financial circles. Grave and longstanding problems of public health, housing, education, and nutrition, all exacerbated by the war, awaited the new regime.

In power, the Sandinista-led revolutionary coalition sought to destroy the Somoza regime and its economic power base, to replace its brutality and inequities with a fairer, more humane, and less corrupt system, and to reactivate the economy. The Sandinistas themselves wanted to move the economy toward socialism in order to improve the lot of the lower classes, to build a participatory democracy under their own leadership, and to integrate all Nicaraguans into the national social and political system. Others in the coalition disagreed about much of the Sandinistas' revolutionary program and hoped to wrest power from or share it with the FSLN. Such differences over the ends of the revolution quickly established the lines of political conflict and shattered the anti-Somocista alliance.

U.S.-Nicaraguan Relations and the Contra War. The Sandinistas feared that the United States might try to reverse the Nicaraguan revolution, as it had other reformist or revolutionary Latin American governments (Guatemala in 1954, Cuba in 1961, the Dominican Republic in 1965, and Chile in 1973). Although the Carter administration had criticized and opposed Somoza, it had worked tenaciously to keep the Sandinistas from power. Even before the FSLN took over, President Carter authorized the CIA to fund certain segments of the press and labor movement.[19]

The Carter administration offered the new regime a nervous gesture of friendship in the form of diplomatic recognition, emergency relief aid, and the release of suspended loans from prior years' aid packages in 1979, and a new $75 million loan commitment in 1980. In 1979–1980 the Sandinistas had fairly good working relations with the United States but warily regarded U.S. links to several thousand national guardsmen who had escaped to Honduras and the United States. First the Argentine military and then the CIA organized the ex-Somocista forces, which began to conduct terrorist attacks on Nicaragua from their Honduran refuge.[20] In 1981 the incoming Reagan administration began trying to reverse the Nicaraguan revolution and destabilize the Sandinista government. Reagan accused Nicaragua (with little evidence) of trafficking arms to El Salvador's rebels and cut off the balance of the Carter administration's $75 million loan and wheat purchase credits.

The United States thereafter steadily escalated its harassment, pressure, and aggression against Nicaragua. Military pressure included massive aid to build up the Honduran military, continuous "maneuvers" in Honduras, and intensive espionage from air, sea, and land. The United States worked continuously to isolate Nicaragua diplomatically from its neighbors in Central America. These pressures, sweetened with generous U.S. aid, persuaded both Honduras and Costa Rica to provide sanctuary to anti-Sandinista rebels. The United States blocked a possible peace agreement among Central American nations negotiated by the Contadora nations (Mexico, Panama, Colombia, and Venezuela). Washington convinced multilateral lending and development agencies to cut off credit to Nicaragua, and on May 7, 1985 embargoed trade with Nicaragua. U.S. propaganda—as energetic as it was inaccurate—discredited and defamed the revolutionary government of Nicaragua and exalted the Sandinistas' enemies.

The centerpiece of the Reagan administration's strategy for Nicaragua was a proxy military-political effort to topple the Sandinistas. In 1981 Reagan gave the CIA $19.8 million to support and augment an exile army of anti-Sandinista counterrevolutionaries known as the "Contras." Their nucleus consisted of former National Guard officers and soldiers and political allies of the former dictator. From 1982 on, attacks across the Honduran border occurred almost daily. Contra forces regularly sabotaged bridges and other economic targets and had taken almost a thousand civilian and military lives within Nicaragua by the end of 1982.

By 1983 there existed major Contra groups; the most important were the Honduras-based Nicaraguan Democratic Force (Fuerzas Democráticas Nicaragüenses—FDN) and the Costa Rica-based Revolutionary Democratic Alliance (Alianza Revolucionaria Democrática—ARDE) and two Miskito Indian groups. A Contra political directorate was organized by the United States to present a palatable public front and facilitate continued funding by Congress. In 1983 the Contras began extensive guerrilla operations within Nicaragua, especially in the rugged northeast and southeast. The CIA added to the destruction by blowing up Nicaraguan oil storage tanks and pipelines and mining harbors on both coasts. The CIA also supported the Contras with intelligence, funding, and training (including a style manual on sabotage for Contra foot soldiers and a more sophisticated training book for Contra leaders that recommended assassination of pro-Sandinista civilians).[21]

By 1985 the Contras had 15,000 persons under arms but had achieved few successes against the Nicaraguan military. They had, however, established a clear record of economic sabotage and atrocities and had killed 13,000 people. In the mid-1980s, the U.S. Congress reacted to these developments by withdrawing funding for the Contra war and legally restraining U.S. efforts to topple the Sandinistas. The Reagan administration responded with covert efforts to fund and assist the Contras that included operations (some flatly illegal) by the National Security Council's Col. Oliver North and other executive agencies. North brokered an illicit arms deal with Iran to provide off-the-books funds for the Contras. The United States also promoted huge gifts of cash to the Contras by private domestic donors, compliant foreign governments, and allegedly even drug-smuggling interests.[22]

When these efforts came to light in October 1986 they became known as the Iran-Contra scandal, and placed further U.S. funding to the Contras in doubt. Reagan then pressed the Contras to intensify their offensive. Supported by a CIA-run military supply operation in 1987, this offensive brought the war to its destructive peak and raised the death toll for the entire war to just under 31,000. Despite more combat operations within Nicaragua, the Contras' military successes remained limited. After the Central American Peace Accord was signed in August 1987, the Contras eventually entered negotiations with the Sandinista government (1988), and the war began to wind down. The new Bush administration called for continued U.S. aid to help hold the Contras together. Direct U.S. aid to the Contras by 1989 had totaled over $400 million. In the long run, they would not be formally disarmed and disbanded until mid-1990, months after the Sandinistas lost the externally manipulated election of February 1990.

The Revolutionary Government. What kind of government elicited such antagonism from three U.S. administrations? The FSLN consolidated its political

THE CONTRA WAR. Peasant children in a feeding program at a war refugee agricultural self-defense resettlement camp (photo by Steve Cagan)

dominance over the new government by early 1980 but kept other coalition members on the junta, in the cabinet, and in the Council of State (Consejo de Estado). Though the FSLN's nine-man DNC held ultimate veto power over the nature of the government and its programs, the Sandinistas created a pluralist system that encouraged representatives of the upper-class minority to participate. Upper-class, business, and various political party interests, although in the coalition, could not control policy and therefore became increasingly antagonistic toward the FSLN. The regime maintained a dialogue with major business interests and with a coalition of opposition parties.[23]

The Sandinistas promoted their own brand of democracy emphasizing popular participation in making public policy and services and programs for the poor. At first scornful of national elections because the dictatorial old regime had always manipulated them, the revolutionary government in mid-1980 announced its intention to postpone national elections until 1985. Immediately after the rebel victory, however, local elections had taken place all over Nicaragua. The Sandinistas also promoted numerous grassroots organizations of women, workers, peasants, youth, children, and neighborhoods. Through these organizations hundreds of thousands of Nicaraguans debated and voted on issues, worked on local problems, took part in national health and literacy campaigns, petitioned their government, and met with officials of governmental bodies and national organizations. Encouraged by the regime, organized labor grew rapidly. Labor's demands for higher wages, however, soon ran afoul of government needs for economic austerity and the FSLN desire for dominance within the movement.

The Sandinistas argued from the outset that the new system must tolerate diversity of political opinion because they had come to power as part of a coalition, because they sought a mixed economy that necessitated cooperation by the privileged classes, and because the international climate required political pluralism for the survival of the revolution. When the junta added new pro-Sandinista groups to the Council of State in 1980, several other party groups cried foul and began to coalesce into an open opposition to the government. The climate for political opposition within the revolution remained open, but not completely free. Other parties suffered from constraints on their press coverage and public activities under the State of Emergency decreed in response to the Contra war in 1982, and pro-regime crowds *(turbas)* sometimes harassed critics of the regime, especially between 1982 and 1984.

The Council of State passed opposition-influenced election and party laws that set elections for president and National Assembly (to replace the junta and Council of State) in November 1984. The government lifted most restrictions on parties and the press for the campaign; it allowed free and uncensored access to government radio and television. A vigorous campaign ensued among seven parties. International election observers and the press[24] concurred that no fraud or intimidation by the FSLN occurred. Observers found the election marred by U.S. pressure that contributed to a conservative coalition's decision not to participate and one party's presidential candidate attempting to drop out late in the campaign. Daniel Ortega Saavedra, DNC member and coordinator of the junta, became president with 63 percent of the total vote. Opposition parties divided about one-third of the National Assembly.

The National Assembly immediately became a constituent assembly tasked to write a new constitution. Contrary to U.S. criticism, the constitution drafting was open and democratic. The resulting document provided for the rule of law, protection of human rights, checks and balances, and competitive elections to be held at six-year intervals.[25] The new election system, constitution, and government structures formalized and institutionalized the revolutionary regime. It left the Sandinistas in power, but presiding over a regime that had much in common with other electoral democracies—the government accepted constitutional restraints and could be replaced in an election.

Despite the external attacks and obstruction, the Sandinistas began their revolution successfully. They shaped a new governmental system, reactivated and reshaped much of the war-ravaged economy, and implemented numerous social programs. They provided expanded health services, and national vaccination and health education campaigns significantly lowered rates of polio, malaria, and infant mortality. A massive literacy crusade raised literacy rates from slightly under 50 percent to about 87 percent. Agrarian reform programs promoted increased national self-sufficiency in food production, formed thousands of cooperative farms, and distributed considerable farmland to individuals and cooperatives.[26]

The growing Contra war, however, forced the government to reorganize to defend the revolution and postponed or undermined many social and economic programs. By 1987 over half of the national budget went for military expenditures and the armed forces had been expanded to 60,000 regulars and 100,000 militia. Social reforms, medical, health, and educational programs and public services suffered from the heavy military spending. Medical care deteriorated, garbage pickup and water service in Managua were curtailed, schools went without supplies and repairs, buses and taxis rusted for lack of parts and repairs. From 1979 through 1983 regular visitors to Nicaragua noticed evident material progress, but from 1984 on signs of decay and lost ground proliferated.

The Sandinistas' human rights performance, though not perfect, was good for a revolutionary regime and considerably superior to that of Somoza and all other Central American governments except Costa Rica.[27] The government moved swiftly to prevent its own supporters and forces from perpetrating human rights abuses in the chaotic days after seizing power. It established a new Sandinista Police and Sandinista Popular Army and worked to curtail abuse of authority by their officials. It humanely treated captured National Guard troops and officials, who were investigated, tried for their crimes, and sentenced. International human rights agencies have criticized the unfair procedures of the Special Tribunals used to try the 6,300 former guardsmen, but these special courts dismissed charges against or acquitted 22 percent of the prisoners. Despite the heinous crimes of some, no one was executed. By 1985 more than half of those sentenced had completed their sentences, been pardoned, or been released.[28]

Despite *La Prensa*'s receiving U.S. CIA funding,[29] the regime allowed the opposition daily newspaper to operate for several years without censorship. During that period, however, the government briefly closed the paper several times for publishing false information in violation of the press law. Under the mounting pressure of the Contra war, the revolutionary government in 1982 decreed a state of emergency that suspended many civil guarantees. This implemented prior censorship of news content of all media, including the FSLN's own *Barricada.* In 1984 before the election censorship eased and most civil rights were restored. Deepening war in 1985–1986 brought the reinstitution of many rights restrictions. The government closed *La Prensa* indefinitely in June 1986 for endorsing U.S. aid to the Contras,[30] but permitted it to reopen without prior censorship after the Central American Peace Accord was signed in 1987.

Two areas of human rights proved problematic for the revolutionary government. In 1982 the growing Contra war prompted relocation of 8,000 Miskito Indians from their homes in the war zone along the Río Coco. Poorly handled, the relocation angered Miskitos, caused thousands to flee, and led many to join anti-Sandinista guerrilla groups. "The external conflict created a context in which Miskito demands for self-determination were seen by the Sandinistas as separatist and related to U.S. efforts to overthrow the government by arming indigenous insurgents and by attempting to turn world opinion against the Sandinistas through false accusations of 'genocide.'"[31] Real abuses of Miskito rights worsened tensions in the area,[32] but no credible observers concurred with U.S. charges of a "genocide" of the Miskitos.[33] By late 1983 the government changed course and began autonomy talks with Atlantic Coast indigenous peoples, aimed at increasing local self-determination. In 1985 it permitted the Miskitos to return to their homes, tensions subsided, and Miskito support for the Contras waned. The autonomy law passed in 1987.

Religious practice remained generally free in Nicaragua under the revolution, but the government became increasingly intolerant of those who expressed anti-regime political goals through religious practice or groups. The government admitted many foreign missionaries of various sects and permitted churches to take part in the literacy crusade of 1980–1981. Many Catholics and numerous Protestant congregations had provided logistical support to the FSLN during the insurrection and supported the new government. The Catholic Church hierarchy, however, strongly and increasingly opposed Sandinista rule. Church-regime conflict became overt by 1982. Missionaries from certain Protestant sects were denied entry to Nicaragua, and pro-FSLN groups on one occasion occupied properties of one sect before being evicted by the police.[34]

Relations between the government and Catholic Church nosedived during and after the trip of Pope John Paul II to Nicaragua in 1983. Each side apparently deliberately provoked the other during the planning and execution of the visit.

Archbishop Miguel Obando y Bravo—long hostile to the Sandinistas—had become the leader of the internal opposition by 1984. From that time through the end of the Sandinista period, Obando (elevated to cardinal in 1985) and Catholic bishops repeatedly denounced government policy. Despite some efforts to seek dialogue with the Church, the Sandinista government periodically closed Catholic Radio and deported a dozen foreign-born priests active in opposition politics. In 1986, when Bishop Pablo Antonio Vega endorsed U.S. aid for the Contras, the government exiled him.[35] Following the signing of the Central American Peace Accord in 1987, Vega and other priests were permitted to return to Nicaragua.

In summary, assailed by increasing domestic criticism, worsening economic woes, and the continued Contra war, the revolutionary government's human rights performance began to deteriorate in 1982. Things improved around the 1984 election, but declined again after 1985. Repression of government critics and opponents remained much less violent than in Guatemala and El Salvador but included intimidation, harassment, and illegal detention of opponents, independent union leaders, and human rights workers; press censorship; curtailment of labor union activity; and poor prison conditions. In 1988, however, the human rights climate improved again as the government offered concessions to the opposition and announced national elections for early 1990.[36]

The Economy. Economic policy, moderate and pragmatic, diverged from models followed by other Marxist-led governments. The revolutionary government accepted the international debt it inherited from the Somoza regime, and obtained hundreds of millions of dollars in grants and "soft" loans from mostly Western governments and international organizations. And though it confiscated the properties of the Somozas and their cohorts, it preserved a private sector that accounted for between 50 and 60 percent of GDP. Early on, the economy recovered much of its prewar production. Agrarian reform did not heavily emphasize state farming, but rather responded to peasant demands for individual or cooperative smallholdings.[37] Though error-plagued, agrarian policy included credit and pricing policies to encourage production by the largest, export-oriented private farmers. U.S. pressures to curtail Western credit to and trade with Nicaragua forced increasing reliance on the Eastern bloc for credit, other aid, and trade in the mid-1980s.[38]

Nicaraguan capitalists nevertheless felt insecure and reluctant to invest under the revolution. Contributing to their sense of insecurity were the business sector's lack of control of politics, the Sandinista leadership's Marxist philosophy, and substantial change in the rules of the economic game when the revolutionary government nationalized the import-export sector, a key source of profits and of control over the business environment. Moreover, industry suffered from the general decline of the Central American Common Market's import-substitution development model, a worldwide recession, and the U.S. credit and trade embargoes.[39]

The Sandinista government adopted several policies to benefit the majority of poor Nicaraguans—wage increases, food price subsidies, and expanded health, welfare, and education services. As economic austerity pressures grew, however, the newly expanded labor movement was legally prohibited from striking (many strikes were nonetheless tolerated). Because taxes fell short of needs, the government borrowed heavily abroad. Security and social welfare spending eventually exceeded tax and foreign credit resources. To maintain continued critically needed foreign credit, the government by 1986 began enacting currency devaluations and cuts in food subsidies and social programs.

The war, economic mismanagement, austerity measures, withdrawal of Soviet-bloc economic aid, and declining public and private investment drove rapid inflation of consumer prices.[40] Shortages grew rapidly between 1985 and 1989, and popular living standards and services deteriorated. "Urban wages in 1988 had fallen, according to some statistics, to only 10 percent of 1980 levels."[41] Inflation reached 1,200 percent in 1987 and then a mind-boggling 33,602 percent in 1988. Only new and harsher austerity programs in late 1988 and early 1989 brought inflation for 1989 down to 1,690 percent.[42] These policies, however, weakened social services and benefits for the common citizen and threw thousands of government employees out of work.

Replacing the Revolution

The 1990 Election. By 1989 the U.S.-orchestrated Contra war and policies of economic strangulation had brought severe economic hardship to Nicaraguans. U.S. policymakers knew that, in any democratic system, when economic conditions get bad, voters tend to vote incumbents out of office. Washington also knew that the Nicaraguan people had wearied at the Contra war's destruction, not the least of which was the 30,865 who had died by the end of 1989.[43] Thus by the late 1980s internal conditions in Nicaragua had changed so radically that U.S. strategy toward the 1990 elections altered significantly from that of 1984.

The U.S. strategy for Nicaragua's 1990 election followed two tracks. One was to denounce the electoral laws, procedures, and conditions in case the Nicaraguan people might defy conventional wisdom and reelect the FSLN. The groundwork was thus laid to denounce as fraudulent an unexpected Sandinista victory. The second track was to work to ensure opposition victory. Washington used millions of covert and promised overt dollars[44] to weld a united opposition (the National Opposition Union—UNO) out of 14 disparate and squabbling microparties[45] and then to promote its candidates—in particular, presidential candidate Violeta Barrios de Chamorro. The United States thus "micromanaged the opposition"[46] and applied massive external pressure on the electorate. The Contra war escalated sharply from voter registration in October 1989 onward.[47] President Bush called President Ortega "an animal . . . a bull in a china shop,"[48] and received Violeta Chamorro at the White House. The United States promised that both the war and the economic embargo would end should she win.

Despite widely credited pre-election polling indicating the contrary, UNO scored a clearcut victory on February 25, 1990. Chamorro won about 55 percent of the valid presidential votes compared to Daniel Ortega's 41 percent. Of 92 seats in the National Assembly, UNO captured 51, the FSLN won 39, and two independent parties took one apiece. On April 25, 1990, Daniel Ortega placed the sash of presidential office on the shoulders of Chamorro.

The Chamorro Years, 1990–1997. The Chamorro era provides challenges to interpretation.[49] On the one hand, the new administration's economic and social policies were harshly austere. Per-capita GDP stagnated from 1990 through 1996, the worst economic performance in Central America, and real wages remained far below their levels in prior decades (Appendix, Table A.1).[50] Indeed, according to the United Nations Development Program's Human Development Index (based on per capita income, education levels, and life expectancy), Nicaragua's rank among nations had dropped from 85th in the world when Chamorro took office to 117th by the time she left.[51] On the other hand, her administration tamed runaway inflation and, after several years, restarted modest economic growth (Appendix, Table A.1). President Chamorro worked hard to make peace and bind up the political wounds of the Nicaraguan family. She viewed reconciliation as essential for successful governance in the short run and eventual democratic consolidation.

The Chamorro administration did not introduce economic neoliberalism to Nicaragua. The Sandinistas had first implemented harsh structural reforms in the late 1980s in response to hyperinflation caused mainly by spending on the Contra war. But the Chamorro administration embraced neoliberalism with enthusiasm and intensified its implementation. "The Nicaraguan government signed its first Contingency Agreement with the IMF in 1991, and then signed a comprehensive Enhanced Structural Adjustment Facility (ESAF) with the Fund in 1994, followed by a second ESAF in 1998."[52] Government properties were privatized, public expenditures cut, budgets balanced, and tariffs lowered. The downsizing of government, cutbacks in social services, privatization of state enterprises, and credit policy that favored export agriculture over peasant production of domestic foodstuffs combined to exacerbate the misery of ordinary Nicaraguans. For example, the U.S. Agency for International Development (USAID) in managing U.S. loans and thus shaping agricultural credit policy, imposed "efficiency criteria" that starved the peasant agricultural sector. "Deprived of credit and other state services and therefore the means to compete in the market, peasants were forced to sell their land."[53] Unemployment, underemployment, drug addiction, crime, homelessness (especially among children), and domestic violence all soared.

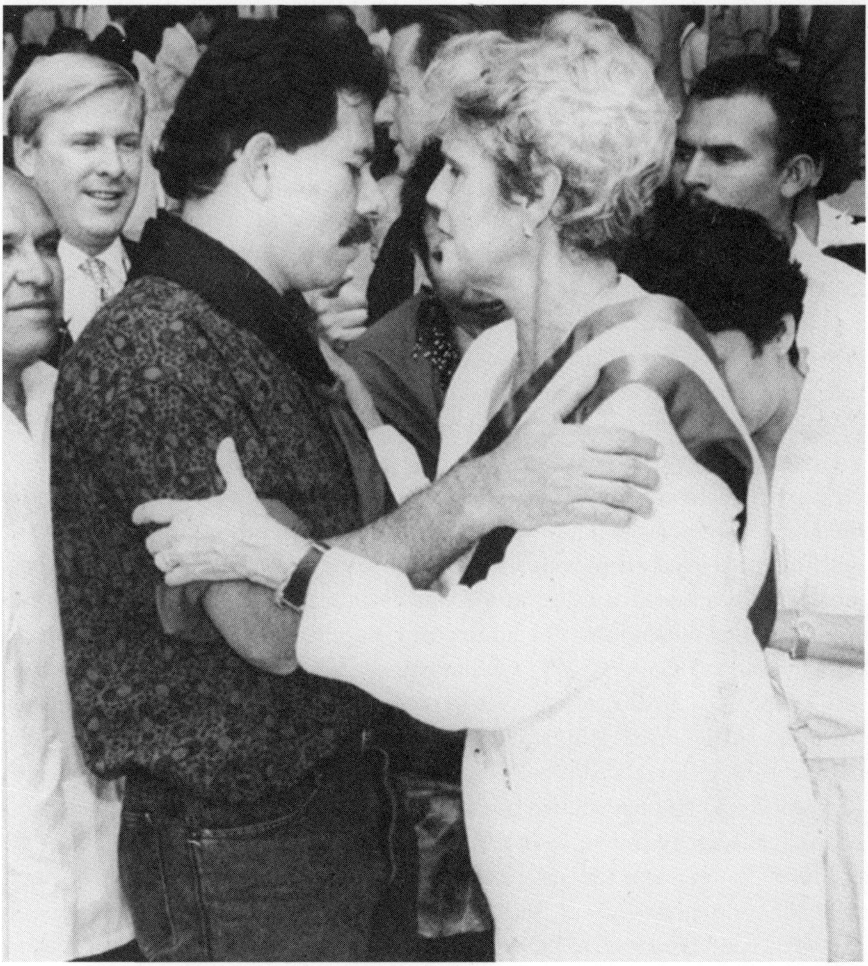

THE END OF AN ERA. Revolutionary President Daniel Ortega places the sash of office on the shoulders of his U.S.-approved successor, Violeta Barrios de Chamorro, on April 25, 1990 (photo courtesy of *Barricada*)

Other social programs changed rapidly after the Sandinistas were voted out. Ideologically conservative administrators reshaped public education drastically. They replaced carefully drafted Sandinista-era textbooks with U.S.-approved and financed generic texts, many of them years out of date. The demobilization of the Contras and the bulk of the national armed forces threw tens of thousands of young men into the economy with little training or experience. The Chamorro administration failed to fulfill promises to give land and resettlement benefits to ex-combatants. Sporadically, throughout the 1990s, rearmed Contras, ex-Sandinista military, and mixed units of both renewed guerrilla activity or took up banditry in rural areas. Organized armed conflict gradually declined, but remnants remained into the late 1990s.[54]

Despite losing almost 3 percent of its population in the insurrection and Contra wars between 1978 and 1990, Nicaragua overall progressed toward national reconciliation and democratic consolidation in the Chamorro years. Grassroots organizations representing the poor played a significant role. The Rural Worker's Association (ATC), the National Union of Farmers and Ranchers (UNAG), and mixed groups of ex-combatants helped negotiate the privatization of state farms and transfer of some land to former workers and ex-combatants. The National Workers' Front (Frente Nacional de Trabajadores—FNT) did the same in the privatization of urban state-owned properties. When the government was unresponsive, grassroots groups demonstrated and protested to force government respect for their interests.

President Chamorro resisted pressures from the United States and domestic right-wingers to engage in a vengeful "de-Sandinization" program. Instead, she wisely allowed Sandinista General Humberto Ortega to remain as head of the military. Thus assured that there would not be an anti-Sandinista bloodbath, the FSLN accepted the rapid demobilization of the army from over 80,000 to less than 15,000 (and by 1998 to 12,000). On the part of the military, "senior commanders recognized that the only way to guarantee the military's survival was to sever its partisan ties to the FSLN and accept increased civilian control."[55] In addition, the Chamorro government, the FSLN leadership, and a wide spectrum of politicians engaged in frequent bargaining, negotiation, and pact making. This ultimately resulted in a majority consensus in the National Assembly, which made possible the promulgation of a new Military Code (1994) that unlinked the armed forces from the FSLN, some revisions of the 1987 constitution (1995), and the passage of a Property Stability Law 209 (1996) that set a framework for dealing with property disputes arising out of the revolutionary period. Clean elections held on the Atlantic Coast in 1994 also boded well.

However, many problems arose. President Chamorro's gestures of reconciliation toward the Sandinistas alienated parts of the diverse UNO coalition. A nasty dispute over constitutional reforms to strengthen the National Assembly, expand the Supreme Court, and prevent presidential self-succession paralyzed the government for much of 1994 and 1995.[56] Many ex-UNO party leaders had won positions as mayors in Nicaragua's largest cities. Nurtured by USAID funding destined exclusively for municipalities that had voted the Sandinistas out, these individuals cultivated popular support with public works patronage. Under their leadership, the old Liberal Party—the majority party of Nicaragua until corrupted by the Somozas—resuscitated as various splinter groups and then fused under the banner of the Liberal Alliance (Alianza Liberal—AL).

A leading figure of this era was Arnoldo Alemán, a lawyer and farmer who had been a Liberal since the Somoza era. During the revolution he developed a hatred for the Sandinistas because they nationalized the bank he worked for, seized his agricultural properties, and put him under house arrest while his wife was dying. Elected mayor of Managua in 1990, Alemán governed the city as a neo-populist. His U.S. aid funds paid for visible public works programs and patronage and jobs for supporters. He courted poor constituents and blamed the Sandinistas for the country's problems. With financial and moral support from Cuban and Nicaraguan exiles in Miami, he and other Liberal mayors built the Liberal Alliance. Alemán won the AL presidential nomination for 1996.

The Sandinistas experienced serious problems during the Chamorro administration. As lame ducks in 1990, the FSLN government passed unseemly laws transferring much state property to top Sandinistas (dubbed *la piñata*). Out of power, the old guard discredited itself further by clinging to leadership when challenged during a party reform effort in 1994. A schism resulted; the breakaway Sandinista Renovation Movement (Movimiento de Renovacion Sandinista—MRS) in 1995 took the vast majority of the intellectual and leadership talent out of the FSLN, leaving mainly hard-line supporters of former president Daniel Ortega, now the party's virtual *caudillo*.[57] Ortega easily won the FLSN presidential nomination.

The 1996 Election and Alemán Administration. For many, the 1996 election left much to be desired. In the highly polarized pre-election atmosphere, the right wing had insisted on a series of last-minute changes in the electoral law and personnel of the Supreme Electoral Council (Consejo Supremo Electoral—CSE). These changes and inadequate funding caused confusion, disorganization, and increased partisanship on electoral boards around the country. Anomalies occurred in voter registration, the campaign, preparation and delivery of materials, operation of polling places, voting, vote reporting, and vote tabulation. Ultimately the Supreme Electoral Council threw out the votes from hundreds of precincts.

However, the Liberal Alliance triumphed by a margin that made the discarded presidential votes immaterial. AL presidential candidate Alemán (51 percent of the vote) beat perennial FSLN candidate Ortega (38 percent). With 86 percent of the electorate voting, the Liberals took 42 National Assembly seats, the FSLN 36 seats, and nine minor parties split 15 seats. Both Ortega and another presidential candidate denounced the Liberal victory as illegitimate, but later the FSLN accepted the outcome.[58]

Contemporary Nicaraguan Politics

Harboring a hatred of the Sandinistas and having not participated in the bargaining that rewrote the rules of the political game in the mid-1990s, Alemán and his

AL plurality in the Assembly questioned the Chamorro-era laws on the military and property and the 1987 constitution. The AL and allies maneuvered to deprive the FSLN of their rightful number of seats on the executive body of the National Assembly, which caused a prolonged period of retaliatory general strikes, demonstrations, angry invective, renewed armed insurgency, FSLN boycotts of the National Assembly, constitutional challenges, sporadic attempts at public dialogue, and behind-the-scenes bargaining between the leaders of the two major political forces. Eventually, international and domestic pressure forced a compromise. In late 1997 negotiations between the FSLN and the government resolved the thorny property issue with a quickly passed Law of Urban and Rural Reformed Property after a brief debate. It guaranteed formal land titles for many of the smallholder beneficiaries of untitled property distribution during the 1980s and 1990s, indemnified people who lost property, and required major beneficiaries of *la piñata* to pay for their larger confiscated houses.[59]

By 1998 and with the settlement of the property issue, a "new normalcy" was beginning to emerge in Nicaragua. The International Monetary Fund renewed support that had been suspended for two years; and a multilateral donor's group of various countries and organizations pledged loans of $1.8 billion over four years to promote macroeconomic stability, the development of agriculture, and governability. A second round of clean (though low turnout) local elections were held in the Atlantic region. As this was happening, however, the leaders of the two major parties each suffered personal scandals. Escalating rumors of corruption engulfed Alemán and would eventually lead to his prosecution and imprisonment. For his part, Ortega's thirty-year-old stepdaughter accused him of having sexually abused her for many years.[60] Although Alemán delayed his legal difficulties until after leaving office and Ortega clung to his role as leader of the FSLN, both leaders suffered irreparable damage to their prestige. Nor did Nicaragua's economic and political elite unite itself under neoliberal globalist leaders as others did in Central America during this era. Robinson identifies two feuding capitalist groups, one modernizing and externally oriented group identified with the Central Bank, globalist think tanks, and U.S. and multilaterally backed financial institutions, the other linked to the old "agro-export oligarchy . . . imbued in the traditional politics of partisan corruption and patronage."[61] Political and economic leadership would remain divided and national economic development largely stagnated.

Late in 1998, hurricane Mitch unleashed widespread flooding, deaths, and infrastructure damage that worsened Nicaragua's already deeply depressed economy and challenged the Alemán administration. Much of the north of the country suffered heavily, with severe damage to areas producing most of the nation's basic grains and coffee. The storm killed over 2,800 people, destroyed or damaged almost 42,000 homes, left 65,000 in shelters, and overall harmed 370,000 people—

roughly one Nicaraguan in twelve. Hurricane Mitch's damage to the economy would persist for several years.

In 1999 with the economy still reeling from the storm, the caudillos of the FSLN and AL again unexpectedly conspired to their mutual benefit. With both men facing legal problems, Ortega and Alemán forged a broad pact to reform the constitution and electoral law. One provision guaranteed losing presidential candidates and the immediate ex-president seats in the Legislative Assembly, which brought with it immunity from prosecution for both leaders. The Alemán-Ortega pact also packed the Supreme Court, strengthened both party leaders within their own parties, and rewrote the electoral law to especially advantage the Liberal Constitutionalist Party (PLC, Partido Liberal Constitucionalista) and FSLN at the expense of all other smaller parties and political movements. Immediate impacts of the new law included a sharp curtailment of the number of smaller-party deputies elected to the 2001–2006 Assembly and a reduction of the number of parties certified to compete in future votes.

In 2001 the Liberal Alliance nominated Alemán's vice president, business leader Enrique Bolaños Geyer, to run for the presidency against FSLN nominee Daniel Ortega. Ortega led Bolaños in the polls until shortly before the election. However, following the September 11 terrorist attacks in the United States, the Bush administration engaged in a smear campaign against Ortega, labeling him a "terrorist."[62] The notion that the U.S. "war on terror" could spread to Nicaragua under an Ortega administration, revived memories of the Contra war. In addition, the United States convinced the Conservatives to align with the Liberals to prevent ticket-splitting among the right. In the end, Bolaños prevailed, winning 56 percent of the vote to Ortega's 42 percent. The Sandinistas won 38 Assembly seats to the AL's comfortable majority of 53. The Conservative Party, once second to the Liberals, captured only one Assembly seat and almost suffered de-certification as a party. Though fallen from their revolutionary era dominance, the Sandinistas had clearly supplanted the Conservatives as the Liberals' opposition in the post-revolutionary political system.

Shortly after his election, Bolaños worked with the National Assembly to repeal the amnesty law for ex-presidents embodied in the Alemán-Ortega pact as a part of his anti-corruption campaign. In 2002 the National Assembly stripped Alemán of his immunity and he was immediately placed under house arrest on charges of laundering $100 million to party candidates and embezzling $1.3 million for his own personal enrichment. In 2004 Alemán was sentenced to a 20-year jail term. Bolaños himself was beset by charges of campaign finance fraud, which led his opponents to call for his impeachment. Bolaños sought the aid of the OAS in fighting off what he charged to be a politically motivated attempt by both Alemán and Ortega supporters to remove him from office.

Bolaños's pursuit of Alemán's prosecution was a major source of conflict within the PLC, which was controlled by Alemán supporters. Bolaños eventually left the party and helped to found the Alliance for the Republic (APRE), a center-right alternative to the PLC, in advance of the 2004 municipal elections. The FSLN benefited from the problems on the right, picking up seats throughout the country. Most importantly, the FSLN won the mayorality of Managua. The beleaguered PLC lost some 100,000 votes while Bolaños's party also had a poor showing.[63] It was, however, a shallow victory for the Sandinistas as abstention rose above 50 percent, and was more than 70 percent in some areas.[64]

Conclusions

Global economic forces, economic assistance from the United States, and cooperation among Central American regimes in response to recessions of the 1940s and 1950s led to the formation of the Central American Common Market. It produced rapid economic growth in the 1960s and 1970s that, because of internal policies aggravated by the 1972 Managua earthquake and 1973 oil price spike, worsened living conditions for the majority of working-class Nicaraguans. This mobilized many people into the political arena in the mid-1970s in search of better working and living conditions or modest reforms. When the Somoza regime brutally cracked down on its critics, the repression caused alliances to be forged among a broad front of opponents, radicalized their originally narrow demands into revolutionary ones, and united the opposition behind the once-weak FSLN. The new rebel coalition marshaled progressively greater resources, whereas those of the regime deteriorated, leading the revolutionaries to power.

The beginning of the revolutionary transformation of Nicaragua in July 1979 was a moment of Central American history no less important than the National War of 1857 or the establishment of the Panama Canal. However, when the Sandinistas consolidated their domination over the revolution, they catalyzed powerful internal and external political forces into more drastic actions in the isthmus. The revolutionary government made important steps toward democracy and responded to external and domestic critics by setting up an election system, holding the 1984 election and with the adoption of the 1987 constitution. Internal opposition to the FSLN's program continued to develop, and the United States mobilized and financed an armed counterrevolution from abroad. Eventually, the Contra war and related programs of economic strangulation caused such economic deterioration and misery that a majority of the Nicaraguan people voted to replace their revolutionary government with one acceptable to Washington. The April 1990 administration change from Daniel Ortega to Violeta Barrios de Chamorro dramatically confirmed Nicaragua's transition to democracy, which had begun with the election of 1984 and was completed with the promulgation of the constitution of 1987.

Viewed from the vantage point of 2005 Nicaragua presented ample cause for concern. The country's dramatic social deterioration—generated by the Contra war and externally imposed economic strangulation—had been accelerated by government indifference and increasingly strict neoliberal "reforms" in the post-Sandinista period. The sad effect is clearly reflected in the dramatic decline in Nicaragua's standing in the United Nations Human Development Index mentioned above. In addition, corruption, political polarization, and truly squalid, self-serving deal making among elites had become common features on the political landscape.

But to end on that note alone would be to omit some important positive points, legacies, perhaps, of the Sandinista revolution. The abuse and murder of street children—a serious post-transition problem in the three countries to the north—was practically nonexistent in Nicaragua, where revolutionary education had stressed the dignity of the poor, including street children. Political assassination—still a problem in El Salvador and Guatemala—remained rare in Nicaragua. Further, though modified and damaged somewhat by pacts between Liberal and Sandinista party elites, the country's democratic institutions survived. Although the corruption of the Alemán administration was reminiscent of the Somoza era, his successful prosecution represented a significant departure from politics as usual. Finally, the electorate's faith in the quality and efficacy of Nicaragua's elections could be seen in turnout rates normally higher than in most other Central American countries.

6

El Salvador

To the casual visitor El Salvador's most striking characteristic is its overpopulation. Foreigners sometimes argue that the tiny country lacks the resources to support its teeming population, but other densely populated countries (The Netherlands, Japan, China) manage to feed their people. El Salvador's real problem is extreme maldistribution of resources brought about, as in the rest of northern Central America, by centuries of external dependence and elite control.[1]

After 13 years of extreme political violence, as insurgents challenged military regimes and their civilian elite allies for power in the 1980s and early 1990s, El Salvador's warring factions agreed to adopt formal civilian democracy. In 1992, the country became more stable—and did so more quickly—than most observers would have expected. Given the historical record of El Salvador's elites, its government's embrace of very conservative economic policies, and the nation's role in the world economy, the country appeared likely to indefinitely maintain debilitating socioeconomic inequalities. Yet as the twenty-first century began, El Salvador was arguably more politically peaceful than at any time in the previous century.

Historical Background

During most of its first century after independence in 1823, a Liberal elite controlled El Salvador. Guatemalan intervention occasionally imposed Conservative rulers, but they were exceptions. Like their regional counterparts, Salvadoran Liberals staunchly advocated free enterprise and economic modernization to better link the country to the world economy. They promoted economic and service modernization to build up agricultural exports. The elite regarded the mestizo and Indian masses as both obstacles to progress and as an essential labor supply.

El Salvador entered the national period with most of its economy built around the production, extraction, and export of indigo dye. By the mid-nineteenth century, cheaper European chemical dyes sharply cut international demand for the deep blue colorant, forcing El Salvador's elite to turn to coffee production. The best land for coffee was the higher, volcanic terrain previously disdained by large landowners. The mountain slopes, however, were occupied by mestizo and Indian communal farmers whose ancestors had been displaced from the valley floors by the Spanish. The would-be coffee growers used their control of the government to appropriate good coffee land.

In 1856, the state mandated individual communes to plant at least two-thirds of their lands in coffee or be confiscated. Lacking the considerable capital necessary to buy and plant coffee trees and wait several years for a crop, many communes were wiped out. Those that survived the 1856 law collapsed in the early 1880s when legislation simply outlawed communal holdings. The government also passed "vagrancy" laws that effectively forced the now-landless peasants to work on the coffee plantations. Outraged by this legalized theft of their land and forced-labor schemes, peasants launched several unsuccessful popular uprisings in the late nineteenth century. Coffee's promoters prevailed, and the privileged classes brought El Salvador into the twentieth century with one of the most unequal patterns of land distribution in all of Latin America. A coffee elite, henceforth known (inaccurately) as the "fourteen families," controlled a lion's share of the country's resources. Coffee cultivation continued expanding into the twentieth century. In 1929, for instance, the socially conscious editor of *La Patria* wrote: "The conquest of territory by the coffee industry is alarming. It . . . is now descending into the valleys displacing maize, rice and beans. It is extended like the conquistador, spreading hunger and misery, reducing former proprietors to the worst conditions—woe to those who sell!"[2]

By the 1930s, the situation reached a political breaking point. The Great Depression had lowered the demand and price for Salvadoran exports. Predictably, the coffee elite attempted to cushion this blow by cutting the already miserable wages of the plantation workers. Meanwhile popular hopes for justice were greatly fueled by an aberrant period of democratic reform in 1930–1931 and then dashed by the rise of yet another reactionary dictatorship, led by General Maximiliano Hernández Martínez. The turmoil and economic travail spawned an ill-coordinated peasant uprising in January 1932, which the government and landowners crushed with the massacre of over 30,000 peasants (few actual insurgents). The promoter of these uprisings, a charismatic Marxist intellectual, Augustín Farabundo Martí, was captured before the revolt and shot and beheaded in its wake. His memory, like that of Sandino in Nicaragua, would continue to affect the country decades later.

The five decades following the rise of General Hernández Martínez and the 1932 massacre (known to this day as the "Slaughter"—*la Matanza*) forms an epoch in Salvadoran history. Whereas before the Liberal elite normally ruled through civilian dictators drawn from among themselves, they henceforth entrusted the government to an uninterrupted series of military regimes. Ruling dictatorially, Hernández Martínez protected the interests of the coffee elite and initiated modernization projects that some of the elite opposed. Post–World War II reform demands from labor and middle-class elements and from within the military ended the Hernández Martínez regime in 1944. In 1948 the armed forces restructured its system of rule by establishing a military-dominated political party, the Revolutionary Party of Democratic Unification (Partido Revolucionario de Unificación Democrática—PRUD). Despite its name, the party promoted neither revolution, democracy nor unity but instead provided the military "an impressive machine of patronage and electoral mobilization."[3] In 1960 the PRUD was replaced by its own clone, the National Conciliation Party (Partido de Conciliación Nacional—PCN).

After 1948 the Salvadoran armed forces—supported by much of the national bourgeoisie, which it defended—ruled essentially on behalf of themselves and became increasingly powerful and corrupt. Military rule developed a cycle of "change" that maintained the status quo. Responding to popular unrest and national problems, progressive young military officers who pledged to institute needed reforms would overthrow an increasingly repressive regime. Then conservative elements of the army with backing from the oligarchy would reassert themselves and drop the recent reforms. This would provoke civil unrest, followed by increased repression, disaffection by another reformist military faction, and a new coup.[4]

One such cycle produced the PRUD between 1944 and 1948. Another cycle culminated in the PRUD's restructuring itself into the PCN in 1961. On January 25, 1961, just after John F. Kennedy's inauguration in the United States, a conservative coup encouraged by the Eisenhower administration took place in El Salvador. Although Kennedy recognized the new government, under the aegis of the Alliance for Progress he apparently also pressured the interim junta to begin implementing mild democratic and social reforms.

The U.S.-created Alliance for Progress and the Central American Common Market (CACM) promoted rapid economic growth in El Salvador. The government developed infrastructure while bourgeois elements and foreigners invested in manufacturing and commerce. The mid-1960s became a time of reformist rhetoric and growing popular hope for change. During this period the opposition

Christian Democratic Party (Partido Demócrata Cristiano—PDC) formed. The PDC's popular leader, José Napoleón Duarte, espoused gradual reformism of the sort supported by the Alliance. Duarte twice won the mayoralty of San Salvador.[5]

A significant process of political transition had begun, aided by rapid economic growth. But this reformism quickly faded in a now-familiar pattern. The mild reforms and the PDC's progress alarmed the oligarchy. El Salvador's establishment press had labeled President Kennedy a "Communist" for promoting agrarian reform. When the PDC's Duarte apparently won the 1972 presidential election, the military answered the oligarchy's call. The regime threw out the election results, installed rightist Col. Arturo Armando Molina as president, and then arrested, tortured, and exiled the defrauded candidate.

Global Forces and Insurrection

Effects of Rapid Economic Growth. The CACM, the Alliance for Progress, and new investment caused rapid economic growth in El Salvador. GDP per capita—overall economic activity in proportion to population—grew faster than 2 percent a year between 1962 and 1978. But as in Nicaragua, the benefits of general economic growth were very unevenly distributed. Consumer prices in El Salvador inflated at a mild rate of about 1.5 percent per year from 1963 to 1972. The OPEC oil price shock, however, drove inflation up to an average of 12.8 percent annually from 1973 through 1979.[6]

In contrast to prices, real working-class wages in El Salvador declined sharply between 1974 and 1980. Wages lost an estimated one-fifth of their real purchasing power between 1973 and 1980. Moreover, Salvadorans' median income was consistently the second lowest in Central America. The reader should bear in mind that, taking into account the maldistribution of income, the disposable annual income of the poorest half of the population probably amounted to no more than a U.S. dollar or two per day, while food and clothing costs were little less than they would have been in the much more prosperous United States. Thus even for those lucky enough to be employed throughout the CACM boom period, officially set wages thus steadily lost effective purchasing power.

Despite the rapid industrialization and productivity growth, the capital-intensive production of consumer goods generated relatively few new jobs for the growing workforce—just the opposite of what CACM and Alliance promoters hoped it would do. Moreover, changes in the agrarian economy pushed hundreds of thousands of peasants off the land, also swelling joblessness. Estimates place unemployment in El Salvador at around 16 percent in 1970. By 1978 the unemployment level, aggravated by oil prices and investor fear generated by the insurrection in Nicaragua, was estimated to have risen to 21 percent. After 1980 unemployment rose even more sharply because of the El Salvador's own developing insurrection. Nervous investors closed some plants and disrupted Central American trade forced others to close.[7]

During the 1970s, wealth became concentrated in fewer hands.[8] After 1950 much of the nation's best agricultural land had been converted to capital-intensive cultivation of export crops (in particular cotton) at the expense of subsistence-farming tenants, squatters, and smallholders. During the 1960s, pressure upon the land increased dramatically—the overall number of farms grew by 19 percent, but the land under cultivation shrank by 8 percent. The 1965 agricultural minimum wage law caused the number of *colonos* and *aparceros* (peasants cultivating for subsistence a plot of land donated by the owner) to drop to one-third of the 1961 level by 1971, and the amount of land so employed to drop to one-fifth of the earlier level.[9]

Thus, in the 1960s a dramatic change in Salvadoran rural class relations greatly increased rural poverty. There was a sharp increase in rental and ownership of tiny (less than 2.0 hectares) farms, but the average size of these small plots shrank. Despite an increase in the number of small plots, the number of newly landless peasants more than tripled between 1961 and 1971. Large farms (over 50 hectares) also shrank in number and size as their owners sold part of their holdings for capital to invest elsewhere. Many members of the rural bourgeoisie moved some of their wealth into the fast-expanding industrial sector during the 1960s and 1970s. They invested in modern, capital-intensive industries that generated large profits. Industrial production and industrial worker productivity grew rapidly while real industrial wages and level of employment actually declined.

Experts on the Salvadoran economy contend that workers' share of the burgeoning national income deteriorated while production and investment became more centralized.[10] Major coffee growers invested roughly four times as much in industry as any other Salvadoran group, and attracted joint ventures with about 80 percent of the foreign capital invested in the country. Moreover, while total industrial output more than doubled between 1967 and 1975, the number of firms actually producing goods diminished by some 10 percent, concentrating wealth and income among the owners of the industrial sector.[11] In Montgomery's words, "The old saying that 'money follows money' was never truer than in El Salvador. . . . These investment patterns not only contributed to an ever-greater concentration of wealth, but confirm that the traditional developmentalist assumption that wealth . . . will 'trickle down' in developing nations is groundless."[12] Orellana agreed: "The majority of Salvadorans, excluded from the benefits of that growth, were prevented from adequately satisfying their basic needs."[13]

Although El Salvador's capitalist elite apparently grew both relatively and absolutely wealthier during the mid-1970s, this pattern changed abruptly in 1979. The Nicaraguan revolution's impact on El Salvador's economy, plus the onset of extensive domestic popular mobilization and political unrest within El Salvador itself in 1978, brought about a sharp decline in investment and economic growth, beginning in 1979. Falling coffee prices and the breakdown of Central American trade due to the exhaustion of the CACM import-substitution growth model accelerated the recession. El Salvador's rapid GDP growth of the mid-1970s reversed and became a 3.1 percent *decline* in overall production and a 5.9 percent *drop* in GDP per capita in 1979. This economic contraction became so severe and persistent that it would require El Salvador 15 years to return to 1980 per-capita production levels. This deep depression not only harmed the interests of El Salvador's coffee producers and industrialists but also brought massive layoffs among their employees.[14]

In summary, the development model followed by the Salvadoran state under the Central American Common Market increased overall production as well as the share of national wealth controlled by the national capitalist class. The Salvadoran working classes became not only relatively but absolutely poorer during the 1970s, and markedly so. The purchasing power of working-class wage earners in El Salvador dropped sharply, beginning in 1973. Joblessness and underemployment rose steadily during much of the 1970s and accelerated late in the decade. When one considers the miserable earning power of the average poor Salvadoran, these facts compellingly demonstrate how gravely living standards eroded during this period. Such adversity, measured for most in such fundamentals as how much food they could put on the table each day, provided powerful political grievances to large numbers of Salvadorans.

Popular Mobilization. Although the military's PRUD-PCN Party always controlled the national government, new opposition parties from across the ideological spectrum appeared during the 1960s.[15] An early sign of growing political opposition was the appearance of two reformist parties: the social democratic National Revolutionary Movement (Movimiento Nacional Revolucionario—MNR) in 1959 and the Christian Democratic Party (Partido Demócrata Cristiano—PDC) in 1960. The Democratic National Union (Unión Democrática Nacionalista—UDN), a coalition of leftist elements, formed in 1967.[16] The PDC and MNR briefly formed a legislative coalition with dissident deputies from the ruling PCN in the late 1960s. This coalition anticipated a major reform push by the National Opposition Union (Unión Nacional Opositora—UNO), an electoral coalition of the PDC, MNR, and UDN. UNO's presidential candidate, José Napoleón Duarte, apparently won the 1972 election but was denied the office by fraud. UNO reportedly also won the 1977 presidential election, but was again defrauded of victory.

Myriad organizations (from unions to self-help organizations to peasant leagues), many promoted by the Church and by the new political parties, developed rapidly during the late 1960s and the 1970s. The number of cooperatives rose from 246 to 543 between 1973 and 1980.[17] Labor union membership among blue-collar and middle-class workers rose steadily from the late 1960s, reaching 44,150 in 1970 and 71,000 by 1977; several unions, especially those of public employees, began making more militant demands.[18] The number and frequency of strikes rose dramatically in 1974 and following years as inflation ate away at living standards.

Development programs sponsored by the Catholic Church, PDC, and even the U.S. Agency for International Development (USAID) swelled the number of working-class organizations in El Salvador during the 1960s and early 1970s. Catholic Christian base communities (CEBs) spread widely through urban and rural poor neighborhoods. In the 1970s CEBs increasingly made political and economic demands on behalf of the poor. Numerous peasant organizations also developed during this period, in part encouraged by the Molina regime's mid-1970s land reform proposals. Peasant leagues began demanding land reform and higher wages. The United Popular Action Front (Frente de Acción Popular Unida—FAPU), a coalition of labor, peasant, and university student organizations, and the Communist Party of El Salvador (Partido Comunista de El Salvador—PCS), formed in 1974. FAPU was the first of several such coalitions that would eventually build a very broad opposition network.

Between 1970 and 1979 five Salvadoran guerrilla organizations arose to challenge the PCN regime militarily (see Appendix, Table A.4). Each also forged a coalition with unions and other popular organizations after 1974. These five broad front coalitions greatly enhanced opposition capability and resources, facilitating strikes and mass demonstrations and providing other material resources for the armed opposition.

Government Repression and the Opposition. After 1970, successive military regimes responded to swelling popular mobilization with growing repression.[19] A rightist paramilitary organization with direct ties to public security forces, the Nationalist Democratic Organization (Organización Democrática Nacionalista—ORDEN), formed in the late 1960s. ORDEN, whose acronym spells the Spanish word "order," recruited tens of thousands of peasants from among former military conscripts. It sought to suppress peasant organization and provided an anti-Communist militia. ORDEN quickly built a grisly record. It attacked and killed striking teachers in 1968 and thereafter became increasingly involved in the murder of persons involved in organizing workers, peasants, or political opposition to the regime.

President Molina (1972–1977) and his handpicked successor Carlos Humberto Romero (1977–1979), both military officers, with close links to key sectors of the agrarian oligarchy, staunchly opposed political and economic reform. As the first guerrilla actions began to occur and labor and peasant organization membership grew after 1973, regular security forces became much more overtly repressive. In 1974 National Guard and ORDEN forces murdered six peasants and "disappeared" several others affiliated with a Church-PDC peasant league. On July 30, 1975, troops killed at least 37 students protesting the holding of the Miss Universe pageant in San Salvador. Regular government troops in the capital massacred an estimated 200 UNO supporters as thousands protested fraud in the 1977 presidential election. From 1975 on, "death squads," a label that McClintock characterized as a misnomer employed deliberately to disguise political terror by regular security forces and ORDEN,[20] became increasingly active. (As discussed elsewhere in this book, their use in El Salvador is just one example of U.S.-sanctioned death squad activity throughout the Americas beginning in 1969.)[21] Beginning with the public assassination of opposition legislator and labor leader Rafael Aguinada Carranza in 1974, death squads assassinated and kidnapped dissidents, Catholic social activists, and priests and attacked Church property. Eighteen Catholic clergy and religious personnel, including Archbishop Oscar Arnulfo Romero, were murdered between 1977 and 1982.[22]

Levels of political repression in El Salvador reached such heights in the late 1970s that official mortality statistics began to reflect the curve of terror. Following a big increase in labor disputes in 1977–1979, two separate indicators of violence shot upward. The government's own annual tally of violent deaths, reported in official statistical abstracts, rose from normal background levels of an average of 864 murders per year for 1965–1966 to 1,837 in 1977, and then skyrocketed to 11,471 violent deaths in 1980.[23] A Catholic human rights agency reported that political murders rose from an average of about 14 per year for 1972–1977 to 299 per year for 1977–1978, 1,030 by 1979, 8,024 in 1980, and 13,353 in 1981.[24]

Statistics convey little of the intensity and nature of governmental abuse of human rights in El Salvador. The following violations became commonplace: searches of persons and residences on a massive scale; arbitrary, unmotivated, and unappealable arrests by secret police/military agencies; widespread and systematic use of physical and psychological torture; violent kidnappings; arbitrary and indefinite retention (often without charges) of prisoners; use of illegally obtained "confessions" extracted through torture or intimidation; official refusal to provide information about detainees; judicial corruption; extremely poor prison conditions; systematic impunity for human rights violators; government antagonism toward humanitarian, human rights, and relief agencies; and intimidation and harassment of prisoners or released prisoners and of their families. Among commonplace types of torture used by the military and police of El Salvador were the following:

> Lengthy uninterrupted interrogations during which the prisoner is denied food and sleep; electrical shocks; application of highly corrosive acids to the prisoner's body; hanging of prisoners by the feet and hands; hooding prisoners [for long periods]; introduction of objects into the anus; threats of rape; disrespect-

> ful fondling and rape; threats of death; simulation of death of the prisoner by removing him from the cell, blindfolded and tied, late at night, and firing shots [toward the prisoner but] into the air; all manner of blows; . . . [and] threats of rape, torture, and murder of loved ones of the prisoner. Among the thousands of murdered detainees, the signs of torture reach uncommon extremes of barbarism: dismemberment [of various types], mutilation of diverse members, removal of breasts and genitals, decapitation . . . and leaving of victims' remains in visible and public places.[25]

After this escalation of government repression in the mid-1970s four large opposition coalitions formed. Each linked various labor, peasant, and student groups to one of the guerrilla organizations. FAPU formed in 1974, the Revolutionary Popular Bloc (Bloque Popular Revolucionario—BPR) in 1975, the 28th of February Popular Leagues (Ligas Populares 28 de Febrero—LP–28) in 1978, and the Popular Liberation Movement (Movimiento de Liberación Popular—MLP) in 1979. By allying with each other and with armed rebels, the opposition coalitions' constituent groups committed themselves to revolutionary action. Together these confederations could mobilize hundreds of thousands of supporters into demonstrations and strikes and could raise funds and recruits for the guerrillas. Guerrilla groups also raised large war chests by kidnapping wealthy Salvadorans for ransom. After mid-1979 arms flowed to the guerrillas from private dealers in Costa Rica. Other arms came through Nicaragua for a short period during 1980 and early 1981.[26]

Growing opposition mobilization, the escalation of regime and rebel violence, the incapacity of the Romero government to address national problems, career frustration among certain groups of military officers, and apprehension about the Sandinistas' victory in Nicaragua in July 1979 led to a first major regime change in El Salvador. Disgruntled senior officers and reformist younger officials ousted President Romero, a former general, on October 15, 1979. The coup temporarily allied these military factions with opposition social democrats of the MNR, the Christian Democrats (PDC), and some business factions. The Carter administration gambled that the reformist inclinations of the junta's members might stem the rising revolutionary tide and immediately endorsed the coup and reformist military regime it established.[27] The coup and new junta thus made palatable the redemption of U.S. arms transfers to the Salvadoran military.

This new regime allowed some new civilian players (the MNR, PDC) and ousted some others (especially the PCN's Romero and his allies) and, with U.S. encouragement, proposed socioeconomic reforms. Nevertheless, the new junta failed to stem the rapidly escalating official violence. Rightist elements quickly emerged on top and expelled some of the reformers in early 1980. This prompted the MNR and most of the Christian Democrats to abandon the junta. However, the support of the United States added a crucial new element to the political game and continued pressure for socioeconomic reform. The coup thus ushered in a reformist military regime that "signalled the exhaustion of traditional forms of political control and the search for a more viable system of domination. The old power apparatus was severely shaken."[28]

The October 1979 coup briefly raised opposition hopes for major changes, but the quick restructuring of the junta and spiraling official violence soon alienated much of the center and left and changed opposition tactics. Further unification of the opposition took place early in 1980: The five guerrilla groups joined to form the Farabundo Martí National Liberation Front (FMLN) to increase their political and military coordination. Opposition forces then forged the Revolutionary Coordinator of the Masses (Coordinadora Revolucionaria de Masas—CRM) in January 1980 and continued massive strikes, protests, and guerrilla warfare. Several parties and mass coalitions, including the MNR and much of the PDC, then united into the Revolutionary Democratic Front (FDR). The FDR and FMLN soon allied to form the joint political-military opposition organization FMLN-FDR, which coordinated overall opposition revolutionary strategy, fielded some 4,000 troops and 5,000 militia, and controlled several zones of the country.

The FMLN-FDR adopted a platform for a revolutionary government, established governmental structures in their zones of control, and began planning to take over power.[29] In recognition of this powerful challenge to junta's sovereignty, Mexico and France recognized the FMLN-FDR as a belligerent force and thus increased the rebels' legitimacy. The FMLN-FDR's representatives operated openly in Panama, Nicaragua, Mexico, Colombia and even the United States.

Outcome of the Challenge to Sovereignty. Momentum in the contest over sovereignty shifted toward the Salvadoran opposition in 1979 and 1980. The rebels had built a massive and cooperative popular base, acquired considerable financing, and mobilized several thousand men and women under arms. The October coup momentarily linked the major opposition parties, a reformist military faction, and key middle-sector proponents of democracy in an effort to implement major structural reforms and curtail government violence. Within weeks, however, rightist elements pushed moderates from the junta and escalated violence. This subverted the reformist opposition's tentative accession to power and blocked its reform attempts. The restructuring of the junta in early 1980 thus closed one middle (and less violent) path to change and convinced much of the moderate center-left into alliance with the armed opposition. On January 30, 1980, Guillermo Ungo and other moderates resigned from the junta and cabinet. When the junta reconstituted itself with more conservative elements of the Christian Democrats and government violence continued, the FDR formed (April 1980), followed by the FMLN (October 1980). By late 1980, guerrilla troops had seized effective control of much of Morazán, La Unión, and Chalatenango provinces, so that "1981 opened with the army badly stretched and the undefeated FMLN poised for a major offensive."[30]

The government found itself and its support in disarray. The first junta itself was divided, had scant support from the mass organizations and almost none from the private sector. When the conservative remnant of the PDC joined the junta in 1980, the major organization representing Salvadoran capital, the National Association of Private Enterprises (Asociación Nacional de Empresas Privadas—ANEP) boycotted the government in outrage. Rightist elements within and outside the military attempted several times to overthrow the junta. The poor battlefield performance of the armed forces' 15,000 ill-trained troops throughout 1980 appeared to foretell imminent doom for the regime.

Help for the junta came from outside the country. The U.S. government decided to provide military aid to the failing Salvadoran military and thus profoundly altered the balance of forces between the regime and insurgents. Military aid and advice and economic assistance worth $5.9 million sent during the waning days of the Carter administration began to rescue the Salvadoran regime. The incoming Reagan administration then greatly boosted U.S. technical assistance and financing. By 1985, U.S. military aid to El Salvador had reached the sum of $533 million. Over 12 years of the Salvadoran civil war, U.S. aid (military plus civilian) totaled about $6 billion.[31]

The Reagan administration, which heavily supported the PDC's Duarte, helped contain rightist opposition to the government and assisted with programs ranging from agrarian reform to constituent assembly elections.[32] U.S. training, arms, munitions, aircraft, and intelligence held the Salvadoran army together long enough to increase its size and capability so that it could effectively fight the FMLN. Unlike what had occurred in Nicaragua, where aid was withdrawn, U.S. assistance in El Salvador rescued the official armed forces and prolonged the conflict. "The principal reason for the extended nature of the war was the capacity of the junta to hold its piecemeal military apparatus together . . . to ward off guerrilla offensives [and hold] the population in a state of terror. . . . It could only have achieved this or, indeed, survived for more than a few weeks with the resolute support of the U.S., which Somoza was, in the last instance, denied."[33]

The development of the Salvadoran government after 1979 depended heavily upon several interacting forces—hard-liners in control of the armed forces, major business interests, extremist anticommunist ideologues of the sort represented by Roberto D'Aubuisson and his Nationalist Republican Alliance Party (Alianza Republicana Nacionalista—ARENA), and the Carter, Reagan, and first Bush administrations. Indeed, another regime transformation occurred mainly because of pressure by the United States. These Salvadoran actors agreed to replace the junta with a transitional civilian-led government marked by the advent of constitutional reform and elections. The war still went badly for the military during the early 1980s, but massive U.S. economic, military, and technical assistance held off the FMLN.

The right fiercely opposed much of the reform and especially including moderates in government, but their dependence on U.S. aid undermined their resistance. Throughout most of the 1980s, the United States championed José Napoleón Duarte's faction of the PDC as the only political force that could help legitimize the struggle against the armed opposition. Backed by the immense financial, technical, and political resources of the United States, Duarte was installed in the presidency and the PDC took a majority of the legislative seats via the 1984 presidential and 1985 legislative elections—both of very dubious quality.[34] Thus began a new and shaky civilian transitional government that would eventually provide the institutional and legal foundation for greater democracy. The short-term goal of the United States in 1984 was to establish new political rules with formal civilian leadership and to broaden the spectrum of participants. This liberalization would provide enough political space to moderates to keep them from aligning with the FMLN. Although detested as a "Communist" by the Right and distrusted by the military, Duarte with his U.S. backing was indispensable to both because they needed U.S. aid to avoid defeat. U.S. pressure upon the military and right was sufficient to protect the Duarte/PDC civil government, but could neither control radical rightist forces nor compel them to permit social reform. In a very real sense, Duarte formally held the office of president without ever really coming to power.

U.S. presence in El Salvador during the Duarte period thus created an unstable and artificial coalition among highly incompatible elements. The Duarte government exercised no control over the security forces or war.[35] Duarte's early initiatives to negotiate with the FMLN-FDR were effectively blocked by both the Salvadoran military and the United States. Both wished to win the war rather than negotiate with the opposition. The constitution written in 1982–1983 effectively barred those aspects of agrarian reform that might have eased the social pressures contributing to the rebellion. The transitional government could not muster support from the business community or conservative parties for badly needed economic austerity measures. Duarte's main base of mass support, the PDC's allied labor unions, grew increasingly frustrated and uncooperative in the late 1980s. The inefficacy and growing corruption of the PDC, aggravated by internal divisions, led to the party's defeat by ARENA in the 1988 legislative elections. On March 19, 1989, moderate-appearing ARENA candidate Alfredo Cristiani won the presidential election, with party strongman Roberto D'Aubuisson discreetly in the background.

Presiding over this second administration in El Salvador's civilian transitional government, "Freddy" Cristiani came from one of his country's wealthiest aristocratic families. A graduate of Georgetown University, diplomatic and fluent in English, he quickly won acceptance by the U.S. government and media as a worthy

PRIMERO DE MAYO (MAY DAY) DEMONSTRATION IN EL SALVADOR, 1988. People with signs representing grass-roots organizations; government response (photos by Steve Cagan)

ally despite his affiliation with ARENA. In fact, although no champion of social justice, Cristiani proved more moderate than many had expected. Among Cristiani's negatives were that he did little to improve the quality of elections held during his presidency or to clean up the nation's corrupt judiciary. On the positive side, his ARENA credentials helped him with the armed forces and, with the assistance of the Central American Peace Accord and eventual U.S. acquiescence, permitted him to negotiate for peace with the FMLN.[36]

War and Peace. The conflict in El Salvador during the 1980s became a bloody stalemate. The rebels held their own against and adapted to increasingly powerful and sophisticated military pressure until 1984–1985. FMLN troop levels rose to around 10,000 by 1984. However, U.S. training, aid, and intelligence helped the regime's forces steadily gain ground in the mid-1980s as transport, logistics, and tactics improved. By 1986 government troop strength rose to 52,000 from the 1980 level of 15,000. By 1985–1986 this began to affect the rebels, whose strength in the field apparently shrank to about 5,000, where it remained roughly static into the late 1980s.[37] The rebel troop decline owed partly to growing government air power's shrinking the guerrilla-controlled zones, and partly to an FMLN strategy shift. Civilian casualties in rebel-held zones escalated. In 1988 and 1989 the guerrillas revealed new capacity to operate effectively in urban areas. When the ARENA-led congress refused to postpone the March 1989 presidential election in response to an FMLN offer to return to peaceful civic competition, the FMLN attempted to disrupt the election by causing widespread power outages and disruption of transportation.

A dispassionate summary of some of the horror of El Salvador's civil war includes the following: Virtually all objective observers attribute at least 80 percent of the country's 70,000 deaths between 1979 and 1992 to the military, the police, and ORDEN.[38] A Reagan administration, worried about retaining U.S. Congressional funding for the Salvadoran government, pressured the country's military, police, and ORDEN to curtail sharply the numbers of deaths and disappearances in 1983 and 1984. Despite such efforts—in themselves revealing how much of the repression emanated directly from the security forces—increasing combat operations kept the casualty rate up in the mid-1980s. The violence was so bad that more than one in six Salvadorans fled the country. Even for those untouched by personal losses, the war, migration, and capital flight deepened the nation's depression and increased human misery. From 1980 through 1987 the economy slowed down by almost 10 percent of its 1980 per capita production level.[39]

The Central American Peace Accord signed in Esquipulas, Guatemala, in August 1987 raised hopes for a negotiated settlement of the Salvadoran war, but little progress was made until the early 1990s. Starting in late 1982, the rebels had pushed for a compromise settlement rather than outright victory. In their opinion, a direct takeover of the government would have brought the type of U.S.-sponsored surrogate war and economic strangulation they observed inflicted on

FMLN REBELS. Female guerrillas in northern Morazón Province, 1988 (photo by Steve Cagan)

the Sandinistas in Nicaragua.[40] Throughout the 1980s, however, the United States and the Salvadoran right opposed a negotiated settlement, opting instead for outright victory. Accordingly, although the Salvadoran government went through the motions of engaging in sporadic negotiation, no real progress occurred for some time. Indeed, the Esquipulas agreement even triggered a sharp upswing in the number of murders by the "death squads"–security forces.

The year 1989 brought things to a head. That spring the FMLN offered to participate in the upcoming presidential elections if the government would agree to postpone them for a six-month period so democratic safeguards could be put in place.

The government went ahead with the elections without the FMLN. ARENA candidate Alfredo Cristiani, who campaigned on peace and economic recovery, easily defeated Christian Democrat Fidel Chávez Mena. Cristiani immediately began implementing neoliberal reforms, starting with the banking and financial sectors in hopes of establishing El Salvador as the financial center of Latin America.

Frustrated at having failed to secure a delay in the elections, the rebels escalated their military operations in outlying areas to demonstrate their strength and convince the government to negotiate seriously. When this pressure also failed, the FMLN in late 1989 mounted a major and prolonged military offensive in the capital city, San Salvador. The military responded by murdering many noncombatants it viewed as sympathetic to the rebels. Most shocking were the murders of six prominent Jesuit priests-intellectuals, their housekeeper, and her daughter on the campus of the Central American University the night of November 16, 1989. High-ranking officers including the chief of staff of the army and the head of the air force authorized this atrocity, perpetrated by a unit of the U.S.-trained Atlacatl Battalion.[41] The guilty generals went free, but two years later a colonel and a lieutenant who had apparently acted under their orders became the very first Salvadoran officers convicted of human rights violations in the twelve-year history of that bloody war.

The guerrilla offensive of late 1989, the embarrassment of the Jesuit massacre and other atrocities, and the end of the Cold War apparently convinced the United States to opt for a negotiated settlement in El Salvador. As a Rand Corporation specialist who wrote a report on El Salvador under contract to the U.S. Department of Defense put it, "The security concerns that impelled the policy have all but evaporated along with the East-West contest. . . . 'Winning' in El Salvador no longer matters much. A negotiated solution, or even 'losing' would no longer carry the same ominous significance."[42] President George H. W. Bush decided in the early 1990s to support the peace process. This cleared the way for a marathon and ultimately successful effort by outgoing United Nations Secretary-General Javier Pérez de Cuellar to bring the warring parties together. Toward the end, U.S. diplomats such as U.N. Ambassador Thomas Pickering and Assistant Secretary of State Bernard Aronson pushed the Salvadoran government to make concessions. Finally, even ARENA founder Roberto D'Aubuisson—in a last public gesture before dying of cancer—endorsed the peace proposal.

Government and Politics Since the Peace Accord

The 1992 peace agreement began altering Salvadoran politics by ushering in a civilian democracy that allowed participation by a broad ideological spectrum. Under U.N. supervision, the government drastically reduced the size of the army and made progress in depoliticizing the services, retiring and reassigning senior officers, and reforming military education. The military abolished its infamous U.S.-trained rapid deployment forces, the Treasury Police, and the National Guard.[43] The government dismantled the National Police and replaced it with a new National Civil Police (Policía Nacional Civil—PNC). Under civilian authority, the PNC drew its

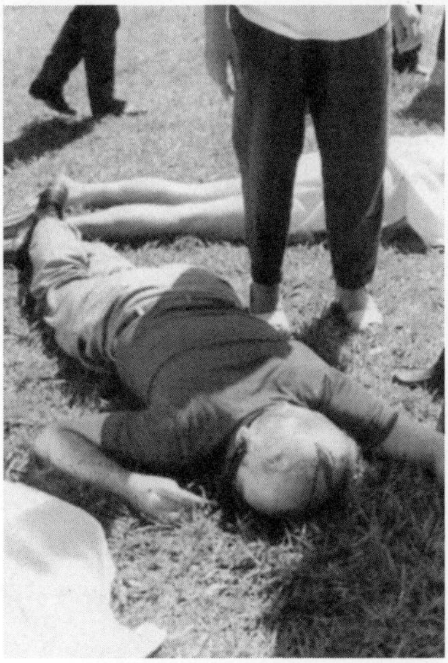

COMING TO A HEAD IN NOVEMBER 1989. The rebel offensive in San Salvador (photo by Arturo Robles, courtesy of CRIES, Managua). A scene from the aftermath of the murder of Jesuit intellectuals at the Central American University by a unit of the U.S.-trained Atlacatl Battalion (photo by Laurel Whitney, reprinted from *Envio* with the permission of the Central American University, Managua)

personnel from both the FMLN and government ranks.[44] A "truth commission" began to investigate the civil war. In March 1993 El Salvador's Truth Commission Report found that 95 percent of the human rights abuses committed since 1980 were the fault of the armed forces and "death squads." Five days later, a general amnesty law was passed by the legislative assembly ensuring that there would be no legal recourse, either criminal or civil, for crimes committed during the war.

The FMLN demobilized its forces by early 1993 and engaged openly in electoral politics. The 1994 elections, dubbed the "election of the century," marked the first truly democratic elections in El Salvador's history. Parties from across the political spectrum vied for seats in the legislature, mayoralities, and the presidency. The FMLN joined a center-left coalition with Democratic Covergence (Convergencia Democrática—CD) in the presidential election. While CD candidate Rubén Zamora managed to force a runoff, he was easily defeated by ARENA's Armando Calderón Sol in the second round of voting. ARENA also won a majority of the seats in the legislative assembly, nearly double those of the FMLN.

Calderón Sol intensified the neoliberal reforms of his predecessor, privatizing the telecommunications and energy sectors and reducing tariffs.[45] The economic growth that characterized the Salvadoran economy during the early 1990s declined later in the decade, resulting in increasing tensions between the industrialists and agrarian elites within ARENA.[46] Additionally, the neoliberal model had done little to address poverty, unemployment, or the growing crime problem. Discontent with neoliberal policies helped the FMLN make significant gains in the 1997 legislative and municipal elections. While ARENA won the most seats, it lost nearly 210,000 votes (a reduction of 39 to 28 seats) while the FMLN gained nearly 82,000 (an increase of 21 to 27 seats).[47] The FMLN alone or in coalition also won 54 mayoralties, including San Salvador. The tensions within ARENA also aided the right-wing PCN, which increased its representation in the legislature by 7 seats. The Christian Democrats posted significant losses, dropping from 18 to 7 seats.

The repositioning of the FMLN as a political party was bolstered by its electoral successes, although there was considerable debate over the direction of the party. One faction, the *renovadores,* favored modernizing the party and finding a compromise with the neoliberals. The other, the *orthodoxos,* believed that the FMLN's potency at the ballot box was a sign that the party should outright reject the neoliberal model. Following a prolonged and heated nominating convention, the FMLN selected former guerrilla and renovador Facundo Guardado as its candidate for president in the 1999 elections. Guardado was easily defeated by ARENA's Francisco Flores, 52 to 29 percent. The sizable loss resulted in considerable fracturing within the FMLN as two groups began to vie for control of the party. Guardado blamed the orthodoxos for the loss while the orthodoxos blamed Guardado's abandonment of the socialist platform for the loss. Guardado resigned as the party's general coordinator, and the orthodoxos assumed control of the party.[48]

Like the two previous ARENA administrations, the Flores administration was committed to the implementation of the neoliberal model. The privatization program hit a snag in 1999 when plans to privatize the services within the health-care sector resulted in a five-month strike by health-care workers. Flores' unwillingness to negotiate with the workers played poorly during the campaign. According to one poll, only 37 percent rated Flores as doing a good job and a majority said that the economy and crime had gotten worse during the first year of his administration.[49]

The FMLN again benefited from the growing unpopularity of ARENA's policies and became El Salvador's largest political party following the 2000 municipal and legislative elections. The FMLN gained four seats in the Legislative Assembly and won 77 (ten in coalition races) mayoralties. In what was expected to be a preview of the 2004 presidential election, FMLN coalition candidate and San Salvador mayor Hector Silva soundly defeated ARENA candidate and businessman Luis Cardenal in the mayoral race in the capital. ARENA's losses in the 2000 elections resulted in a major reshuffling of ARENA's executive committee, including the resignation of its director, former president Cristiani. The PCN continued to take advantage of ARENA's losses, gaining three seats in the legislature and 15 mayoralities. Many, however, chose not to vote. As evidence of the decreasing confidence in Salvadoran politics, voter turnout was only 38 percent—down from 45 percent in 1997.[50]

ARENA's poor showing in the election and El Salvador's economic malaise did not derail Flores's commitment to the neoliberal model. In a highly controversial move, Flores successfully pushed through the dollarization of the economy in January 2001. Two major earthquakes in January and February 2001 compounded the effects of El Salvador's economic slowdown. The quakes exposed the neglect of social services under the neoliberal program, as hospitals and other services were easily overwhelmed. Although seemingly resolved in 2000, the issue of privatizing certain health services reemerged prior to the 2003 municipal and legislative elections. Health-care workers engaged in a second strike throughout the campaign. When San Salvador mayor Hector Silva intervened to mediate the conflict, the FMLN became furious and accused him of violating party procedure. The FMLN maintained its 31 seats in the Legislative Assembly while ARENA lost two seats in the 2003 municipal and legislative elections. Additionally, the FMLN retained its mayoral post in San Salvador despite losing very popular two-time mayor Hector Silva as a candidate.

Flores's tenure, widely regarded as uncompelling, was marked by two prolonged health-care strikes, economic stagnation, and a troubling gang problem. Combined with the FMLN's momentum from the 2003 elections, it appeared that ARENA could lose the 2004 presidential elections. To toughen its image prior to the 2004 presidential election, the Flores government pushed for harsh anti-gang measures. Known as *mano dura* (effectively, but not literally, "iron fist"), the legislation, which criminalized gang membership, was criticized by human rights advocates domestically and internationally.

The FMLN, firmly in the control of the orthodoxos, was again unable to turn its electoral successes in the legislative and municipal races into a presidential win in 2004. The selection of former commandante and Communist Party leader Shafick Handal as its presidential candidate was unpopular both at home and abroad. The U.S. was extremely uneasy over the idea of an FMLN victory, as Handal vowed he would withdraw Salvadoran troops from Iraq and adamantly opposed the Central American Free Trade Agreement (CAFTA). Former U.S. Ambassador Rose Likins and other State Department officials warned of a deterioration in U.S.-Salvadoran relations under a Handal administration.[51] ARENA's candidate, former sportscaster Antonio Saca, seized the opportunity to exploit a potential rupture in the relationship by focusing on the country's dependence on remittances, which exceeded $2 billion annually. Several U.S. congressmen also suggested that an FMLN victory should result in a review or termination of temporary protected status (TPS) for Salvadorans living in the United States and a reconsideration of remittance policies.[52]

In the end, Handal's unpopularity and U.S. interference in the elections thwarted an FMLN victory. ARENA's Saca easily defeated Handal in the first round of voting, 57 percent to 36 percent. Former San Salvador mayor Hector Silva ran on the United Democratic Center (Centro Democrático Unido—CDU) coalition ticket with the Christian Democrats, but the CDU-PDC failed to win 5 percent of the vote. The 2004 presidential elections were the most polarized since the "elections of the century" a decade earlier. ARENA frequently invoked Cold War imagery and rhetoric, lambasting Handal as a terrorist bent on turning El Salvador into another Cuba. Surprisingly, the outcome of the election had little effect on the orthodoxo control of the FMLN and Handal remained at the helm of the party. For its part, ARENA was bolstered by Saca's resounding victory. Despite three successive, lackluster administrations, ARENA managed to win the election with a virtual unknown.

Conclusions

El Salvador became a markedly different place after the peace accords. On the positive side, foreign assistance smoothed transition to civilian democracy, encouraged the formation of hundreds of civil society organizations, and trained former combatants for new occupations. The FMLN contested elections and won seats in the legislature, mayorships, and city councils. Human rights violations declined and political liberties improved, while the press became more free and able to engage in investigative reporting and commentary critical of the government. Undoubtedly moved by this improved climate, Salvadorans' support for the government rose substantially, and public opinion suggested some prospect for democratic consolidation. On the negative side, the human rights climate remained somewhat troubled and evidence persisted of potential for violent political repression. Crime escalated and remained very high. Efforts were under way to reform the courts and criminal laws, both in disarray in the mid 1990s.[53] The economy declined in the mid-1990s and early 2000s, and two severe earthquakes in 2001 added to the country's socioeconomic woes.

On balance, then, at this writing, El Salvador had made progress toward consolidating its democracy, although much remained to be accomplished with regard to institutional development, individual security, and human rights. The nation's elites had accommodated themselves to the transnational model and were making progress at low-intensity electoral democracy. A citizenry long brutalized by repression and civil war remained cautious in their political participation, but began expressing increased support for democracy and for the new regime.

7

Guatemala

Guatemala's long, violent passage from military authoritarian rule to electoral democracy followed a different path from Nicaragua's but one similar to El Salvador's. The rapid economic change and repression that drove turmoil and regime change, however, were similar in all three nations. In Guatemala, as in El Salvador, rebels and power holders fought a protracted civil war marked by three regime changes, the last of which established a democracy, curtailed military power, and permitted former rebels into the political arena. Unlike El Salvador, Guatemala's military governments had largely kept rebels at bay without much visible involvement by the United States.

Historical Background

Though Guatemala is unlike the rest of modern Central America in having a large, unintegrated indigenous population, it shares historical legacies with nineteenth-century Nicaragua and El Salvador. In all three countries, an early period of Liberal-Conservative conflict was followed by a consolidation of Liberal control. The Liberals implemented "reforms" that produced profound socioeconomic realignments and shaped contemporary social and political problems.

The Liberals took control of Guatemala in 1871 and dominated it, with minor exceptions, until the 1940s. Liberal dictator-president Justo Rufino Bárrios (1873–1885) pushed to modernize by building roads, railways, a national army, and a more competent national bureaucracy. He promoted the new crop, coffee, and encouraged foreign investment. Barrios opened Church and Indian communal lands to cultivation by large landowners (latifundists). By 1900 coffee accounted for 85 percent of Guatemala's exports. Landownership was increasingly concentrated in the hands of latifundist coffee growers who also dominated Guatemalan economics and politics. Forced from their land, indigenous Guatemalans fell prey to debt-peonage and "vagrancy" laws, enacted and enforced by the coffee-grower dominated government, that coerced them to labor on coffee plantations.

In the late nineteenth century, the construction of a railroad to the Atlantic coast created the banana industry. Early in the twentieth century, the U.S.-based United Fruit Company (UFCO), formerly mainly a shipper/exporter, squeezed out Guatemalan banana growers. UFCO eventually owned key public utilities and vast landholdings. The Liberal development program continued in the twentieth century. In politics, Manuel Estrada Cabrera's brutal dictatorship (1898–1920) inspired Nobel laureate Miguel Angel Asturias's chilling novel of state terror, *El Señor Presidente.* Big coffee plantations, many foreign owned, continued expanding at the expense of small subsistence farmers.

When the world economy collapsed in 1929, Guatemala's exports plummeted and worker unrest grew. President Jorge Ubico, who assumed dictatorial control of government in 1931, violently suppressed unions, Communists, and other political activists while centralizing power in the national government. Ubico continued to promote the development of government and economic infrastructure (banks, railways, highways, telephones, the telegraph, and electrical utilities). Although originally an admirer of European Fascists Mussolini and Franco, Ubico took the opportunity provided by World War II to confiscate over $150 million in German-owned properties, mainly coffee plantations. He amended vagrancy laws to require Indians to work a certain number of days per year for the state and thus effectively converted the government into Guatemala's major labor contractor.

Labor unrest, middle-class democratization pressures, and a loss of U.S. support caused Ubico to resign in 1944. Student- and labor-backed military reformers called elections for later that year. Educator and former exile Juan José Arévalo Bermejo, who described himself vaguely as a "spiritual socialist," won the presidency. During his five-year term, Arévalo began numerous reforms: instituting social security, a labor code, professionalization of the military, rural education, public health promotion, and cooperatives. Arévalo vigorously encouraged union and peasant organization and open elections. Arévalo's economic policies, described as an "explicit attempt to create a modern capitalist society,"[1] did not address the root of the country's social problems—extreme maldistribution of land—a legacy of the "liberal" reforms.

In 1950 Guatemalans elected a young army officer, Jacobo Arbenz Guzmán, to succeed Arévalo. Arbenz sought to deepen the revolution's social reforms despite growing conservative and U.S. opposition. In 1951 he legalized the Communist Party, called the Guatemalan Labor Party (Partido Guatemalteco del Trabajo—

PGT), which began actively organizing labor and promoting agrarian reform. Over 500 peasant unions and 300 peasant leagues formed under the Arbenz government.[2] A 1952 Agrarian Reform Law began the confiscation and redistribution of farmland to 100,000 peasants.

Arbenz's reforms and peasants and worker organization threatened the rural labor supply system and shifted economic power toward workers and peasants and away from latifundists and employers. The threatened interests took action when Arbenz nationalized land belonging to United Fruit, offering compensation to the company at its previously declared tax value. This, of course, troubled several high Eisenhower administration officials with ties to UFCO. The nationalization, the presence of a few Communists in the government, and Arbenz's purchase of light arms from Czechoslovakia caused the United States to label the Arbenz government Communist. In 1953 the United States set out to destabilize Guatemala's Arbenz administration with financial sanctions, diplomatic pressure in the Organization of American States, and Central Intelligence Agency (CIA) disinformation and covert actions. The CIA engineered a conspiracy with a disloyal rightist army faction. In June 1954 the tiny, CIA-supported National Liberation Army, led by Col. Carlos Castillo Armas, invaded Guatemala. The armed forces refused to defend the government and Arbenz had to resign.[3]

Colonel Castillo Armas, head of the National Liberation Movement (Movimiento de Liberación Nacional—MLN), assumed the presidency with the backing of the United States and the Catholic Church. With ferocious anticommunist propaganda, the counterrevolution dismantled the labor and peasant movements, killed and jailed thousands, repressed political parties, revoked the Agrarian Reform Law, and returned confiscated lands to their former owners. The government suppressed working- and middle-class and prorevolutionary organizations and "there began a continuing . . . promotion of upper-sector interests."[4] Military and business sectors gained political influence within the government. Foreign policy became closely identified with the United States, and U.S. and multilateral aid programs promoted economic growth by financing extensive infrastructure development.

The MLN became a political party during the late 1950s, drawing together coffee plantation owners, municipal politicians and bureaucrats, owners of midsized farms, and certain military elements united in anticommunism and in their hostility toward the 1944–1954 revolution. Confusion followed Castillo's assassination in 1957 and the army imposed Gen. Miguel Ydígoras Fuentes as president. The Ydígoras government promoted Guatemala's participation in the Central American Common Market, permitted CIA-backed anti-Castro Cuban forces to train in Guatemala in preparation for the Bay of Pigs Invasion of 1961, and continued police terror against supporters of the revolution and labor and peasant leaders.

Continued violence and corruption in the Ydígoras government prompted an abortive coup by reformist army officers in 1960. Escaped remnants of the plotters formed the nucleus of the first of several rebel groups. The leaders of the Revolutionary Armed Forces (Fuerzas Armadas Revolucionarias—FAR) and the 13th of November Revolutionary Movement (Movimiento Revolucionario del 13 de Noviembre—MR-13) eventually adopted a Marxist-Leninist ideology and guerrilla war strategy patterned after that of Cuba's Fidel Castro. U.S. military aid to Guatemala increased rapidly, but early military operations against the guerrillas proved ineffective. Military dissatisfaction and a desire to block the next election culminated in Col. Enrique Peralta Azurdia's overthrow of Ydígoras in 1963, after which counterinsurgency operations expanded rapidly.

In 1965 the military decided to return the government nominally to civilians, and the 1966 election campaign was generally free and open.[5] The Revolutionary Party (Partido Revolucionario—PR) candidate, Julio César Méndez Montenegro, who denounced the twelve-year counterrevolution, won the presidency. After Méndez took office, however, counterinsurgency accelerated and military control of politics deepened despite the civilian president. The army's 1968 Zacapa campaign, heavily U.S.-backed and U.S.-trained, killed an estimated ten thousand civilians, dealt the guerrillas a severe blow, and earned its commander, Col. Carlos Arana Osorio, the sobriquet of "the Butcher of Zacapa."

After one decade of reform/revolution followed by another of counterrevolution, Guatemalan society was deeply polarized. Some on the right feared the 1966 election signified the breakdown of the counterrevolution and required drastic action. Several right-wing "death squads" formed and commenced terrorizing persons vaguely associated with the left and reformist politics. Regular national security forces (army and police), peasant irregulars armed by the government in areas of insurgency, and right-wing terrorist groups permitted and encouraged by the regime conducted a terror campaign against the government's political opposition (although many victims were apolitical) and effectively intimidated, demobilized, and disarticulated much of it.

In these circumstances the presidential election of 1970—though conducted cleanly by the Méndez government—resulted in victory for Col. Carlos Arana Osorio, the nominee of both the MLN and the military's own Institutional Democratic Party (Partido Institucional Democrático—PID). With U.S. aid at its historic peak during his administration, Arana consolidated the military's political power and deepened its corruption. An aggressive economic modernization program created huge public-sector enterprises and projects (some under army control) to increase the financial autonomy of the armed forces and the amounts of graft available to top officers. Terror against unions, political parties, and suspected critics of the regime escalated anew.

Global Forces and Conflict

The political situation of the late 1960s, with a counterinsurgency-oriented military regime confronting an ongoing insurgency, seemed to offer little prospect for economic growth. Much of the violence, however, took place in Guatemala's indigenous highlands or lowlands jungles and away from urban areas. This allowed parts of Guatemala—even during the conflict—to experience the rapid economic growth driven by Central American Common Market and Alliance for Progress policies.

Income. Under the economic guidance of the military-business partnership, Guatemala experienced the same rapid economic growth seen in Nicaragua and El Salvador. Per-capita GDP grew at an average of 3.0 percent from 1962 through 1971, and 2.6 percent annually from 1972 through 1980. During the CACM boom, per-capita GDP in constant 1986 dollars rose 70 percent, the second highest growth rate in Central America.[6]

As in Nicaragua and El Salvador, however, Guatemalan economic growth did not increase the income of the poor. The average annual change in the consumer price index, which was only 0.7 percent from 1963 through 1972, rose to 12.3 percent per annum for 1973–1979. Real wages did not keep up with inflation. Working-class wages peaked in 1967, then declined throughout the 1970s. In 1979 the purchasing power of real working-class wages had declined by one-fourth of 1967 levels.[7] Income distribution became markedly less equal during the CACM boom. Between 1970 and 1984 income distribution concentrated increasingly in the hands of the wealthiest fifth of the people, whose share of national income rose from 46.5 to 56.8 percent between 1970 and 1984. The income share of Guatemala's poorest fifth shrank from 6.8 to 4.8 percent for the same years. The share of the middle three-fifths of income earners also shrank, from 46.7 percent in 1970 to 38.4 percent in 1984.[8]

Employment. Official unemployment statistics for Guatemala indicate a steady growth of unemployment even during the years of the fastest CACM-induced growth. Official unemployment rates rose from 4.8 percent in 1970 to 5.5 percent in 1980, and then nearly doubled to 10.0 percent by 1984. Estimated underemployment rates rose from 24.5 percent in 1973 to 31.2 percent in 1980 to 43.4 percent in 1984.[9]

Wealth. Guatemalan data on wealth distribution are scarce, but several studies permit inferences.[10] Land, has long been unequally distributed. The agrarian census of 1950 reported that farms smaller than five *manzanas* (roughly 3.5 hectares) made up 75.1 percent of the farms but only occupied 9.0 percent of the cultivated land. The 1.7 percent of farms larger than 64 *manzanas* (45 hectares) made up an astonishing 50.3 percent of the cultivated land.[11] The 1979 agricultural census revealed that inequality of landownership in Guatemala had increased, becoming the most extreme in Central America. The rapid rural population growth shrank the amount of arable land per capita from 1.71 hectares/capita in 1950 to less than 0.79 by 1980.[12]

In the late 1970s, agrarian unemployment among indigenous people began rising while wages deteriorated. This change was accompanied by reports that communally and privately held land in the indigenous highlands was being appropriated by Ladinos (mestizos). Concentration of landownership caused highland people to outmigrate to the cities or to public lands newly opened for colonization in the Petén and Izábal. However, military officers and politicians amassed much land in those departments by driving many small-holders off their new plots in the region.[13] In 1976 a great earthquake devastated the western highlands and further worsened the poverty of tens of thousands of indigenous peasants.

While worker productivity in manufacturing grew steadily from the 1950s through the 1970s, the real wages and share of national incomes of the working and middle classes declined sharply during the 1970s. The main beneficiaries of increasing productivity were foreign and national investors.[14] During the same period, the ownership of the means of industrial production became steadily more concentrated in a decreasing number of large firms. Private-sector pressure-group organization became more extensive and sophisticated.[15] In some industries modernization of production and growing ownership concentration displaced many workers.

Guatemala's upper classes prospered during most of the 1970s because of the CACM industrialization boom and relatively high coffee prices, but conditions began to deteriorate in 1981 when economic output began a decline that lasted through 1985. The causes of this recession included declining commodity prices, political unrest elsewhere in Central America and capital flight. Thus, Guatemala's sharp general recession (as distinct from deteriorating real working-class wages) began around 1981 and deepened in 1982. This slump, which lagged four years behind a similar one in Nicaragua and two years behind El Salvador's, seriously eroded the economic position of Guatemalan economic elites. Some became critical of the economic management of successive military presidents and began rethinking their commitment to the regime.

Popular Mobilization. Reformist elements promoted important changes under Guatemala's democratic governments of 1944–1954, but after the 1954 coup they suffered badly. The MLN government and the armed forces embarked upon a program of demobilization that decimated the ranks of reformist politicians, unionists, and indigenous people who had supported the Arévalo and Arbenz governments. Marxist guerrilla opposition to the regime first appeared in 1962, but suffered a severe setback from the heavy general repression and from an intense counterinsurgency campaign in the late 1960s.[16]

Popular mobilization rekindled during the 1970s as real wages fell and income distribution worsened. Mobilization, however, lagged behind that in Nicaragua and El Salvador, probably because of Guatemala's heavier repression and its ethnic divisions.[17] Increased unionization and industrial strikes during the government of Gen. Eugenio Kjell Laugerud García (1974–1978) followed a decline in manufacturing wages in the early 1970s. Laugerud momentarily relaxed repression of unions in 1978 and a wave of strikes occurred. The 1976 earthquake's devastation of lower-class housing mobilized slum dwellers into two confederations. These groups pressed for housing assistance and in 1978 organized a transport boycott to protest increased bus fares. The FAR resurfaced and two new, indigenous-based guerrilla organizations, the Guerrilla Army of the Poor (Ejército Guerrillero de los Pobres—EGP) and the Organization of the People in Arms (Organización del Pueblo en Armas—ORPA) also appeared. All grew rapidly and began overt military activity in the late 1970s.

During the 1960s and 1970s the Christian Democratic Party (Partido Demócrata Cristiano de Guatemala—PDCG) promoted hundreds of agrarian cooperatives and a labor union movement to build a constituency and organizational base. As in El Salvador and Nicaragua, Christian base communities appeared throughout much of poor rural and urban Guatemala during the early 1970s. Christian base communities (CEBs) organized community and labor groups among Guatemala's long quiescent indigenous populace. Despite military rule and repression, civil society and opposition parties multiplied. The PDGC and other reform-oriented centrist and leftist parties including the Democratic Socialist Party (Partido Socialista Demócrata—PSD) and the United Front of the Revolution (Frente Unido de la Revolución—FUR) called for new policies and ran for office. Citizens organized, but also lost confidence in elections because the military regime fraudulently manipulated several presidential elections to block opposition victories. Abstention by registered voters rose from 44 percent in 1966 to 64 percent in the 1978 national election.[18]

State Response and Opposition. Guatemalan rulers intensely repressed labor union activists, students, peasant groups, indigenous peoples, opposition parties, and other dissidents during the post-1954 counterrevolution. Somewhat relaxed during the early 1960s, repression of the same groups escalated sharply from 1966 on. In that year both private and public security force death-squad terrorism began, consistently taking dozens of lives a month. The army's aggressive 1968–1970 counterinsurgency campaign decimated the Revolutionary Armed Forces (FAR) and the Edgar Ibarra Guerrilla Front (Frente Guerrillera Edgar Ibarra—FGEI) guerrilla movements.

In the political turmoil of the 1978 election, all parties again nominated military officers as presidential candidates. Soon after Gen. Lucas García took office, government forces brutally crushed the Guatemala City bus fare protests. As opposition parties grew in 1978–1979, security force death squads assassinated dozens of national and local leaders of the Democratic Socialist and Christian Democratic parties and of the reformist United Front of the Revolution (FUR). Hundreds of union leaders, university faculty, and student leaders also disappeared or were assassinated during the Lucas government.

In the countryside, peasant organizations led by the Peasant Unity Committee (Comité de Unidad Campesina—CUC) stepped up organizing. The CUC staged a major strike against sugar planters in 1980. In 1978 and 1979 the regrouped FAR and ORPA began military activity in the western highlands. Soon afterward the Guerrilla Army of the Poor (EGP), also with strong indigenous support, resumed combat against the regime in the highlands. Estimates placed the number of guerrilla troops at around 4,000 by 1982; the rebels' popular support was widespread. Army counterinsurgency escalated to include massacres of indigenous villagers to discourage support for the guerrillas.

From 1960 on the U.S. Embassy tracked Guatemalan political murders, most committed by government security forces and rightist death squads.[19] The average political murder rate, mainly in urban areas, rose from about 30 per month in 1971 to 75 per month in 1979 and then soared to a nearly 303 per month by 1982.[20] Some experts believe army counterinsurgency operations in rural areas to have killed many more than urban-area violence. Despite such massive human rights violations, Guatemala continued to receive new economic assistance from the United States that totaled over $60 million from 1979 through 1981.[21] Guatemala's truth commission, the Historical Clarification Commission, later referred to the period from 1978–1985 as the "most violent and bloody period of the confrontation." Deaths likely totaled 200,000.[22]

The armed forces, the backbone of the regime headed by General Lucas, confronted three critical problems in 1982. First was the extensive indigenous support for the guerrillas in the western highlands and growing unrest in the countryside elsewhere. Second was the economy, which slowed in 1979–1980, then contracted sharply in 1981–1982. Third, the Lucas government, failing on several fronts, deteriorated and lost many allies. When news leaked out that President Lucas had perpetrated another election fraud in 1982, younger army officers overthrew him and installed Gen. Efraín Ríos Montt as president. This coup began a gradual process of successive regime changes that took fourteen years to complete.

The coup leaders' apparent dual strategy was to increase repression to crush the rebels and demobilize growing opposition while simultaneously reforming the political rules of the game with elections and eventual civilian rule under military tutelage. In the first phase President Ríos Montt abolished the old rules by annulling the 1965 constitution and the electoral law, dissolving the Congress, suppressing political parties, and imposing a state of siege. Pursuing the political reform agenda largely obscured by the regime's de facto nature, a Council of State wrote a new electoral law and called for July 1984 elections for a constituent assembly to draft a new constitution.

On the military agenda, repression escalated again as the Guatemalan army mounted a new rural counterinsurgency campaign in indigenous zones. Ríos Montt's press secretary Francisco Bianchi justified the campaign: "The guerrillas won over many Indian collaborators. Therefore, the Indians were subversives, right? And how do you fight subversion? Clearly, you had to kill Indians because they were collaborating with subversion. And then they would say, 'You're massacring innocent people.' But they weren't innocent. They had sold out to subversion."[23] The army massacred numerous whole villages and committed many other atrocities against suspected guerrilla sympathizers. The army forced the relocation and concentration of Indians, many of whom were pressed into work on modern, army-owned farms producing vegetables to export, frozen, to the United States. The military formed army-controlled, mandatory "civil self-defense patrols" involving virtually all adult rural males. Estimates of the rural counterinsurgency's death toll range up to 150,000 persons between 1982 and 1985. U.S. Embassy violence statistics tended to overlook such massacres because embassy staff could not easily verify the incidents.[24] The counterinsurgency war made at least 500,000 persons, mostly Indians, into internal or external refugees.[25] Robinson contends that the war's dislocation of the rural indigenous population contributed to the development of a new supply of cheap labor that would support Guatemala's embrace of the neoliberal economic model.[26]

Unable to detect much meaningful political reform under Ríos Montt, centrist political activists hunkered down or fled, while those of the leftist opposition attempted to forge coalitions to enhance their power and resource base.[27] The Democratic Front Against Repression (Frente Democrático Contra la Represión—FDCR) appeared in 1979. It included numerous unions and the PSD and FUR. Two years later, several of the FDCR's more radical elements—including the peasant federation CUC—split away from the FDCR and formed the January 13th Popular Front (Frente Popular 13 de Enero—FP-13). In 1982 both the FP-13 and the FDCR endorsed yet another coalition effort led by a group of prominent regime opponents. This third group was the Guatemalan Committee of Patriotic Unity (Comité Guatemalteco de Unidad Patriótica—CGUP). The nation's guerrilla groups also united into the Guatemalan National Revolutionary Union (Unidad Revolucionaria Nacional Guatemalteca—URNG) in 1982 and issued a revolutionary manifesto challenging the regime's sovereignty.

The URNG's drive for a broader coalition soon bogged down, possibly a victim of the regime's efforts to reestablish civilian rule. Labor unions remained reluctant to form political links that might jeopardize their legal status—even with legal political parties.[28] The government curtailed rightist terrorism in urban areas somewhat after 1982, despite intensifying rural counterinsurgency. When President Ríos

Montt's increasingly erratic public behavior embarrassed the military reformists, they deposed him in August 1983 and replaced him with General Oscar Humberto Mejía Victores. Political reforms moved forward: The electoral registry was reformed and a new voter registration undertaken. The constituent assembly, elected in 1984, produced a new constitution that took effect in May 1985. President Mejía immediately called for elections, and the regime allowed some long-suppressed political forces of the center and left to resurface and contest the election.

Elections for president, Congress, and municipalities took place in late 1985. Although military pressure excluded left parties, centrist parties participated. Though held against a backdrop of three decades of brutal demobilization, the election itself was generally free from rightist terror against opposition parties. The Christian Democrats, led by presidential candidate Vinicio Cerezo Arévalo, won the presidency and a majority of the Congress in clean elections in November and December 1985.[29] Party spokesmen affirmed that they participated in the 1984 and 1985 elections and the constituent assembly because they believed the military seriously intended to reduce its role in governing.[30] This opening to civilian politicians in the mid-1980s helped dissuade the opposition parties from allying with the revolutionary left.

The 1985 election ushered in the second of Guatemala's critical regime changes in its long-term, military-managed liberalization. It culminated in a civilian transitional regime with new electoral rules and institutions for competing for public office and with a broader spectrum of political actors allowed into the arena. Powerful economic sectors that once supported military rule, reeling from three more years of miserable economic performance, began to embrace the prospect of a government and economy managed by elected civilians. Citizens noted the new arrangements and showed hope for an end to Guatemala's long, violent political nightmare by voting. Compared to prior elections, Guatemalans voted at much higher rates—78 percent in 1984 and 69 percent in 1985. The turnout increase was greatest in urban areas where violence had diminished and political freedom increased.

The Civilian Transitional Regime and the Civil War

The civilian transitional regime confronted critical, interconnected needs. The first was to end the civil war, but President Cerezo and his successors had only limited power over either the armed forces or the rebels. The second was to consolidate civilian rule and further progress toward democracy. To accomplish this, any settlement would have to pacify the rebels and curtail the military's great power in national political life. Constituencies that supported the war needed to be persuaded to accept civilian constitutional rule. Third, Guatemala needed economic recovery, but the economy continued to deteriorate. Progress on these fronts was halting and often seemed elusive. During the Cerezo administration, however, globally oriented capitalists, intent on modernizing the economy by reducing the power of the traditional agro-export elite, coalesced around several economic organizations and think tanks actively encouraged by a U.S. Agency for International Development (USAID) program of Private Enterprise Development. "The emerging New Right groupings began to explore the development of the transnational project in Guatemala and to gain an instrumental hold over the state in policy development. . . . At the behest of this emerging private sector bloc, the government approved a series of liberalization and deregulation measures."[31]

President Cerezo actively promoted the August 1987 Central American Peace Accord, which provided a rough, internationally endorsed blueprint for promoting political reconciliation, dialogue, and formal democratization. Cerezo's effort to end the civil war, however, stagnated because the military and rebels failed to cooperate fully. Cease-fire talks with the URNG in Madrid fell apart. Dialogue between the government and other national political and economic forces was limited. Indeed, the guerrilla war intensified in late 1987 as the URNG and the army sought to improve their positions.[32]

The balance of resources between the warring parties began to shift gradually in the government's favor. Although Guatemala's economic and military assistance from the United States remained a tiny fraction of that received by El Salvador (Appendix Table A.3), the military's and government's institutional capabilities remained fairly high. Political reform helped isolate the rebels from a broader political coalition while the army's rural counterinsurgency program increasingly denied them access to their indigenous supporters. Economic performance improved after 1987. Moreover, the military's retreat from executive power, the election of a new government, and new initiatives to improve the abysmal human rights situation (enactment of *habeas corpus* and *amparo* laws, a human rights ombudsman, and judicial reforms)[33] increased the government's domestic and external legitimacy.

Despite a promising beginning, the Cerezo administration performed poorly in many areas. Business groups, opposition parties, and labor criticized Cerezo and the Christian Democratic Party (Partido Demócrata Cristiano de Guatemala—PDCG) for many shortcomings: corruption, indecision and policy errors, economic problems, failure to address the needs of the poor, and lack of progress on human rights. Social mobilization increased. Several external human rights monitors and the government's own human rights ombudsman denounced continuing army and police human rights abuses against labor activists, union members, homeless street children, students, human rights advocates, religious workers, political party leaders, and foreigners.[34]

Peace talks had begun in Oslo, Norway, but too late to benefit Cerezo and the PDCG. Well before negotiations commenced, the URNG changed its goals from military victory to winning a negotiated settlement. In the early 1990s, several factors reinforced that decision, including the difficulty of fighting while cut off from its indigenous base and potential moderate allies, the Soviet bloc's collapse, and the electoral defeat of Nicaragua's Sandinistas. The army's new willingness to negotiate reflected erosion of its support among the bourgeoisie, increasing criticism of military human rights violations, and the continuing attrition of the war. The negotiations progressed little during Cerezo's term.

Cerezo's dismal record handicapped the Christian Democratic Party in the 1990 election. Parties of the old right (landed oligarchy and military) such as the MLN and PID declined. To take their place new parties appeared, several of them representing transnationally oriented economic elites who had been gaining rapidly in influence. These included the Union of the National Center (Unión del Centro Nacional—UCN), the Solidarity Action Movement (Movimiento de Acción Solidaria—MAS), and National Advancement Party (Partido del Avance Nacional—PAN). The vote was relatively free and clean, although the left remained excluded. Barely half of Guatemala's dispirited voters turned out for the two rounds of 1990 elections (a major decline from 1985). Voters having rejected the discredited PDCG, the presidential runoff was between two new right conservatives, newspaper publisher Jorge Carpio Nicolle of the PAN and engineer Jorge Serrano Elías of the MAS. The victor was Serrano, a Protestant with a populist flair, who promised to push the peace negotiations.[35]

Serrano, a former minister in Ríos Montt's cabinet, appointed numerous military officials to his government. He responded with unexpected vigor to human rights violations by detaining and prosecuting military officials, and energetically pursued peace negotiations. However, when the economy slumped further in 1991, Serrano imposed a package of tough structural adjustment measures informed by the transnational capitalist sector and its think tanks.[36] Adversely affected popular groups protested widely, and the security forces replied with a typical barrage of human rights abuses.

Serrano plunged the civilian transitional regime into crisis on May 25, 1993, when (apparently supported by part of the military) he attempted an *autogolpe* ("self-coup"). He illegally dissolved the Supreme Court and Congress, censored the press, restricted civil liberties, and announced his intention to rule by decree. Citizens, civil society organizations, and governmental institutions responded to the *Serranazo* with energetic protests. The United States, the Organization of American States, and other external actors quickly warned Guatemalan political actors, the military included, that the international financial institutions so essential to Guatemala's economic recovery would look with great disfavor on a deviation from constitutional practice.[37]

Internal resistance and external pressure undermined the Serranazo and kept the civilian transitional regime on track. The Court of Constitutionality (Corte de

Constitucionalidad—CC), backed by an institutionalist military faction, removed Serrano from office under provisions of the 1985 constitution. Congress elected Ramiro de León Carpio, the human rights ombudsman, to finish out the presidential term. President de León, unaffiliated with a political party but backed by a broad array of civil organizations, then pushed for a package of constitutional reforms enacted by Congress and ratified by popular referendum in January 1994. This initiated the election of a new Congress in August 1994 to serve out the rest of the term.[38]

Peace negotiations gained forward momentum in 1994 under the mediation of the United Nations.[39] A January "Framework Accord" established a timetable and provided for an Asamblea de la Sociedad Civil (Assembly of Civil Society—ASC) made up of most political parties and a diverse array of nongovernmental organizations, including women's and indigenous groups, to advise negotiators. Progress came steadily thereafter: In March 1994 negotiators signed a critical human rights accord that established a United Nations human rights monitoring mission that commenced its work in November. There followed agreements on the resettlement of refugees and a historical clarification commission to study the long-term violence (June 1994) and an accord on indigenous rights (March 1995).[40]

As negotiations continued into 1995, another national election took place. Guatemala City mayor Alvaro Arzú of the National Advancement Party (PAN) announced his candidacy, as did Efraín Ríos Montt of the right-wing populist Republican Front of Guatemala (Frente Republicano de Guatemala—FRG). The Ríos candidacy prompted a legal battle because the constitution barred participants in prior de facto regimes from becoming president. The election tribunal ruled against the former dictator. A sign of the left's growing confidence in its ability to participate in the system came when a coalition of leftist groups formed a political party, the Frente Democrático Nueva Guatemala (New Guatemala Democratic Front—FDNG) to compete in the election. The URNG also suspended military actions during the final weeks of the campaign. In the November 1995 general election the FDNG took six of 80 seats in Congress, the PAN 43, and the FRG 21, with turnout up from the 1990 election. The FDNG and various indigenous civic committees won several mayoral races. Arzú, a business leader active in the new transnationally oriented coalition, narrowly won the presidency in a January 1996 runoff.[41]

Alvaro Arzú took office under worsening political portents,[42] but moved decisively to advance peace by shaking up the army high command and police, meeting with rebel leaders, and embracing negotiations. There followed an indefinite cease-fire between the URNG and the army in March 1996, an accord on socioeconomic and agrarian issues (May 1996), and another on civil-military relations (September 1996) that would increase civilian control of the armed forces, limit military authority to external defense, and replace the violent and corrupt national police.

The Peace Accords and Contemporary Guatemalan Politics

On December 29, 1996, the government and the URNG signed the Final Peace Accord in Guatemala City, ending 36 years of civil war.[43] This agreement on new political rules embraced the previously negotiated accords and marked the establishment of an electoral democratic regime. The military came under increased civilian authority and found their responsibilities curtailed. Police reform commenced. The rebels of the URNG, many groups of the left, the new FDNG, and indigenous peoples—previously repressed or otherwise excluded—gained access to the political system as legal players. The URNG agreed to demobilize its forces and participate within the constitutional framework. A broad array of civil society organizations, including those representing the bourgeoisie (heretofore ambivalent about the peace process and new democratization), embraced the new regime.

Arzú's economic program of neoliberal reforms (privatization of electricity and telecommunications, budget cuts, fiscal reforms, trade and foreign exchange liberalization, and reduction of regulation) appeared destined to promote new economic growth but at the cost of worsening the nation's highly unequal distribution of income and increased poverty.[44] There remained potential that violent forces antagonistic to the democratic project and needed socioeconomic reforms might undermine the new regime. Nothing more clearly revealed the challenges of the consolidation of civilian democracy in Guatemala than the murder of Auxiliary Archbishop Juan Gerardi Conedera on April 26, 1998. Two days after the Catholic Church's Human Rights Office issued a report on civil war political violence to Guatemala's Historical Clarification Commission, Bishop Gerardi—one of its authors—was bludgeoned to death. Police quickly arrested an unconvincing suspect, but a death squad long connected to the presidential guard later claimed credit for the murder and began intimidating other Catholic human rights workers.[45] The investigation eventually placed the blame on two captains and a sergeant in the army and a priest. In June 2001, Col. Disrael Lima Estrada, Capt. Lima Oliva, Sgt. Jose Villanueva, and Father Mario Orantes were convicted in his death.[46] Although an appeals court overturned the conviction the following year, Guatemala's Supreme Court later upheld their convictions and sentences.[47] In 1999 the Historical Clarification Commission (CEH) released its report, *Guatemala: Memory of Silence,* finding that more than 200,000 died in the war and as many as 1.5 million were displaced. The report attributes 93 percent of the acts of violence committed during the war—the height of which was the period 1978–1984—to the army and state security forces (Civil Patrols).[48] The report found that the killings rose to the level of genocide, as 83 percent of the victims were Maya.[49] Some 626 massacres of Mayan communities were attributed to the state.[50] The report also found that U.S. military assistance to Guatemala "had significant bearing on human rights violations during the armed conflict."[51] Shortly after the unveiling of the report, U.S.

President Bill Clinton publicly apologized for the role of the United States in supporting state security forces during the war.[52]

The report's findings and recommendations on preservation of memory, victim compensation, national reconciliation, and strengthening democracy and human rights were downplayed by President Arzú. Arzú also openly rejected the commission's recommendations to create a commission to investigate and purge army officers for acts of violence, stating that the military had already investigated itself and "purified" its forces. The peace accords received another blow in May 1999 when voters defeated a referendum on constitutional reforms (including judicial and military reform), required to implement some provisions of the accords, by a margin of 55.6 percent.

Growing social violence and socioeconomic woes were the main issues of the 1999 elections. The FRG nominated Alfonso Portillo after the party's leader, retired General Efraín Ríos Montt, was declared ineligible to run for office due to his role in the 1982 coup. After failing to win a majority in the first round of voting, Portillo easily defeated the PAN candidate, Guatemala City Mayor Oscar Berger, in a runoff. The FRG also dominated the Congress with 63 of 113 seats and elected Ríos Montt as Congress president.[53] The New Nation Alliance (Alianza Nueva Nación) leftist coalition, which included the URNG, had a better than expected showing with 13 percent of the vote (9 seats).

Considered a populist by some, Portillo fared little better than Arzú in addressing Guatemala's persistent socio-economic problems. Initiatives aimed at addressing poverty, such as increasing the minimum wage, kept Portillo at odds with the Guatemalan business community throughout his term. The few advances of the Portillo government were tempered by its failure to combat Guatemala's crime wave, including continuing attacks on human rights workers, or to promote further implementation of the peace accords. Rather than reduce and reform the role of the military in Guatemalan society, Portillo and Rios Montt ousted reformist military officers appointed by President Arzú and replaced them with ones more likely to sympathize with the FRG administration. "Contrary to the regional trend, the corrupt FRG government also significantly increased the military's budget and duties," gave command of the military to "an unsavory trio of discredited former army officers allegedly associated with past human rights abuses and organized crime."[54] Indeed, the Portillo government gained notoriety for high levels of corruption.[55] In 2003 Guatemala was decertified by the U.S. government for its failure to contain the counternarcotics trade in the country.[56] Under Portillo, Guatemala seized a mere fraction of previous cocaine tonnage, despite evidence that transshipments actually increased.[57] In addition, the USDEA (Drug Enforcement Administration) estimated that Guatemala's patently corrupt Department of Anti-Narcotic Operations (Departamento de Operaciones Anti-Narcóticos) stole more than twice the amount seized in 2002.[58]

The 2003 presidential campaign season was tumultuous. In May 2003, the FRG nominated Rios Montt as its presidential candidate. When he attempted to register as a candidate, he was refused on the grounds that he was forbidden by the constitution from running due to his role in the 1982 coup. The Supreme Electoral Tribunal (Tribunal Supremo Electoral—TSE) agreed and denied his first and second appeals. His request for an injunction was denied by the Supreme Court of Justice (Corte Supremo de Justicia—CSJ). He then appealed to the Court of Constitutionality, which granted the injunction and authorized his registration. When the CSJ suspended registration in protest, Montt arranged for thousands of demonstrators to stage a violent protest in Guatemala City to demand his registration.[59] While the protests drew widespread criticisms of Montt's actions, including from the U.S. State Department, the CC ordered the TSE to register him. Although he came in a distant third, Rios Montt won nearly 20 percent of the vote.[60] His presence was enough to force a runoff election between National Unity of Hope (Unidad Nacional de la Esperanza—UNE) candidate Alvaro Colom and Great National Alliance (Gran Alianza Nacional—GANA) candidate Oscar Berger. With voter turnout less than 50 percent, Berger defeated Colom in the second round 54.1 percent to 45.9 percent. GANA also won 47 Congressional seats, with the FRG winning 43, the UNE 32, and the PAN 32.[61]

Berger, who campaigned on job creation and renewed support for the peace accords, swiftly appointed indigenous rights activist and Nobel Peace laureate Rigoberta Menchú to oversee the implementation of the peace accords and noted human rights attorney Frank La Rue as head of the president's human rights office.[62] Speaking at a ceremony on the fifth anniversary of the truth commission, Berger apologized for the war and pledged to compensate victims.[63] The Supreme Court rulings in the Myrna Mack and Bishop Gerardi trials also helped to refocus attention to the peace accords and human rights. Additionally, Berger replaced problematical senior military commanders and pledged to reduce the size of military (by 35 percent) and its budget (fixed at 0.33 percent of GDP).[64]

As in other Central American countries, Guatemala experienced a surge in social violence after the end of the civil war. In the first six months of 2004, nearly 2,000 people were murdered. Berger responded to the crime wave by firing both the interior minister and chief of police.[65] In a somewhat more controversial move, Berger then ordered 1,600 soldiers to join the police in combatting crime.[66] One horrific trend was the murders of more than 1,183 young women between January 2002 and June 2004.[67] Many of these women were raped and tortured before they were murdered; some were decapitated or burned beyond recognition. While government and media sources attributed many of these killings to gangs, few were investigated.[68] In an effort to curb gang activity, Berger signed an agreement with the governments of El Salvador, Honduras, and Nicaragua that would allow warrants issued in one country to be shared with all signatories. Gang members responded by decapitating a man and pinning a note to his body warning Berger against anti-gang laws.

Conclusions

The year 2004 marked the fiftieth anniversary of the U.S. coup that led to the overthrow of the Arbenz government, ending Guatemala's democratic revolution. The 36-year civil war that followed left some 200,000 dead, and many more missing and displaced. The 1996 peace accords notwithstanding, turmoil of every sort persisted into the Berger administration. Although initial appointments by the Berger administration and an increasing willingness on the part of Guatemala's courts to address the military's impunity for its crimes signal some positive change, much work remained to be done. When the United Nations peacekeeping and verification unit MINUGUA departed at the end of 2004 after monitoring the peace process since the 1990s, significant elements of the peace accords still had not been implemented. Little had been done to address the rights of Guatemala's indigenous population, and marginalization and systemic racism persisted. Land occupations by campesinos, another legacy of Guatemala's inequitable society, led to unrest and brutality in the countryside. While human rights abuses declined, activists and workers remained targets of violent repression. Crime and impunity, including both the proliferation of gangs and continued activity by security forces, threatened Guatemala's fragile peace. In sum, Guatemala still had far to travel before winning a meaningful peace.

8

Honduras

Honduras suffered serious negative effects from the Central American Common Market growth boom and the ensuing political and economic turmoil of the 1980s and 1990s. Governed by the armed forces well into the 1980s, Honduras shared many of the regime characteristics of El Salvador, Guatemala, and prerevolutionary Nicaragua. Nevertheless, unlike the other authoritarian regimes, Honduras managed mostly to escape the violent upheaval of those neighboring states. Indeed, Honduras owed its relative stability to a general strategy similar to that followed in Costa Rica. The government made policy that alleviated some of the effects of eroding popular living standards, and either avoided or ameliorated brutal political repression. Meanwhile, external pressure converted the nation's economic policies to harmonize with the neoliberal rules of the international economic game and groups sympathetic to these pressures rose to prominence in the political system.

Historical Background

Honduras is an unusual and paradoxical country. By a geological quirk, its soil lacks the rich volcanic material prevalent throughout the region's other countries. Geographically isolated, with broken terrain and poor transportation facilities, Honduras did not develop a significant export economy in the nineteenth century and remained mainly a subsistence economy. Though the common people of Honduras were even poorer than their Nicaraguan, Salvadoran, or Guatemalan counterparts, Honduran history reveals little mass rebellion or guerrilla warfare. Until the 1970s, the country was a calm eddy in Central America's troubled waters.

Indeed, it has not been the masses of citizens but Honduran party and military elites, often under pressure from such foreign actors as the United States, who have intermittently roiled Honduran political waters.

Several factors have contributed to this relative social and political stability in the face of mass poverty. Honduras never really developed so coherent or powerfully privileged an elite class as did its three neighbors, Nicaragua, El Salvador, and Guatemala. Of course, there have always been rich Hondurans, but their wealth remained regionally based. Unlike the rest of Central America, coffee became a significant export crop for Honduras only after World War II and thus did not drive much wealth accumulation or greatly shape social classes there.

When commercial banana production was introduced at the turn of the twentieth century, foreigners, not Hondurans, were responsible. The banana industry developed along the sparsely populated northern coast and displaced few peasant or Indian communal holdings. Indeed, though generally poor in quality, land was nearly always plentiful in Honduras; thus, poor peasants could usually find free or cheap land to farm. Virtually no land shortage developed until the mid-twentieth century, when foreign market demands and urban population growth led wealthier Hondurans to begin a process of concentrating landownership.

These economic development patterns had other ramifications.[1] First, with no need to quell an angry, dispossessed, and exploited rural working class, the Honduran army remained rather weak well into the twentieth century. Second, the banana industry contributed to labor relations unlike those seen in neighboring nations. Because banana companies were foreign owned, Honduran governments were not very keen on keeping banana workers' wages down. Indeed, rising wages meant more basic consumption and thus helped Honduran entrepreneurs. Moreover, because banana production was less labor intensive than, for instance, coffee production, the companies could pay higher wages without becoming less competitive. Strikes were frequent, but Honduran governments felt less inclined to forcibly suppress workers and the companies more willingly made wage concessions than often proved true in other countries or in the production of other crops. Thus, although labor unions were not formally legalized until 1954, they had existed informally and operated fairly freely for many decades. Over the long haul, Honduras developed a much larger (and politically more potent) organized workforce than other Central American countries.

In another contrast with neighboring nations, the Liberal/Conservative debate began much later in Honduras. In the nineteenth century, the country was dominated by a succession of nonideological caudillos who simply succeeded each other by force of arms. Party development began in earnest when a Liberal, Marco Aurelio Soto, was president (1876–1883). True to the Liberal vision of the era, he began efforts to modernize the nation, build a service infrastructure and state apparatus, and attract foreign investors. By the end of the century the Honduran Liberal Party (Partido Liberal de Honduras—PLH) was formed. Liberals dominated the political scene until the 1930s. Their conservative counterpart—the National Party (Partido Nacional—PN)—was born in 1923, but was able to take power only when the PLH split in the 1932 election. National Party caudillo Tiburcio Carías Andino was elected in 1932 and held the presidency until 1949—giving Honduras its longest period of political stability.

Following Carías's retirement, Liberal-National conflict intensified. The Liberal Party's electoral strength recovered with the rapid expansion of labor union movement in the early 1950s. PN efforts to deny the Liberals power prompted the army in 1956 to seize power in order to end the dispute; there followed a year of military rule. When the military relinquished power, PLH candidate Ramón Villeda Morales swept the 1957 election. Villeda's government signed the Central American Common Market accords and passed several modernizing social policies, including social security, labor, and agrarian reform laws. Despite such legislative symbols of progress, Honduras remained the poorest country in Central America.

From the mid-twentieth century onward, Honduras developed problems and patterns more typical of the rest of Central America. As noted earlier, land hunger first became a real problem during this period. This was due in part to appropriation of peasant-occupied lands by larger landholders as the latter sought to take advantage of increased internal and external commodity markets. Another important cause was a sudden rise in population growth rates due to improved public health conditions and practices developed during World War II. The rapid increase in demand for land in the 1950s and 1960s led to greater tension between classes and increasing peasant mobilization.

An additional growing similarity between Honduras and other Central American nations came from the militarization of its political system. With the advent of the Cold War, labor unrest in the banana plantations was commonly blamed on "Communist agitators." As part of its general regional strategy to contain "communism," the United States "concluded several agreements to train and equip the loosely organized armed forces of Honduras, and from the early 1950s through 1979 more than 1,000 Honduran personnel had had U.S. training."[2] Although from the 1950s through the 1970s there was virtually no guerrilla opposition to the Honduran government, much of the U.S. military training of the era dealt with counterinsurgency and put a strong emphasis on "national security." In 1973–1980 U.S. aid to Honduras rose sharply compared to earlier periods, especially military assistance (Appendix, Table A.3).

Not surprisingly, the increasing factionalism and conflict within and between the Liberal and National parties left a power and leadership vacuum. This vacuum and the growth of the military's strength drew the armed forces more deeply into politics. Even though civilian caudillos had run the country for the first half of the twentieth century, after the 1956 coup the armed forces for four decades ruled the nation directly or powerfully influenced civilian rulers from just offstage.

The Honduran military behaved, although not well, more benignly than its counterparts in neighboring states until the 1980s. The military acted more as an arbiter between other political groups than as an agent of a ruling class. It tolerated labor, peasant, and political party organizations, and allowed Catholic clergy to carry the "social gospel" to the poor and to build grass-roots organizations. And especially after the birth of the Alliance for Progress and Central American Common Market, there was much talk of basic socioeconomic reforms, some directly promoted by military governments.

In 1963 Air Force Col. Oswaldo López Arellano overthrew Villeda Morales and assumed power in coalition with National Party figures. The regime began to repress labor and peasant activism and to enlarge and strengthen the armed forces. Conservative economic policies, disadvantageous trade relations built into the Central American Common Market, and the 1969 war with El Salvador led to growing public unrest as López's presidency ended. The failure of the successor National-Liberal coalition to deal with growing national turmoil prompted López Arellano, now a wealthy general, to seize power again. This time, supported by labor, peasant groups and other progressive elements, he implemented several populist programs, including an agrarian reform.

Military participation in rule changed character in the late 1970s. Embarrassed by a bribery scandal, López transferred power in 1975 to Col. Juan Alberto Melgar Castro, the first of two hard-line military dictators who abandoned López's populist reforms and curtailed civilian participation in national administration. Melgar was overthrown in 1978 by Col. Policarpio Paz García. Despite the rapid changes in regimes, the military strove to promote national economic development and turned away from social programs. Although the Melgar and Paz regimes largely ignored questions of social justice, they remained relatively respectful of basic human rights and permitted certain civil and political liberties. There were no death squads, no systematized tortures, and no rash of disappearances. The press remained relatively free and boisterously critical of the military regimes.

Despite their developmentalist goals, the armed forces proved inept as rulers and economic managers. By the late 1970s corruption scandals, deepening economic difficulties, the fall of the Somoza regime in Nicaragua, and growing pressures from spurned civilian politicians created powerful incentives for the military to abandon power. Although the Carter administration never severed military assistance to Honduras, it pressured General Paz to relinquish power. Under such internal and external pressures, the military called elections in 1980 for a constituent assembly that would rewrite the constitution. In November 1981, presidential elections were held.

Liberal candidate Roberto Suazo Córdova won a clear majority and took office in January 1982. The Liberal victory surprised many who believed the armed forces would interfere in the vote to favor its erstwhile PN allies. Col. Gustavo Alvarez Martínez became head of the armed forces. The new Reagan administration put heavy pressure on Honduras to assist U.S. efforts against the Sandinistas in Nicaragua and Salvadoran guerrillas operating in Honduran territory. A U.S. military spokesman neatly summarized the U.S. appraisal of the situation: "Honduras is the keystone to our policy down there."[3] Suazo and Alvarez accepted the presence of U.S. troops on continuous "maneuvers," the construction and expansion of military bases and facilities in Honduras, and even U.S. training of Salvadoran troops on Honduran territory. Sanctuary and overt cooperation were provided to the Contra army that the United States was developing to attack Nicaragua's Sandinista government. Honduras thus became the active ally of the U.S. military strategy for Nicaragua and El Salvador.[4] Wags described the country as an aircraft carrier—the U.S.S. *Honduras.* In exchange for all this, Honduras received hundreds of millions of dollars in U.S. assistance—especially military aid (Appendix, Table A.3).

This U.S. military assistance program rapidly expanded the size and power of the armed forces and permitted Alvarez to overshadow and intimidate the civilian president and Congress. Relations with Nicaragua deteriorated badly. By 1984 the U.S.-financed Contra forces in Honduras had begun to rival in number the Honduran military and had severely disrupted public order along the Nicaraguan border. By 1983 Honduras developed death squads made up of public security force and Nicaraguan exile elements; political disappearances and murders became increasingly commonplace. As repression grew and domestic political tensions rose, several small leftist guerrilla groups appeared and began operations—a novelty in Honduras. Though weak and fragmented, the Honduran guerrilla movement grew as the 1980s proceeded. In the next section we will examine this period in more detail and try to explain why such problems—strikingly similar to those in Nicaragua, El Salvador, and Guatemala—did not push Honduras down the path toward civil war.

Weathering Global Forces

Honduras was the Central American nation least altered in social and economic structure by the Common Market. In the late 1970s, Honduras reminded many observers of the rest of the region several decades before. Honduras's economic performance was certainly the least successful of the five CACM nations in terms of overall growth. Much of its new investment went into agriculture. Honduras's agricultural sector remained the largest in the isthmus, having only declined from 70 percent to 63 percent of the workforce between 1960 and 1980. Even though the manufacturing workforce more than doubled (from 6 to 13 percent) between 1950 and 1983, the Honduran industrial sector remained the smallest in Central America.[5]

Despite its relatively slow development, Honduras experienced a sustained period of overall economic growth. Per-capita GDP grew an average of almost 1.5 percent per year between 1962 and 1971. As a consumer but not an exporter of manufactured consumer goods, Honduras developed trade imbalances with other CACM nations, especially neighboring rival El Salvador. These imbalances and resulting economic difficulties worsened after the 1969 war with El Salvador. Economic growth slowed to only 0.4 percent from 1972 through 1979. Overall, per-capita GDP in Honduras rose from $1,700 in 1960 to $2,280 by 1980, a slow but sustained 34 percent increase (an average of 1.7 percent annually). After 1980, the per-capita GDP economic growth basically stagnated, declining slightly to $2,224 in 1990 and to $2,049 in 2000.[6]

Income. Our theory about the onset of rebellion in Central America argues that severe declines in real working-class wages and living conditions play an important role in mobilizing many people into labor, political, and protest organization and activity.[7] Because many urban and rural wage earners in Central American societies live on earnings that give them little or no margin of safety, a drop in their real earnings (wages corrected for inflation) can have catastrophic effects on their ability to survive. A rapid erosion of life chances can be a powerful impetus to join political or labor groups seeking redress of such problems.

Wage data on Honduras reveal that wage workers lost ground relative to other income earners in the mid-1970s, but then recovered much of their purchasing power by 1978–1979. Wages fluctuated somewhat but experienced no sustained declines like those occurring in Guatemala, El Salvador, and Nicaragua at the same time. Honduran working-class wages fell in 1974 and 1975, recovered in 1976, fell again in 1977, and then rose to above 1973 levels again in 1978 and 1979. Real working-class wages in Honduras declined again in 1981, recovered in 1982, but then declined every year afterward into the early 1990s, sparking considerable labor unrest in the 1990s. In sum, while working-class earnings and living standards did decline in Honduras during the mid-1970s, these declines were less severe and sustained than those in neighboring countries, apparently because the government permitted real wage rates to recover much of their earlier purchasing power.[8] After 1982, however, Honduran workers gradually lost ground again.

Income Distribution. Another way to examine the amount of economic class disparity in Honduras is to explore shifts in the distribution of income among classes.

One measure of changing income inequality pattern during the 1970s is the share of national income paid out as employee compensation. A decrease in the level of employee compensation would indicate a relative shift of income away from salaried and wage-earning workers and toward investors and entrepreneurs. Data on Honduras reveal that between 1970 and 1975, the employee-compensation share of all national income fluctuated somewhat, but overall tended to increase. Honduran employee compensation improved markedly in the early 1970s.[9] Overall, it appears that wages and salaries in Honduras continued to rise until the early 1980s.

In summary, Honduras during the 1970s and 1980s presented a clear contrast to Nicaragua, El Salvador, and Guatemala in both relative and absolute income trends. In Honduras, wages fluctuated during but tended to recover within a year or two after sharp declines. As shown in Chapters 5, 6, and 7, however, in the neighboring three countries during the same period, real and relative income for working-class citizens suffered sustained and severe declines.

Wealth. Honduras also did not undergo the marked increases in class inequality observed in Nicaragua, El Salvador, and Guatemala during the 1970s. Although Honduras was a member of the CACM and experienced the rapid energy-driven consumer price increases of the mid-1970s, data reveal that these factors affected wealth distribution in Honduras (and Costa Rica) less than in the rest of the isthmus.

The least industrialized nation in the CACM, Honduras underwent the least dramatic changes in socioeconomic structure in the first two decades of the Common Market. During the 1970s, therefore, it experienced smaller and slower wealth and income inequality increases than those affecting Guatemala, El Salvador, and Nicaragua.[10] As noted above, working-class wages tended to recover from inflation in the late 1970s and income distribution did not sharply disfavor wage and salary earners. Honduran governments vigorously encouraged the growth of export agriculture in the 1960s and 1970s, and colonizable agricultural land continued to be available until the late 1970s. Both of these factors helped to prevent a rapid growth of rural unemployment. Because of widespread peasant organization and mobilization during the 1960s and 1970s, the government began an ambitious agrarian reform program.[11] From 1975 to 1979 the Honduran program distributed some 171,480 hectares to roughly 10 percent of Honduran landless and land-poor campesino families.[12] Although the agrarian reform distributed only about one-fourth of its goal and was widely criticized as insufficient and co-optative, it nevertheless constituted a major transfer of wealth toward campesinos. After 1980, peasant organizations, facilitated by the 1970s reform legislation, invaded much additional land in what amounted to an informal or quasi-legal redistribution program.[13] Efforts by the government of Rafael Leonidas Callejas to scale back agrarian reform land transfers sharply in 1991 provoked violent clashes between peasants and the government. The government quickly restored the program.

Popular Mobilization. In Honduras,[14] popular mobilization generally increased during the 1960s and 1970s.[15] The already large union movement grew. The greatest growth came among peasant wage workers and landless peasants organized into land occupation movements by several federations. The Catholic Church promoted some rural mobilization in the 1960s but generally retreated from it in the 1970s. The Liberal Party remained out of power during military rule from 1963 through 1981. The National Party collaborated with the first López Arellano regime in the 1960s but was frozen out afterward. Two small new centrist parties developed during the 1970s. These were the Christian Democratic Party of Honduras (Partido Demócrata Cristiano de Honduras—PDCH) and the Innovation and Unity Party (Partido de Inovación y Unidad—PINU). When elections resumed in 1979, however, neither PINU nor the Christian Democrats had captured a major share of the support of the Liberal or National parties.

Business and private-sector organizations also multiplied and became more active in pressing policy demands upon the state during the 1960s and 1970s. Although its relative underdevelopment had heretofore left Honduras without a unified bourgeoisie or dominant upper-class sector, economic elites became much more active in politics during the 1980s. Robinson argues that, spurred by USAID encouragement and by a decade of heavy U.S. military and diplomatic presence in the country, bourgeois groups linked to the emergent transnational economy formed and began to influence both the main national parties and the military. In the process, "clusters came together, penetrated, and largely captured both [Liberal and National] parties by the 1990s, but without the coherence" in business and political organizations such forces had achieved in El Salvador or Guatemala.[16]

Several small leftist guerrilla groups appeared in Honduras during the 1970s and early 1980s (see Appendix, Table A.4).[17] In 1960 a pro-Castro splinter from the Honduran Communist Party (Partido Comunista de Honduras—PCH) formed the Morazán Front for the Liberation of Honduras (Frente Morazanista para la Liberación de Honduras—FMLH), a guerrilla group sporadically active in the 1960s and early 1970s. In 1979 the FMLH reappeared. In 1978, the PCH spun off more dissidents who formed the Popular Movement for Liberation (Movimiento Popular de Liberación—MPL), known as the "Chichoneros." The MPL's most spectacular action was the taking hostage of 80 San Pedro Sula business leaders in 1982. The Lorenzo Zelaya Popular Revolutionary Forces (Fuerzas Populares Revolucionarias "Lorenzo Zelaya"—FPR), founded by a pro-Chinese faction of the PCH, appeared in 1981 and conducted various acts of urban political violence. The Revolutionary Party of Central American Workers of Honduras (Partido Revolucionario de Trabajadores Centroamericanos de Honduras—PRTCH), the Honduran branch of a regional revolutionary group, was founded in 1977. In 1983 the guerrilla groups formed the National Directorate of Unity (Dirección Nacional de Unidad—DNU) to coordinate their activities on the revolutionary left. Despite the rise of armed opposition, insurgent violence in Honduras remained low compared to neighboring nations.

One new guerrilla group, the Army of Patriotic Resistance (Ejército de Resistencia Patriótica—ERP-27), appeared in Honduras in 1989. However, reconciliation efforts and a government amnesty program for political prisoners and exiles resulted in the release of more than 300 persons from jail in 1991. Several exiled guerrilla leaders from four different groups also returned to Honduras from exile, and four Chichoneros announced their intention to abandon armed struggle and form a new political party.[18]

Overall, then, the levels of popular and elite mobilization of various sorts increased in Honduras during the 1970s and continued into the 1980s. Indeed violent political participation occurred in protest of regime policies even reaching the level of incipient guerrilla struggle by various leftist factions. However, the state never sufficiently repressed legitimate mass mobilization to the point of triggering armed resistance as a last resort, as had been true in Nicaragua, El Salvador, or Guatemala.

Government Response to Popular Mobilization. From 1963 through 1982, the armed forces governed Honduras. The military authoritarian regime of the 1960s and 1970s included elements with developmentalist and populist orientations and less inclined to control all aspects of national life than the militaries of El Salvador and Guatemala. For instance, during the early 1970s the second military government of Gen. Oswaldo López Arellano (1971–1975) accommodated burgeoning campesino mobilization and developed a populist agrarian reform program. A conservative faction of the armed forces led by Col. Juan Alberto Melgar Castro deposed López for the second time in 1975. Labor repression then increased, marked by a massacre of 14 protesters at Los Horcones in 1975. Yet in an astounding departure from what would have happened in neighboring nations, the government then used civilian courts to prosecute, convict, and imprison army officers implicated in the massacre.[19]

Violent regime repression of opponents (illegal detentions, disappearances, and murders) rose significantly in Honduras in the early 1980s, but still remained moderate by Central American standards.[20] For instance in 1982, a year when Guatemala and El Salvador each had over ten thousand political disappearances and murders, Honduran human rights activists reported a total of only forty assassinations and "permanent disappearances."[21] Political parties, unions, peasant leagues, and a free press operated openly and likely helped restrain human rights violations by vigorously denouncing government abuses of authority.[22]

Honduran security forces took numerous measures to curtail armed opposition, including forming rural militias called Civil Defense Committees (Comités de Defensa Civil—CDCs) in several areas, and stepped up counterinsurgency efforts. Right-wing elements, apparently involving some Nicaraguan exiles and enjoying military complicity, began to kidnap, torture and murder suspected subversives and government critics in the early 1980s. By 1982, "extra-judicial action [had become] standard operating procedure for the Honduran armed forces in dealing with violent opposition. The methods include[d] disappearances, torture, use of clandestine detention centers, and . . . execution of prisoners."[23]

One key aspect of the Honduran case was the process by which the armed forces returned formal power to civilians. Despite the growing institutional strength of the military during the 1960s and 1970s, the Honduran armed forces never controlled the state apparatus so extensively or aggressively as did the militaries of neighboring countries. Moreover, as the punishment of military officials for the Los Horcones massacre revealed, the Honduran military never fully exempted itself from accountability to the law and constitution.

In a clear indication of how leaders' choices can divert a nation from catastrophe, the military authoritarian regime headed by then-president General Policarpio Paz García voluntarily embarked on political reform rather than choosing the massive repression undertaken by the rulers of Honduras's three immediate neighbors. Popular unrest had grown in the mid- and late 1970s, and its repression by the army and military-dominated police, the Public Security Forces (Fuerzas de Seguridad Pública—FUSEP) brought increasing pressure for reforms from the Carter administration. The military government's blatant corruption had become an increasing embarrassment, and the military's traditional National Party allies became somewhat disaffected from the regime. Finally, events unfolding elsewhere in the isthmus in 1979 troubled the military leadership: Nicaraguan revolutionaries ousted the repressive despot Somoza, destroyed his National Guard, and began a revolution. Popular mobilization and growing violence in El Salvador portended similar problems there.

Rather than risk civil war, revolution, or destruction of the military, General Paz García and the senior military officers' council decided to return power to civilians, ushering in a brief reformist military regime. The change to a civilian transitional regime was swift. General Paz García called an election for a constituent assembly in 1980. The Liberal Party, long mistrusted by the armed forces, captured a near majority of the constituent assembly. With Paz García holding the provisional presidency to maintain military ascendancy, the Liberals drafted a new constitution, which set elections for a new, civilian government for 1981.

Confounding the expectations of many observers, the armed forces permitted both traditional parties (including the Liberals' social-democratic Left) and the two new groups (PINU and the Christian Democrats) to take part in a generally free and open 1981 election. And again contrary to widespread expectations, the military did not rig the 1981 elections on behalf of its longtime PN allies. Liberal candidate Roberto Suazo Córdova won a clear majority in a clean election, and General Paz García relinquished the presidency in early 1982.[24]

So began the transitional civilian democratic regime in Honduras, engineered by the armed forces to prevent civil war and further institutional damage to the military itself. For well over a decade the military would remain very powerful in the transitional civilian regime, resistant to civilian control and feared by civilian politicians. Military power remained largely exempt from civilian control until the mid-1990s, blocking transition to full formal democracy. Indeed, during the 1980s, the Honduran military's power and resources actually increased despite its giving up the formal reins of power. U.S. military assistance to Honduras during the 1980s ballooned from $3.1 million per year for 1977–1980 to $41.5 million annually for 1981–1984 and eventually hit $57.7 million per year for 1985–1988 (Appendix, Table A.3). The United States provided this military aid (and copious economic assistance) in exchange for the Honduran armed forces' help with U.S. efforts to contain revolutionary movements in neighboring El Salvador and Nicaragua. In trade for effectively ceding control over much of southern Honduras to the Nicaraguan Contras, cooperation with the U.S.-advised Salvadoran armed forces against the FMLN, and a heavy U.S. military presence, the Honduran military waxed rich in U.S.-built bases and U.S.-supplied equipment and training. Human rights abuses by the army and FUSEP increased during the mid-1980s.

The prospects for civilian rule appeared to dim in the early 1980s. U.S. military assistance expanded the power of the armed forces and permitted General Alvarez to overshadow and intimidate the civilian president and congress. Opposition violence and repression rose under Alvarez's leadership of the military. But in 1984 senior armed forces officers unexpectedly ousted Alvarez from his command because he had deepened Honduras's role in the U.S.-Nicaragua imbroglio, allowed Salvadoran troops to train in Honduras and disregarded the military's tradition of corporate decisionmaking.

In another poor augury for democratic prospects, in 1985 President Suazo himself precipitated a constitutional crisis by seeking to retain power. The armed forces, labor movement, and United States applied counterpressure and blocked Suazo's efforts to amend the constitution.

The military's adherence to constitutional rule helped save the trappings of civilian democracy in 1985, but the civilian transition remained wobbly. The 1986 election brought José Azcona Hoyos, the leading Liberal candidate, to the presidency. Azcona represented a new modernization-oriented agro-industrial and manufacturing faction of the Liberal Party. These neoliberals, known as the Alianza Liberal Popular (Popular Liberal Alliance—ALIPO), came mostly from the northern region around San Pedro Sula. During Azcona's term protests grew over Honduran support for the U.S.-backed, anti-Sandinista Contras. Other continuing obstacles to effective civilian rule were the military's great power, elite commitment to democracy that sometimes appeared desultory, and continued human rights violations by the military and FUSEP. Economic difficulties accumulated in the form of anticipated cutbacks in U.S. economic and military aid, a sharp contraction in GDP per capita (1989–1991), rapid consumer price increases, and declines in real wages.[25]

When the National Party defeated the Liberals in a clean election in 1990, President Azcona peacefully passed power to Rafael Callejas of the National Party. Callejas, leader of a reformist faction of urban businessmen and economic technocrats, brought the neoliberal wing of the National Party to power. Since its economy, despite considerable capital flight, had been buoyed up by heavy U.S. aid, Honduras had been able to avoid the full neoliberal structural adjustment imposed on the rest of the region. But when the end of the Sandinista revolution in Nicaragua augured curtailed U.S. aid to Honduras, pressures mounted to embrace neoliberalism. Callejas agreed in March 1990 to the first of three major structural adjustment programs negotiated with the IMF, USAID, and other international lenders. Two more structural adjustment packages promoting economic austerity, free markets, nontraditional exports, tourism, free trade zones, and assembly plant manufacturing *(maquiladoras)* followed over two successive administrations.[26]

The peaceful transfer of power from a ruling party and president to a victorious opponent in 1990 was a step toward democracy, but prospects for full transition to a civilian democratic regime remained in question. Since the Contras withdrew from Honduras in 1990 and 1991 following the 1990 Nicaraguan election and peace accord, Honduran anger about them subsided. An amnesty law passed in 1991 allowed members of armed insurgent groups to abandon their violent opposition and some eventually rejoined legal politics. This effectively dismantled the tiny revolutionary left. The Callejas administration's embrace of neoliberal reforms attracted much new foreign capital and dozens of assembly plants. Callejas's neoliberal austerity measures and devaluation of the lempira, however, spawned hardship, labor unrest and popular protest. The security forces often harshly repressed such mobilization, but the military and government exercised continuing restraint. In late 1990 the military high command chose a new commander who curtailed and punished abusive military behavior and reconciled with guerrilla, peasant, and labor leaders. Human rights abuses were investigated and some perpetrators punished.[27]

The opposition Liberals won Honduras's 1993 presidential and Congressional elections. President Carlos Roberto Reina, a human rights leader, campaigned on a promise to curtail the military power and corruption. For a second time the incumbent government relinquished power to a victorious opponent, another step forward in democratic consolidation. However, the military commander, General Luis Discua, immediately showed displeasure with Reina's proposals to end the draft, cut the military budget, and transfer the police agency FUSEP to civilian control. Despite military objections, Reina and Congress passed and ratified the constitutional reform transferring FUSEP to civilian control. Ironically, and as in El Salvador and Guatemala, the ensuing police reform process led to a crime wave. Congress revised the draft law and allowed the military draft to lapse and military force levels to decline. This reduction in military power signaled a critical political game rule change and effectively reduced the military's role within the regime. We believe these changes marked 1996 as the year of Honduras's effective transition to civilian democracy.[28]

Contemporary Honduran Politics

Reina's successor, Liberal Carlos Roberto Flores Facussé, took office in January 1998 after yet another clean election. Despite campaign rhetoric critical of IMF policies, Flores' economic plan proposed to strengthen the neoliberal model through the expansion of the maquila industry, increasing tourism, and expansion of the agro-export sector.

The neoliberal reforms of the 1990s exacerbated decades of environmental degradation, including deforestation and soil erosion, as many migrated to the cities seeking employment in the burgeoning maquila industry.[29] This combination proved deadly in October 1998 when Hurricane Mitch struck Honduras. More than 11,000 were killed, and 2 million were left homeless.[30] Many of those affected were migrants who had settled on the crowded hillsides surrounding Tegucigalpa, which were washed away. The hurricane caused nearly US$4 billion in economic losses, devastating the agricultural and shrimping sectors. Honduras was granted relief under the World Bank's Heavily Indebted Poor Countries (HIPC) initiative, which permitted the suspension of payments on its US$4.4 billion debt, which had consumed 46 percent of its annual budget, and creditors canceled US$900 million of its debt balance.

This restructuring of Honduras's debt and the extension of additional loans required the Flores administration to pursue structural adjustment policies while pledging to reduce poverty. After selling the airports, Flores attempted to privatize the telecommunications and energy industries. When the privatization of Hondutel failed, the IMF froze the distribution of loans and demanded that the government accelerate its privatization and poverty reduction programs. The pressure on the Flores government to further implement neoliberal policies complicated efforts to rebuild and address rising poverty and unemployment after Mitch.

Oddly, the hurricane disaster aided the consolidation of civilian rule in Honduras. Its military was extremely incompetent in responding to Mitch, thus undermining its stature. The military's influence was further reduced as President Flores completed the police reform and passed critical constitutional amendments that brought the military under the direct control of the civilian chief executive for the first time since 1957. Army officers responded by plotting to overthrow Flores, although the coup never occurred. Flores then demonstrated his authority over a divided and restive military when in 1999 he dismissed its uniformed commander and most of the army's top echelon. Thereafter the military was obedient to presidential directives and refrained from any interference in civilian policy making.[31]

Civil society, especially human rights and indigenous groups, increasingly and energetically denounced the human rights abuses of the 1980s and 1990s. The government began investigating past military rights abuses. This investigation notably included a civilian judge's seizure of the files of military intelligence and counterintelligence services that implicated numerous high-ranking officers. But there remained evidence that serious human rights problems persisted, marked by renewed activity by death squads and the assassination in February 1998 of Ernesto Sandoval, a leader of the Human Rights Committee of Honduras (Comité de Derechos Humanos de Honduras—CODEH), Honduras's leading human rights agency.[32]

Despite notable gains in redefining the role of the Honduran military, Flores's administration was beset by persistent poverty, sluggish growth, and a violent crime wave, all of which were exacerbated by Hurricane Mitch. Two Liberal administrations succeeded in managing the transition to democracy but failed to address Honduras's mounting socioeconomic problems. After some controversy regarding his eligibility, the National Party's Ricardo Maduro defeated Liberal Party candidate Rafael Pineda in the 2001 presidential elections. The former central bank president pledged to crack down on crime and corruption, acting quickly to reduce government perks by selling off hundreds of government luxury vehicles. Initial attempts to limit immunity for crimes and human rights abuses and reduce the number of elected officials failed in Congress. The National Party won only 61 of 128 seats, making it the first time since the 1981 transition that the governing party did not control Congress. A later coalition with the Christian Democrats gave the Nationals a legislative advantage over the Liberal's 55 seats.

Honduras's prolonged crime wave was a major theme of the 2001 elections. In 2000, the murder rates in Tegucigalpa and San Pedro Sula were 51 and 95 per 100,000, respectively, making Honduras one of the most violent countries in the hemisphere.[33] Much of the crime wave was blamed on gang activity, which had proliferated in those two cities over the previous decade. The rise in gang violence was bad for business as numerous maquilas and other businesses relocated to more favorable settings following the kidnappings of prominent foreign businessmen. It was estimated that nearly 500 gangs (or *maras*) had more than 100,000 members, including the infamous Mara Salvatrucha and Mara 18. Maduro, whose own son was killed in a bungled kidnapping, continued his predecessors' militarization of the police force through his Operación Guerra Contra la Delincuencia, which sent 10,000 officers into the streets and appointed a military official as the head of security.[34] Maduro's hard line against gangs, including a mandatory twelve-year sentence for being a gang member, often resulted in retaliation by gang members. In December 2004 gang members opened fire on a public bus in San Pedro Sula, killing 28 people. A note left at the scene stated the act was in opposition to the possible reimposition of the death penalty.

A related aspect of the crime wave was the extrajudicial killings of Honduran youth, primarily street children presumed to be involved in gang activity. Between 1998 and 2002 more than 1,500 youths were murdered, most of them males under the age of 18.[35] Human rights organizations, such as Amnesty International and Casa Alianza, claimed that some of the deaths could be attributed to "social cleansing" by state and private security forces. One United Nations report was particularly critical of the impunity with which these murders were committed, citing a failure to investigate and prosecute the crimes.[36] Mounting criticism from the human rights community forced the government to commission its own report, which implicated police and security forces in a small percentage of the killings.

Maduro's economic plan promised to further aggravate social unrest. After contentious negotiations with the IMF, the technocratic administration pledged to reinvigorate the privatization process. Meeting the demands of the international financial community and reducing poverty and fighting violent crime were at odds with one another. While Maduro attempted to reduce the number of elected officials and other bureaucrats, he resisted a reduction in public employment. Civil society was increasingly well mobilized against plans to privatize key state-owned utilities and government services. In 2003 government plans for civil service reform and the privatization of water drew some 25,000 people into the streets in protest.[37]

Conclusions

During the 1970s Honduras at least partly ameliorated the growing inequalities affecting working-class victims of rapid economic change, while employing only moderate repression. Under military governments of the late 1970s and civilian transitional Suazo and Azcona governments in the 1980s, repression, while higher than in Costa Rica, remained much lower than the sanguinary levels of the remaining three isthmian countries. We emphasize that the Honduran armed forces exercised only *comparative* restraint in repression. The Honduran military killed some 1,000 victims during the 1980s and 1990s, which, though terrible in its own right, paled in comparison to the staggering toll of over 300,000 lives taken by the security forces of Somoza's Nicaragua, El Salvador, and Guatemala during the 1970s and 1980s.

Such repression notwithstanding, the Honduran security forces voluntarily transferred nominal control of executive and legislative power to a constitutional regime, a political reform of symbolic significance to Hondurans. Second, despite specific differences in their policies, Honduras and Costa Rica during the 1970s permitted working-class wages to recover previous purchasing power after declines and shifted some wealth and income to certain lower-class groups. Thus modest socioeconomic reforms to ameliorate the effects of growing poverty, combined with some restraint in repression and accommodative political reforms, saved Honduras from the abyss of internecine violence that beset three of its neighbors and enabled Honduras to maintain relative political stability.

The similarities in amelioration of poverty and the creative management of state response to mobilization by Costa Rica and Honduras, nations otherwise quite distinct from each other, strongly suggest that the slaughter and chaos of insurrection, revolution, and civil war were not inevitable in the Central America of the late 1970s. A relatively poor, military-dominated regime and a more prosperous democracy each responded to the growing tide of opposition mobilization with policy choices that almost certainly saved many thousands of lives.

One area of similarity between Honduras and all other Central American nations was the adoption of neoliberal economic policies by Honduran governments by 2000. The armed forces had once employed populist wealth transfers (land reform) and other social policies to purchase political stability, but such state-led programs would necessarily diminish sharply under neoliberal austerity. With these externally demanded economic model reforms, new political sectors amenable to neoliberalism rose to preeminence within both the Liberal and National parties. While these changes made Honduras's new civilian democratic regime acceptable to the prevalent international economic regime, they also stripped the government of state resources and policy tools that had helped avoid rebellion in the 1980s. The neoliberal model thus greatly restricted Honduras's ability to respond to the profound socioeconomic crises plaguing the country. At this writing, as much as 80 percent of the Honduran population remained in poverty, nearly half of those in extreme poverty. Crime and unemployment were rampant, breeding insecurity in an already vulnerable population. Honduras's debt burden, although reduced following Hurricane Mitch, continued to exceed spending on basic services. Thus, the greatest threat to the future of Honduran democracy appeared to be the government's incapacity to address the most basic needs of its people.

9

Political Participation, Political Attitudes, and Democracy

Classical democratic theory defines democracy as citizen participation in the rule of a society. Political participation embraces not only such well examined phenomena as voting and partisan activity, but such less studied yet important activities as community-level activism, contacting public officials, civil society engagement, and protest behavior. Citizen participation in public, community, and economic life conveys citizens' demands to government, and thus to some extent constrains the actions and expectations of officials and elites. Classical democratic theorists argue that a society is more democratic when the number of citizens who take part in politics is greater, their political activities are more varied, and the arenas affected by citizen action are broader.[1] This chapter employs data from recent surveys to explore the breadth and range of political engagement in Central America's mostly fledgling democracies.

Political participation, however, will tell us only part of the story about Central Americans and democracy. We are interested in the extent to which the five nations have begun to consolidate their formally democratic regimes. Democratic consolidation, the institutionalization of democratic expectations and rules within a polity, rests in part on the attitudes and norms of citizens.[2] Political systems become more consolidated—secure and well established—the more citizens share democratic attitudes, reject authoritarian norms and military rule, and express support for their democratic polities. We will thus examine these attitudes among Central Americans.

Participation and attitudes do not develop in a vacuum. Political contexts, both domestic and external, are critical to both participation and attitudes. Importantly, all five countries in Central America became civilian democratic regimes by the 1990s, but many factors other than regime type have shaped levels and styles of citizen political engagement and political attitudes. As we know, Central American political histories vary widely, as do levels of political repression, the age of democratic regimes, and economic environments. In some countries with undemocratic regimes, democratic norms have nevertheless spread or been adopted by citizens through contact with more democratic societies as their citizens traveled and worked abroad, or through media exposure, or because such norms became useful in struggling against repression.[3] The behavior of regimes, and by extension their international sponsors, affects the participation and attitudes of citizens, and thus shapes the region's prospects for democratic consolidation.[4] At the individual level, citizens' own educational and economic resources diverge, as do their experiences with official corruption and crime. This chapter, therefore, examines how isthmian nations' politico-economic contexts and their citizens' experiences, resources and social positions affect their political attitudes and system support as we seek insight into the prospects for democratic consolidation.

Citizen Participation

We turn first to a comparative examination of political participation. Table 9.1 presents data on the levels of engagement in various political activities of Central Americans.[5] Being registered to vote varies considerably from nation to nation. Some countries require voter registration and issue a mandatory and combined national identity-voter registration card. Others separate national civil registration and voter registration. Costa Rica's highly institutionalized Tribunal Supremo de Elecciones (Supreme Electoral Tribunal—TSE) has operated for several decades and achieved 99 percent registration of Costa Ricans in 2004. Lower registration rates elsewhere appear to occur because other countries make less conscientious efforts at registering all eligible citizens (El Salvador and Guatemala), the newness and inexperience of some civil registries (Nicaragua), and changing rules and procedures. The lowest national rate of voter registration (76 percent) our survey found was in Guatemala, where voting is not mandatory. We compared these data to those from a similar survey from the early 1990s and detect an upward trend in registered voters of several percentage points in Costa Rica, El Salvador, and Nicaragua. El Salvador had the greatest registration gain (14 percent) between 1991 and 2004.[6] This is, in part, a result of the implementation of a new voter and identification card (the Documento Unico de Identidad), which required the Tribunal Supremo de Elecciones to engage in a massive re-registration drive in advance of the 2004 elections.

Other factors held equal, voter registration in 2004 tended to be higher in Central America's poorer countries and in its less repressive ones. Older people and more educated people tended to be more faithful in registering to vote.[7]

Reported voter turnout in each country's most recent presidential election averaged around 75 percent, except for Guatemala at 65 percent (Table 9.1). These reported turnout rates are likely higher than true turnout rates because a few voters—perhaps 5 percent—usually report having voted when they did not. Nevertheless, Central Americans are very active voters compared to the United States, where turnout in recent presidential elections has hovered around 50 percent. We surmise that Central Americans are active voters because of the region's recent experiences with dictatorship, political violence, and fraudulently manipulated elections. Having free elections is likely a refreshing opportunity and one much valued in the region. Also high turnout may be encouraged because each isthmian country is small and the political arenas are thus less remote than in a country as large as the United States.

We compared these 2004 data to those from a similar Central American survey from the early 1990s and discover a downward trend in voter turnout with one major exception.[8] Reported voter turnout in the most recent presidential election declined a few percentage points in Guatemala and Nicaragua, but fell 15 percent in Costa Rica and 18 percent in Honduras. The turnout decline in Costa Rica, consistent with national election bureau turnout reports, has been widely noted and analyzed elsewhere.[9] In marked contrast, El Salvadorans reported a 23 percent increase in voting in the most recent presidential election compared to their voting rate in early 1990s.

In 2004, other factors held equal, citizens in Central America's poorer countries and in its less repressive countries turned out to vote more than others. Older and better educated citizens voted at higher rates than younger or less educated citizens.[10] Thus, voter turnout levels mirrored trends in voter registration noted above.

Partisan activity, another measure of political participation in the national arena, requires more time and effort than voting. Our surveys asked about having attended meetings of political parties. Table 9.1 reveals that Central American averages varied widely around the regional mean of 13 percent. The lowest party attendance reported was in Costa Rica, at a surprisingly low 6 percent. We suspect this low level may stem from Costa Rica's two major parties having adopted primary elections in the 1980s, which reduced the use of local party meetings. Costa Rica's party system, however, is experiencing a period of rapid and significant change. The once-dominant National Liberation Party (PLN) suffered defections and severe electoral reversals in the 1998 and 2002 elections.[11] Citizens may thus be less engaged with parties in Costa Rica because of continuing citizen disaffection with the party system, and because both the PLN and PUSC experienced major corruption scandals since the mid 1990s.

Levels of political party meeting attendance elsewhere divide into two distinct levels. Almost one-fifth of Hondurans and Nicaraguans report attending party meetings. This contrasts sharply to Guatemalans' and Salvadorans' party meeting attendance at 9 and 12 percent, respectively. Guatemala's and El Salvador's transitions to formal democracy are among the region's most recent, and in both violent repression afflicted certain parties' members and political candidates. Their citizens may thus have remained reluctant to expose themselves as party activists by attending meetings, or to report having done so in a survey.[12] In Nicaragua and Honduras party activity was much freer and more open during the 1980s and 1990s, likely accounting for the higher levels reported there. Other factors held constant, poorer Central Americans, men, and urban dwellers are more active in party meetings.[13]

The third type of political participation linked to elections is campaign involvement. The survey asked people whether they had ever attempted to persuade someone how to vote, or worked for a political campaign or candidate (Table 9.1). In these electioneering activities and in spite of low party attendance levels, Costa Ricans stand out as the most active Central Americans. This makes sense given Costa Rica's lengthy democratic tradition and low repression levels. In the rest of the countries, between 19 percent (Nicaragua) and 28 percent (Guatemala) of respondents reported trying to persuade someone how to vote. Salvadorans (8 percent) and Guatemalans (10 percent) were the least likely to have worked for a candidate or campaign (8 percent). In contrast, Nicaraguans (14 percent and Hondurans (15 percent) were almost as active as Costa Ricans. Again we note lower involvement among citizens of Guatemala and El Salvador, the two countries with the highest historic repression levels and the most recently ended civil wars. Other factors held constant, citizens of more prosperous countries but also the more repressive countries were more active in campaigning; older citizens, men, and the more educated engaged in campaigning more than younger citizens, women, and those with less education.[14]

Outside the electoral arena, communal activism—collective self-help or community improvement work—has a vibrant history in Central America and provides a means to address local problems and needs. Communal activism persisted even during intense political conflict and repression. This may have been possible because collective self-help activity among neighbors probably did not appear to challenge authoritarian regimes.[15] Respondents to our 2004 survey (Table 9.1) revealed that regionwide one person in five at least occasionally attended a communal organization meeting. Within the previous two years one in three had "contributed or tried to contribute to the solution of some problem" of their communities. Guatemalans and Hondurans were the most engaged in communal activism, but in one form or another it was commonplace everywhere. Between the early 1990s and 2004, reported attendance at communal association meetings had declined about 10 to 12 percent in Costa Rica, Guatemala, and Nicaragua but remained steady elsewhere.[16]

Participation through civil society (formal organizations) provides citizens a way collectively to promote their interests. Table 9.1 presents comparable data on the percent of citizens attending meetings at least "from time to time" in church-related, school-related, and business and professional organizations. Over two thirds of Guatemalans and Hondurans reported intermediate involvement in church-related groups. Forty-five percent of Costa Ricans and Hondurans reported intermediate attendance at school-related groups. Fewer than one in fifteen respondents regionwide reported business-professional group activity, with Guatemalans and Nicaraguans more active than others. The most striking information concerning civil society activism in Table 9.1 is the overall mean group activism level. Salvadorans reported far less engagement in organizations than the rest of their Central American neighbors, while Hondurans were the most involved in civil society.

We compared these 2004 data to those from a similar Central American survey from the early 1990s and discovered that Central Americans everywhere but Nicaragua reported big increases (13 to 31 percentage points) in involvement in church-related groups. This may be attributable to a widely observed growth of evangelical Protestant proselytism and the formation of myriad church congregations in the 1990s. In contrast, school-related group attendance declined between 7 and 14 percentage points in El Salvador, Guatemala, and Nicaragua; it was flat elsewhere. Involvement in professional and business groups declined regionwide.[17]

Other factors constant, Central American citizens in 2004 engaged more in civil society activism where both political repression and economic risk (indicating a relatively insecure investment climate) were higher. This highlights the importance of organizations to those operating in Central America's more unstable political and economic environments. It likely reflects a strategy of citizens in turbulent politico-economic contexts to pool efforts and share risks in pursuit of their interests in diverse social and economic arenas (economic, communal, religious, and civic).[18]

Citizens typically contact public officials to demand services, seek benefits, or call the government's attention to some problem. About three Central Americans in ten reported contacting a local public official. Costa Ricans, Guatemalans, and El Salvadorans were the most prone to do so, and Hondurans the least. In contrast, contacting national legislative deputies was something only one in 11 2004 survey respondents reported, with only small variation across the region. Guatemalans and Salvadorans, the most active in contacting local officials, were the least likely to contact a legislator. This may reflect the higher recent levels of repression in both countries than elsewhere in the region. Previous research has shown that participation in the local arena (municipal government and local organizations) provides venues for citizen activism even in very repressive regimes, possibly because it is less scrutinized by or threatening to national authorities.[19]

Overall and holding other factors constant, contacting rates were higher among citizens of both the poorer countries but also the less repressive ones. Among individual traits contributing to contacting public officials were being poorer, older, more educated, a rural resident, and a male.[20]

A last type of political participation is protest behavior. An average of one in eight Central Americans reported having taken part in a protest or demonstration, but the variation between countries is striking. Nicaraguans (18 percent) and Costa Ricans (15 percent) were most likely to have protested, and Salvadorans (6 percent) the least likely. El Salvador's history of violent repression of opposition groups may account for the small number of self-reported protesters there. Nicaragua has experienced high levels of protest activity in the post-revolutionary era as working-class groups, unions, and organizations linked to the FSLN have challenged many of the austerity and privatization plans of recent governments. Costa Rica's high protest rate does not square with the country's placid image, but Costa Rica in fact has a lively record of citizens demonstrating and of positive government response to protest.[21] Other factors held constant, protesters were more prevalent in both the less economically and politically stable countries. Region-wide, protesters tended to be more educated and older, and more of them were men.[22]

To sum up, according to 2004 survey data Central Americans engaged the political system through high voter turnout, campaigning, attendance at party meetings, contacting officials, and even protesting. There were national patterns worth noting. In the region's oldest and most successful democracy, Costa Rica, citizens were less active in political parties and community activism but the most active election campaigners and protesters. Guatemalans were the most active in civil society, and Salvadorans the least. Overall, Hondurans were probably the most widely and deeply engaged of Central Americans. Thus, to the extent that democracy involves participation in politics, one may conclude that Central America was indeed democratic.

Among the individual and systemic traits that affected within-system participation overall (a combined measure of all the participation variables except protesting), other factors held constant, higher systemic levels of political terror, being slightly better off, and being female reduced participation. Factors that increased participation were perceiving the political system to allow free participation, being older, and (most strongly) having more education.[23] These findings reveal that certain factors that could be controlled by national political elites—access to education, levels of political violence and repression and, therefore, the perceived civil and political liberties climate—constituted keys to increased democratic participation in Central America as the twenty-first century began. Thus the ruling elites' choices about public policy and governmental behavior, factors we have repeatedly cited as a key to the quality of political and economic life in Central America, remain central to citizen participation.

TABLE 9.1 POLITICAL PARTICIPATION RATES BY COUNTRY, CENTRAL AMERICAN NATIONS, 2004

	Costa Rica	*El Salvador*	*Guatemala*	*Honduras*	*Nicaragua*	*Regional Mean*
Type of Political Participation						
Voting Behavior						
Registered to vote (%)	99	94	76	91	87	89
Voted in last presidential election (%)	74	76	65	73	75	73
Attend political party meetings (%)	6	9	12	19	20	13
Campaigning						
Attempted to persuade someone how to vote (%)	30	21	28	25	19	25
Worked for a political campaign or candidate (%)	16	8	10	15	14	13
Communal Activism						
Attend community improvement group* (%)	14	19	27	28	18	21
Worked with others to solve community problem (%)	34	31	34	37	29	33
Civil Society Activism*						
Church-related group (%)	52	39	69	69	51	56
School-related group (%)	44	36	36	45	41	40
Business-professional group (%)	7	5	9	7	9	7
Mean group activism **(%)	34	26	38	41	33	35
Contacting Public Officials						
Local official (%)	32	34	32	22	30	30
Legislative deputy (%)	11	8	8	11	9	9
Protest participation (%)	15	6	11	9	18	12

*Percentages are for reporting attendance at meetings of each group "from time to time" or more frequently, at least an intermediate or higher level of involvement.

**Average of all three types of groups listed above (church, school, and business-professional) for at least the intermediate-level of involvement ("from time to time").

SOURCE: 2004 Survey by U.S. Agency for International Development.

Citizen Attitudes

Latin American political culture has had a strong authoritarian component marked by deference to authority, preference for strong leaders, intolerance of regime critics, and antidemocratic norms. Central American countries shared these cultural traits, which were almost certainly reinforced by the protracted periods of authoritarian rule discussed elsewhere in this volume. In contrast, however, prior research has reported higher democratic norms than anticipated among Nicaraguans—equal in fact to those of Costa Ricans—during the late 1980s despite Nicaragua's limited experience with democracy.[24] The recent emergence of formal democracy in four of five countries and questions about the commitment of Central Americans to democracy calls for us to assess[25] the balance between authoritarian and democratic norms among Central Americans today.

To evaluate political attitudes we begin with a question asking whether the country needs "a strong leader who does not need to be elected or worry about elections." As Table 9.2 reveals, only 13 percent of Central Americans agreed with this patently authoritarian statement in 2004, a viewpoint clearly inimical to democracy and probably dangerous to it if widely held. Individual country samples ranged widely around this regional mean, with Costa Ricans and Salvadorans the least in agreement. Guatemalans (at 18 percent) and Hondurans (22 percent) gave the highest share of authoritarian responses. Region-wide, fewer than one person in seven held this authoritarian view, which shows that most Central Americans reject as an ideal that leadership should be unrestrained by elections. There nonetheless remained substantial numbers of pro-authoritarians in Guatemala and Honduras. Other factors held equal, this authoritarian norm was most widely held in the more repressive countries of the region, and by its younger, less educated, and urban-dwelling citizens.[26]

Probing further, our survey asked people whether "there are ever any circumstances under which a military coup might be justified." Here the answers will little comfort those who prefer Central America's civilian-led democratic governments to military regimes. About half of the respondents region wide agreed that there might arise circumstances under which a military coup would be justified. Nicaraguans embraced this idea the least (32 percent),[27] but Salvadorans (64 percent) and Hondurans (55 percent) were the most accepting of the notion. Costa Rica, which has had no military rule for eight decades and no coups since the 1940s, surprises with almost half of its respondents envisioning circumstances that might justify a coup. Other factors held constant, residents of the economically and politically more stable countries justified coups, a somewhat baffling finding. We conjecture that perhaps residents of the more economically and politically stable countries could view the idea of a coup as a possible defense against some hypothetical turmoil that might threaten their relative stability. Coup justifiers tended to be younger, less educated, and urban dwellers.[28]

When interviewers asked what specific hypothetical problems might justify a military takeover of their governments, Central Americans cited official corruption (61 percent), followed closely by crime (56 percent), and by inflation (55 percent). These findings reveal that, region-wide, Central Americans' commitment to civilian rule remains partly contingent on the performance of their regimes. Threats to personal and economic security (crime and inflation) and problems of public corruption (which also affects those who must pay bribes) deeply trouble many—even in the more stable countries. Should crime, corruption, or inflation (or all three) become sufficiently bad, armed forces or other plotters against the constitutional order might be able to count on the forbearance or even support of a coup d'état claiming to rectify such problems.

Shifting to citizens' democratic norms, Table 9.2 reports the national means for an index of agreement with basic general participation rights for citizens of a democracy. On a scale of one to 100 (from the least to the most democratic), the citizens of all five countries averaged well into the positive end of the scale, with a clear national bias in favor of general democratic participation rights. Costa Ricans and Nicaraguans scored the highest (81 and 78 points, respectively), and Guatemalans scored the lowest (at 66 points) but still strongly democratic. Other factors held equal, people living in more stable countries and those with more education supported basic participation rights more.

Comparing support for general participation rights between an early 1990s survey and this one in 2004, we found a decline in the scale scores regionwide. Costa Ricans, Salvadorans, and Guatemalans recorded a decline of four to five points on the scale, and Hondurans and Nicaraguans about a ten-point decline. Central Americans had not abandoned their support for general participation rights as of 2004, to be sure, but we view the decline of support for participation rights with concern.[29]

Another measure, on a similar one to 100 scale, shows Central Americans to report less tolerance for participation rights for regime critics (those "who speak badly of our form of government") than for participation rights in general. This index measures citizens' evaluations of one of democracy's more challenging precepts, that of allowing regime critics to take part in politics and try to convince others of their positions. Costa Ricans, Hondurans, and Nicaraguans were the more tolerant; they ranged around a score of 60. In contrast, Salvadorans (with a score of 56 on tolerance) and Guatemalans (with a score of 52), manifested less political tolerance. Other factors held constant, people living in more stable countries and with higher standards of living and more education tended to be more politically tolerant.[30]

Comparing tolerance levels between an early 1990s survey and this one in 2004, we found a mixed result. No meaningful changes occurred in Costa Rica or Nicaragua. In Honduras the scale mean on tolerance declined 10 points. Combined with a similar decline in support for general participation rights in Honduras, this finding suggests a somewhat diminished popular commitment to democracy there since the early 1990s. In contrast, tolerance scale scores rose 6 points in El Salvador and 7 in Guatemala, a positive development in the two countries with the lowest tolerance scores in the region.[31]

A final index of citizens' democratic norms involves their embrace of protest, civil disobedience, and even political violence. Evaluating citizen reaction to these methods is tricky. On the one hand protest and even political confrontation may be necessary to create, nurture, or maintain a democracy. Indeed, Thomas Jefferson argued that popular unrest was essential to democracy.[32] On the other hand, within formal democracies, confrontational political tactics are seldom widely supported by the citizenry, and if engaged in to extremes may threaten a democratic system. Taking part in a "group wishing to violently overthrow an elected government"—one of the items in this index—may indeed be inimical to democracy itself. Bearing in mind these complexities, we see that on a similar 1 to 100 scale regionwide the index average is only 26. There is a strong shared bias against such techniques. Hondurans were the most favorable toward confrontational tactics (24 index mean), and Costa Ricans the least (18 index mean).

Comparing support for civil disobedience and confrontational political methods between the 1990s survey and this one in 2004, we found an increase everywhere but Honduras.[33] In each of the other four countries, support for protest and confrontation in 2004 rose roughly seven scale points from their early 1990s levels. As repression diminished with the end of two civil wars and the development and operation of formal democracy more broadly, Central Americans became more supportive of confrontational tactics. Interestingly, the trend also applies for Costa Ricans who—unlike their neighbors—have enjoyed stable democracy for several decades. Because Costa Ricans also increased their approval of protest and confrontation, we surmise that some of the increase stems from neoliberal economic reforms. Under pressure from foreign lending institutions and governments, debt-strapped regional governments in the 1980s and 1990s cut public services, state jobs, and privatized public sector enterprises. Protests provided affected workers and consumers one of the few tools to influence public policy. We are not surprised that sympathy for confrontational tactics was rising simultaneously with protests of tough austerity measures.

Other factors held equal, Central Americans living in the less repressive countries and also the more stable countries were more favorable toward confrontational political tactics.[34] At the individual level, Central Americans favoring

TABLE 9.2 POLITICAL ATTITUDES BY COUNTRY, CENTRAL AMERICA, 2004

	Costa Rica	*El Salvador*	*Guatemala*	*Honduras*	*Nicaragua*	*Regional Mean*
Attitudes						
Authoritarianism						
"We need a strong leader who does not need to be elected." (% agreeing)	7	6	18	22	13	13
Support for Military Coups						
"There are some circumstances under which a military coup may be justified." (% agreeing)	48	64	46	55	32	49
Democratic Norms						
Support for general political participation rights* (index, range = 1–100)	81	70	66	72	78	73
Tolerance for participation rights for regime critics ** (index, range = 1–100)	62	56	52	60	59	58
Support for civil disobedience and confrontational political methods *** (index, range = 1–100)	25	28	29	34	30	29
"How much would you approve that people take part in a group that wishes to overthrow an elected government by violent means?" (index, range = 1–100).	18	24	29	32	26	26
System Support						
General System Support**** (index, range = 1–100)	71	62	51	53	51	58
Specific Institutional Support***** (index, range = 1–100)	58	57	45	48	44	50

*This index incorporates approval of three behaviors: taking part in a legal demonstration, in a group working to solve communal problems, and in campaigning for a candidate or party.

**This index incorporates approval of four behaviors by critics of the regime: being allowed to vote, carry out peaceful demonstrations, run for public office, and give a speech on television.

***This index incorporates approval of four behaviors: taking part in street blockages, invading of private property, taking over factories, offices, or buildings, or taking part in a group that wishes to overthrow an elected government by violent means.

****This index incorporates level of approval of national political institutions, protection of basic rights, pride in the system, and obligation to support the political system.

*****This index incorporates citizen support/approval for nine different specific government institutions (elections office, legislature, "the government," political parties, supreme court, municipal government, and elections, etc.).

SOURCE: 2004 Survey by U.S. Agency for International Development.

confrontational tactics tended to be poorer, younger, and less educated. This confirms previous evidence that protest may be a preferred political tool for those with few other resources.[35] Lacking the resources availed by social status, money, education, and organization that would provide influence over policy makers, such disadvantaged citizens may view protest and civil disobedience as useful to promote their interests. Interestingly, however, as noted above, other influences held constant, Central America's actual self-reported protesters (not those merely favoring confrontational tactics) tend to be better educated and slightly older than others.[36]

In sum, in 2004, Central Americans in every country clearly tended to disapprove of confrontational political tactics. Yet as we saw above, one respondent in five reported taking part in a political protest. Clearly a substantial minority of Central Americans not only approved of taking political advocacy to the streets, and some did actually protest, whether legally and peacefully or via more confrontational means. When they were asked specifically which types of actions they most agreed or disagreed with, we discovered something striking. Central Americans tended to disapprove the most of occupying buildings, blocking streets, or invading property—actions that create inconvenience or disrupt the lives of others. In sharp contrast, as revealed in Table 9.2, they approved somewhat more (a scale mean of 26 out of 100, with little variation among nations) of people "taking part in a group that wishes to overthrow an elected government by violent means." We interpret this as a willingness (held at least theoretically)—widespread in the isthmus—to tolerate organizing and violence against even an elected government that abuses or fails in its fundamental obligations to the citizenry. Thus we see that, despite the horrors of insurrection and war that widely afflicted Central America from the 1970s well into the 1990s, many of the region's citizens still reserve the right to conspire and rebel against a bad (even if elected) regime.

This finding in turn raises another important issue—how much did Central Americans in 2004 actually support their governments? Table 9.2 presents the mean scores on two measures of the legitimacy of (support for) the political system—general support for the national system, and support for specific national institutions. There we see that the regional mean on the general system support index was 58, in the positive end of the scale. Costa Ricans at 71 scored the highest, not surprising given the country's long record of stable democracy. Particularly noteworthy, however, the low mean general system support scores for Guatemala (51), Honduras (53), and Nicaragua (51).

Comparing general support for the political system between the 1990s survey and this one in 2004, we found very mixed results. General system support declined by seven scale points in Costa Rica, six in Guatemala, and 12 in Nicaragua. In contrast, El Salvadorans reported seven scale points and Hondurans eight scale points higher general system support in 2004 compared to the early 1990s.[37]

Probing further we find that in 2004 Central Americans were less satisfied with specific national institutions than with their political systems in general. The regional mean on specific institutional support was only 50, the scale's midpoint, and average support scores for Guatemalans (45), Hondurans (48), and Nicaraguans (44) fell in the disapproving (non-supporting) end of the scale. With regard to specific institutions, therefore, only Costa Ricans and Salvadorans held positive support scores. Guatemalans, Hondurans, and Nicaraguans somewhat disapproved of their institutions.

These support scores may provide our best indicator of how consolidated Central America's new democratic governments had become as of 2004. Costa Rica and El Salvador appeared be in the strongest positions regarding consolidation of their democratic institutions, though some of Costa Rica's trends were worrisome. In contrast their isthmian neighbors remained, both generally and specifically, somewhat less politically supportive of their governments. To anyone worried about democratic consolidation, these lower political support scores for Guatemala, Honduras, and Nicaragua indicate a potential for trouble. Even more troubling are downward support trends over time in Guatemala and Honduras. These data suggest that three of the region's five democratic regimes were only weakly supported—several years after regime change and despite their citizens' generally democratic norms and shared repudiation of authoritarianism.

Factors Shaping Attitudes and Participation

We see that in 2004 Central Americans were active in their political systems in diverse ways—behaving democratically—but that their attitudes demonstrated some ambivalence. On the one hand, most people reported strong democratic norms and repudiated authoritarian leadership. On the other hand a large minority reported being willing to countenance others seeking to overthrow elected regimes, while a majority believed a military coup could be justified if corruption, crime, or inflation were sufficiently bad. Moreover, citizens of Guatemala, Honduras, and Nicaragua averaged system support at or below the midpoints of the scales. These national means on the tilting point between system legitimacy and illegitimacy reveal great ambivalence about these democratic regimes. Indeed, even Costa Rica, though firmly in the positive end of the support scales, experienced a steady decline in political support indicators from the 1980s to the early 2000s.[38] This raises the question of what might account for such indifferent support. What factors may contribute to low system support?

We suspect that several factors shape support for regimes. These include Central America's differing sociopolitical contexts (historical background, repression, and economic activity), where citizens stand within the society (individual wealth and education), and citizens' experiences and beliefs (sense of freedom to take part; experiences of corruption and crime victimization).

Table 9.3 summarizes some indicators of these possible influences on Central Americans' support for their regimes. We assume that the higher a country scores on each of these factors, the lower will be its general and specific political support scores. First, contextual measures reflect considerable variation in the situations of the different nations. Real GDP per capita in constant terms in 2000—a measure of relative economic development—ranged from $5,870 for Costa Rica to $1,767 for Nicaragua. Second and third are measures of political and economic stability. *The Economist* uses experts to rank Central American countries on a scale of 1 to 100 for their political risk (the stability of their political systems, with higher scores being better) and on a similar scale for economic risk (the degree of the stability of their economies). *The Economist*'s political risk ranking for the fall of 2003 for isthmian countries ranged from a high of 77 for Costa Rica to a low of 51 for Guatemala. The other countries ranged in the mid to upper 60s on the scale. *The Economist*'s similarly constructed economic risk scores were much worse for the region. They ranged from a regional best in El Salvador of 60 down to 29 for Nicaragua. Expert outside observers clearly viewed national economic and political stability in Central America as varying separately from each other. Large discrepancies prevail between the political stability (higher) and economic stability (lower) measures for Costa Rica, Honduras, and Nicaragua.

A fourth context measure is the Political Terror Scale for 2001, which evaluates the general level of political repression present in the countries. On a scale of one to five, a good score (low terror) has a value of 1.0. Repression had been much higher in the region (except Costa Rica) in prior years, but by 2001 things had improved. Costa Rica had the region's best (lowest) terror score, with Guatemala and Honduras tied for worst at 3.

Individuals' life experiences that might lower political support may well include being victims of crime and political corruption. If the state cannot reasonably protect citizens from criminals and if public officials regularly extort bribes, citizens thus victimized may withdraw their support from their regime. Table 9.3 shows that 15 percent of Central Americans reported being crime victims, with little variation across the region. A different index of the severity of the crime victimization that weights violent crime more heavily than nonviolent ones reveals that Salvadorans experienced somewhat more severe crimes and Guatemalans somewhat less than their regional neighbors. An index comparing citizens experiences with official corruption (having to pay bribes to various types of officials) reveals that corruption is lowest in Costa Rica (an index score of .20 on a scale of 0–5), while the scores for the other countries are all higher (.26 to .29).

Finally, perceptions of the climates for political participation and civil liberties protection may also color system support. We suspect that people who express fear

TABLE 9.3 POSSIBLE SOURCES OF LOW POLITICAL SUPPORT IN CENTRAL AMERICA

Variables	*Costa Rica*	*El Salvador*	*Guatemala*	*Honduras*	*Nicaragua*	*Region*
Political-Economic Context						
Real Gross Domestic Product per Capita, 2000 (US $)*	5,870	4,435	3,914	2,049	1,767	3,607
Political Risk Score (1 = very unstable to 100 = very stable)**	77	64	51	68	68	66
Economic Risk Score (1 = very unstable to 100 = very stable)**	47	60	52	46	29	47
Political Terror Scale* (1 = very low repression to 5 = high repression)**	1	2	3	3	2	2.2
Personal Experience******						
Crime victimization (% reporting)	15	17	13	14	15	15
Official corruption experience index (range 0 = low to 5 = high)	.20	.26	.28	.29	.19	.26
Perceptions of Political System******						
Perceived freedom to participate in politics (index, range 0 = low to 2 = high)	1.6	1.5	1.4	1.6	1.5	1.5
Perceived national civil liberties climate (index, range 0 = low to 4 = high)	1.8	1.6	1.5	1.5	1.6	1.6

*SOURCE: Alan Heston, Robert Summers, and Bettina Aten, *Penn World Tables,* Center for International Comparisons at the University of Pennsylvania (CICUP), October 2002.

**SOURCE: *The Economist,* www.eiuresources.com/ras/default.htm, accessed March 5, 2005.

***SOURCE: Mark Gibney, *Political Terror Scale 1980–2003,* accessed June 17, 2004 at www.unca.edu/politicalscience/faculty-staff/gibney.html; and Freedom House, *Freedom in the World 2004,* www.freedomhouse.org/research/freeworld/2004/table2004.pdf, accessed June 24, 2004.

****Both items drawn from 2004 Survey by U.S. Agency for International Development.

that they are not free to participate in politics in various arenas, and those who perceive the human rights climate to be adverse, will support their regimes less than those viewing these factors more favorably. Table 9.3 contains indexes of both sorts of perceptions. We note that the national index averages in the table portray a generally positive view of freedom to participate in politics across the region. Evaluation of the civil liberties climate ranges a bit more widely and has a lower mean within the scale's range, indicating less the citizenries' confidence in this arena. The lack of variation across the region only indicates regional homogeneity on this perception. It does not, however, preclude that individuals with negative perceptions on these items might withhold their support for their regime.

We come now to the big question for Central America: How do these factors affect support for political institutions and for the political systems in general? Do they, as anticipated, actually raise or lower citizens' support? Does a climate of political repression or one's perception of political corruption reduce system support—in effect, lower the legitimacy of a regime? Does a higher level of political stability or high level of economic growth contribute to support and thus possibly to democratic consolidation?

The answer is straightforward: Yes, most of these contextual factors, experiences, and perceptions do indeed influence political support of both kinds—general support for the system and for specific institutions. Statistical analysis (not included here to save space)[39] reveals that (in descending order of importance) the following factors elevate general system support: greater political and economic stability, less political terror, a positive view of the civil liberties climate, lower perceived corruption, greater economic development (GDP per capita), and lower crime victimization. Similarly, support for specific national institutions goes up significantly (in descending order of importance) with greater economic stability, less political repression, a well-perceived civil liberties climate, greater political stability, and lower experience of political corruption.[40] Finally, urban dwellers had higher levels of both general system support and specific-institution support. This seems quite reasonable given that throughout the isthmus Central America's urban populations enjoyed much better living conditions, better services, and life standards than rural residents.

Finally, perceptions of the climate for political participation and civil liberties protection may also color system support. We suspect that people who fear that they are not free to participate in politics and those who perceive the human rights climate to be adverse will support their regimes less. Table 9.3 contains indexes of both sorts of perceptions. We note that the national averages in the table portray a generally positive view of freedom to participate in politics across the region. Evaluation of the civil liberties climate ranges a bit more widely and has a lower mean within the scale's range, indicating less confidence in this arena. The lack of variation across the region, however, in no way suggests that individuals with negative perceptions on these items would not withhold their support for the regime.

Conclusions

Early in the twenty-first century, Central Americans were accommodating themselves to their mostly still young democratic regimes. They were conducting themselves in a manner necessary to and consistent with democracy by participating in politics in diverse arenas and ways, and by sharing political values congruent with democratic polities. Collectively and country by country they strongly supported basic democratic norms and repudiated authoritarian rule. These findings augured well for democracy in the region—insofar as popular behavior and values could support democratic rules of the game. But the matter was more complicated than that—these actions and attitudes would necessarily interact with the complex national and international environments in shaping democratic consolidation.

Central Americans held important reservations about their polities. Their commitment to the regimes of the moment appeared less than solid. Dependent on certain adverse conditions, particularly severe corruption, crime, or inflation, well more than half of Central Americans believed that a coup d'état might be justified. And just less than half of Central Americans approved of organizing to violently overthrow an elected government. As of 2004, support for confrontational political tactics had apparently grown across the region since the 1990s. No strangers to previous bad regimes and economic turmoil, Central Americans thus appeared willing to extend their rulers only so much rope. Many people appeared, at least in the abstract, willing to opt for protest and rebellion should their governments badly violate the social contract. Our public opinion data show that citizens' political support for their regimes was strongest in Costa Rica and El Salvador. In contrast, Guatemala, Nicaragua, and Honduras all had regime support levels that were much lower, and in the former two the support had waned since the early 1990s. Guatemala, Honduras, and Nicaragua thus appeared to have elevated risks for political instability. Challenges to poorly consolidated democratic regimes of course might come from either democratic forces or antidemocratic ones. Thus we cannot easily predict whether increased turmoil would strengthen or weaken formal representative democracy as it exists in Guatemala, Honduras, or Nicaragua.

Given this only partly encouraging panorama of public opinion, what might these countries' rulers or even outsiders do to increase the prospects for democratic stability in Central America, especially in the three wobblier cases? What actions might increase political support for these regimes? Some things, especially the larger contextual variables, are very hard to manipulate in the short or medium term—especially the economies. Honduras and Nicaragua were very hard up economically in real terms. Their disadvantages relative to the region's other three nations, and especially to the larger world economy, had worsened in recent decades. From the 1980s through the 1990s Nicaragua's economy moved dramatically and tragically backward—*de-developing* to reach 1950s levels of productivity.

On the positive side, there remained several locally manageable factors. Elites (power holders) could, if willing, promote increased comity among political elites and greater accord on democratic rules of the political game. If accomplished, this could increase political stability and lower political risk. Governments could, if they would, address problems of political and economic corruption with legal reforms and prosecution of bribe takers. While powerful vested interests might oppose such reform, if implemented it could improve the economic climates, attract greater domestic and foreign investment, and would undoubtedly garner approval from corruption-weary citizens. Further, reducing political repression by improving police and military training and curtailing acts of official violence and repression could boost political support in the middle term by reducing fear and encouraging greater participation. Obviously, efforts to reduce crime could strengthen citizen political support for civilian democratic regimes over time. Thus, these measures were arguably at least partly within reach, and could help each country move toward democratic consolidation.

The difficult and distressing fact, however, was that much of this potential for progress rested on the will and actions of elites and, to a significant extent, on foreign actors such as the United States. On the bright side, elites in Guatemala, Nicaragua, Honduras, and El Salvador had made some progress and real concessions to their narrowly construed economic and power interests over the last decade or two—albeit accomplishing this only when pressed very hard by outside actors and by rebels from below. These concessions led to formal electoral democracy, reduced repression, and better lives for many. Political support in El Salvador rose much higher than we would have ever expected a decade or so ago, given the national elite's grim historical record.

Based especially on the early successes in Costa Rica and the Honduran and Nicaraguan regime changes of the 1980s, we see that elite-led reform is not impossible in Central America, even absent pressure for it from the international arena. But how likely might be further such reforms that could contribute to democratic consolidation? In our opinion, as we wrote this the prospects for such reform and work for consolidated democracy among the political and economic elites of Nicaragua, Honduras, and Guatemala were very modest at best. The citizens were manifestly ready to take part in and support democracy. Indeed they had already embraced it. This put the ball in the elites' end of the court, and also in the court of the international community, whose economic and political preferences loom large in local elites' choices.

That leaves us with two critical questions: First, could and would national elites give the region's citizens enough economic progress and reform that the people would continue to support their fledgling democracies and not opt again to rebel? As argued repeatedly in the preceding chapters and in Chapter 10, after decades of the United States promoting repression that blocked democracy, the international community eventually came together to encourage Central American regimes to adopt "low-intensity" democracy (formal electoral civilian regimes) as the Cold War waned. At the same time, however, external actors led by the United States promoted new economic policies that constrained the ability of Central American governments to promote economic development favoring the poor majority. Neoliberal orthodoxy, imposed from abroad and embraced by the new economic and political elites of the region's civilian democracies, had stripped governments of many tools to promote social welfare or invest in human capital. Thus, even if local ruling elites were willing to promote equitable development—as they had once done in Costa Rica, Nicaragua and even Honduras—neoliberalism would reduce their ability to make such choices. Key international actors had pressured Central American nations to adopt the neoliberal development model and would pressure them to keep it. Thus prospects for economic growth with equity seemed modest indeed.

Second, how might Central American citizens respond, through their attitudes and participation, to continued poor economic performance, increased inequality, or to increasing poverty? (All these, recall, helped mobilize Central American unrest in the 1970s and 1980s.) At the time of this writing, Central American citizens showed enthusiasm for democracy, but many also expressed willingness to use confrontational and even violent political means. Protests of neoliberal policies and their effects were reported around the isthmus in the late 1990s and early 2000s. We suspect that with reduced prospects that growth would be accompanied by even a modicum of distributive equity, Central America could eventually become again more politically turbulent. We know that in the 1990s and early 2000s civilian democratic regimes presiding over deteriorating popular living standards in the Andean region—Venezuela, Bolivia, Ecuador—experienced protest mobilization, unrest, and violence. Would the same happen in Central America, or would regional elites instead choose to adapt the neoliberal model slightly to allow for a more equitable distribution of the fruits of growth? The answer to this question would depend heavily on the behavior of one powerful international actor, the United States. The past performance of this important actor—the subject of our next chapter—would not lead one to optimism.

10

Power, Democracy, and U.S. Policy in Central America

Central American politics derive in part from the unique internal social, economic, and political evolution of each of the republics, but they are also influenced by the United States. U.S. proximity and the gross disparities in population and national wealth between the region's major hegemon and its tiny neighbors have long caused U.S. policy to greatly affect the region. The results have sometimes been quite detrimental to the well-being of Central Americans. We argued in earlier editions that Washington's apparent definition of its interests in Central America and its strategies for achieving them were fundamentally flawed during the Cold War: short-termed, reactive, and excessively concerned with stability. The U.S. effort to contain leftist influence and insurgency in the region from the 1960s through the 1990s is described case by case in Chapters 4 through 8. Here we focus on U.S. policies that, at a minimum, intensified political conflicts that by the early 1990s had killed over 300,000 people (mainly civilians), nearly ruined the economies of the region and displaced millions, left countless others jobless, orphaned, or physically or psychologically maimed. U.S. policy was by no means the only cause of the Central American tragedy, but it contributed importantly to its onset and evolution.

The Cold War between the U.S. and the Soviets ended in 1990, and Central America's revolutionary-counterrevolutionary conflict wound down to end in 1996. U.S. fears of Communist-inspired uprisings and subversion accordingly, waned and the United States scaled back its overt and covert intervention in the region. Nevertheless Washington's policy in the region in the late 1990s and early 2000s remained quite interventionist and retained much of the ideological framework that shaped U.S. Cold War intervention. The particular tools of U.S.

involvement in Central America changed more than the underlying policy and objectives themselves.

Although the tactics and style of U.S. policy toward the isthmus evolved, overall U.S. objectives remained remarkably constant. The main goals were always to protect U.S. economic and security interests by keeping as much control as possible over events and policies in Central America—minimizing perceived security threats while maximizing economic interests and utility. Even in times of lofty rhetoric about good neighborliness, the Alliance for Progress, human rights, or democracy, U.S. policies consistently focused on maintaining political stability and influence over friendly governments. Concerned about the Cuban revolution, President Kennedy promoted the Alliance for Progress to encourage economic development and democracy in Latin America. He simultaneously increased U.S. military assistance throughout the region. Intended to augment the capacity of Latin American armed forces to contain communism and protect democracy, U.S. military aid under Presidents Kennedy, Johnson, and Nixon also helped armies topple democratic regimes and intensify human rights abuses. Ironically, the presence of U.S.-backed, rights-abusing dictatorships helped spark insurgencies in Central America from the 1960s throughout the 1980s.

Although the intensity of U.S. involvement in the isthmus diminished after 1990 and Central America virtually vanished from the news, Washington in the early 2000s continued to promote U.S. security and economic interests by keeping leftist politicians out of power, and by aggressively promoting economic policies and development models that conform to U.S. interests.

The Problem of Power

Power is the basic currency of politics. Simply put, groups within a given polity generally receive benefits and attention from the prevailing political regime in rough proportion to the amount of power they can bring to bear on that regime. The powerful receive the most; the powerless, little or nothing. Charles W. Anderson argued that the traditional "power contenders" in Latin American society—the Church, the military, the rural and urban economic elites—allow new groups to enter and receive benefits from the political system only when these groups demonstrate their own "power capabilities."[1] We argued in Chapter 2 that regime changes in Central America—especially struggles for democratization—have involved conflict and the reconfiguration of relationships among traditional power contenders and new groups from the middle and working classes.

Power capabilities vary from group to group. The Church exercises authority through the traditional belief systems and moral suasion. The military holds much of the means of violent coercion. Economic elites use their wealth to influence events. In contrast, lower-class groups have scant resources but can wield influence by organizing and carrying out strikes, protests, and the like. But the incontrovertible fact is that the majority of Central Americans—peasants, urban and rural workers, and slum dwellers—usually lack the organization that would give them real power capabilities. During the Cold War, when such groups attempted to develop power through organization, existing powerholders saw them as subversive, labeled them Communist, and violently repressed them. Accordingly, because Central America's poor majorities have held little power, policy usually has been unresponsive to their plight. We have seen country by country how this lack of responsiveness generated grievances, and how some regimes suppressed these grievances, thus making violence the people's last recourse.

Great power disparities between the small privileged upper class and its emerging middle-class allies and the underprivileged, impoverished majority generated the Central American crisis of the late twentieth century. As we noted in earlier chapters, power relationships in the five countries had deep historical roots. It is no accident that Costa Rica, with the most egalitarian society, and Honduras—an economic backwater that never developed a cohesive and exploitative elite—were least affected by turmoil. It is also not surprising that Guatemala, El Salvador, and Nicaragua, the countries with the greatest historically rooted power disparities, experienced the region's highest levels of violence. Their elites, long accustomed to their lopsided power advantage, resisted sharing power and making the sacrifices needed for the genuine development of all sectors of society.

Democracy

Democracy provides a powerful base of legitimacy for contemporary governments. Indeed, most regimes today claim to be democratic. The problem is that the term *democracy* is contested and its meaning debated. Socialist theorists usually stress distributive economic and social criteria, whereas those from the industrially developed West emphasize political rules—often narrowly procedural ones. In the United States, one definition with which few would quarrel is that democracy is "government of, by, and for the people." However simple this definition may sound, it sets forth two conceptual elements fundamental to effective democracy: first, that the system should be as participatory as possible, and, second, that it should facilitate general well-being.[2]

In the 1980s the United States promoted civilian rule and elections in Central America. When these appeared Washington proclaimed the birth of "democracy" in its client states, Guatemala, El Salvador, and Honduras, but condemned its alleged absence in revolutionary Nicaragua. Only in 1990, when the besieged Nicaraguan people elected the U.S.-backed Violeta Barrios de Chamorro president, was Nicaragua finally recognized as democratic by Washington. Closer inspection, however, makes this U.S. interpretation difficult to sustain.[3] All four countries held nationwide, internationally observed elections. The elections in three countries—excluding El Salvador's in the 1980s—were internationally acclaimed as procedurally clean. But democracy requires much more than simply holding procedurally correct elections or establishing formal civilian rule. A critical issue is popular participation in elections and in other political affairs.

The elections in Guatemala in 1985 and 1990 as well as those in El Salvador in 1982, 1984, 1988, 1989, and 1991 were held against a background of state-sponsored terror that had taken tens of thousands of lives and had disarticulated most mass-based civic and political organizations. Candidates perforce came mainly from center to far right parties, and independent or critical media outlets were nonexistent. Repression confined most citizen participation in formal national politics mainly to voting; only a tiny minority of center and right-wing party activists engaged in campaigns. In Nicaragua in 1984 and 1990, in contrast, there was no program of state-sponsored terror; organizations representing the poor majority had been encouraged to develop, grow, and make demands on government. Opposition parties and elite interest groups also existed quite openly and participated in politics. In stark contrast, international human rights organizations concurred that the systematized torture, murder, and disappearance of political opponents that was widespread and institutionalized in Guatemala and El Salvador did not occur in Nicaragua. Though important rightists boycotted the 1984 Nicaraguan election, three parties on the FSLN's right and three on their left challenged the Sandinistas. Nicaragua's antiregime media (including *La Prensa* and Radio Católica), though partly censored, carried an anti-Sandinista message to the voters. The six participating opposition parties enjoyed extensive uncensored free time on state-sponsored radio and television.

One may also question the U.S. application of the term *democracy* in Central America during the Cold War by asking: Were there governments "for the people"? In whose interest did they rule? The Sandinista revolution made efforts to deliver benefits to the people. By 1984, even its critics credited the government with "significant gains against illiteracy and disease."[4] Nicaragua also made advances in agrarian reform, housing, social security, and the status of women. Eventually the U.S.-backed Contra war forced the diversion of public spending away from social welfare and to the military budget. By the 1990 election most social programs had been sharply reduced, and the country was mobilized for war. Nicaragua's disastrous economic and political situation in 1990 led its citizens to use the democratic election system established by the revolutionary regime to vote the FSLN out of office and end the revolution. Thus the Sandinista handover to the opposition in 1990 not only flowed from democratic rules of the game that were already in place but dramatically reconfirmed Nicaragua's transition to a civilian democratic regime in 1987.

In El Salvador and Guatemala, in contrast, the process of regime change toward democracy during the last decade of the Cold War proceeded differently. In both, the reformist military regime that overthrew the authoritarian military regime acted with so much violent repression that many observers detected no meaningful transformation of the political systems. When each country's reformist military regime ceded rule to a transitional civilian government, skepticism abounded about how much real power these elected civilian rulers had while their militaries still held veto power over key matters. The civilian politicians, however, gradually gained independence from the armed forces as Cold War threats diminished, and formerly excluded power contenders were eventually allowed to take part. Honduras followed a similar path of gradual transition to democracy, albeit without a civil war or such intense repression.

Eventually all four countries established formally elected civilian regimes under heavy pressure from the United States, but the quality of their democracies still remained to be determined in the early 2000s. Some argue that not only must formal rules of democracy and popular participation without massive repression exist but, more important, qualitative and socioeconomic foundations must also exist. To truly participate and thus influence decisions in a formally democratic country, the poor majority needs the fundamental human and political resources provided by socioeconomic well-being. By the late 1990s Nicaragua, El Salvador, Guatemala, and Honduras all had formal civilian democracies, but poverty and income and wealth maldistribution left poor citizens largely without the socioeconomic requisites of an effective democracy.

Critics have accordingly tagged the four new democracies of Central America as "low intensity democracies" or "polyarchies" to distinguish them from more egalitarian regimes of rule "by the people and for the people."[5] The rankings on comparative democracy indexes (see Table 2.3) for Nicaragua, El Salvador, Guatemala, and Honduras confirm the middling to poor performance of these formally democratic regimes. Thus elites—albeit including a broader circle of power contenders than in the 1970s—continued to dominate the polities and poorly meet democracy's basic norms even under formally elected civilian regimes.

Mobilization

The decades following World War II were marked by a growing awareness that something was seriously wrong in Latin America. Those who viewed mass poverty as rooted in an extremely unequal distribution of power began advocating a greater diffusion of power. In the 1940s and 1950s, social democratic and Christian democratic parties talked of "penetrating" the masses, of creating and fortifying party-oriented labor, peasant, and neighborhood organizations that would unify and express the interests of the masses. From the 1950s onward, educators such as Paulo Freire of Brazil, aware that mass empowerment would require the emergence of a socially, politically, and linguistically literate citizenry, began promoting, through adult education, consciousness-raising programs that encouraged poor people to examine and question their social condition.[6]

Jolted by the Cuban revolution in 1959, the United States at first supported reform in Latin America with programs like the Alliance for Progress (to promote economic growth) and the Peace Corps (to promote community development by mobilizing, educating, and empowering poor people to solve their own problems). For a while, thousands of idealistic U.S. citizens worked with Latin America's poor and promoted collective self-help programs. Others promoted popular participation and mass mobilization. The U.S. Agency for International Development (USAID) encouraged Central American governments to develop community action and improvement programs and cooperatives, many hundreds of which were started across the region. Ultimately both local and U.S.-sponsored mobilization caused a surge of democratic participation by ordinary Central Americans. Before long, however, a strong reaction set in. Disinclined to respond to the legitimate demands of the newly articulate poor, some Central American elites viewed this mobilization as a nuisance or a threat. They chided Peace Corps volunteers for associating with "Communists"—that is, the poor people in the community action organizations. Eventually, when the central governments, too, conveyed their displeasure to U.S. diplomats, the Nixon administration officially terminated Peace Corps involvement in community action. This graphically illustrates how keeping good relations with pro-U.S. regimes mattered more to Washington than promoting popular participation and democratization.

The Latin American Catholic Church promoted the most extensive mobilization in the hemisphere in the 1960s. Even in the 1950s, some important Church figures such as Dom Helder Câmara of Brazil had begun calling for social justice and an uplifting of the oppressed majority in what came to be called "liberation theology." By the end of that decade and the beginning of the next, they found a powerful ally in the Vatican as Pope John XXIII embarked on his pivotal *aggiornamento,* or updating, of the Catholic Church. Part of this process, as expressed by the Second Vatican Council, was the new focus on the problems of Latin America, by then the largest single segment of world Catholicism. This, in turn, stimulated Latin American Catholics to engage in an even deeper examination of the human problems of their region.

The high-water mark of such concern came at the Second General Conference of Latin American Bishops at Medellín, Colombia, in 1968. Focusing on poverty

GRASS-ROOTS MOBILIZATION. A protest march in San José, Costa Rica (photo by John Booth). Adult education in Nicaragua as depicted in a revolutionary mural (photo by Thomas Walker)

and exploitation in Latin America, the bishops used a form of structural analysis not unlike the "dependency" explanation we discussed in Chapter 2.[7] They argued that Catholic clergy should make a "preferential option for the poor," and to do so should promote Christian base communities (comunidades eclesiales de base—CEBs), or grassroots organizations, in which people of all classes would discuss the social problems of their community or country in light of the social gospel. In addition, natural community leaders or lay delegates of the word would be trained to preach the social gospel and act as community organizers.[8]

The Medellín bishops conference deeply affected Latin America, and especially Central America. No doubt to the astonishment of many conservative bishops who had perfunctorily signed the high-sounding Medellín declarations, thousands of priests and nuns—and even a few bishops—began implementing the ideas of the conference almost immediately. By the 1970s, extensive grassroots mobilization was taking place through newly created CEBs in the four countries of northern Central America. Tens of thousands of poor people were becoming aware of themselves as human beings made in the image of God and having rights to fair treatment, dignity, and justice from their governments and employers. Though the objectives and tactics of the CEBs were nonviolent, the elite-dominated governments of the region predictably viewed them as highly subversive. Again the label "Communist" was applied and, eventually, tens of thousands of Catholics, including dozens of priests and nuns and even one archbishop, died in the repression that was mounted to reverse their mobilizing effort.

By the mid- to late 1970s, social mobilization had become widespread throughout northern Central America. Peasants had joined unions and federations and created cooperative organizations concerned with production and marketing. Urban workers had expanded the labor movement. Teachers, medical personnel, students, and women had all become more organized and active. As we noted in Chapter 8, the Honduran regime chose to accommodate or only mildly repress mobilization. Such relative moderation is probably the major reason why Honduras avoided open insurrection. In Somoza's Nicaragua, Guatemala, and El Salvador, however, the more entrenched and powerful elites chose violent demobilization rather than accommodation to deal with new popular demands. In these three, state repression begot responding violence, as previously moderate citizens in increasing numbers opted for insurrection. In Nicaragua, mobilization, responding repression, and insurrection ultimately led to a revolutionary coalition victory in 1979. In Guatemala and El Salvador, in contrast, the scale and cruelty of state-sponsored terrorism (with especially heavy U.S. material support—see Appendix Table A.3) curtailed or reversed civilian mobilization and stalemated rebels on the battlefield.

The mobilization that had brought about the Nicaraguan revolution continued and was encouraged by the new government thereafter. Prior to the victory, Catholics from the Christian base movement had joined with nationalist Marxists from the FSLN and others to organize a variety of grassroots organizations. These included the Rural Workers' Association (Asociación de Trabajadores del Campo—ATC), the Sandinista Workers' Federation (Central Sandinista de Trabajadores—CST), the Association of Women Confronting the National Problem (Asociación de Mujeres Frente a la Problemática Nacional—AMPRONAC), the Civil Defense

Committees (Comités de Defensa Civil—CDCs), and the Sandinista Youth (La Juventad Sandinista).[9] After 1979 the CEB movement also continued and other grassroots organizations emerged, such as the National Union of [small] Farmers and Ranchers (Unión Nacional de Agricultores y Ganaderos—UNAG). By 1984, the U.S. Embassy in Managua estimated that between 700,000 and 800,000 Nicaraguan citizens—around half of all adults—were in such organizations.[10]

Grassroots organizations performed many functions—defending the revolution, political socialization, mobilizing volunteers to carry out social programs, and providing venues for political participation, which ordinary people had never experienced previously. The local organizations held internal elections, discussed local needs organized to solve them, petitioned their government for everything from material and financial support to major changes in government policy, and named representatives to the planning boards of government economic and social service entities.[11] Sometimes such organizations abused their power or engaged in petty corruption, but overall they gave many ordinary Nicaraguan citizens the first opportunity in their lives to participate meaningfully in politics.

In addition to the grassroots organizations, the Sandinista-led government used education to advance participation and democracy. Borrowing the techniques of Catholic educator Paulo Freire and using tens of thousands of volunteers, the revolutionary government undertook a basic literacy crusade its first year in power. The drive lowered rates of adult illiteracy and won Nicaragua the United Nations prize for the best literacy crusade of the year. Thereafter, continued attention was paid to maintaining and increasing literacy and generally improving the educational level of all Nicaraguans. In addition to building the skills of the workforce and socializing Nicaraguans to support the revolution, a central motive for the heavy emphasis on education was to "empower" the people—to create a citizenry capable of intelligent self-government.[12]

The Roots of U.S. Policy in Central America

At least until the end of the Cold War, the United States had certain legitimate, and widely consensual, security interests in Central America. Most agreed that it was in the interest of the United States that no Soviet bases, troops, advanced weapons, or nuclear arms be present in the isthmus, and that no country in the region form a military alliance with the Soviet Union. It was and remains in the interest of the United States that Central American societies enjoy sufficient prosperity, democracy, and political stability that their citizens not turn massively to exile or refuge. Similarly, Central American nations needed peace among themselves and their military forces to be appropriately sized and in balance with each other. An arms race or increased intraregional conflict might have caused a war in

Central America, sparked direct U.S. military intervention there, or threatened the security of the Panama Canal or important trade routes. However, many critics of U.S. policy in Central America believe that U.S. actions during the Cold War actually harmed rather than advanced these interests. In order to understand how this came about, we must review the roots of U.S. policy.

U.S. interests in Central America have evolved over time and have sometimes been subject to intense debate within the United States. During the nineteenth century, encouraging trade, coping with massive British naval power, and transit across the isthmus were important U.S. concerns. As U.S. sea power supplanted British dominance in the late nineteenth century and as the United States rapidly industrialized, the desire to establish and control a transisthmian canal led to U.S. intervention in Panama in 1903. Once canal construction and operation were under way, the United States used troops in Panama and Nicaragua to assure a continuing canal monopoly and protect the canal itself. U.S. diplomats (sometimes assisted by the marines) often heavy-handedly promoted U.S. business and geopolitical interests throughout Central America in the early twentieth century. During World War II, the United States sought to protect the Panama Canal from Axis interference through cooperative security arrangements with Central American governments.

During the Cold War, U.S. interests in Central America continued to focus upon economic and security concerns. The containment of Soviet-inspired communism was the major force driving U.S. policy. Despite the boom brought about by the Central American Common Market, U.S. investments in Central America remained modest compared to those in most other parts of the world. Nevertheless, promotion of a "healthy business climate" in Central America also heavily influenced U.S. policy choices.

Washington viewed the effervescent mobilization in Central America throughout the second half of the twentieth century as problematical. Although a cause for hope for millions of poor people and a true step toward democracy, mobilization worried some of Central America's entrenched elites. They viewed the process with alarm and responded with state terror to discourage participation. Hearkening to their cries of "Communist subversion," Washington, too, joined the fray. It is interesting to consider that the U.S. government—whose citizens tenaciously defend their own right to participate in civic and interest organizations—allied itself with the privileged minority in Central America in its campaign against participatory mobilization. U.S. policy in the region perhaps responded more to domestic political fears, misperceptions, and rhetoric in the United States and the fears of local elites than to the reality of the situation in the isthmus.

As a capitalist country, the United States made consistent efforts to promote capitalism and to protect U.S. business interests at home and abroad. Policymakers in the White House, State Department, and Congress tended to formulate national security—especially in Central America and the Caribbean—as much in terms of business interests and trade as along military and geostrategic lines. Radical and even merely reformist political doctrines, commonly (but often incorrectly) labeled "Communist" by local elites, were usually viewed as incompatible with U.S. interests. From the early twentieth century on, the impulse to contain this "threat of communism" motivated conservative politicians and cowed their critics. U.S. politicians feared being depicted by their adversaries as having "lost ground" to communism. After World War II, and especially with the Cuban revolution, the fear of Soviet-inspired communism in our backyard shaped U.S. policy in Central America. Thus even U.S. politicians and policymakers sympathetic to socioeconomic reform and democracy supported demobilization in Central America when reformers' demands were labeled "subversive" by Central American elites or by interested U.S. observers.[13]

Much of the U.S. preoccupation with communism in Central America, however, was tragically ill founded and largely inappropriate.[14] (We examine communism in Central America below). Ill advised or not, most U.S. administrations from the 1940s through the 1980s strongly believed that communism threatened, and they transmitted this concern to Latin American military establishments as part of the doctrine of national security. This doctrine, in turn, served to justify a systematic and widespread demobilization campaign in Central America.

As taught in war colleges and military training centers around the hemisphere, the doctrine of national security was a product both of U.S. anticommunism and Latin American elaboration. It originated in an elaborate national security apparatus (i.e., CIA, National Security Council) created in the United States in the late 1940s. In 1950, National Security Council document "NSC-68" described an expanding Communist menace and urged huge increases in military expenditures. Even though George Kennan, the originator of the concept of containment of communism, by then felt that the threat described in "NSC-68" was exaggerated, it nevertheless became the blueprint for U.S. behavior in the early Cold War. Its ideas spread to Latin America through U.S. training programs for virtually all of the military establishments of the hemisphere.

Latin America in the 1950s and 1960s provided fertile ground for these Cold War security concepts. Though local Communist parties were weak and there were few, if any, obvious external threats to the security of any of the elite-based governments, the privileged classes and their military allies found it convenient to portray popular mobilization and protest as subversive and part of a Moscow-controlled plot. In this setting, national security ideas from the United States were quickly adapted and refined into a full-fledged ideology, complete with training centers, native military philosophers, literature, and annual meetings of the Latin American Anti-Communist Confederation. The ideology was geopolitical, viewing national and international politics as a zero-sum game between communism and the "free world." Whether in foreign or domestic affairs, a loss of territory, allegiance, or influence for one side was seen as a gain for the other. Internal politics became a battlefield. Social, economic, and political justice became largely irrelevant or seen as a point of entry for threatening ideological influences.

The national security doctrine was also inherently elitist. Its believers held the military uniquely capable of understanding the national good and, therefore, having the right to run the state and make decisions for society as a whole if military leaders judged that civilian politicians were performing poorly. The doctrine directly equated democracy with a visceral anticommunism. Accordingly, strange as it may seem, the harshly authoritarian anticommunist "national security states" created under this ideology were often described by their apologists as "democratic."

All opposition to national security states—and most forms of civilian organization except those on the right—were viewed as subversive and "Communist" or "Communist-inspired." Brutal demobilization and atomization of civilian society were accepted as appropriate. U.S. personnel on occasion actively promoted the use by their Latin American colleagues of what they euphemistically called "counterterror" (the widespread use of extralegal arrest, torture, and murder designed to quiet so-called subversive groups).[15] Most Latin American militaries and police received technical and material assistance and training including techniques of counterterror. It is not surprising, therefore, that the tactics of torture, murder, and disappearance employed by security forces and government-sponsored death squads were similar from country to country.[16]

By the late 1960s and early 1970s, the USAID's benignly titled Office of Public Safety had close links to the security forces of Brazil, Uruguay, and Guatemala, countries with radical demobilization programs using death squads, torture, murder, and disappearance.[17] In the early 1970s these links became a public scandal in the United States and throughout the world. The U.S. Congress investigated the links between U.S. government programs and state-sponsored terror in Latin America. In 1974, Congress formally terminated U.S. police and internal security aid programs and ordered the U.S. Department of State to submit yearly reports on the human rights performance of all states to which the U.S. government supplied aid. But these measures did not solve the problem. In practice, State Department human rights reports seemed to be influenced and colored more by the status quo–oriented policy goals of Washington than by the objective reality of the countries supposedly being described.[18] And though some of the most objectionable U.S. links were discreetly terminated, state-sponsored terror and direct or indirect U.S. material aid to rights-violating regimes and forces continued. Starting in 1982, the Reagan administration began successfully petitioning an increasingly red-baited Congress to make exceptions to the 1974 prohibition against U.S. assistance to police and internal security forces for El Salvador, Guatemala, and Honduras.

Communism in Central America

Because so much U.S. policy turned on the question of communism in Central America, we must explore its meaning and influence. Most Central American insurgents and many of the area's intellectuals found Marxist and, in some cases, Leninist analysis useful in understanding the reality around them. Nevertheless, it is misleading to equate the intellectual acceptance of those analytical tools with a commitment to a Communist agenda or political subservience to the Soviet-oriented international Communist movement. Most Central Americans were too pragmatic and nationalistic to accept such control. Indeed, Soviet-oriented Communist parties fared poorly in Central America. Communists, socialists, and anarchists—many of them European exiles—influenced Central American intellectual life and labor movements in the early twentieth century. The Communists, followers of Karl Marx, received a boost over their leftist competitors because of the Soviet revolution in Russia. Although always targets of repression, Communists gained leadership roles in Central American labor movements in the 1930s. The Soviet alliance with the West during World War II gave the region's tiny Communist parties and their more successful unions a brief political opening in the early 1940s. Although repression of the left resumed in most countries after 1945, brief exceptions occurred in Costa Rica in the 1940s and Guatemala in the early 1950s, where Communist elements were junior partners with more conservative parties in government coalitions. Communist parties generally fared poorly because of the Soviet practice of limiting local parties' flexibility to pursue national solutions. The Stalin-Hitler pact of 1939 discredited Communists in Central America and elsewhere. Soviet insistence in later years that Latin American Communists seek accommodation with local dictators further tarnished their already poor image. Moscow so restrained local Communist parties that, in the 1960s, less patient advocates of sociopolitical reform resigned in disgust and emulated Castro's successful insurgency.

Throughout most of their histories, therefore, local nationalists—including most other Marxists—mistrusted the small, Moscow-oriented Communist parties of Central America. Most Central American revolutionaries and intellectuals remember that the Cuban Communist Party, in its determination to follow Soviet orders to peacefully coexist with Fulgencio Batista, opposed Fidel Castro until just before the rebel victory. Costa Ricans recall that their local Communist Party, the region's largest, backed the regime of strongman Rafael Calderón Guardia, who lost the 1948 civil war to anticommunist social democratic forces. Since then the Costa Rican Communists never won more than five of the 57 seats in the Legislative Assembly, and after the mid-1980s their influence faded almost to nil.

Nicaraguans remember that the Communist-led labor movement collaborated with the Somoza dictatorship in the 1940s. They recall that the founders of the FSLN broke away from the pro-Soviet Nicaraguan Socialist Party because the latter offered no solutions to Nicaragua's problems and that only just before the FSLN victory did the local Communists join the rebel cause. Even in El Salvador, local Communists joined the insurrectionary effort just shortly before the would-be "final offensive" of late 1980 and early 1981. In Nicaragua after the rebel victory, no Moscow-oriented Communist Party played more than a peripheral role in the new government. Furthermore, in the election of 1984, the three Communist parties, which had lambasted the FSLN for allegedly selling out the revolution, garnered only 3.8 percent of the total vote.[19] After 1984, Nicaragua's traditional Communists remained in opposition to the FSLN.

In summary, during the Cold War traditional Central American Communist parties exercised their greatest influence on labor movements and in brief periods of limited participation in rule in Costa Rica and Guatemala. However, at their strongest they remained weak, unpopular, opposed to revolution and subservient to Moscow.

Central America's Marxist revolutionary movements were more complex than the region's traditional Communist parties. Most of the principal leaders of Nicaragua's FSLN, El Salvador's FMLN, and Guatemala's URNG were Marxist-Leninists. They shared socialism's predilection for distributive justice as an answer for their unjust societies. Their revolutionary strategy followed Castro's in Cuba—guerrilla warfare against regime and armed forces supplemented by tactical alliances with other social and political forces. Marxist-Leninist rebels, as we noted earlier, gained popular support and power largely because of the repressiveness of the regimes of Nicaragua, El Salvador, and Guatemala. In Nicaragua, the Sandinistas built their support base and broad coalition as the most viable alternative for those brutally repressed by the Somoza regime. Intense repression blocked moderate, centrist options for reform and redress of grievances in El Salvador and Guatemala, which drove many into Marxist-led guerrilla movements.

Marxist-Leninist rebels regarded Cuba as a friend and ally and received some Cuban aid in their struggles. Soviet and Eastern bloc assistance to insurgents was limited, in keeping with Moscow's skepticism about their chances for success. Once the Sandinistas won power in Nicaragua, however, their links to the Soviet bloc became overtly friendly and Moscow became more cooperative. After the West refused Nicaraguan military assistance in 1980 and anticipating increased U.S. hostility, the Sandinistas turned to Cuban and Soviet arms and advice for reorganizing their security forces.[20] As U.S. antagonism mounted in the early and mid-1980s, Nicaragua rapidly strengthened its links to the Eastern bloc to counter an expected invasion, fend off the Contras, and replace embargoed Western aid, trade, and credit.[21]

Despite such links, the Sandinistas remained pragmatic in most policies. Instead of imposing Soviet-style Stalinist centralism and one-party political monopoly of the revolution (as Castro did in Cuba), they remained committed to a mixed economy and political pluralism. Although the Sandinistas never tried to hide that they found parts of Marxist and Leninist analysis useful, their social, economic, and political policies revealed them to be pragmatic and nationalists rather than orthodox Communists.

Nicaragua's critics made much of the Sandinista government's friendly relationship with the socialist bloc, but that link should be put in perspective. Nicaragua increased not only its ties to the Eastern bloc but also ties with many non-Communist regimes. Nicaragua increased trade, aid, and diplomatic relations with governments as disparate as those of Brazil, Canada, Chile, France, Libya, the People's Republic of China, the Scandinavian countries, and Spain. While Nicaragua frequently voted with the USSR in the United Nations, it sometimes abstained (e.g., on votes on Afghanistan and the Korean Airlines shootdown) or voted against the USSR on important UN issues (e.g., the matter of sending a peacekeeping force to Lebanon). Nicaragua's UN voting record from 1979 through 1985 revealed that, although Nicaragua often voted against U.S. positions and with positions backed by the USSR, it agreed almost as often with most Latin American countries, especially with Mexico.[22] Although Nicaragua eventually relied almost exclusively on the socialist bloc for military supplies, the Sandinistas had first asked the United States to help standardize its military equipment. In spite of the Pentagon's endorsement of that Nicaraguan proposal, the Carter administration—facing a conservative, Cold War opponent in the 1980 election campaign—chose the politically safe option of rejecting that request.[23]

Like the Sandinistas, other Central American insurgents appeared to be Marxist-Leninists with respect to revolutionary strategy, but pragmatic and nationalistic in concrete policy matters. They recognized that U.S. influence in the isthmus would probably doom any purely Communist regime or government, especially one that allowed Soviet troops or missiles within its borders. Moreover, evidence of the failure of Stalinist political and economic centralism abounded throughout the socialist world in the 1980s. To assume that the Sandinistas or Central America's other Marxist rebels would ape failed systems was unrealistic.

Thus, though the United States had been intensely worried about communism in Central America for four decades, its concerns appear overblown. Communist parties were weak. Marxist-Leninist guerrillas had not prospered in Honduras and Costa Rica, where regimes were not excessively repressive. The excessive U.S. concern about communism produced misguided, counterproductive policies—the ugliest of which was to assist repressive regimes in their campaigns of demobilization.

Demobilization in Central America

Despite some death-squad activity in Honduras in the early 1980s, systematic mass demobilization programs occurred largely where traditional elites were the most powerful and entrenched—Guatemala, El Salvador, and Nicaragua under the Somozas. In Guatemala and El Salvador, demobilization took the form of state-sponsored terror. In Nicaragua it came as state-sponsored terror prior to the Sandinista victory of 1979, and U.S.-sponsored Contra terror from 1981 onward. Whatever the form, the objective remained constant—to atomize and make docile the ordinary citizenry of Central America. This would facilitate rule by traditional, conservative, pro-U.S. elites or, where necessary, their replacement with friendly, if ineffective, reform-oriented moderates.

Demobilization—or at least the U.S. link to it—lasted longest and was most brutal in Guatemala.[24] It commenced with the U.S.-sponsored overthrow of elected reformist President Jacobo Arbenz in 1954. Scant hours after Carlos Castillo Armas was imposed as president, a mysterious Committee Against Communism—comprised of CIA personnel—seized Guatemalan government, political party, and labor and peasant union documents and began compiling what would soon become known as the Black List. Before the year was out, the names of an estimated 70,000 individuals connected with the former government or with grassroots or political organizations from that era were included on that list of suspected Communists. That August, the Castillo Armas government issued a Law Against Communism, which declared, among other things, that anyone included on the "register," as it was formally called, was thenceforth banned from public employment and subject to indefinite imprisonment without trial.

Though this register ultimately became a death list, this took some time because the Arévalo and Arbenz governments had partially succeeded in training the Guatemalan security forces to respect human rights. However, in the ensuing decade the U.S. government became increasingly involved in Guatemalan affairs, blocking a return to democracy in the early 1960s and providing ever-escalating doses of security assistance, advice, and training. Meanwhile, previously nonviolent politicians, frustrated by the closing of the democratic option, turned to open rebellion. By the late 1960s, the insurgents and the opposition in general were labeled "terrorists" and a program of state-sponsored "counterterror," was begun. Featuring the torture, murder, and disappearance of thousands of suspected

Communist subversives, this demobilization program was carried out both directly by uniformed security forces or indirectly by government-sanctioned death squads.

By the early 1970s, the rural areas had been "pacified." Terror now moved to the cities as General Carlos Arana Osorio, former coordinator of the rural pacification effort and now president, began eliminating alleged "subversives" (e.g., party leaders, intellectuals, media persons, and labor organizers) among the urban population. The mid-1970s brought a period of eerie calm. But soon, as corrupt military officers began taking over traditional indigenous lands and peaceful protests were met with violence, the whole cycle began again. Many indigenous people came to support reemerging guerrilla groups, and the regime responded with more terror in rural areas, particularly in the early 1980s.

From 1977 through the mid-1980s, the United States formally cut off military aid to the Guatemalan regime because of human rights abuses. However the significance of that fact is more apparent than real (Appendix Table A.3). U.S. military training continued, and under the Reagan administration, some U.S. material aid to the Guatemalan military, previously banned, was relabeled nonmilitary and resumed. What is more, Israel—the biggest recipient of U.S. aid in the world—took up much of the slack as a supplier of military equipment and training to the Guatemalans during this period.[25]

The demobilization campaign of the late 1970s failed to eradicate leftist rebels, and the growth of corruption in the regime and deepening economic difficulties led to the 1982 coup and a reformist military government. Its first leader, General Ríos Montt, sharply increased violent demobilization, but the economy eroded further and some of the military's allies distanced themselves from the regime. Military leaders then ousted Ríos Montt, replaced him with General Mejía Victores, and decided to return nominal control of the executive and legislative branches to civilians. Washington approved the armed forces' plan to formally transfer power to civilians and supported the election of 1985 and resulting civilian transitional regime. The Reagan administration, frustrated by the Congress's refusal to authorize funds for direct military aid to Guatemala's unsavory military regimes, viewed switching to an elected civilian president, Vinicio Cerezo, as a useful cosmetic change that would make it easier for Washington to provide military and economic assistance to Guatemala.

For two presidential terms, the civilian transitional government in Guatemala slowly progressed toward controlling the armed forces, ending the civil war, and reducing the demobilization campaign. Before taking office, moderate Cerezo had to promise not to prosecute military personnel for human rights violations. Although rights abuses continued, no prosecutions occurred, and Cerezo refused to allow the International Red Cross to open a Guatemalan office. Powerful economic groups blocked proposed socioeconomic reforms, and some business interests conspired unsuccessfully with rightist military radicals to overthrow the regime. Elected in 1990, Conservative President Jorge Serrano Elías made little progress on social problems, human rights abuses by the military, or peace talks with the rebels. Serrano then attempted the disastrous self-coup of 1993 and was ousted from office by Congress and the judiciary. The resolution of this constitutional crisis strengthened the hands of those seeking peace and deeper democracy in Guatemala. Serrano's replacement, Ramiro de León Carpio, advanced the peace talks. Elected in 1995, de León's successor, Alvaro Arzú, completed peace negotiations, began curbing the military, and instituted a more inclusive, formal civilian democratic regime.

El Salvador, too, suffered a process of demobilization in the 1970s and 1980s in which the United States played a major role. Admittedly, demobilization was nothing new to that country. The military, acting on behalf of the elite, perpetrated tremendous violence against poor people in the early 1930s when the world depression had set off local mass-based reform pressure. The resulting "slaughter" *(la matanza)* took the lives of around 30,000 people. But the violence of the late twentieth century achieved new levels of carnage that were estimated as of 1988 as at least 70,000 dead and 500,000 displaced.[26]

The demobilization campaign was a response to the unusual burst of mobilization of the early to mid-1970s. At first demobilization by the regimes of Arturo Molina and Humberto Romero occurred at moderate but well-publicized levels. International criticism, however, led the Carter administration to suspend most U.S. military assistance. However, when Somoza was overthrown by revolutionaries in Nicaragua, alarm swept Washington, and a quick decision was made to resume military aid to El Salvador lest it be the next country to "fall." Such an apparent policy reversal could be sold to the U.S. Congress only if a civilian-military, reformist government were to come to power. Washington viewed the most acceptable civilians as the Christian Democrats.[27] Reformist elements in the armed forces, private sector, and opposition parties that shared Washington's desire to block a revolutionary outcome began plotting against General Romero.

The coup d'état took place on October 15, 1979. The civilians on the first junta and in the government were Social Democrats, Christian Democrats, and unaffiliated moderates, but the junta changed rapidly. Conservative interests blocked the reformists, and human rights abuses by the military actually increased. Within three months the first civilians resigned from the junta in protest. The junta replaced those who resigned with individuals from the conservative wing of the Christian democratic movement and military hard-liners from within the military replaced moderate officers.

U.S. military aid to El Salvador resumed after the coup. Despite fanfare about moderation and reform, torture, murder, and disappearances soared far above levels under the previous military governments.[28] In February 1980, U.S. Chargé d'Affaires James Cheek met with Christian Democrats in the government and urged that El Salvador institute what he called "a clean counter-insurgency war" that would give the armed forces greater leeway against suspected subversives. Though some Christian Democrats resisted, Cheek's suggestions were implemented in March through Decree 155, which imposed a state of siege and gave the military draconian powers to deal with civilians.[29] Throughout the rest of the Carter administration and for several years into the Reagan period, security forces systematically dismantled grassroots party and interest organizations and largely disregarded human rights. U.S. officials publicly blamed the tens of thousands of killings first on "violence of the right and the left" and later on "right-wing death squads." The government and even the military were falsely depicted in the United States as composed of moderates earnestly trying to control violence.

Congress eventually pressured El Salvador and the White House to reduce the shocking level of human rights abuse in El Salvador. In 1982 and 1983, with congressional approval for further military aid hanging in the balance, the Reagan administration sent emissaries to San Salvador to pressure the Salvadoran government and military to curtail the killings.[30] As a result, for the next several years—though the aerial bombardment of civilian populations in rebel-controlled areas actually escalated—the so-called death-squad killings declined. But by then, the demobilization had largely succeeded. The leaders and many members of most grassroots party and interest organizations to the left of the conservative Christian Democrats had been killed, driven underground, or forced into exile. The two opposition newspapers had been terrorized into extinction. And the Catholic Church, having suffered the martyrdom of Archbishop Romero and numerous clergy and lay activists, had been cowed into a much less critical posture.

News of the reformist military's bloody record in the early 1980s made continued U.S. economic and military aid from the U.S. Congress progressively less certain. President Reagan then pressured El Salvador to move toward an elected, constitutional government. The junta called an election in 1982 for a constituent assembly to draft a new constitution. With terror at its apogee, parties of the extreme right won a majority of seats in the Constituent Assembly. U.S. pressure brought a slackening in the violence, and Washington essentially forced the right-dominated Constituent Assembly to appoint a moderate figurehead, Alvaro Magaña, as interim president. In 1984, with terror somewhat curtailed, Salvadorans cast their presidential vote for the U.S.-funded and endorsed center-right Christian Democratic candidate, José Napoleón Duarte, a popular reformist ex-mayor of San Salvador. This ushered in a civilian transitional regime, but one that for years had limited power over public policy. Duarte's ability to rule and promote reforms was hamstrung by the constitution written by the rightist-dominated Constituent Assembly and by the overweening power of the armed forces.

By the time of the 1988 legislative elections, President Duarte was dying of cancer and his administration had proven itself corrupt. After the Esquipulas peace accord in August 1987, death squad terror again escalated as the Salvadoran right attempted to sabotage its implementation. Not surprisingly, voters in the 1988 and 1991 legislative and 1989 presidential elections abandoned the Christian Democrats and moved sharply to the right.

Nicaragua suffered demobilization both before and after the revolutionary victory of 1979. The Somoza regime conducted one wave from 1975 through July 1979. U.S.-backed Contras carried out the second wave from 1981 through mid-1990. Together, these campaigns took nearly 81,000 lives; around 50,000 in the earlier period and almost 31,000 in the latter. Though some of the deaths counted here were those of combatants, most were civilians.

The barbarity of the Somoza regime's efforts to pacify Nicaragua and perpetuate itself in power is well documented.[31] Worth mentioning, however, is the close relationship that existed between the U.S. government and Somoza's National Guard. In 1979 Somoza's guard had more U.S.-trained personnel than any other military establishment in Latin America, not just proportionally, but absolutely.[32] More Nicaraguan officers and soldiers had been trained by the United States than was true of the military of any other Latin American country, including a comparative giant like Brazil, with almost 40 times Nicaragua's population. U.S. military aid and the training of Nicaraguan military personnel ceased fully only after Guard massacres of civilians in several cities in September 1978. As in Guatemala, Israel immediately picked up the slack by supplying the Guard with automatic weapons and other equipment. U.S. military attachés remained in Nicaragua until months before Somoza fell, and helped spirit many of Somoza's officer corps into exile after the rebel victory.

The Reagan administration chose the Contras as its instrument to demobilize Nicaragua under the revolution. This counterrevolutionary force of remnants of the National Guard, first organized by agents of the Argentine military soon after the Sandinista victory, received a big infusion of funds when President Reagan signed National Security Decision Directive Number 17 in November 1981. Although young people who had never served in Somoza's National Guard eventually came to constitute the majority of the lower ranks, Contra officers were mostly ex-Guardia officers.[33] The United States manipulated and funded the Contras from the early 1980s on. Revolutionary agrarian policies and military recruitment alienated enough peasants to turn the Contras into a strong social movement. This deeply worried the revolutionary government and armed forces.[34]

The demobilization tactics employed by the counterrevolutionaries and their U.S. backers shifted over time. At first some in the CIA clearly believed that the Contras could serve as authentic and ultimately successful guerrillas. However, when the Contras in their first two years employed crude terrorist tactics, the CIA commissioned its famous manual for Contra officers, *Psychological Operations in*

SOCIOPOLITICAL DEMOBILIZATION. Scene at a Somoza National Guard body dump on the outskirts of Managua in the summer of 1979 (photo courtesy of *Barricada*)

Guerrilla Warfare.[35] Although criticized in the United States for its instructions on the selective assassination of government officials and for its cold-blooded ideas on the hiring of professional gunmen to create martyrs from among the opposition at antigovernment rallies, the overall thrust of the document is relatively moderate. The manual sought to teach the Contras to focus their terror narrowly and intelligently. Though selective assassination was advocated, the Contras should not terrorize the population and should behave respectfully enough to win a civilian base that might eventually help them isolate and defeat the Sandinistas.

Some Contra units apparently followed the tactically sound CIA advice. Pockets of civilian support developed in remote, lightly populated central departments of Boaco and Chontales and in the north. But the Contras mostly failed to achieve such discipline and behaved brutally.[36] This, coupled with their widespread image in Nicaragua as U.S. mercenaries and direct descendants of Somoza's hated Guardia Nacional, meant that, by the mid-1980s it was clear to most informed observers that the Contras could never rally enough popular support to overthrow their government.

Although the Contras grew in numbers in the mid-1980s as they recruited increasingly disgruntled peasants, their military accomplishments remained limited. The Contras forced the Sandinista army to improvise its own counterinsurgency strategy, which prevented the rebels from taking or holding territory. The military buildup, however, eventually disrupted the economy and undermined support for the government. As CIA awareness of the Contras' limitations grew, Contra tactics changed to employ terror and sabotage to disrupt the economy, government, and society. Terror and sabotage became the principal and most effective instruments of demobilization. Contra units attacked rural social service infrastructure such as schools, health clinics, day care centers, and food program storage facilities; economic infrastructure such as cooperative or state farms, bridges, power lines; cooperative or grassroots organizations; and persons connected to those three. Among the nearly 31,000 Nicaraguans killed in the Contra war were 130 teachers, 40 medical personnel, and 152 technicians.[37] The Contras planted antitank mines on rural roads, killing and mutilating hundreds. This tactic was aimed at undermining the rural economy and alienating people from the government while forcing heavy defense spending that would undermine social services, cause inflation, and seed urban popular discontent.

The Contra terror campaign of the late 1980s bore fruit. Social services were curtailed, or eliminated in some remote areas. Agricultural output declined, the economy went sour, and inflation went through the roof. Membership in grassroots organizations, which had climbed through 1984, stagnated in 1985 and 1986, and then declined in 1987–1988 as economic dissatisfaction rose and making ends meet became ever harder. Opposition protests and union resistance to austerity programs grew in 1986–1987, and the government began to repress its opponents and curtail civil liberties.

By the February 1990 national elections, the U.S.-sponsored program of demobilization had so undercut the Sandinistas' legitimacy and intimidated the populace that the victory of the U.S.-endorsed candidate, Violeta Barrios de Chamorro, was all but inevitable. No doubt a plurality of those who voted for Chamorro had opposed the revolution all along; even in the comparatively good times of 1984, the opposition had received nearly one-third of the vote. But another segment of the Chamorro voters consisted of citizens who quit supporting the Sandinistas as they watched government programs deteriorate and the economy collapse in the late 1980s. Finally, another segment consisted of people who, although they favored the revolution, were simply unwilling to face the punishment the United States had signaled would continue should the FSLN win. Typical of this group was a generally pro-Sandinista woman who, on the day following the election, was berated by an army veteran for having betrayed the Fatherland in voting for UNO. She was the mother of two draft-age boys, and she responded indignantly that she was not going to sacrifice her boys "for the fucking Fatherland!"[38] The latter two blocs of votes, which very likely provided the winning margin for UNO, appear to have been a product of U.S. policy.

U.S. Policy in the Post–Cold War Period

The end of the Cold War at the beginning of the 1990s brought a dramatic shift in U.S. foreign policy. Since the Soviet Union and the socialist bloc no longer existed as a perceived threat to U.S. interests, Washington could begin responding to Central American reality on its own terms. Accordingly, the United States immediately reversed its policy toward the civil wars in El Salvador and Guatemala. U.N.-backed efforts at achieving negotiated settlements between guerrilla forces and the governments of those countries—long opposed by the United States—were now enthusiastically endorsed. In Nicaragua, though Cold War policy lingered a bit longer, President Clinton eventually appointed a new U.S. ambassador, John Maisto, who quickly observed that it was time for the United States to leave the "hangups of the Cold War" behind and treat all civilian forces in that country—including the Sandinistas—as legitimate.[39]

The post–Cold War shift in U.S. policy toward the region greatly facilitated the achievement of negotiated peace settlements in El Salvador (1992) and Guatemala (1996) and the various intra-elite accords on modifying the rules of the political game that took place in Nicaragua in the mid-1990s. This not only bolstered prospects for the consolidation of civilian democratic regimes in all three war-ravaged countries but actually helped bring them about in the first place in the two late comers, El Salvador and Guatemala. In 1994, the Summit of the Americas set a new agenda for hemispheric relations by focusing on such issues as the genuine promotion of democracy, sustainable development, and regional trade. The Clinton administration embraced a policy of engagement rather than interference, even apologizing for the U.S. role in the Guatemalan civil war. But this less interventionist and more cooperative approach ended abruptly under the administration of George W. Bush. The rehabilitation of several Cold War–era ideologues instrumental in Reagan administration policies in Central America signaled a regression in policy.[40] Rather than emphasizing the promotion and support of democracy in Central America, the new Bush administration subverted it by interfering and manipulating elections in Nicaragua (2001) and El Salvador (2004).

Other aspects of U.S. policy, however, had not changed—principal among them, the promotion of a strongly capitalist economic model. Using heavily U.S.-influenced international lending agencies—the International Monetary Fund, the World Bank, the Inter-American Development Bank—to wield both carrot and stick, Washington insisted on harsh "structural adjustment" policies, which, though they resulted in overall growth, also tended to concentrate income and hurt the poor majority. By the late 1990s, the dynamic contradictions between income-concentrating neoliberalism and the consolidation of civilian democracy—both promoted by the United States—were coming to the fore.

The necessity to secure the U.S. economic agenda in the region resulted in the support of "low-intensity democracy," which emphasizes the election of "favorable" candidates over the democratic process. Using economic and diplomatic intimidation, the Bush administration sought to affect electoral outcomes in Nicaragua, El Salvador, and, to a lesser extent, Guatemala, by recasting the Latin American left (formerly labeled "Communists") as "terrorists." This is what Robinson calls the "promotion of polyarchy" in U.S. policy, which is intended to make the region "safe" and "available" for capital.[41] The result is a form of democracy that is defined by electoral competition among elites, the neutralization or demobilization of mass movements, and the subordination of politics to global capital. With few exceptions, these policies have benefited local elites and global capital rather than the average citizen.

One key element of the U.S. economic agenda in the region was the creation of a free trade zone. In 1989 the first Bush administration launched the idea of a hemispheric free trade area. In 1994 the North American Free Trade Agreement (NAFTA) became the first of what was hoped to be a series of free trade agreements throughout the Americas. Discussions for a free trade zone between the second Bush administration and the five Central American countries began in 2001. In early 2002 the Bush administration announced negotiations for a Central

American Free Trade Agreement (CAFTA), which would take the place of the Caribbean Basin Initiative (CBI).[42]

CAFTA would give the U.S. increased access to the Central American market by reducing tariff barriers and removing investment barriers.[43] The removal of investment barriers would allow U.S. companies to compete for the provision of public services, part of the IDB's prescription for reforming the public sector.[44] This topic was a major sticking point in the negotiations between the United States and Costa Rica, specifically over its telecommunications and insurance sectors. While the other Central American countries had zealously pursued privatization policies from the late 1990s onward, Costa Rica, responding to domestic pressure, had not privatized any of its state-owned industries since 1995. After protests and a strike by public employees, Costa Rica withdrew for a while from CAFTA talks over U.S. insistence that it open these sectors. However, the Costa Rican government ultimately said it would consider such policies. Like NAFTA, the agreement also would further reduce state autonomy by allowing U.S. corporations to sue their host countries over "unfair" regulations.[45] There was also some disagreement over protection for key commodities, particularly U.S. sugar and textile subsidies which could result in dumping (selling excess commodities at below market prices in order to suppress real market prices, a violation of international trade norms), and intellectual property rights as they pertained to access to generic drugs.[46] The agreement was signed by the five Central American countries and U.S. in May 2004, but as of this writing still required ratification from each of the signatories' legislatures.[47]

By the 1990s, whereas coffee and bananas were once the foundations of Central American economies, migrants to the United States had become the new monocrop. Remittances (money sent home by workers abroad) had become a vital part of the Central American economies.[48] In 2001 Central Americans sent home US$3.6 billion in remittances, more than foreign direct investment or official development aid.[49] By 2002 remittances, which grew steadily throughout the 1990s, accounted for 30 percent of Nicaragua's GDP, 15 percent in El Salvador, and 12 percent in Honduras.[50] Remittances added from 11 to 35 percent to the available income in all but Costa Rica.[51] Remittances, also referred to as "migradollars," have mitigated some of the costs associated with neoliberal policies by providing "income" to both the urban and rural poor.

These remittances were made possible, of course, by the steady migration flow from Central America to the United States. Salvadoran presence in the United States was so significant that Salvadorans commonly referred to the United States as "Department 15" (the country is formally divided into 14 departments). Hundreds of thousands of Central Americans (mostly Salvadoran) were in the United States on temporary protected status (TPS), having fled civil wars (El Salvador, Guatemala, Nicaragua) or natural disasters (Honduras and Nicaragua after Mitch,

El Salvador after the 2001 earthquakes).[52] Should TPS end when the current extensions were to expire in 2006, migrants would be forced to return to their home countries, and the economic impact would be devastating. Not surprisingly, newly elected presidents Maduro and Saca—like various of their predecessors—made visits to the United States shortly after their inaugurations seeking the renewal of TPS for their populations. President Saca visited the United States again after the extension was announced, visiting Salvadoran communities and urging them to re-register as part of a TPS education and registration campaign by the Salvadoran embassy.[53]

Remittances and TPS provided a means for U.S. manipulation of El Salvador's 2004 presidential elections.[54] ARENA's campaign claimed that an FMLN victory would have a significant impact on remittances from Salvadorans living in the United States, which exceeded US$2 billion in 2002. This idea was reinforced by comments from three U.S. Congressmen five days before the election to the effect that an FMLN victory should lead to a review of the TPS of Salvadorans and a restriction on remittances.[55] The unequivocal message was that an FMLN victory would threaten remittances.

The dependence on the renewal of TPS, as well as a continued reliance on U.S. economic assistance, led some Central American countries to provide military support to the U.S. "war on terror," in particular to the war in Iraq. In 2003 El Salvador, Nicaragua, and Honduras (the three Central American countries that enjoyed Temporary Protected Status for their populations in the U.S.) joined the U.S. war by sending troops to Iraq. Guatemala's President Berger initially pledged to commit troops, but quickly rescinded the offer in the face of widespread opposition to the plan. Even Costa Rica (with no formal army) joined the "coalition of the willing" by declaring its support for the war. However, Costa Rica's courts later forced withdrawal of even this symbolic support because it violated the nation's statutory posture of international neutrality. By early 2004, only El Salvador remained in Iraq.[56]

In the Latin American context, the U.S. "war on drugs" became intertwined with the "war on terror." That was easy because the Revolutionary Armed Force of Colombia (Fuerza Armada Revolucionaria de Colombia—FARC) was known to tax production of all goods produced within its area of control. But FARC's involvement, though it was less active in the narcotics trade than Colombia's rightist paramilitary forces, allowed the United States to label it (and by extension guerrillas and former guerrillas elsewhere) as "narcoterrorist." Central America was an important route for the transshipment of cocaine, and the U.S. enlisted the aid of regional governments in its counter-narcotics policies. The result of the growing U.S. effort to contain narcotics transshipments was a partial remilitarization of the isthmus in the form of increased U.S. military aid.[57] In 2000 the U.S. established its own anti-narcotics military base, or Forward Operating Location (FOL), in El

Salvador.[58] Additionally, there were a number of U.S. DEA operations in the region that focused on intelligence, training, and interdiction. Under Operation Central Skies, the United States provided army helicopters, police and security training, logistics support, and personnel to local security forces in Costa Rica, El Salvador, Guatemala, and Honduras. Increasing political and economic pressure was applied to Central American states to cooperate in the U.S. "war on drugs," going so far as to "decertify" Guatemala (a U.S. declaration of that country's noncooperation and withholding of certain assistance) following a dramatic decline in narcotics seizures there.

Added to all this, Central America's recent problem with gangs was another curiously transnational phenomenon. The gang culture pervading most of the Central American countries was imported by repatriated Central Americans who had lived in U.S. inner cities. This new gang activity greatly aggravated Central America's crime wave, particularly in El Salvador, Guatemala, and Honduras. Gangs were responsible for countless murders (many of them quite brutal), kidnappings, and robberies and engaged in drug trafficking and human smuggling. In response El Salvador, Guatemala, and Honduras passed controversial anti-gang laws, and in 2004 all but Costa Rica signed an agreement to coordinate anti-gang measures and share arrest warrants. The U.S. "war on terror" coincided nicely with the Central American "war on gangs." Indeed, a *Washington Times* story claimed that an al-Qaeda leader met with leaders of Mara Salvatrucha in Honduras.[59] While officials from Central American countries later disputed the story, there was little doubt that some recognized the opportunity to militarize the war on gangs under the guise of the war on terror.[60] Both Guatemala and Honduras sent military forces into the street to battle gangs, endangering the recently developed balance between new civilian police forces and the old style of military-dominated internal security.

Conclusions

U.S. policy in Central America during the Cold War was not only destructive and ill advised but, more importantly, counterproductive to the interests of both the United States and those of the peoples of the isthmus. Responding more to domestic political pressures in the United States and to outmoded conceptions of security and economic interests than to the concrete reality of Central America, it jousted with a vastly overblown threat of communism for more than four decades. As a result, the United States sided with a tiny exploitative elite in demobilizing strategies that took the lives of over 300,000 people. Furthermore, U.S. policy did violence to both the concept and the practice of democracy in the region. Power and democracy go hand in hand. As long as U.S.-advised military forces used counterterror to quiet and exclude from the political arena a wide spectrum of civil society, the transition to civilian democratic regime types was made impossible.

The end of the Cold War facilitated peace and democracy in the region. The U.S. imperative shifted from fighting communism to promoting the so-called Washington Consensus and democratization. While there was support for democratic transitions in the 1990s, evidence clearly demonstrates Washington's preference for "low-intensity democracy." The emerging war on the terrorism-drug-gang nexus created a climate of insecurity that further endangered the region's democracies, all in an attempt to make the region safe for investment. Such policy threatened to create externally oriented democracies, which serve the needs of the U.S. policymakers and international capital rather than those of the Central American people.

11

Reflections and Projections

We should now reflect on some of the patterns that have emerged from our examination of Central America over the last four decades and project or speculate about the region's possible future. Keep in mind that decades of involvement with the subject have taught us that it is far easier to sum up than to predict. We freely admit that our individual and joint writings—like those of most other observers over the years—are strewn with faulty predictions.

Reflections: Repression, Mobilization, and Democratic Transition

The Crises

As we have noted previously, the crises in Central America in the latter half of the twentieth century arose from several factors: (1) centuries of socioeconomic formation; (2) rapid economic growth in the 1960s followed by a sharp economic crisis in the mid-1970s; (3) elite and government intransigence in the face of mobilization driven by the economic crisis; and (4) international Cold War politics—notably the behavior of the United States. We disagree with the Kissinger Commission report of 1984, which argued that the violent upheavals of the 1970s and 1980s occurred mainly because of Soviet bloc/Cuban meddling in "our backyard."[1]

Clearly the crises of the twentieth century can, in part, be traced to the early social and economic formation of what are now the five major Central American countries. In the colonial period, Guatemala, El Salvador, and Nicaragua developed relatively strong, largely Hispanic ruling classes, which exploited the majority nonwhite, largely indigenous masses to produce primary export products. Inequality and repression were established from the start, and elite factionalism became intense by the end of the colonial era and in early independence. Thus both the political and economic pressures encouraged violent, military-dominated polities. In the other two countries, less exploitative systems developed, but for different reasons. In Costa Rica, where native peoples had either been killed or driven out of the central highlands, there was practically no racially distinct underclass to exploit. Moreover, divisions among elites were minor. So civilian rather than military government became the norm for long periods, and military rule when it occurred was an aberration. Honduras, on the other hand, the poorest part of the region, never really developed the powerful, self-confident, and exploitative elite minority seen in its three immediate neighbors.

These differing social formations meant that, in the twentieth century, the governing elites of these five countries essentially became conditioned to respond differently to local sociopolitical crises. Honduran and Costa Rican elites responded with relative moderation and accommodation whereas those of Guatemala, El Salvador, and Nicaragua exhibited intransigence and employed violent repression. Where accommodation or even mere cooptation—as was frequently the case in Honduras—prevailed, social peace was preserved. Where intransigence and repression ruled the day, insurgent forces emerged, gained legitimacy, and either toppled the government (Nicaragua) or held government forces at bay for years in protracted civil wars (Guatemala and El Salvador).

At this juncture external interference actually exacerbated a problem it was intended to solve. Seized by inflated Cold War fears of Soviet penetration into Central America, the United States misinterpreted mobilizing popular demands for social justice and democracy. Listening almost exclusively to the voices of an intransigent local elite and a foreign policy establishment deeply suspicious of the left, Washington rallied to the trumpets of anticommunism. Thus, in the 1950s—at the height of McCarthyism at home—the CIA helped overthrow Guatemala's first experiment in socially progressive democracy. The United States then beefed up the military and police establishments of all four of the local dictatorships and began to train local militaries to implement repression and counterinsurgency. This began in Guatemala and Nicaragua in the 1960s, in El Salvador in the 1970s, and in Honduras in the 1980s. In the face of such increasingly violent intransigence, and with democratic avenues of redress closed, guerrilla movements formed and expanded—first in Guatemala and Nicaragua, then in El Salvador, and still later in Honduras. We believe that, had local dictatorships been less protected by U.S. arms, less encouraged by U.S. support, and more constructively responsive to the demands of mobilized civil society and the needs of the suffering majority, accommodation might have taken place and thus obviated the conversion of opposition and mobilized demand making into insurrectionary movements.

Central America's Unique Patterns of Transition

Central America is a remarkable laboratory for the study of democratic transition in that it presents several types of regime change. Of the five countries, Honduras—with its fragile state and weak elite—historically oscillated between military and civilian rule. Under pressure by the Carter administration to become more democratic and with top military officers keenly aware of both the Nicaraguan revolution next door and the growing institutional cost to the military of remaining in power, Honduras moved quickly from military authoritarian through reformist military to, nominally, transitional civilian democratic regimes in the early 1980s. This occurred just as the Reagan administration chose Honduras as a staging ground for attacks on the Nicaraguan revolution and Salvadoran insurgency. Ironically, for a few years in the early 1980s repression perpetrated by certain military units escalated dramatically while the elected government took a back seat to the U.S.-supported military. But such extremism was out of character and by the mid-1980s the military had brought its own excesses somewhat under control. The early and tentative years of the transitional civilian democratic regime in the 1980s gave way to full civilian democracy with greater civilian control of the military and armed forces reform by 1996.

Costa Rica, in contrast, experienced its democratic transition mainly during the first half of the twentieth century, a process that drew upon several factors: inauguration of extensive education in the late nineteenth century; expansion of working-class organizations and other civil society that gained considerable momentum during the 1930s; a tradition of civilian rule and elections—albeit elitist and often fraudulently manipulated; and a critical division of the ruling *cafetalero* elite in the 1940s. This culminated in the brief civil war and democratic revolution of 1948–1949. Its resolution, the constitutional revision of 1949, and a working agreement among political elites from the 1950s on provided the bases for a continuing and successful civilian democratic regime. Although buffeted by the turmoil and violence that convulsed the region in the 1970s and 1980s, Costa Rica maintained its stability and democratic practices throughout with accommodation of opposition, good human rights performance, and public policy that improved middle- and working-class living standards.

In the other three countries' transitions from dictatorship in the 1970s to democracy in the 1980s and 1990s took place literally at gunpoint. In each country economic strains in the 1970s led to opposition and popular mobilization for change, to which each government responded with violent intransigence. For Nicaragua, El Salvador, and Guatemala in the 1970s, there appeared no viable option to insurrection.

In Nicaragua, the FSLN overthrew the Somoza dictatorship in 1979 and instituted the revolution. Moderate in comparison to other Marxist-led regimes, the

Sandinistas moved the Nicaraguan revolution from de facto rule with wide grassroots democratic participation (1979–1984) to civilian government (1985–1987). They culminated Nicaragua's institutional reforms and instituted a civilian democratic regime with the promulgation of a new constitution. By 1990, however, the economic and political damage of the Contra war, U.S.-orchestrated economic strangulation, and some aspects of revolutionary policy had polarized and virtually beggared the country. Nicaraguans availed themselves of their electoral institutions to reject continuing rule by the Sandinistas and to end the revolution by electing Violeta Barrios de Chamorro.

Guatemala and El Salvador passed from military authoritarian regimes through military reformist regimes and civilian transitional regimes and ultimately to civilian democracy by way of civil war and elaborately negotiated peace settlements. Although they originally dreamed of overthrowing their respective dictatorships and establishing revolutionary regimes, both the FMLN of El Salvador (by 1982) and the URNG of Guatemala (by 1986) had discarded that objective as unrealistic. They had witnessed U.S. policy toward the revolutionary government of Nicaragua and had become convinced, in the words of Rubén Zamora (the leader of the Salvadoran FMLN's political wing), that outright "victory would be ashes in our mouths."[2] The United States, and hence, its two client governments, would resist negotiated settlements until after the end of the Cold War. The United States and key elites in El Salvador and Guatemala, including the armed forces, pursued a moderating and gradualist reform strategy of using elections and transition to nominally civilian government to enhance governmental legitimacy and deny rebels a broader coalition. In the post–Cold War environment and with the Nicaraguan revolution over, Washington and local actors eventually accepted peace agreements similar to those envisioned by the guerrillas a decade earlier. Thus civilian democratic regimes, with former rebels included in the political arena and newly restrained militaries, emerged from decades of violent conflict.

The legacy of "transition at gunpoint," as seen in Nicaragua, El Salvador, and Guatemala, appears mixed. On the one hand, all three countries now had at least formally democratic political institutions, and civil and political conditions were far better than those that had existed prior to the onset of guerrilla activity. In addition, since all three transitions (especially that in Nicaragua) had required considerable grassroots participation, democracy in the 1990s and 2000s would feature increased involvement on the part of ordinary people. This situation stood in marked contrast to transitions to democracy in the Southern Cone of South America where, ordinary people, largely demobilized by previous dictatorships, were for a decade or more hesitant to participate in normal institutions of civil society.

However, certain negative aspects were also visible in Central America's unusual transitions to democracy. The rapid demobilizations of tens of thousands of government and insurgent fighters on both sides in all three countries, abundant arms left over from the conflicts, and police reforms that cashiered large numbers of officers in Guatemala and El Salvador. These factors produced high levels of armed criminal delinquency—and in Nicaragua, sporadic renewed insurgency—that threatened both individual and state security. For several years the new or reformed police agencies created by the regime transitions or peace accords could not cope with the resulting surge in violent crime. Moreover, as in all civil wars, the fratricidal armed conflict of the 1970s and 1980s and accompanying personal loss and black propaganda had left a legacy of deep polarization and partisan hatred that would likely impede the normal functioning of civil politics for years to come. As we wrote this in late 2004, crime in the form of gangs, carjackings, armed assaults, and drug trafficking remained major problems in several countries.

Finally, the legacy of bitter competition between the United States and the three revolutionary movements during the 1970s and 1980s would likely play a role in post–Cold War politics for some time to come. For instance, in the 1996 Nicaraguan election, when the gap in the polls between conservative Arnoldo Alemán and his FSLN opponent Daniel Ortega suddenly narrowed, the U.S. State Department strayed far from Washington's official policy of neutrality and made repeated statements indicating U.S. disapproval of Ortega. The United States also applied similar pressure against the same FSLN candidate in the 2001 Nicaraguan presidential election, and overtly expressed its preference that El Salvador's FMLN lose the 2004 presidential election. Such expressions of apparent U.S. preference may well have influenced the votes in these cases.[3] This phenomenon raised an important question: Would perceived U.S. disapproval of old Cold War enemies act as a barrier to the normal alternation in power in potentially emerging two-party systems in Nicaragua and El Salvador?

Projections: Prospects for Democratic Consolidation

The External Setting

This brings us to an examination of the prospects for democratic consolidation in Central America. As we note below, most of the theories on this subject focus on domestic considerations that promote or impede consolidation. In Central America, however, we believe that it makes little sense to discuss such factors as if these countries existed in a vacuum. In fact, Central America's international environment, particularly the behavior of the United States, is—and long has been—one of the most important factors shaping local regime types. This should not be surprising because the United States emerged from World War II as the world's most powerful nation and by the end of the twentieth century had become the world's only superpower. Washington exercised tremendous influence over the tiny nearby Central American republics through its diplomacy, aid programs, demonstrated willingness to project military power into the region, close relationships with local militaries, and virtual veto power over the decisions of critically important international lending agencies such as the International Monetary Fund, the World Bank, and the Inter-American Development Bank.

Although it is probably true that most U.S. policy makers throughout the twentieth century would have preferred democratic forms of government,[4] it is also clear that this preference frequently took a back seat to the pursuit of U.S. economic and security interests. Security trumped democracy especially during the Cold War when concern with containing a perceived Communist threat overwhelmed any squeamishness U.S. policy makers may have had about Central American dictators.[5] Even when the Reagan and first Bush administrations pushed for the election of civilian governments in El Salvador and Guatemala, they continued to support local military establishments whose campaigns of counterterror against a wide spectrum of civil society made such elections far from democratic. What is more, until the Cold War ended, the United States opposed (and hence delayed) negotiated settlements that would have allowed for greater civil rights and fuller democracy.

With the Cold War over in the 1990s, the United States reversed policy—promoting peace settlements and much freer and more meaningful democratic processes. For example, U.S. aid helped finance and provided technical assistance for the Nicaraguan election of 1996. With this type of U.S. backing, democracy in Central America had an unusual window of opportunity. However, because there was no telling whether or how long this propitious international setting would last, it was especially important that Central American democracy be consolidated internally. Accordingly, it is appropriate at this point to discuss domestic components of democratic consolidation—both in theory and in the concrete reality of Central America in the early 2000s.

Internal Factors

By the end of the twentieth century, all the Central American nations had elected, civilian, constitutional regimes, a circumstance that would have seemed inconceivable as recently as 1980. In each newly democratized nation, power had changed hands through peaceful elections among civilian candidates several times. This remarkable change from authoritarian to civilian democratic regimes aroused much interest among scholars.[6] As we have so frequently argued in the preceding pages, Central America's old (Costa Rica) and new (all the rest) civilian democratic regimes all faced difficult political and economic challenges. The new democracies, in particular, stood at a critical juncture where their political actors had to work to conserve their fledgling democratic regimes from powerful and often unpredictable forces.

In practical terms, the preservation of democracy in Central America would require the four newer democratic regimes to devise predictable and widely acceptable political structures and processes more like those that existed in Costa Rica since the 1950s. These would need to be able to sustain citizen participation and protect the individual political rights that guarantee the participation of civil society. This process of preserving the new democracies of the isthmus is *democratic consolidation.*[7]

Students of democratic consolidation, some focusing specifically on Latin America, have identified several important consolidation factors. Among the most important is (1) the development of an elite settlement, a consensus among a broad array of elites (the leadership of major social, economic, and political forces) to accept and accommodate each other's participation in the political game, to accept democratic procedures, and to allow the mass public and civil society to take part in politics.[8] Such accords, typically shaped by what Larry Diamond and Juan Linz call "founding democratic leadership,"[9] may derive from explicit pacts among elites or may simply evolve over time. However such settlements initially occur, they must allow for some evolution so the regime can adjust to change and accommodate new power contenders.[10]

Another important element is (2) the emergence of an autonomous civil society (political participation and organized interest activity). Such participation by the civil society—especially in matters of economic policy making—is essential to communicate citizens' needs to government and to restrain state power. Among other factors that contribute to consolidation are: (3) the development of a mass culture of support for democratic norms; (4) strong but moderate political parties; (5) a strong legislature; (6) a strong and effective government; (7) a small military that is allegiant to civilian leadership; (8) some deconcentration of wealth or amelioration of poverty; (9) moderate economic growth; and (10) as noted above, the support of important external actors.[11]

To evaluate each of these ten points for all five Central American countries would necessitate another entire volume and is well beyond the scope of this chapter. Nevertheless, a brief review of several of them will tell us something useful about the prospects for democratic consolidation in Central America.

Prospects

We have already noted the importance of these consolidation factors—the support of external actors for democracy—so we need not detain ourselves further with it other than to reaffirm that the United States will play a major role here. As long as U.S. foreign policy values and reinforces democracy in Central America, local elites will operate within important constraints that will make it easier for them to play by democratic rules. Unfortunately, not all the news is encouraging here. As we have noted, the United States interfered in elections in El Salvador

(2000, 2004) and Nicaragua (1990, 1996, 2001) to discourage voting for candidates from the parties of the once-revolutionary left. U.S. endorsement of, and suspected involvement in, the abortive 2002 coup d'état against Venezuela's constitutionally elected populist president Hugo Chávez in 2002 and its active role in the removal of popularly elected Haitian President Jean-Bertrand Aristide in 2004 deviated sharply and prominently from the pattern of recent U.S. commitment to the integrity of democratic and constitutional order in Latin America. Some wondered whether the United States would continue to support democratic rules of the game in the region or might again return to embracing U.S.-friendly autocrats.

Since the 1980s other key outside actors, of less influence than the United States but nevertheless of import, have also encouraged democracy in Central America. Indeed, several of these, including most European countries and the Catholic Church, favored and contributed in various ways to democratization and democratic consolidation. These pressures appear likely to continue for the middle term. Central America's Latin American neighbors—many new democracies themselves—used diplomacy to promote Central American peace and democracy during the 1980s when direct U.S. armed intervention in the isthmus seemed likely. Most Latin American governments appeared likely to continue to prefer civilian democracy, but several regimes in the Andean region had very fragile, at-risk democratic institutions. Multiple democratic breakdowns in Latin America would weaken regional support for electoral democracy in the isthmus and might encourage antidemocratic actors.

Elite Settlement. Had there emerged broadly inclusive inter-elite agreements about democratic rules of the game? Costa Rica's elite settlement had been in place for decades, a cornerstone of that nation's political stability. Progress toward elite settlement elsewhere was somewhat less certain. In the late 1980s John Peeler, an expert on Costa Rica's elite settlement and on democratization, expressed doubt about the progress toward democratic elite settlements in the other countries of the isthmus.[12] Since then, however, several specific accords and pacts have been signed among formerly warring elites in Nicaragua (ending the Contra war in 1990), El Salvador (the 1992 peace accord), and Guatemala (the 1996 peace accord). Governments and their armed opponents agreed to nominally democratic political rules, formerly excluded players were allowed into the legal political arena, clean elections were held, and power was subsequently transferred peaceably from incumbents to victorious opponents. Peeler's assessment of Central American formal electoral democracies in the early 2000s became more optimistic; he notes that the newer isthmian democracies had achieved both of his democratic stabilization criteria and at least one of two of his consolidation criteria.[13]

On the negative side, in Nicaragua, broken government promises and economic hard times led former combatants—ex-Contra and ex-army alike—for several years to return to arms in small-scale insurgency and banditry. Ex-combatant violence, however, had largely vanished by the time of this writing. In El Salvador and Guatemala, although the peace agreements held, periodic assassinations of human rights activists and candidates for office clearly revealed that some political actors wished to intimidate some players, disrupt the accords, or destabilize the democratic regimes. Similar violence also took place in Honduras. While the courts blocked the efforts of former military dictator Efraín Ríos Montt to return to Guatemala's presidency in 1999, Ríos Montt did become majority leader of the Congress, seeding doubt about his movement's commitment to democracy. Levels of repression and political terror in the four newer Central American democracies remained at middling or higher levels in the early 2000s, contrasting with Costa Rica's minimal repression (Table 2.3). Democracy and civil liberties scores for these four countries also remained problematically low by standards for electoral democracies, and again notably worse than in Costa Rica.

In summary, the willingness of Central American elites to play by democratic rules had reached a historic high level as this went to press, but there remained doubts and pockets of resistance. Elites had not come to control rights violations nor had they all demonstrated commitment to democratic norms. It was clear that we simply might not know for many more years whether elites would come to trust each other and accept democracy as the only political game as they had in Costa Rica's smoothly cooperative settlement. On balance, however, middle-run prospects for democratic elite settlements appeared reasonably good.

Civil Society and Participation. How much autonomous civil society and political participation had developed in Central America? Turning first to political participation, recent surveys of urban citizens in all Central American nations (Chapter 9) reported a wealth of voting and registration, electioneering, contacting of public officials, organizational activism, and communal self-help in all five nations. The range and breadth of political activity among urban citizens was remarkable, especially given the history of turbulence in some countries. Indeed, in the early 1990s, the factor that most curtailed participation was high national levels of repression. Because repression declined somewhat in the 1990s after peace deals were signed and military and police reform implemented, we expected that citizen participation should increase after formal democratization. The analysis of citizen engagement in 2004 (Chapter 9) indicated several things that contributed to higher participation: lower national-level repression and a better individual perception of the civil liberties climate, greater national political stability, and a higher level of economic development.

Focusing on civil society, there was evidence that activism within most kinds of organizations increased Central Americans' support for democracy and political activity. In the early 1990s, higher national levels of civil society activism were associated with higher levels of democracy within the region.[14] These studies of participation and civil society gave reason for optimism about democratic consolidation in Central America. Central Americans in 2004 were active in diverse organizations, with considerable variation by group type among the nations. Some trends were found in civil society activism between the early 1990s and 2004. Civil society activism fell sharply in Nicaragua in the late 1980s and after the 1990 FSLN electoral defeat, despite the Sandinista government's history of mobilizing support through organizations.[15] Over the 1991–2004 period, during which repression declined in the four newer democracies, engagement in Church-related groups rose sharply everywhere but Nicaragua. In contrast, involvement in school groups and activism in professional and business groups declined in most of the region. Perhaps this selective organizational demobilization trend across the region indicated that civil society activism cooled as political conflict subsided.

Intriguingly, the 2004 surveys revealed that, other factors held constant, higher levels of repression and poorer economic performance correlated with greater civil society activism by Central Americans. That citizens of the less economically successful and more repressive of these newly democratized nations could and did use civil society to pursue their interests indicates how vital civil society activity remained to Central America's democratic future.

Public Attitudes and Culture. Did the broad general public of Central America support democratic rules of the game? In the early 1990s, high levels of repression reduced popular support for democratic liberties. Thus the waning of state repression might lead one to expect that, other things equal, citizen support for democratic liberties would increase. The surveys just mentioned explored citizen support for various kinds of participation and for citizens' rights and liberties. In summary, large majorities of Central Americans favored democratic liberties in the early 1990s and in 2004 (Chapter 9). However, the 2004 level of democratic norms had declined somewhat rather than increased since the early 1990s. The data indicate that the troubling finding of diminished support for general participation rights owed significantly to the poor national economic performance observed in some countries. Political stability, in contrast, contributed to more support for participation rights, more tolerance for dissenters, and higher support for civil disobedience.

In 2004, most citizens strongly rejected the idea of an authoritarian leader, but surprisingly almost half could envision circumstances that might justify a coup d'état. Guatemalans and Salvadorans had the region's lowest levels of general democratic norms and tolerance. Support for confrontational political methods rose everywhere except Honduras between the early 1990s and 2004, likely due to diminished repression.

Regionwide, Central Americans' evaluation of governmental legitimacy (specific support for the system—Table 9.2) in 2004 balanced on the midpoint of the scale—that is, neutral. Country by country, Guatemalans, Hondurans and Nicaraguans regarded their governments somewhat unfavorably, while Costa Ricans and Salvadorans held more positive views. Comparison with early 1990s survey data suggests that the system support of Costa Ricans, Guatemalans, and Nicaraguans had declined, while support rose among Salvadorans and Hondurans. As of 2004, Costa Rica and El Salvador appeared to be consolidating popular support for their political institutions, though some of Costa Rica's trends appear worrisome. In contrast, three of the region's five democratic regimes were only weakly supported—several years after regime change and despite their citizens' generally democratic norms and shared repudiation of authoritarianism. Higher levels of system support were driven by higher political and economic stability, higher levels of economic development, lower repression, less victimization by crime, and a lower perception of crime. In short, government and economic performance had much to do with citizen support for the democratic regimes in Central America at the beginning of the twenty-first century.

Party Systems. To what extent did Central America approach the model of other stable democracies in having two strong but moderate (ideologically centrist) political parties? Costa Rica for years came closest with its dominant main parties, the social democratic PLN and the moderate conservative PUSC, that regularly traded ruling power. The PLN, however, fared poorly in the 1998 and especially the 2002 election, raising the prospect that it might collapse. A major corruption scandal then arose around two successive Social Christian Unity Party presidents in the early 2000s and suggested the PUSC was also in trouble. Honduras's center-right National Party and the center-left Liberal Party between them had effectively dominated the political arena for decades and had since the 1990s regularly traded off ruling power through elections.

Two other countries had strong parties, but they are more ideologically polarized than centrist and less evenly matched than in Costa Rica and Honduras. El Salvador's ARENA, once on the far right, moderated somewhat after the mid-1980s and dominated the presidency and legislature from the Cristiani administration (1988) into the late 1990s. The Salvadoran Christian Democratic Party declined and virtually vanished by the 1990s. On the Salvadoran left was the former guerrilla insurgent coalition FMLN, which had joined the legal political struggle and (though weaker than ARENA) made large gains in legislative and city council elections in 1997 and 2000. ARENA again defeated the FMLN in the 2004 election.

In Nicaragua the FSLN moderated its leftist stances in the early 1990s and remained relatively strong. Despite losing three successive national elections (1990, 1996, and 2001), the FSLN frequently captured mayoral offices including that of the capital Managua. Indeed, in 2004 it was the front runner in mayoral victories. The Liberal Alliance, in 1996, had reconstituted a strong Liberal coalition and succeeded itself in power in 2001. Recent election law reforms implemented by the FSLN and Liberals tilted the playing field steeply against other Nicaraguan parties, keeping them tiny, personalistic, and fractious. At this writing the Liberals were divided by the scandal that sent a former Liberal president to prison in 2003. However, Nicaraguans' pattern of forming anti-Sandinista electoral coalitions together with a, by then, well-established pattern of overt U.S. anti-Sandinista involvement in Nicaraguan politics lead us to question whether the FSLN had much chance of winning back the presidency.

Guatemala had several small and medium-sized ideological or personalistic parties of varying ages. The Christian Democrats of Guatemala, once a candidate for a strong, centrist role, failed to consolidate their position of electoral leadership during the presidency of Vinicio Cerezo Arévalo and declined badly after their 1990 election defeat. President Alvaro Arzú's PAN won the 1995 election in a runoff. The PAN subsequently fared poorly in presidential races, losing in 1999 with Oscar Berger as its candidate. Berger won the presidency in 2003 but as the candidate of a coalition GANA. The URNG and FDNG had won some legislative seats but appeared unlikely to have much presidential success. At this writing Guatemala's party system remained the most fragmented in the region.

In summary, only Costa Rica and Honduras clearly met the two-party, centrist model. Costa Rica's two major parties, however, were in serious trouble in the early 2000s. Though both had other very small parties, El Salvador and Nicaragua were developing into two-party polarized polities. Although there remained real questions as to whether the ex-guerrilla organizations FSLN and FMLN could ever win their respective nations' presidencies, they had taken part effectively in legislative and municipal contexts. To the extent that the two-party, centrist model might contribute to democratic consolidation, Costa Rica and Honduras appeared to have some advantage. Something similar could develop in El Salvador and Nicaragua should the polarized big parties further moderate their politics and continue to learn to work together in the legislative and municipal arenas.

Armed Forces. To what extent were the region's militaries small and loyal to civilian rule? In the Central American isthmus as recently as 1990 this question was risible, but by the late 1990s there had been significant progress. In 1990, only one government approached the criterion of having a small and allegiant military—Costa Rica had dismantled its army in 1949—but all the other countries had large armies swollen by war (or in Honduras by foreign aid to support U.S. geostrategic goals in the region). After 1990, though, change came rapidly. After settling the Contra war in 1990, the new Nicaraguan government reduced the size of its military by 80 percent, civilianized the police, passed a new military code, and professionalized and renamed the army (now the Nicaraguan Army). Nicaraguan military behavior after 1990 suggested a willingness to accept civilian control. With the end of the Salvadoran and Guatemalan civil wars the armies of both countries underwent substantial force cuts and came under increased civilian influence. Top officers were retired and reassigned. In a troubling trend, Guatemala's military became somewhat resurgent in national politics during the early 2000s. In the mid-1990s the long truculent Honduran military submitted to reforms that included abolition of the draft, reassignment of officers, and civilianization of the police.

No one familiar with the history of Central America's recently reformed militaries could be wholly sanguine about their prospects for loyalty to their civilian governments, but by the late 1990s armies of the isthmus were out of power, discredited by their past abuses and poor performance as rulers, and lacking the former financial and political support of the United States (demobilization was no longer a major issue for Washington). Expert observers of the regions' armed forces reported trends that were mostly encouraging for democracy (Guatemala possibly excepted) as the twenty-first century began.[16] Central American militaries had become smaller, less human rights abusive, and more cooperative with civilian officials. Ruhl calls the decline in the political power of the area's militaries "a great achievement for the region" and characterizes the status quo in all four as falling between "democratic control" and "conditional subordination" to civilian authorities.[17] We view these changes as indisputable goods and a positive omen for democratic consolidation in the middle-term future.

Globalized Economies and Democracy

While we have focused most of our attention on the transformation of Central America's political regimes into civilian democracies by the 1990s, it is important to point out that the region's economies also changed in the 1980s and 1990s in ways that will shape Central America's future for decades to come. For the last three decades of the twentieth century, civil war, energy price increases, deteriorating terms of trade, excessive external borrowing, and the collapse of the Central American Common Market bedeviled the region's economies. In varying degrees, each at some time faced or experienced severe economic crisis and required international help. In exchange for international credit required to ameliorate or prevent economic ruin, the United States, the World Bank, and the International Monetary Fund exacted fundamental economic transformations. Under this intense outside pressure, and with the collaboration of modernizing local capitalists, all Central American countries eventually altered their economic models to embrace neoliberalism.

Neoliberal economic reforms pressed upon Central America's reduced government spending on social welfare, education, and infrastructure. Governments streamlined payrolls, reduced budget deficits, privatized publicly owned corporations and services, curtailed regulatory efforts, and generally reduced the state's role in their economies. They slashed tariffs and import quotas to open up Central American economies to foreign goods and investment, aggressively promoted nontraditional exports, and sought national advantage in the international economy in tourism and as suppliers of cheap labor for light manufacturing and assembly plants. These nearly revolutionary reforms brought some new investment from within and from abroad and contributed to economic recovery in some countries. Neoliberalism advanced the economic fortunes of the local capitalists who took advantage of the new openings to the world capitalist economy and the reforms their international lending allies demanded. And with the aid of their external allies these economic actors gained new political power in the emerging civilian democratic regimes of the region.

Neoliberalism, however, had negative consequences. It shrank the capacity of Central American governments to improve the general welfare of their citizens, promote economic growth, and invest in human capital. Governments with international financial monitors and externally imposed structural adjustment agreements found themselves with more unemployed citizens who earned relatively lower average wages, and fewer government resources to redistribute income or ameliorate poverty. Governments thus had fewer tools with which to promote their citizens' general welfare. The new openness of their economies to the world undermined local manufacturing. New assembly plants had to compete in a global economy, which exerted relentless downward pressure on wages in those industries and left them vulnerable to relocation to the next cheaper labor market to develop. The prospect for continued foreign investment in assembly plants remained very uncertain, and deterioration of the welfare of the poor majority of Central Americans seemed increasingly likely. Social pathologies such as urban gangs, narcotics use, prostitution and sex tourism, violent crime, and public corruption increased across the region in the 1990s and early 2000s. Trimmed-down states found themselves unable to respond effectively to these growing problems.

These pernicious economic trends, derived from Central America's traditional economic weaknesses, its elites' scant enthusiasm for reform, and the effects of neoliberal economic policies, appeared likely to have pernicious effects on democracy in the region. Flawed by their poor human rights performance, the democracies that emerged from regime transformation in Central America were widely and rightly criticized. Neoliberalism's economic effects appeared certain to continue to limit the capacity of their citizens to participate effectively in politics because many would never gain the economic resources and human capital required to influence public decisions. Central American nations, operating leanly and meanly under the rules of the global economy, would lack both the resources and will to lift up their citizens and improve their life chances. Thus, at the time of this writing, it appeared that the low-intensity democracy encouraged by neoliberalism might well remain the best that Central Americans, with the possible exception of Costa Rica, might be able to expect for many decades to come.

Conclusions

On balance, then, there were both positive and negative signs for the consolidation of formal civilian democracies in Central America as the twenty-first century began. In political terms, collectively the citizens of the isthmus enjoyed more human rights and greater political freedom than ever before. Central American opinion on balance clearly preferred democracy to dictatorship. Political elites were playing by formal democratic rules, and key institutional and external factors seemed likely to continue to support democratic regimes. The great experiment of the Nicaraguan revolution—a regime that pushed for much more participatory democracy and greater social justice than the polities that survived it—had failed under a combination of fierce U.S. pressure and its own errors.

Critics derided the new democracies of Central America as "low-intensity" or "light" democracies, and there was merit to the criticism. Formal democratic rules and procedures in a socioeconomic context of enormous inequality and widespread and growing poverty would provide the legions of poor and unorganized Central Americans only modest influence over public policy. The great neoliberal economic experiment imposed upon all five countries of the region by international financial institutions and major donor nations, at least in the short run, exacerbated inequality and poverty. Thus the only long-run hope for increased resources for the poor majority under neoliberal development models—and thus for increased popular political power and the deepening of democracy—appeared to be for the economies of the region to produce sustained and rapid growth. The realistic prospects for such growth appeared to range from modest in the countries with more robust economies (Costa Rica and El Salvador) to grim in the nearly prostrate Honduras and Nicaragua. Holding forth the prospect of renewed political turmoil in the region, opinion surveys—almost certainly reacting to the poor economic performance of the region's nations—showed that in the early 2000s many Central Americans remained willing to use confrontational political means.

Thus, what Central America, aside from Costa Rica, had achieved was low-intensity democracy with very modest prospects for achieving government of, by, and for the people. On the other hand, low-intensity democracy is, we believe, better than no democracy at all, especially in one regard well known to all Central Americans. At least 300,000 lost their lives to authoritarian repression during the decades-long struggle for formal democracy. Civilian governments—especially with curtailed militaries—intimidate, imprison, maim, and kill much less than do military regimes. Under Central America's civilian democratic regimes, fewer will suffer the repression experienced under military regimes. Inequalities and economic limitations notwithstanding, citizens able to organize, contact officials, vote, and protest can defend and pursue their interests more effectively than those who cannot. In this sense, through the formal democratization of their polities in the traumatic 1970s, 1980s, and 1990s, millions of ordinary Central Americans won the right to become protagonists in their own political reality.

Appendix

TABLE A.1 SELECTED ECONOMIC DATA FOR CENTRAL AMERICA, BY COUNTRY, 1950–2004

	Costa Rica	*El Salvador*	*Guatemala*	*Honduras*	*Nicaragua*	*Region*[a]
Gross Domestic Product (GDP)[b]						
1960	1,646	1,985	4,045	1,112	1,461	10,249
1970	2,932	3,437	6,911	1,905	2,849	18,034
1980	5,975	4,723	11,987	3,243	2,950	29,978
1990	6,313	6,334	12,923	3,985	2,587	32,143
2003	11,486	10,508	20,617	5,932	3,672	45,339
GDP per capita[c]						
1960	1,332	772	1,020	575	879	891
1970	1,694	958	1,373	725	1,388	1,207
1980	2,222	1,044	1,732	886	1,065	1,393
1990	2,094	1,210	1,404	775	663	1,209
2003	2,854	1,554	1,589	803	862	1,405
Percent change in GDP/capita						
1960–70	27	24	31	26	58	35
1970–80	31	9	26	22	–23	15
1980–90	6	16	–18	–13	–38	–13
1990–2003	36	28	13	4	3	16
Percent[d] employed in agriculture						
1960	51	62	67	70	62	63
1980	29	50	55	63	39	47
1999	20	9	23	13	29	19[g]
Percent[d] employed in manufacturing						
c. 1950	11	11	12	6	11	10
1983	16	14	15	13	15	15
1999	22	31	19	32	25	28[g]
Percent GDP from manufacturing						
1960	14	15	13	12	16	14
1980	22	18	17	16	25	18
2004	29	31	19	32	25	27[g]
Remissions as percent of GDP						
1990	.0	7.4	1.4	4.4	0.0	2.6[g]
2002	.8	13.5	7.3	11.1	9.4	8.4[g]
External debt[e]						
1980	2.7	.9	1.2	1.5	1.2	7.7[f]
1990	3.8	2.1	2.8	3.5	10.7	22.8[f]
2002	2.0	2.7	1.8	6.8	15.6	28.9[f]

(continues)

TABLE A.1 *(continued)*

	Costa Rica	*El Salvador*	*Guatemala*	*Honduras*	*Nicaragua*	*Region*[a]
Debt as a percent of GDP						
1970	11.5	5.2	3.6	9.5	10.9	8.2[g]
1982	110.3	42.0	17.6	69.4	121.5	72.2[g]
1991	73.0	36.7	29.8	118.9	649.1	181.5[g]
2003	21.1	30.1	13.9	66.4	85.9	43.5[g]
Debt service ratio						
1990	15.4	13.0	11.2	18.0	58.3	23.8[g]
2002 (or most recent)	13.7	6.7	13.8	12.9	25.7	14.56[g]

[a]Weighted averages unless otherwise specified.

[b]In millions of 1986 U.S. dollars; regional value is sum for all nations.

[c]In 1986 U.S. dollars.

[d]Of economically active population.

[e]Disbursed total external debt, in billions of current U. S. dollars.

[f]Sum of country totals.

[g]Unweighted mean.

Sources: John A. Booth and Thomas W. Walker, *Understanding Central America* (Boulder: Westview Press, 1993), Table 2; Inter-American Development Bank, *Economic and Social Progress in Latin America: Natural Resources. 1983 Report* (Washington, DC, 1983), Tables 3 and 58; Inter-American Development Bank, *Economic and Social Progress in Latin America: Science and Technology. 1988 Report* (Washington, DC, 1988), Table E-1 and country tables; Inter-American Development Bank, *Economic and Social Progress in Latin America: Natural Resources. 1994 Report* (Baltimore: Johns Hopkins University Press, 1994), Tables B-2, E-11 and country tables; Inter-American Development Bank, *Economic and Social Progress in Latin America, 1997 Report: Latin America After a Decade of Reforms* (Washington, DC: 1997), Tables B-1, B-2, B-10, E-1, and country profiles; Banco Interamericano del Desarrollo (Inter-American Development Bank), *Situación económica y perspectivas: Istmo Centroamericano y República Dominicana* (Washington, DC, May 2004), accessed January 6, 2005, iadb.org/regions/re2/SEPmayofinalMhung.pdf, pp. i–v; U.S. Central Intelligence Agency, *The World Factbook* (Washington, DC: 1993), country reports, and U.S. Central Intelligence Agency, *The World Factbook* (Washington, DC, 2004), accessed January 6, 2005, cia.gov/cia/publications/factbook/, country reports.

TABLE A.2 Selected Social Data for Central America, by Country, 1960–2004

	Costa Rica	*El Salvador*	*Guatemala*	*Honduras*	*Nicaragua*	*Region*[a]
Population (in millions)						
1960	1.2	2.6	4.0	1.9	1.5	11.2[b]
1980	2.3	4.5	6.9	3.7	2.8	20.2[b]
2003	4.2	6.6	12.3	7.0	5.3	35.4[b]
Population density estimate (persons/km.^{2})						
1998	72.3	293.8	106.3	55.2	39.4	80.5
Mean annual population growth						
1961–70	3.4	3.4	2.8	3.1	3.2	3.3
1970–80	2.8	2.3	2.8	3.4	3.0	3.0
1980–90	2.8	1.6	2.9	3.4	3.4	2.8
1990–96	2.4	2.2	2.9	3.0	2.5	2.7
2004	1.5	1.8	2.6	2.2	2.0	2.0
Percent indigenous population						
1978	1	2	60	2	2	14
2004	1	1	43	7	5	11
Percent urban population						
1960	33.2	36.4	34.0	22.5	41.7	33.6
1996	49.3	48.4	41.8	48.6	74.1	50.2
Percent literate						
1960	86	42	40	30	32	42
c. 2000	96	80	70	76	67	78
Primary school enrollment ratio[c]						
1980	107	75	73	98	94	89
1990	101	81	78	108	94	92
c. 2002	108	112	103	106	105	107
University enrollment						
c. 2001[c]	20	17	8	14	12	14
Life expectancy at birth						
1980–85	73	57	59	60	60	60
c. 2003	78	70	66	66	69	70
Infant mortality/1,000 live births						
c. 1993	14	40	62	49	56	55
c. 2003	9	33	36	32	32	28
Religious identification (percent) *c.* 1985						
Catholic	97	93	79	94	88	90
Protestant	3	4	6	3	8	5

(continues)

TABLE A.2. *(continued)*

[a]Unweighted average for region unless otherwise specified.

[b]Sum for region.

[c]As percent of population of university age.

Sources: John A. Booth and Thomas W. Walker, *Understanding Central America* (Boulder: Westview Press, 1993), Appendix Table 3; Inter-American Development Bank, *Economic and Social Progress in Latin America: Science and Technology. 1988 Report* (Washington, DC, 1988), pp. 384, 408, 416, 440, 464; Inter-American Development Bank, *Economic and Social Progress in Latin America, 1992 Report* (Washington, DC, Johns Hopkins University Press, 1992), country tables; Inter-American Development Bank, Economic and Social Progress in Latin America: Natural Resources. 1994 Report (Baltimore: Johns Hopkins University Press, 1994), country tables; Inter-American Development Bank, *Economic and Social Progress in Latin America, 1997 Report: Latin America After a Decade of Reforms* (Washington, DC: 1997), Tables A-1 and A2; Banco Interamericano del Desarrollo (Inter-American Development Bank), *Situación económica y perspectivas: Istmo Centroamericano y República Dominicana* (Washington, DC, May 2004), accessed January 6, 2005 at iadb.org/regions/re2/SEPmay ofinalMhung.pdf, pp. i–v; María Eugenia Gallardo and José Roberto López, *Centroamérica: La crisis en cifras* (San José, Costa Rica: Instituto Interamericano de Cooperación para la Agricultura-Facultad Latinoamericano de Ciencias Sociales, 1986), Tables 2, 4, 7, 8, and 10; Tom Barry and Deb Preusch, *The Soft War: The Uses and Abuses of U.S. Aid in Central America* (New York: Grove Press, 1986), p. 129; U.S. Central Intelligence Agency (1993: country reports); and U.S. Central Intelligence Agency, *The World Factbook* (Washington, DC, 2004), accessed January 6, 2005, cia.gov/cia/publications/factbook/, country reports; and United Nations Educational, Scientific, and Cultural Organization, UNESCO Statistical Yearbook, 1997 (Paris and Lanham, MD: UNESCO Publishing and Bernam Press, 1997), Tables 1.2 and 3.9.

TABLE A.3 MEAN ANNUAL U.S. MILITARY AND ECONOMIC ASSISTANCE TO CENTRAL AMERICA, 1946–1992

	Costa Rica	*El Salvador*	*Guatemala*	*Honduras*	*Nicaragua*	*Region*[a]
			Military Assistance[b]			
1946–1952	–	–	–	–	–	–
1953–1961	.01	.03	.19	.14	.24	.62
1962–1972	.16	.72	3.31	.90	2.36	7.45
1973–1976	.03	2.08	.83	2.23	.28	5.45
1977–1980	1.25	1.60	1.25	3.13	.85	6.98
1981–1984	3.95	98.85	.00	41.48	.00	144.28
1985–1988	3.93	112.78	5.20	57.73	.00	179.64
1989–1992	.10	63.10	2.35[c]	25.60	.00	91.15
Overall Mean 1946–1992	.83	23.86	1.63	12.38	.69	38.24
			Economic Assistance[b]			
1946–1952	1.00	.40	1.65	.42	1.03	4.50
1953–1961	5.80	1.23	13.48	3.90	3.73	28.14
1962–1972	9.41	11.95	14.52	8.42	12.95	56.07
1973–1976	14.10	6.10	19.60	24.43	26.90	91.13
1977–1980	13.65	21.85	17.28	27.88	18.63	99.56
1981–1984	112.75	189.43	21.13	79.53	16.55	419.39
1985–1988	171.13	383.38	135.90	179.33	.10	869.84
1989–1992	5.83	287.68	116.73	150.18	206.80	837.22
Overall Mean 1946–1992	36.48	78.72	32.73	42.06	26.83	216.83

[a]Includes only Costa Rica, El Salvador, Guatemala, Honduras, and Nicaragua.

[b]Millions of U.S. dollars.

[c]The George H.W. Bush administration canceled Guatemala's 1990 military assistance of $3.3 million for human rights reasons. That left the aid delivered at less than originally appropriated for the period.

SOURCES: G. Pope Atkins, *Latin America in the International Political System* (New York: The Free Press, 1977), Tables D, E, and G. Pope Atkins, *Latin America in the International Political System* (Boulder: Westview Press, 1989), Tables 10.2 and 10.4; and Office for Planning and Budgeting, U.S. Agency for International Development, *U.S. Overseas Loans and Grants and Assistance from International Organizations: Obligations and Loan Authorizations, July 1, 1945–September 30, 1992* (Washington, DC, Congressional Information Service, microfiche, 1993).

TABLE A.4 Central American Rebel Groups, 1959–1989

	Costa Rica	*El Salvador*	*Guatemala*	*Honduras*	*Nicaragua*
1959					various groups[b] (1959–1961)
1960				FMLH[a]	
1961					FSLN
1962			MR-13 FAR, FGEI[c]		
1963					
1964					
1965					
1966					
1967					
1968					
1969					
1970		FPL			
1971			ORPA		
1972		ERP	EGP		
1973					
1974					
1975		FARN			
1976		PRTCS			
1977				PRTCH	FSLN splits[d]
1978			PGT-DN	MPL	
1979	La Familia	FAL			reunification of FSLN, MPU-FPN[e]
1980	PRTC	FMLN[f] FMLN-FDR[g]	 MRP-Ixim		
1981			URNG[h]	FPR	
1982					
1983				DNU[i]	
1984					
1985					
1986					
1987					
1988					
1989				ERP-27	

[a]Only sporadically active through late 1979, when it resumed armed struggle.

[b]Of some 20 groups formed, only the FSLN survived beyond 1963.

[c]MR-13 disappeared after late 1960s counterinsurgency campaign; core of FAR survived to renew guerrilla activity in 1978; core of FGEI survived counterinsurgency and helped form EGP.

[d]Under heavy counterinsurgency pressure, FSLN split into three factions with tactical differences.

[e]MPU-FPN coalitions linked broad-front political opposition with FSLN.

[f]MLN included all five Salvadoran guerrilla organizations.

[g]FMLN-FDR linked FMLN guerrillas with broad-front political opposition coalition.

[h]URNG linked the guerrilla groups EGP, FAR, ORPA, and the PGT-DN; MRP-Ixim not a member.

[i]DNU linked the MPL, FPR, and FMLH guerrilla organizations.

TABLE A.5 COMPARATIVE DATA ON CENTRAL GOVERNMENT EXPENDITURES (PERCENT OF BUDGET)

	Costa Rica		*El Salvador*	*Guatemala*		*Honduras*	*Nicaragua*
	1978	*1983*	*1984*	*1978*	*1984*[a]	*1976*	*1976*
1. Defense	2.7	3.0	24.6	11.0	13.7	10.5	12.8
2. Education	24.5	19.4	15.5	13.0	12.7	20.7	16.9
3. Health	3.6	22.5	8.1	7.1	7.5	14.7	4.1
4. Social security/ welfare	28.3	14.5	3.7	4.1	3.9	4.7	19.9
5. Total percent on education, health and social security/ welfare (2 + 3 + 4)	56.3	56.3	27.3	24.2	24.1	40.1	40.9
6. Ratio of human services to defense (5:1)	21:1	19:1	1:1	2:1	2:1	4:1	3:1

[a]Slightly different budget breakdowns are used between Wilkie and Perkal and Wilkie and Lorey on the one hand and Inforpress Centroamericana on the other. The 1984 Guatemala data for the social security and welfare category on this measure are assumed to be the same as Inforpress's "labor" and "government" lines combined.

SOURCES: James W. Wilkie and Steven Haber, eds., *Statistical Abstract of Latin America, Volume 21* (Los Angeles: University of California at Los Angeles-University of California Latin American Center Publications, 1981), Table 2323; James W. Wilkie and David Lorey, eds., *Statistical Abstract of Latin America, Volume 25* (Los Angeles: University of California at Los Angeles-University of California Latin American Center Publications, 1987), Table 30; and Inforpress Centroamericana, *Central America Report*, 1985, p. 5.

Acronyms

AID	Agency for International Development
AL	Liberal Alliance (Alianza Liberal) (N)*
ALIPO	Popular Liberal Alliance (Alianza Liberal Popular) (H)
AMNLAE	Luisa Amanda Espinosa Nicaraguan Women's Association (Asociación de Mujeres Nicaragüenses Luisa Amanda Espinosa)
AMPRONAC	Association of Women Confronting the National Problem (Asociación de Mujeres Frente a la Problemática Nacional) (N)
ANEP	National Association of Private Enterprises (Asociación Nacional de Empresas Privadas) (ES)
APRE	Alliance for the Republic (Alianza para la República) (N)
ARDE	Revolutionary Democratic Alliance (Alianza Revolucionaria Democrática) (CR-based contra forces)
ARENA	Nationalist Republican Alliance Party (Alianza Republicana Nacionalista) (ES)
ASC	Assembly of Civil Society (Asamblea de la Sociedad Civil) (G)
ATC	Rural Workers' Association (Asociación de Trabajadores del Campo) (N)
BPR	Revolutionary Popular Bloc (Bloque Popular Revolucionario) (ES)
CACM	Central American Common Market
CAFTA	Central American Free Trade Agreement
CBI	Caribbean Basin Initiative

*Abbreviations of countries: CR = Costa Rica; ES = El Salvador; G = Guatemala H = Honduras; N = Nicaragua

CC	Court of Constitutionality (Corte de Constitucionalidad) (G)
CD	Democratic Convergence (Convergencia Democrática) (ES)
CDC	Civil Defense Committee (Comité de Defensa Civil) (N & H)
CDS	Sandinista Defense Committee (Comité de Defensa Sandinista) (N)
CDU	United Democratic Center (Centro Democrático Unido) (ES)
CEB	Christian base communities *(comunidades eclesiales de base)*
CEH	Historical Clarification Commission (Comisión de Esclarificación Histórica) (G)
CGUP	Guatemalan Committee of Patriotic Unity (Comité Guatemalteco de Unidad Patriótica)
CIA	Central Intelligence Agency
CODEH	Human Rights Committee of Honduras (Comité de Derechos Humanos de Honduras)
COSEP	Superior Council of Private Enterprise (Consejo Superior de la Empresa Privada) (N)
COSIP	Superior Council of Private Initiative (Consejo Superior de la Iniciativa Privada) (N)
CPI	consumer price index
CRIES	Regional Coordinating Body for Economic and Social Research (N)
CRM	Revolutionary Coordinator of the Masses (Coordinadora Revolucionaria de Masas) (ES)
CSE	Supreme Electoral Council (Consejo Supremo Electoral) (N)
CSJ	Supreme Court of Justice (Corte Supremo de Justicia) (G)
CST	Sandinista Workers' Federation (Central Sandinista de Trabajadores) (N)
CUC	Peasant Unity Committee (Comité de Unidad Campesina) (G)
DC	Christian Democratic Party (Partido Demócrata Cristiano) (G)
DINADECO	National Community Development Directorate (Dirección Nacional de Desarrollo de la Comunidad) (CR)
DNC	Joint National Directorate (Dirección Nacional Conjunta) (N)
DNU	National Directorate of Unity (Dirección Nacional de Unidad) (H)
EGP	Guerrilla Army of the Poor (Ejército Guerrillero de los Pobres) (G)
EPS	Sandinista People's Army (N)
ERP	Revolutionary Army of the People (Ejército Revolucionario del Pueblo) (ES)
ERP-27	Army of Patriotic Resistance (Ejército de Resistencia Patriótica) (H)

ESAF	Enhanced Structural Adjustment Facility
EXA	export agriculture
FAL	Armed Forces of Liberation (Fuerzas Armadas de Liberación) (ES)
FAO	Broad Opposition Front (Frente Amplio Opositor) (N)
FAPU	United Popular Action Front (Frente de Acción Popular Unida) (ES)
FAR	Revolutionary Armed Forces (Fuerzas Armadas Revolucionarias) (G)
FARC	Revolutionary Armed Forces of Colombia (Fuerzas Armadas Revolucionarias de Colombia)
FARN	Armed Forces of National Resistance (Fuerzas Armadas de Resistencia Nacional) (ES)
FDCR	Democratic Front Against Repression (Frente Democrático Contra la Represión) (G)
FDN	Nicaraguan Democratic Force (Fuerzas Democráticas Nicaragüenses)
FDNG	New Guatemala Democratic Front (Frente Democrático Nueva Guatemala)
FDR	Revolutionary Democratic Front (Frente Democrático Revolucionario) (ES)
FGEI	Edgar Ibarra Guerrilla Front (Frente Guerrillera Edgar Ibarra) (G)
FMLH	Morazán Front for the Liberation of Honduras (Frente Morazanista para la Liberación de Honduras)
FMLN	Farabundo Martí National Liberation Front (Frente Farabundo Martí de Liberación Nacional) (ES)
FNT	National Workers' Front (Frente Nacional de Trabajadores) (N)
FOL	Forward Operating Location
FP-13	January 13th Popular Front (Frente Popular 13 de Enero) (G)
FPL	Popular Forces of Liberation (Fuerzas Populares de Liberación) (ES)
FPN	National Patriotic Front (Frente Patriótico Nacional) (N)
FPR	Lorenzo Zelaya Popular Revolutionary Forces (Fuerzas Populares Revolucionarias "Lorenzo Zelaya") (H)
FRG	Republican Front of Guatemala (Frente Republicano de Guatemala)
FSLN	Sandinista National Liberation Front (Frente Sandinista de Liberación Nacional) (N)
FUR	United Front of the Revolution (Frente Unido de la Revolución) (G)

FUSEP	Public Security Forces (Fuerzas de Seguridad Pública) (H)
GANA	Great National Alliance (Gran Alianza Nacional) (G)
GDP	gross domestic product
HIPC	World Bank's Heavily Indebted Poor Countries
ICE	Costa Rican Electrical Institute (Instituto Costarricense de Electricidad)
IMF	International Monetary Fund
LP-28	28th of February Popular Leagues (Ligas Populares 28 de Febrero) (ES)
MAS	Solidarity Action Movement (Movimiento de Acción Solidaria) (G)
MINUGUA	United Nations Mission in Guatemala (Misión de las Naciones Unidas en Guatemala)
MLN	National Liberation Movement (Movimiento de Liberación Nacional) (G)
MLP	Popular Liberation Movement (Movimiento de Liberación Popular) (ES)
MNR	National Revolutionary Movement (Movimiento Nacional Revolucionario) (ES)
MPL	Popular Movement for Liberation (Movimiento Popular de Liberación) (H)
MPU	United People's Movement (Movimiento Pueblo Unido) (N)
MR-13	13th of November Revolutionary Movement (Movimiento Revolucionario del 13 de Noviembre) (G)
MRP-Ixim	People's Revolutionary Movement-Ixim (Movimiento Revolucionario del Pueblo-Ixim) (G)
MRS	Sandinista Renovation Movement (Movimiento de Renovación Sandinista) (N)
NAFTA	North American Free Trade Agreement
OAS	Organization of American States
OPEC	Organization of Petroleum Exporting Countries
ORDEN	Nationalist Democratic Organization (Organización Democrática Nacionalista) (ES)
ORPA	Organization of the People in Arms (Organización del Pueblo en Armas) (G)
PAC	Citizen Action Party (Partido de Acción Ciudadana) (CR)
PAN	National Advancement Party (Partido de Avance Nacional) (G)
PCH	Honduran Communist Party (Partido Comunista de Honduras)
PCN	National Conciliation Party (Partido de Conciliación Nacional) (ES)

PCS	Communist Party of El Salvador (Partido Comunista de El Salvador)
PDC	Christian Democratic Party (Partido Demócrata Cristiano) (ES)
PDCG	Christian Democratic Party of Guatemala (Partido Demócrata Cristiano de Guatemala)
PDCH	Christian Democratic Party of Honduras (Partido Demócrata Cristiano de Honduras)
PGT	Guatemalan Labor Party (Partido Guatemalteco del Trabajo)
PID	Institutional Democratic Party (Partido Institucional Democrático) (G)
PINU	Innovation and Unity Party (Partido de Inovación y Unidad) (H)
PLC	Liberal Constitutionalist Party (Partido Liberal Constitucionalista) (N)
PLH	Honduran Liberal Party (Partido Liberal de Honduras)
PLN	Liberal Nationalist Party (Partido Liberal Nacionalista) (N)
PLN	National Liberation Party (Partido de Liberación Nacional) (CR)
PN	The National Party (Partido Nacional) (H)
PNC	National Civil Police (Policía Nacional Civil) (ES)
PR	Revolutionary Party (Partido Revolucionario) (G)
PRTC	Revolutionary Party of Central American Workers (Partido Revolucionario de Trabajadores Centroamericanos-Costa Rica)
PRTCH	Revolutionary Party of Central American Workers of Honduras (Partido Revolucionario de Trabajadores Centroamericanos de Honduras)
PRTCS	Revolutionary Party of Central American Workers (Partido Revolucionario de Trabajadores Centroamericanos-El Salvador)
PRUD	Revolutionary Party of Democratic Unification (Partido Revolucionario de Unificación Democrática) (ES)
PSD	Democratic Socialist Party (Partido Socialista Demócrata) (G)
PTS	The Political Terror Scale
PUSC	Social Christian Unity Party (Partido de Unidad Social Cristiano) (CR)
RN	Nicaraguan Resistance (Resistencia Nicaragüense)
SAA	Structural adjustment agreements
TPS	Temporary protected status
TSE	Supreme Electoral Tribunal (Tribunal Supremo Electoral) (CR, ES, G)

UCN	Union of the National Center (Unión del Centro Nacional) (G)
UDEL	Democratic Liberation Union (Unión Democrática de Liberación) (N)
UDN	Democratic National Union (Unión Democrática Nacionalista) (ES)
UFCO	United Fruit Company
UN	United Nations
UNAG	National Union of Farmers and Ranchers (Unión Nacional de Agricultores y Ganaderos) (N)
UNE	National Unity of Hope (Unidad Nacional de la Esperanza) (G)
UNO	National Opposition Union (Unión Nacional Opositora) (N & ES)
URNG	Guatemalan National Revolutionary Union (Unidad Revolucionaria Nacional Guatemalteca)
USAID	U.S. Agency for International Development
USDEA	U.S. Drug Enforcement Agency
USSR	Union of Soviet Socialist Republics

Notes

Chapter 1

1. John A. Booth and Thomas W. Walker, *Understanding Central America* (Boulder: Westview Press, 1989 ed. and 1993 ed.).

2. We except from this generalization Costa Rica, which had enjoyed civilian constitutional government since the 1950s. In 2004 Freedom House ranked Costa Rica as "free" and the remaining four countries of the region "partly free." See Freedom House, *Freedom in the World 2004,* www.freedomhouse.org/research/freeworld/2004/table2004.pdf, accessed June 24, 2004.

3. Booth and Walker, *Understanding Central America,* 3rd ed. (Boulder: Westview Press, 1999), Ch. 5.

4. Our estimate is based on population data from Alan Heston, Robert Summers, and Bettina Aten, *Penn World Table Version 6.1,* Center for International Comparisons at the University of Pennsylvania (CICUP), October 2002; and David E. Ferranti, et al., *Inequality in Latin America and the Caribbean: Breaking with History?* Advance Conference Edition (Washington, DC: International Bank for Reconstruction and Development/The World Bank, October 2003), Table A.5. We estimate this to be the number of people surviving on less than U.S.$2 per day.

5. Here, and in certain other parts of this volume, much of the wording is from Thomas W. Walker's unsigned contribution to: Presbyterian Church (USA), *Adventure and Hope: Christians and the Crisis in Central America: Report to the 195th General Assembly of the Presbyterian Church* (Atlanta, 1983), pp. 57–91, 97–101. The authors wish to thank the Presbyterian Church for its kind permission to publish this material (which Walker wrote in 1982 while he was part of the

UPCUSA [United Presbyterian Church (USA)] Task Force on Central America) here in this form.

6. Population estimates for Central America for 2004 based on Alan Heston et al., *Penn World Table;* U.S. 1998 population projections from the U.S. Census Bureau, *State Populations Ranking Summary: 1995 and 2025:* http://www.census.gov/population/projections/state/9525 rank.

7. The first datum refers to investment from all sources as percent of GDP, from Heston et al., *Penn World Table*; social spending datum from David E. Ferranti et al., *Inequality in Latin America and the Caribbean: Breaking with History?* Advance Conference Edition (Washington, DC: International Bank for Reconstruction and Development/The World Bank, October 2003), Table 4.1.

8. Although it is outside the purview of our study, the United States invaded Panama in 1989 to oust its dictator and install in power the true victors of the 1989 election. Though this is an example of intense attention, the U.S. government's focus on the other five nations during this later period was much less overtly public and confrontational than had been the case under President Reagan.

Chapter 2

1. For a compelling discussion of the argument that economic and political forces shaping Central America derive from the transformation of the global economy, see William I. Robinson, *Transitional Conflicts: Central America, Social Change, and Globalization* (London: Verso, 2003), and especially Ch. 1, and *Promoting Polyarchy: Globalization, U.S. Intervention, and Hegemony* (Cambridge: Cambridge University Press, 1996).

2. See Table 1.1 for 2000 GDP per capita estimates. Latin American GDP per capita estimated from Alan Heston, Robert Summers, and Bettina Aten, *Penn World Table Version 6.1*, Center for International Comparisons at the University of Pennsylvania (CICUP), October 2002, and Inter-American Development Bank (IADB), *Economic and Social Progress in Latin America: 1997 Report* (Baltimore: Johns Hopkins University Press, 1997), Table B–2. U.S. data from U.S. Bureau of Economic Analysis, "National Accounts Data," Table 3, www.bea.doc.gov/bea/dn/niptbl-d/hti#Table 1.Part B, April 8, 1998. Estimate of U.S. GDP per capita based on population estimate of 270 million.

3. For an extended overview of data on Central America's social welfare and inequality within the larger Latin American context, see David E. Ferranti et al., *Inequality in Latin America and the Caribbean: Breaking with History?* Advance Conference Edition (Washington, DC: International Bank for Reconstruction and Development/The World Bank, October 2003).

4. Urban and rural populations and growth rates for 1996 from IADB, *1997 Report,* Table A–2.

5. Wallace W. Atwood and Helen Goss Thomas, *The Americas* (Boston: Ginn and Co., 1929), p. 45.

6. For an overview, see, for instance, Ronald H. Chilcote and Joel C. Edelstein, *Latin America: Capitalist and Socialist Perspectives of Development and Underdevelopment* (Boulder: Westview Press, 1986).

7. For evidence see the Appendix, Table A.5. The exception to this came during the Nicaraguan revolution in the 1980s, during parts of which state spending exceeded half of GDP. Because of the Contra war, however, the revolutionary government cut back many social programs in order to divert funds to defense spending.

8. Robinson, *Transitional Conflicts,* pp. 50–53.

9. This concept of political regimes draws upon Charles W. Anderson, "The Latin American Political System," in Charles W. Anderson, *Politics and Economic Change in Latin America: The Governing of Restless Nations* (New York: Van Nostrand Reinhold, 1967), and also owes something to the conceptualization of John Higley and Michael Burton, "The Elite Variable in Democratic Transitions and Breakdowns," *American Sociological Review* 54, No. 1 (1989), pp. 17–32; and to Gary Wynia's use of the term "political game," in his *Politics of Latin American Development* (Cambridge: Cambridge University Press, 1990), pp. 24–45.

10. Note that any such categorization of regimes is somewhat arbitrary, but we undertake the effort in Table 2.3 to illustrate the extent and the high number of regime changes in Central America. The authors discussed and to some extent disagreed about labeling the regime types and dates of change, especially for Nicaragua, without straying from the regime change criterion (new rules and new coalition) laid out above.

11. Barrington Moore, *Social Origins of Dictatorship and Democracy* (Boston: Beacon Press, 1966).

12. Guillermo O'Donnell, *Modernization and Bureaucratic Authoritarianism: Studies in South American Politics* (Berkeley and Los Angeles: University of California Press, 1973).

13. Juan J. Linz and Alfred Stepan, eds., *The Breakdown of Democratic Regimes* (Baltimore: Johns Hopkins University Press, 1978); Guillermo O'Donnell, Philippe C. Schmitter, and Lawrence Whitehead, eds., *Transitions from Authoritarian Rule* (Baltimore: Johns Hopkins University Press, 1986).

14. Mark J. Gasiorowski, "Economic Crisis and Regime Change: An Event History Analysis," *American Political Science Review* 89 (1995), pp. 882–897; Mark J. Gasiorowski, "An Overview of the Political Regime Dataset," *Comparative Political Studies* 21 (1996), pp. 469–483.

15. Charles W. Anderson, "Toward a Theory of Latin American Politics," in Howard J. Wiarda, ed., *Politics and Social Change in Latin America: Still a Distinct Tradition?* (Boulder: Westview Press, 1992), pp. 239–254.

16. See John Peeler, *Latin American Democracies* (Chapel Hill: University of North Carolina Press, 1985); Deborah J. Yashar, *Demanding Democracy: Reform and Reaction in Costa Rica and Guatemala, 1870s–1950s* (Stanford: Stanford University Press, 1997); and John A. Booth, *Costa Rica: Quest for Democracy* (Boulder: Westview Press, 1998).

17. John A. Booth and Thomas W. Walker, *Understanding Central America,* 2nd ed. (Boulder: Westview Press, 1993), Chapter 5. For an excellent integrated overview of why and how revolutions occur, see T. David Mason, *Caught in the Crossfire: Revolutions, Repression, and the Rational Peasant* (Lanham, MD: Rowman and Littlefield, 2004).

18. Louis Kriesberg, *Social Conflicts,* 2nd ed. (Englewood Cliffs, NJ: Prentice-Hall, 1982), p. 29.

19. John Walton, *Reluctant Rebels: Comparative Studies in Revolution and Underdevelopment* (New York: Columbia University Press, 1984), p. 13.

20. Ibid.; Theda Skocpol, *States and Social Revolutions* (Cambridge: Cambridge University Press, 1979); Mancur Olson, "Rapid Growth as a Destabilizing Force," *Journal of Economic History* 23, No. 4 (1963), pp. 529–552; and Jeffrey M. Paige, *Agrarian Revolution: Social Movements and Export Agriculture in the Underdeveloped World* (New York: Free Press, 1975). For specific applications to Central America, see Charles Brockett, *Land, Power, and Poverty: Agrarian Transformation and Political Conflict in Central America* (Boston: Unwin Hyman, 1988); Timothy Wickham-Crowley, *Guerrillas and Revolution in Latin America* (Princeton: Princeton University Press, 1992); Robert Williams, *Export Agriculture and the Crisis in Central America* (Chapel Hill: University of North Carolina Press, 1986); John A. Booth, "Socioeconomic and Political Roots of National Revolts in Central America," *Latin American Research Review* 26, No. 1 (1991), pp. 33–73; Edelberto Torres Rivas, *Crisis del poder in Centroamérica* (San José, Costa Rica: Editorial Universitaria Centroamericana, 1981); and Mason, *Caught in the Crossfire.*

21. Kriesberg, *Social Conflicts,* pp. 66–106; Charles Tilly, *From Mobilization to Revolution* (Reading, MA: Addison-Wesley, 1978); Rod Aya, "Theories of Revolution Reconsidered: Contrasting Models of Collective Violence," *Theory and Society* 8 (June-December 1979), pp. 39–100; Mason, *Caught in the Crossfire.*

22. Jack A. Goldstone, "An Analytical Framework," in Jack A. Goldstone, Ted Robert Gurr, and Farrokh Moshiri, eds., *Revolutions of the Late Twentieth Century* (Boulder: Westview, 1991), pp. 37–51; Ted Robert Gurr, *Why Men Rebel* (Princeton: Princeton University Press, 1970); Walton, *Reluctant Rebels;* Skocpol, *States and Social Revolutions.*

23. Goldstone, "An Analytical Framework"; and James DeFronzo, *Revolutions and Revolutionary Movements* (Boulder: Westview, 1991), pp. 7–25; Robinson, *Promoting Polyarchy* and *Transitional Conflicts.*

24. Timothy P. Wickham-Crowley, *Guerrillas and Revolution in Latin America: A Comparative Study of Insurgents and Regimes Since 1956* (Princeton: Princeton University Press, 1992).

25. Ronald Inglehart, "The Renaissance of Political Culture," *American Political Science Review* 82 (November 1988), pp. 1203–1230; Mitchell A. Seligson and John A. Booth, "Political Culture and Regime Type: Evidence from Nicaragua and Costa Rica," *Journal of Politics* 55 (August 1993), pp. 777–792; Edward N. Muller and Mitchell A. Seligson, "Civic Culture and Democracy: The Question of Causal Relationships," *American Political Science Review* 88 (September 1994), pp. 645–652; Larry Diamond, "Introduction: Political Culture and Democracy," and "Causes and Effects," both in Larry Diamond, ed., *Political Culture and Democracy in Developing Countries* (Boulder: Lynne Rienner, 1994).

26. Dankwart Rustow, "Transitions to Democracy: Toward a Dynamic Model," *Comparative Politics* 2 (April 1970), pp. 337–363; Adam Przeworski, "Some Problems in the Study of the Transition to Democracy," in O'Donnell, Schmitter, and Whitehead, eds., *Transitions from Authoritarian Rule* (Baltimore: Johns Hopkins University Press, 1986); Samuel P. Huntington, *The Third Wave: Democratization in the Late Twentieth Century* (Norman: University of Oklahoma Press, 1991); Mitchell A. Seligson and John A. Booth, eds., *Elections and Democracy in Central America, Revisited* (Chapel Hill: University of North Carolina Press, 1995).

27. Seymour Martin Lipset, "Social Requisites of Democracy: Economic Development and Political Legitimacy," *American Political Science Review* 53 (March 1959), pp. 69–105; Tatu Vanhanen, *The Process of Democratization* (New York: Crane Russak, 1990); Dietrich Rueschemeyer, Evelyne Huber Stephens, and John D. Stephens, *Capitalist Development and Democracy* (Chicago: University of Chicago Press, 1992); Robert D. Putnam, "Bowling Alone: America's Declining Social Capital," *Journal of Democracy* 7 (Summer 1996), pp. 38–52; and Robert D. Putnam, *Making Democracy Work: Civic Traditions in Modern Italy* (Princeton: Princeton University Press, 1993).

28. Lawrence Whitehead, "The Imposition of Democracy," in Abraham F. Lowenthal, ed., *Exporting Democracy: The United States and Latin America* (Baltimore: Johns Hopkins University Press, 1991).

29. Peeler, *Latin American Democracies;* Larry Diamond, "Introduction: Politics, Society, and Democracy in Latin America," in Larry Diamond, Juan Linz, and Seymour Martin Lipset, *Democracy in Developing Countries,* Volume 4, *Latin America* (Boulder: Lynne Rienner, 1989); John Higley and Richard Gunther, eds.,

Elites and Democratic Consolidation in Latin America and Southern Europe (Cambridge: Cambridge University Press, 1992); and Huntington, *The Third Wave.*

30. Robinson, *Promoting Polyarchy* and *Transitional Conflicts.*

31. For example, Lowenthal, ed., *Exporting Democracy;* Thomas Carothers, *In the Name of Democracy: U.S. Policy Toward Latin America in the Reagan Years* (Berkeley: University of California Press, 1991); Huntington, *The Third Wave;* Dario Moreno, "Respectable Intervention: The United States and Central American Elections," in Seligson and Booth, eds., *Elections and Democracy in Central America, Revisited;* Thomas W. Walker, "Introduction: Historical Setting and Important Issues," in Thomas W. Walker, ed., *Nicaragua Without Illusions: Regime Transition and Structural Adjustment in the 1990s* (Wilmington, DE: Scholarly Resources, 1997); Gary Prevost and Harry E. Vanden, eds., *The Undermining of the Sandinista Revolution* (New York: St. Martin's, 1997); Wickham-Crowley, *Guerrillas and Revolution;* and DeFronzo, *Revolutions and Revolutionary Movements.*

32. Seven training manuals used between 1982 and 1991 were disclosed by the Department of Defense. See U.S. Department of Defense, "Fact Sheet Concerning Training Manuals Containing Materials Inconsistent with U.S. Policy" (Washington, DC: September 1996). See also Dana Priest, "U.S. Instructed Latins on Execution, Torture—Manuals Used 1982–1991, Pentagon Reveals," *Washington Post,* September 21, 1996, pp. A1, A9; Lisa Haugaard, "How the US Trained Latin America's Military: The Smoking Gun," *Envio* 16, No. 165 (October 1997), pp. 33–38.

33. The words of a State Department official who appeared with coauthor Walker on a panel on Central America at California State University, Los Angeles, on April 20, 1979.

34. The Contra war and conflict with the United States would continue during the first three years of the new civilian democratic regime and three remaining years of Daniel Ortega's presidential term, at that time obscuring the profound import of these changes. The 1987 Central American Peace Accord eventually facilitated a negotiated end to the war. In the 1990 election Nicaragua's voters, disillusioned by a collapsing economy and the Contra war, replaced the FSLN administration with the opposition.

35. The Political Terror Scale (PTS) and Freedom House (FH) scores provide useful comparative measures but must be viewed with some caution since they are compiled by evaluators who attempt systematically to glean evidence over time from press coverage of incidents of political violence (PTS) or political rights and liberties (FH). Accordingly, they reflect the biases and fluctuating intensity of coverage of the U.S. newspapers from which they are drawn and their manipulation by U.S. foreign policy makers. These biases are clearly seen in 1980s scores for relatively rights-respectful ("enemy") Nicaragua, which are practically as poor as those for massively rights-abusive ("friends") El Salvador and Guatemala in the same

period. That said, we still find these indexes useful in illustrating change over time within individual countries, especially El Salvador, Guatemala, and Honduras. In those instances they help us to draw reasonably valid inferences about evolving liberties and levels of political violence.

Chapter 3

1. Good histories are Ralph Lee Woodward, Jr., *Central America: A Nation Divided,* 2nd ed. (New York: Oxford University Press, 1985), and Mario Rodríguez, *Central America* (Englewood Cliffs, NJ: Prentice-Hall, 1965). The best short history is Hector Pérez Brignoli, *A Brief History of Central America* (Berkeley: University of California Press, 1989). For a longer treatment, see James Dunkerley, *Power in the Isthmus: A Political History of Modern Central America* (London: Verso, 1988). See also Chapter 3 of John A. Booth, *Costa Rica: Quest for Democracy* (Boulder: Westview Press, 1998).

2. See David Richard Radell, "An Historical Geography of Western Nicaragua: The Spheres of Leon, Granada, and Managua, 1519–1965," Ph.D. dissertation, University of California, Berkeley, 1969, pp. 66–80.

3. *Criollos* (creoles) were people of European origin born in the colonies. Descendants of the conquerors and land grantees, many had wealth but the colonial system restricted their political and administrative power.

4. On the Walker filibuster and its aftermath, see Karl Bermann, *Under the Big Stick: Nicaragua and the United States Since 1848* (Boston: South End Press, 1986).

5. Honduras never really developed a landowning aristocracy; economic and political power remained in the hands of regional *hacendados* and newer urban industrial-commercial-financial entrepreneurs.

6. Enrique A. Baloyra, "Reactionary Despotism in Central America," *Journal of Latin American Studies* 15 (November 1983), pp. 295–319.

7. Ibid., pp. 309–310.

8. In Honduras, agrarian colonization and expanding employment in the modern capitalist sector of agriculture continued to absorb much of the growth of the rural labor force.

9. Victor Bulmer-Thomas, *The Political Economy of Central America Since 1920* (Cambridge: Cambridge University Press, 1987), pp. 177–180.

10. See Appendix Tables 1 and 2 of the 3rd edition of John A. Booth and Thomas W. Walker, *Understanding Central America* (Boulder: Westview Press, 1999).

11. John Weeks, "The Industrial Sector," in Thomas W. Walker, ed., *Nicaragua: The First Five Years* (New York: Praeger, 1985), pp. 281–296; and John Weeks, *The Economies of Central America* (New York: Holmes and Meier, 1985), pp. 101–151.

12. Weeks, *The Economies of Central America,* p. 284.

13. Per capita GDP trends in constant dollar terms from Alan Heston, Robert Summers, and Bettina Aten, *Penn World Table Version 6.1,* Center for International Comparisons at the University of Pennsylvania (CICUP), October 2002.

Chapter 4

1. On the downside, critics argue that Costa Rican exceptionalism is often carried to xenophobic and racist extremes, especially vis-à-vis Nicaraguans. This charge is articulated by Costa Rican scholar Carlos Sandoval-Garcia in *Threatening Others: Nicaraguans and the Formation of National Identities in Costa Rica* (Athens: Ohio University Press, 2004), the Spanish edition of which won the 2002 Costa Rican National Monograph Award.

2. Bruce M. Wilson, *Costa Rica: Politics, Economics, and Democracy* (Boulder: Lynne Rienner Publishers, 1998); John A. Booth, *Costa Rica: Quest for Democracy* (Boulder: Westview Press, 1998); William I. Robinson, *Transnational Conflicts: Central America, Social Change, and Globalization* (London: Verso, 2003).

3. John A. Booth, "Representative Constitutional Democracy in Costa Rica: Adaptation to Crisis in the Turbulent 1980s," in Steve Ropp and James Morris, eds., *Central America: Crisis and Adaptation* (Albuquerque: University of New Mexico Press, 1984), Table 5.1. Other material on the evolution of Costa Rica drawn from Mitchell A. Seligson and Miguel Gómez, "Ordinary Elections in Extraordinary Times: The Political Economy of Voting in Costa Rica," in John A. Booth and Mitchell A. Seligson, eds., *Elections and Democracy in Central America* (Chapel Hill: University of North Carolina Press, 1989); John A. Booth, "Costa Rica: The Roots of Democratic Stability," in Larry Diamond, Juan J. Linz, and Seymour Martin Lipset, eds., *Democracy in Developing Countries, Volume 4: Latin America* (Boulder: Lynne Rienner, 1989), pp. 387–422; Lowell Gudmundson, *Costa Rica Before Coffee* (Baton Rouge: Louisiana State University Press, 1986); and from interviews by Booth with Costa Rican scholars and political experts during author's visits there in August 1987, January 1988, and December 1990. See also Booth, *Costa Rica: Quest for Democracy,* Ch. 3.

4. See Booth, *Costa Rica: Quest for Democracy,* pp. 40–42; Astrid Fischel, *Consenso y represión: Una interpretación sociopolítica de la educación costarricense* (San José: Editorial Costa Rica, 1987).

5. Booth, *Costa Rica: Quest for Democracy,* p. 42, and Fabrice E. Lehoucq and Ivan Molina, *Stuffing the Ballot Box: Fraud, Electoral Reform, and Democratization in Costa Rica* (Cambridge: Cambridge University Press, 2002), Ch. 1.

6. John A. Booth and Thomas W. Walker, *Understanding Central America,* 3rd ed. (Boulder: Westview Press, 1999), Appendix Tables 1 and 2.

7. See Chapter 2 or, for more detail, John A. Booth, "Socioeconomic and Political Roots of National Revolts in Central America," *Latin American Research Review* 26 (1991, No. 1), pp. 33–74.

8. Booth and Walker, *Understanding Central America*, 3rd ed., Appendix Table 6.

9. See also Victor Bulmer-Thomas, *The Political Economy of Central America Since 1920* (New York: Cambridge University Press, 1987), Table 10.7, p. 219; Víctor Hugo Céspedes, Alberto di Mare, and Ronulfo Jiménez, *Costa Rica: La economía en 1985* (San José, Costa Rica: Academia de Centroamérica, 1986), Cuadro 19, p. 71.

10. Booth and Walker, *Understanding Central America,* 3rd ed., Appendix Table 7 and see Table 6.

11. Víctor Hugo Céspedes, *Evolución de la distribución del ingreso en Costa Rica* (San José, Costa Rica: Instituto de Investigación en Ciencias Económicas, Universidad de Costa Rica, 1979), Cuadro 6; and Céspedes et al., *Costa Rica: La economía en 1985,* Cuadro 20, p. 73; David Felix, "Income Distribution and the Quality of Life in Latin America: Patterns, Trends, and Policy Implications," *Latin American Research Review* 18, No. 2 (1983), pp. 3–34.

12. For further data, see John A. Booth, "Representative Constitutional Democracy in Costa Rica: Adaptation to Crisis in the Turbulent 1980s," in S. Ropp and J. Morris, eds., *Central America: Crisis and Adaptation* (Albuquerque: University of New Mexico Press, 1984), p. 171. On the operation and impact of the Costa Rican development model, see John A. Booth, *Costa Rica: Quest for Democracy* (Boulder: Westview Press, 1998), Chapters 3 and 8.

13. Mitchell A. Seligson, *Peasants of Costa Rica and the Development of Agrarian Capitalism* (Madison: University of Wisconsin Press, 1980), pp. 122–170; see also Francisco Barahona Riera, *Reforma agraria y poder político* (San José: Editorial Universidad de Costa Rica, 1980), pp. 221–422; Donaldo Castillo Rivas, "Modelos de acumulación, agricultura, y agroindustria en Centroamérica," in D. Castillo Rivas, ed., *Centroamérica: Más allá de la crisis* (México: Ediciones SIAP, 1983), pp. 210–213.

14. Booth and Walker, *Understanding Central America,* 3rd ed., Appendix, Table A8.

15. E. Lederman et al., "Trabajo y empleo," in Chester Zelaya, ed., *Costa Rica contemporánea,* Tomo II (San José: Editorial Costa Rica, 1979); James Backer, *La Iglesia y el sindicalismo en Costa Rica* (San José: Editorial Costa Rica, 1978), pp. 135–207; Gustavo Blanco and Orlando Navarro, *El solidarismo: Pensamiento y dinámica social de un movimiento obrero patronal* (San José: Editorial Costa Rica, 1984).

16. Rodrigo Fernández Vásquez, "Costa Rica: Interpretación histórica sobre reforma social y acción eclesiástica: 1940–1982," *Estudios Sociales Centroamericanos* 33 (September–December 1982), pp. 221–248.

17. This material is from John A. Booth, "Costa Rica: The Roots of Democratic Stability," in Larry Jay Diamond, Seymour Martin Lipset, and Juan J. Linz, eds. *Democracy in Developing Countries,* Volume 4: *Latin America* (Boulder: Lynne Rienner, 1989); and Booth, "Representative Constitutional Democracy."

18. Booth and Walker, *Understanding Central America,* 3rd ed., see Appendix Tables 5 and 6.

19. "Costa Rica," *Mesoamérica,* April 1990, pp. 11–12; "Costa Rica," *Mesoamérica,* July 1990, pp. 7–8; "Costa Rica," *Mesoamérica,* October 1990, p. 9; "Costa Rica," *Mesoamérica,* November 1990, pp. 9–10; "Costa Rica," *Mesoamérica,* December 1990, p. 11; "Costa Rica," *Mesoamérica,* January 1991, pp. 4–7; "Costa Rica," *Mesoamérica,* February 1991, pp. 4–5; "Costa Rica," *Mesoamérica,* April 1991, pp. 1–2.

20. John A. Booth, "Political Parties in Costa Rica," in P. Webb, S. White, and D. Stansfield, eds., *Political Parties in Transitional Democracies* (Oxford: Oxford University Press, expected 2004 forthcoming); Mitchell A. Seligson and Edward Muller, "Democracy, Stability, and Economic Crisis: Costa Rica, 1978–1983," *International Studies Quarterly* 31 (September 1987), pp. 301–326; and Booth, "Costa Rican Democracy."

21. Booth, "Representative Constitutional Democracy," pp. 173–176; Booth, "Costa Rican Democracy," pp. 39–40; Seligson, *Peasants,* pp. 105–114; U.S. Department of State, *Country Reports on Human Rights Practices* (Washington, DC: U.S. Government Printing Office, February 2, 1981), pp. 241–244. See also Booth, *Costa Rica: Quest for Democracy,* pp. 114–121.

22. This section draws heavily on Booth, "Political Parties in Costa Rica." Data are drawn from Mary A. Clark, "Nontraditional Export Promotion in Costa Rica: Sustaining Export-Led Growth," *Journal of Interamerican Studies and World Affairs* 37 (1995, No. 2), pp. 181–223; Wilson, *Costa Rica: Politics, Economics, and Democracy*, pp. 113–150; Booth, *Costa Rica: Quest for Democracy*, ch. 8; and Booth and Walker, *Understanding Central America*, 3rd ed., Appendix Tables 1, 4, and 5.

23. Robinson, *Transnational Conflicts*, pp. 64–65.

24. Booth, *Costa Rica: Quest for Democracy,* ch. 8.

25. Ibid.

26. Ibid., pp. 166–172 and Table 8.5; election data from Tables 3.4 and 4.1; Booth and Walker, *Understanding Central America,* 3rd ed., Appendix Table 6.

27. Alan Heston, Robert Summers, and Bettina Aten, *Penn World Table Version 6.1* (Philadelphia: Center for International Comparisons at the University of Pennsylvania—CICUP, October 2002); Interamerican Development Bank, country notes, www.iadb.org/exr/country/, accessed June 14, 2004.

28. Robinson, *Transnational Conflicts,* ch. 4.

29. This section draws heavily on Booth, "Political Parties in Costa Rica."

30. Kenneth M. Roberts, "Rethinking Economic Alternatives: Left Parties and the Articulation of Popular Demands in Chile and Peru," and Carlos M. Vilas, "Participation, Inequality, and the Whereabouts of Democracy," both in Douglas A. Chalmers, Carlos M. Vilas, Katherine Hite, Scott B. Martin, Kerianne Piester, and Monique Segarra, eds., *The New Politics of Inequality in Latin America: Rethinking Participation and Representation* (Oxford: Oxford University Press, 1997); and William I. Robinson, *Promoting Polyarchy: Globalization, U.S. Intervention and Hegemony* (Cambridge: Cambridge University Press, 1996).

31. Regine Steichen, "Cambios en la orientación política-ideológica de los partidos políticos en la década de los '80," and Marcelo J. Prieto, "Cambios en las organizaciones políticas costarricenses," in José Manuel Villasuso, ed., *El nuevo rostro de Costa Rica* (Heredia, Costa Rica: Centro de Estudios Democráticos de América Latina, 1992); Wilson, *Costa Rica: Politics, Economics, and Democracy;* and Carlos Sojo, "En el nombre del padre: Patrimonialismo y democracia en Costa Rica," in Manuel Rojas Bolaños and Carlos Sojo, *El malestar con la política: Partidos y élites en Costa Rica* (San José, Costa Rica: Facultad Latinoamericano de Ciencias Sociales, 1995), pp. 84–86.

32. Oscar Alvarez, "Costa Rica," *Boletín Electoral Latinoamericano* 17 (January-June 1997), p. 60.

33. Booth, "Political Parties in Costa Rica," Tables 2 and 3.

34. Ibid., and Manuel Rojas Bolaños, "Las relaciones partido gobierno," in Manuel Rojas Bolaños and Carlos Sojo, *El malestar con la política: Partidos y élites en Costa Rica* (San José, Costa Rica: Facultad Latinoamericano de Ciencias Sociales), pp. 36–50; Booth, *Costa Rica: Quest for Democracy,* Chapter 8; and Wilson, *Costa Rica: Politics, Economics, and Democracy,* p. 161.

35. Booth, "Political Parties in Costa Rica," Tables 2, 3, and 5.

36. Robinson, p. 245.

37. The World Bank Group, Latin America and the Caribbean, *Costa Rica: Social Spending and the Poor,* bln0018.wldbank.org/LAC/lacinfoclient.nsf/d29684951174975c85256735007fef12/f24ea1b7e81104ca85256dde006546f4/$FILE/CR%20Social%20Spend%20Part1.pdf, accessed January 6, 2005.

38. Ibid.

39. Ibid.

40. *Central America Report,* November 2000, p. 6, and June 2001.

41. See Robinson, pp. 142–146.

42. "Protests Put Privatization on Hold," *Central America Report,* April 7, 2000, p. 6; "Telecom Privatization Ruled Unconstitutional," *Central America Report,* May 12, 2000, p. 6.

43. *Central American Report,* May 1999, p. 7.

44. *Central American Report,* September 2003.

Chapter 5

1. Paul Levy, as quoted in Jaime Wheelock Román, *Imperialismo y dictadura: Crisis de una formación social* (México: Siglo Veintiuno Editores, 1975), p. 29.

2. See John A. Booth and Thomas W. Walker, *Understanding Central America*, 3rd ed. (Boulder: Westview Press, 1999), Appendix Table 1.

3. For an extended discussion of this material, see ibid., pp. 69–76 and data in Appendix Tables 5, 6, 7, and 8.

4. Centro de Investigaciones y Estudios de la Reforma Agraria (CIERA), *Informe de Nicaragua a la FAO* (Managua: Ministerio de Desarrollo Agropecuario y Reforma Agraria, 1983), pp. 40–41.

5. Mario A. DeFranco and Carlos F. Chamorro, "Nicaragua: Crecimiento industrial y empleo," in Daniel Camacho et al., *El fracaso social de la integración centroamericana* (San José, Costa Rica: Editorial Universitaria Centroamericana, 1979), Cuadro 2.

6. John A. Booth, *The End and the Beginning: The Nicaraguan Revolution*, 2nd ed. (Boulder: Westview Press, 1985), Ch. 5.

7. See Booth and Walker, *Understanding Central America*, 3rd ed., Appendix Table 8. Note that computational methods vary from nation to nation, so that cross-national comparisons of unemployment rates should not be made. Trends within nations in the table, however, are usefully disclosed.

8. Donaldo Castillo Rivas, "Modelos de acumulación, agricultura, y agroindustria en Centroamérica," in D. Castillo Rivas, ed., *Centroamérica: Más allá de la crisis* (México: Ediciones SIAP, 1983), pp. 202–205; Consejo Superior Universitaria Centroamericana (CSUCA), *Estructura Agraria, dinámica de población, y desarrollo capitalista en Centroamérica* (San José, Costa Rica: Editorial Universitaria Centroamericana, 1978), pp. 204–254.

9. CIERA, *Informe de Nicaragua*, p. 41.

10. Jaime Wheelock Román, *Imperialismo y dictadura: Crisis de una formación social* (México: Siglo Veintiuno Editores, 1975), pp. 141–198; Amaru Barahona Portocarrero, *Estudio sobre la historia contemporánea de Nicaragua* (San José, Costa Rica: Instituto de Investigaciones Sociales, Universidad de Costa Rica, 1977), pp. 33–44.

11. Material from Ricardo E. Chavarría, "The Nicaraguan Insurrection," in Thomas W. Walker, ed., *Nicaragua in Revolution* (New York: Praeger, 1982), pp. 28–29; Booth, *The End and the Beginning*, Ch. 6.

12. George Black, *Triumph of the People: The Sandinista Revolution in Nicaragua* (London: Zed Press, 1981), pp. 70–72; Centro de Información, Documentación y Análisis del Movimiento Obrero Latinoamericano (CIDAMO), "El movimiento obrero," in G. García Márquez et al., *Los Sandinistas* (Bogotá: Editorial Oveja Negra, 1979), pp. 171–176.

13. Michael Dodson and Tommie Sue Montgomery, "The Churches in the Nicaraguan Revolution," in Walker, ed., *Nicaragua in Revolution,* pp. 163–174; Laura Nuzzi O'Shaughnessy and Luis H. Serra, *The Church and Revolution in Nicaragua* (Athens: Monographs in International Studies, Latin American Series No. 11, Ohio University, 1986).

14. See also T. Walker, "Introduction," in Thomas W. Walker, ed., *Nicaragua: The First Five Years* (New York: Praeger Publishers, 1985), p. 20; Julio López C. et al., *La caída del somocismo y la lucha sandinista en Nicaragua* (San José, Costa Rica: Editorial Universitaria Centroamericano, 1979), pp. 98–112.

15. Thomas W. Walker, *The Christian Democratic Movement in Nicaragua* (Tucson: University of Arizona Press, 1970).

16. Omar Cabezas, *Fire from the Mountain,* trans. Kathleen Weaver (New York: New American Library, 1986).

17. Booth, *The End and the Beginning,* Ch. 8.

18. See ibid., pp. 97–104; López C. et al., *La caída del somocismo,* pp. 71–98.

19. "A Secret War for Nicaragua," *Newsweek,* November 8, 1982, p. 44. See also Peter Kornbluh, "The Covert War," in Thomas W. Walker, ed., *Reagan Versus the Sandinistas: The Undeclared War on Nicaragua* (Boulder: Westview Press, 1987), p. 21.

20. Ariel C. Armony, *Argentina, the United States, and the Anticommunist Crusade in Central America, 1977–1984* (Athens: Ohio University Center for International Studies, 1997).

21. Tayacán [the CIA], *Psychological Operations in Guerrilla Warfare: The CIA's Nicaragua Manual* (New York: Vintage Books, 1985).

22. Michael Isikoff, "Drug Cartel Gave Contras $10 Million, Court Told," *Washington Post,* November 26, 1991, pp. A1, A8. For a detailed discussion of other ways in which drug money was used to finance the Contra effort, see Peter Dale Scott and Jonathan Marshall, *Cocaine Politics: Drugs, Armies and the CIA in Central America* (Berkeley: University of California Press, 1991).

23. See also Rose Spalding's *Capitalists and Revolution in Nicaragua: Opposition and Accommodation, 1979–1993* (Chapel Hill: University of North Carolina Press, 1994).

24. E.g., a detailed report by Latin Americanists, *The Electoral Process in Nicaragua: Domestic and International Influences* (Austin, TX: Latin American Studies Association, November 19, 1984); or Booth, *The End and the Beginning,* pp. 215–223.

25. For a balanced treatment of the building of governmental institutions in Sandinista Nicaragua and, in particular, the 1987 constitution, see Andrew A. Reding, "The Evolution of Governmental Institutions," in Thomas W. Walker, ed., *Revolution and Counterrevolution in Nicaragua* (Boulder: Westview Press, 1991), pp. 15–47. For more discussion of the constitution—pro and con—as well as a complete English translation, see Kenneth J. Mijeski, ed., *The Nicaraguan Constitution of 1987: English Translation and Commentary* (Athens: Ohio University Press, 1991).

26. For details, see Walker, ed., *Nicaragua in Revolution,* and *Nicaragua: The First Five Years.*

27. See Michael Linfield, "Human Rights," in Walker, ed., *Revolution and Counterrevolution in Nicaragua,* pp. 275–294.

28. Lawyers Committee for International Human Rights, *Nicaragua: Revolutionary Justice* (New York: April 1985), pp. 33–40.

29. John Spicer Nichols, "*La Prensa:* The CIA Connection," *Columbia Journalism Review* 28, No. 2 (July–August 1988), pp. 34, 35.

30. *Los Angeles Times,* June 27, 1986, p. 15.

31. Martin Diskin et al., "Peace and Autonomy on the Atlantic Coast of Nicaragua: A Report of the LASA Task Force on Human Rights and Academic Freedom," Part 2, *LASA Forum* 17 (Summer 1986), p. 15.

32. Americas Watch, *On Human Rights in Nicaragua* (New York, May 1982), pp. 58–80.

33. See Martin Diskin et al., "Peace and Autonomy on the Atlantic Coast of Nicaragua: A Report of the LASA Task Force on Human Rights and Academic Freedom," Part 1, *LASA Forum* 17 (Spring 1986), pp. 1–16; and Part 2, pp. 1–16.

34. Americas Watch, *On Human Rights in Nicaragua,* pp. 58–80.

35. See O'Shaughnessy and Serra, *The Church and Revolution in Nicaragua,* and *Los Angeles Times,* June 27, 1986, p. 15; June 30, 1986, p. 7; *New York Times,* July 5, 1986, p. 2.

36. "Latin Presidents Announce Accord on Contra Bases," *New York Times,* February 15, 1989, pp. 1, 4; *New York Times,* February 16, pp. 1, 6; "Nicaragua Pins Hopes on Turning Bureaucrats into Farmers," *Dallas Morning News,* February 22, 1989, p. 12A; and Booth's conversations with Mauricio Díaz of the Popular Social Christian Party and Pedro Joaquín Chamorro Barrios, former director of the Nicaraguan Resistance, Montezuma, New Mexico, February 1989.

37. Joseph R. Thome and David Kaimowitz, "Agrarian Reform," in Walker, ed., *Nicaragua: The First Five Years;* and Forrest D. Colburn, *Post-Revolutionary Nicaragua: State, Class, and the Dilemmas of Agrarian Policy* (Berkeley: University of California Press, 1986).

38. See Booth and Walker, *Understanding Central America,* 3rd ed., Appendix Table 9.

39. John Weeks, "The Industrial Sector," and Michael E. Conroy, "Economic Legacy and Policies: Performance and Critique," in Walker, ed., *Nicaragua: The First Five Years;* and interviews by Booth with COSEP members in León, August 1985.

40. See Booth and Walker, *Understanding Central America,* 3rd ed., Appendix, Table 5.

41. Latin American Studies Association (LASA) Commission to Observe the 1990 Nicaraguan Elections, *Electoral Democracy Under International Pressure* (Pittsburgh: LASA, March 15, 1990), p. 19.

42. [United Nations] Comisión Económica para América Latina y el Caribe, "Balance Preliminar de la Economía de América Latina y el Caribe, 1990," *Notas Sobre la Economía y el Desarrollo,* Nos. 500–501 (December 1990), p. 27.

43. This figure is part of eight pages of statistics on the human cost of the war provided to Walker by the Nicaraguan Ministry of the Presidency in January 1990.

44. LASA Commission, *Electoral Democracy,* pp. 24–26.

45. See Eric Weaver and William Barnes, "Opposition Parties and Coalitions," in Walker, ed., *Revolution and Counterrevolution in Nicaragua,* pp. 117–142.

46. An unidentified U.S. official quoted in "Chamorro Takes a Chance," *Time,* May 7, 1990, p. 43. For documentation of the massive U.S. intervention in Nicaragua's 1990 election, see William I. Robinson, *A Faustian Bargain: U.S. Involvement in the Nicaraguan Elections and American Foreign Policy in the Post–Cold War Era* (Boulder: Westview Press, 1992).

47. Coauthor Thomas Walker is in a particularly good position to attest to this upsurge in Contra activity. A member of the LASA Commission to Observe the 1990 Nicaraguan Elections, he was specifically assigned to observe and investigate the campaign and election in the war zone of northern Nicaragua in late 1989 and early 1990.

48. As quoted in "Ortega Livens up San José Summit," *Central America Report* 16, No. 43 (November 3, 1989), p. 340.

49. For a systematic and comprehensive examination of this period see Thomas W. Walker, ed. *Nicaragua Without Illusions: Regime Transition and Structural Adjustment in the 1990s,* (Wilmington, DE: Scholarly Resources, 1997).

50. See also Booth and Walker, *Understanding Central America,* 3rd ed., Appendix Tables 1 and 6.

51. As cited in Nitlapan-*Envío* Team, "President Alemán: First Moves, First Signals," *Envío* 16, No. 187–188 (February–March 1997), pp. 3–4.

52. William I. Robinson, *Transnational Conflicts: Central America, Social Change, and Globalization* (London and New York: Verso, 2003), pp. 78–79.

53. Ibid., p. 79.

54. See, for instance, "Nicaragua: Atlantic Coast Groups Rearm," *Central America Report* 25, No. 22 (June 11, 1998), p. 3.

55. J. Mark Ruhl, "Curbing Central America's Militaries," *Journal of Democracy* 15, No. 3 (July 2004), p. 141.

56. Shelly A. McConnell, "Institutional Development," pp. 45–64 in Walker, ed., *Nicaragua Without Illusions.*

57. The authors interviewed various Nicaraguan political leaders during June and July of 1998, including Víctor Hugo Tinoco, FSLN representative in the National Assembly; Dora María Téllez, professor, former minister of health, and leader of the MRS; René Núñez, a top official of the FSLN; Mariano Fiallos, professor and former head of the CSE; Alejandro Bendaña, author, former foreign ministry official

in the Ortega administration; Antonio Lacayo, businessman, farmer, and former minister of the presidency in the UNO government; Dr. Rigoberto Sampson, mayor of León. There was striking uniformity in their assessment of the FSLN's status.

58. On the election see John A. Booth and Patricia Bayer Richard, "The Nicaraguan Elections of October 1996," *Electoral Studies* 16, No. 3 (1997), pp. 386–393; John A. Booth, "Election Observation and Democratic Transition in Nicaragua," in Kevin J. Middlebrook, ed., *Electoral Observation and Democratic Transitions in Latin America* (La Jolla, CA: Center for U.S.-Mexican Studies of the University of California, San Diego, 1998); *Envío* 15 (December–January, 1996–1997); and Thomas W. Walker, Epilogue, in Walker, *Nicaragua Without Illusions,* pp. 305–311.

59. Nitlapan-*Envío* Team, "An Accord Besieged by Discord," *Envío* 16, No. 196 (November 1997), pp. 3–4.

60. On Alemán's scandal, see David Close and Kalowatie Deonandan, eds., *Undoing Democracy: The Politics of Electoral Caudillismo* (Lanham, MD: Lexington Books, 2004); on the scandal involving Ortega, see Juan Ramón Huerta, *El silencio del patriarca* (Managua: Litografía El Renacimiento, 1998); and "Extractos del testimonio desgarrador de Zoliamérica," *Confidencial* 2 (May 24–30, 1998), pp. 1, 9–11.

61. Robinson, *Transnational Conflicts,* p. 83; see also pp. 82–87.

62. See, for instance, "No aceptan Ortega" in *La Prensa Libre,* February 28, 2001 and "Garza tajante contra el FSLN" in *El Nuevo Diario,* April 6, 2001.

63. "Low Turnout in Nicaragua Elections; Big Win for FSLN," *Noticen,* November 11, 2004.

64. Ibid.

Chapter 6

1. See Tommie Sue Montgomery, *Revolution in El Salvador: Origins and Evolution* (Boulder: Westview Press, 1982); and Enrique Baloyra, *El Salvador in Transition* (Chapel Hill: University of North Carolina Press, 1982).

2. As quoted in Montgomery, *Revolution in El Salvador,* p. 46.

3. Baloyra, *El Salvador in Transition,* p. 35.

4. Tommie Sue Montgomery, "El Salvador: The Roots of Revolution," in Steve C. Ropp and James A. Morris, eds., *Central America: Crisis and Adaptation* (Albuquerque: University of New Mexico Press, 1984), p. 78.

5. See Stephen Webre, *José Napoleón Duarte and the Christian Democratic Party in Salvadorean Politics: 1960–1972* (Baton Rouge: Louisiana State University Press, 1979).

6. For a more detailed discussion and data on the CACM growth boom in El Salvador, see John A. Booth and Thomas W. Walker, *Understanding Central America,* 3rd ed. (Boulder: Westview Press, 1999), Ch. 7 and Appendix.

7. See ibid., Appendix Table 8; Hugo Molina, "Las bases económicas del desarrollo industrial *y* la absorción de fuerza de trabajo en El Salvador," in Daniel Camacho et al., *El fracaso social de la integración centroamericana* (San José, Costa Rica: Editorial Universitaria Centroamericana, 1979), pp. 245–254; Phillip L. Russell, *El Salvador in Crisis* (Austin, TX: Colorado River Press, 1984), pp. 76–78; Victor Antonio Orellana, *El Salvador: Crisis and Structural Change* (Miami: Latin American and Caribbean Center Occasional Paper Series No. 13, Florida International University, 1985), pp. 5–9; Victor Bulmer-Thomas, *The Political Economy of Central America Since 1920* (Cambridge: Cambridge University Press, 1987), pp. 175–229.

8. See especially Tommie Sue Montgomery, *Revolution in El Salvador: Origins and Evolution* (Boulder: Westview Press, 1982); Donaldo Castillo Rivas, "Modelos de acumulación, agricultura, y agroindustria en Centroamérica," in D. Castillo Rivas, ed., *Centroamérica: Más allá de la crisis* (México: Ediciones SIAP, 1983), pp. 204–207; James Dunkerley, *The Long War: Dictatorship and Revolution in El Salvador* (London: Junction Books, 1982), pp. 87–118.

9. Dirección General de Estadística y Censos (DGEC-El Salvador) *Anuario Estadístico, 1981,* Tomos III-V (San Salvador: Ministerio de Economía, 1983), Cuadros 311–01, 311–02; Bulmer-Thomas, *Political Economy of Central America,* pp. 201–207.

10. Orellana, *El Salvador: Crisis,* pp. 5–10; Molina, "Las bases económicas," pp. 245–254.

11. Orellana, *El Salvador: Crisis,* pp. 5–7.

12. Montgomery, *Revolution in El Salvador,* pp. 94–95.

13. Orellana, *El Salvador: Crisis,* pp. 6–7.

14. See Chapter 1, Table 1.1, and Booth and Walker, *Understanding Central America,* 3rd ed., Appendix Table 1.

15. Material based on Montgomery, *Revolution in El Salvador;* Dunkerley, *The Long War,* pp. 90–102; Jorge Cáceres Prendes, "Radicalización política y pastoral en El Salvador: 1969–1979," *Estudios Sociales Centroamericanos* 33 (September–December 1982), pp. 97–111.

16. Russell, *El Salvador in Crisis,* pp. 71–78; Tomás Guerra, *El Salvador en la hora de su liberación* (San José, Costa Rica: n.p., 1980), pp. 103–108; Baloyra, *El Salvador in Transition,* pp. 43–52.

17. DGEC-El Salvador, *Anuario Estadístico, 1981,* Tomos III–V.

18. Rafael Menjívar, *Formación y lucha del proletariado industrial salvadoreño* (San José, Costa Rica: Editorial Universitaria Centroamericano, 1982), pp. 115–162; Russell, *El Salvador in Crisis,* p. 71.

19. See Michael McClintock, *The American Connection,* Vol. 1: *State Terror and Popular Resistance in El Salvador* (London: Zed Books, 1985), pp. 156–209, for details on the rise of repression in El Salvador; see also Inforpress Centroamericano, *Central America Report,* January 20, 1984, p. 23.

20. McClintock, *The American Connection,* pp. 174–177.

21. Even in 2004, recourse to death squads—this time in quelling insurgents in Iraq—was reportedly still being advocated by certain U.S. officials who were veterans of the 1980s anticommunist crusade in Central America. See Michael Hirsh and John Barry, "The Salvador Option: The Pentagon May Put Special-Forces Led Assassination and Kidnapping Teams in Iraq," *Newsweek,* January 8, 2005, http://www.msnbc.com/id/680692/site/newsweek.

22. Tommie Sue Montgomery, "El Salvador: The Roots of Revolution," in Ropp and Morris, eds., *Central America: Crisis and Adaptation,* pp. 86–90.

23. Taken from DGEC-El Salvador, *Anuario Estadístico* for years 1965, 1966, 1968, 1969, 1971, 1977, 1980, and 1981; the figure reported in the table is the total number of "homicides" plus other, unexplained violent deaths.

24. Based on data reported in Baloyra, *El Salvador in Transition,* p. 190; and Richard Alan White, *The Morass: United States Intervention in Central America* (New York: Harper and Row, 1984), p. 44; and Inforpress Centroamericano, *Central America Report,* January 20, 1984, p. 23.

25. Comisión de Derechos Humanos de El Salvador (CDHES), *Primer Congreso de Derechos Humanos en El Salvador* (San Salvador, El Salvador: CDHES, November 1984), pp. 30–31, authors' translation.

26. It is unclear whether the Sandinistas were aware that arms were coming through their territory. When confronted with that charge by U.S. Ambassador Lawrence Pezzullo, Daniel Ortega of the Nicaraguan junta promised to stop the flow if the United States would indicate where it was originating. He was quickly told, the flow was stopped, and the U.S. Department of State then certified that it had stopped. Though no credible evidence of any significant subsequent arms flow from Nicaragua was ever presented, the Reagan and Bush administrations would repeat the charge over and over until it became accepted as fact by the U.S. media.

27. Philip J. Williams and Knut Walter, *Militarization and Demilitarization in El Salvador's Transition to Democracy* (Pittsburgh: University of Pittsburgh Press, 1997), pp. 100–113.

28. Ibid., p. 113.

29. Montgomery, *Revolution in El Salvador,* pp. 140–157.

30. Dunkerley, *The Long War,* p. 175.

31. Benjamin C. Schwarz, *American Counterinsurgency Doctrine and El Salvador: The Frustration of Reform and the Illusion of Nation Building* (Santa Monica, CA: Rand Corporation, 1991), p. v.

32. Baloyra, *El Salvador in Transition;* José Z. García, "El Salvador: Recent Elections in Historical Perspective," in John A. Booth and Mitchell A. Seligson, eds., *Elections and Democracy in Central America* (Chapel Hill: University of North Carolina Press, 1989), pp. 60–89.

33. Dunkerley, *The Long War,* p. 163.

34. For discussions of problems with the U.S.-backed elections in El Salvador in 1982, 1984, and 1985, see Terry Karl, "Imposing Consent: Electoralism vs. Democratization in El Salvador," in P. Drake and E. Silva, eds., *Elections and Democratization in Latin America* (La Jolla, CA: Center for Iberian and Latin American Studies—Center for U.S.-Mexican Studies, University of California, San Diego, 1986), p. 21; Edward S. Herman and Frank Brodhead, *Demonstration Elections* (Boston: South End Press, 1984), pp. 93–152; and García, "El Salvador: Recent Elections," pp. 60–89.

35. See, for instance, Karl, "Imposing Consent," pp. 18–34; and Clifford Krauss, "El Salvador Army Gains on the Guerrillas," *Wall Street Journal,* July 30, 1986, p. 20.

36. On elections see Enrique A. Baloyra, "Elections, Civil War, and Transition in El Salvador, 1982–1994: A Preliminary Evaluation," in Mitchell A. Seligson and John A. Booth, eds., *Elections and Democracy in Central America, Revisited* (Chapel Hill: University of North Carolina Press, 1995). On the military and peace negotiations, see Williams and Walter, *Militarization and Demilitarization in El Salvador,* Chs. 6 and 7; and Ricardo Córdova Macías, "El proceso de diálogo-negociación y las perspectivas de paz," in *El Salvador: Guerra, política, y paz, 1979–1989* (San Salvador: CINAS-CRIES, 1988), pp. 195–219; Ricardo Córdova Macías, *El Salvador: Las negociaciones de paz y los retos de la postguerra* (San Salvador: Instituto de Estudios Latinoamericanos, 1989).

37. Karl, "Imposing Consent."

38. Comisión de la Verdad, *De la locura a la esperanza: La guerra de doce años en El Salvador. Informe de la Comisión,* published in *Estudios Centroamericanos* 158 (March 1993), San Salvador; Booth and Walker, *Understanding Central America,* 3rd ed., Appendix Table 11.

39. Booth and Walker, *Understanding Central America,* 3rd ed., Appendix Table 1.

40. Points made in two lengthy interviews with three official FMLN spokespersons conducted by members of the Central American Task Force of the United Presbyterian Church's Council on Church and Society in Managua in November 1992. Coauthor Walker, a member of that task force, was present for the interviews.

41. Written Statement of Representative Joe Moakley, chairman of the Speaker's Task Force on El Salvador, November 18, 1991; see also the account in Comisión de la Verdad, *De la locura a la esperanza.*

42. Schwarz, *American Counterinsurgency Doctrine,* pp. v, vi.

43. See Philip J. Williams and Knut Walter, *Militarization and Demilitarization,* pp. 151–182.

44. For a discussion of police reform see Jack Spence, *War and Peace in Central America: Comparing Transitions Toward Democracy and Social Equity in Guatemala, El Salvador and Nicaragua* (Boston: Hemisphere Initiatives, November 2004), pp. 59–62.

45. For a detailed discussion of the reforms under Cristiani and Calderón Sol see Jack Spence, David Dye, Mike Lanchin, and Geoff Thale, *Chapultepec: Five Years Later* (Boston: Hemisphere Initiatives, January 16, 1997); Oscar Melhado, *El Salvador: Retos económicos de fin de siglo* (San Salvador: UCA Editores, 1997).

46. Growth averaged 6 percent annually between 1990 and 1995, but dropped to 3.0 percent from 1996 to 2000.

47. José Miguel Cruz, "Por qué no votan los Salvadoreños?" *Estudios Centroamericanos,* 1998, pp. 595–596.

48. Guardado and several others were expelled from the FMLN in 2001.

49. Instituto Universitario de Opinión Pública (IUDOP), *Evaluación del primer año del gobierno de Francisco Flores* (San Salvador: Universidad Centroamericana José Simeon Cañas, 2000).

50. Tribunal Supremo Electoral de El Salvador.

51. "Embajadora E.U.A. advierte contra FMLN," *La Prensa Gráfica,* June 4, 2003; "Peligraría la inversión americana; Entrevista: Rose M. Likins," *La Prensa Gráfica,* June 4, 2003; "Diferencias con FMLN: Noriega pide tomar la mejor decisión," *El Diario de Hoy,* February 7, 2004.

52. "Disturbing Statement out of El Salvador," *Congressional Record,* March 17, 2004, pp. E394-E395; "El Salvador," Congressional Record, March 17, 2004, page E402; "Election in El Salvador," *Congressional Record,* March 17, 2004, p. E389. Authors' note: In place since the 1980s, TPS is a concession by the United States of an exceptional right of many Salvadoran citizens to remain within the United States (there are hundreds of thousands of them) and to work. The maintenance of TPS would guarantee a continuation of the vast amounts of remissions by U.S.-based Salvadorans to their families, a mainstay of the Salvadoran national economy.

53. See, for instance, Freedom House, *Freedom in the World: The Annual Survey of Political Rights and Civil Liberties, 1993–1994* (New York: Freedom House, 1994), pp. 242–243; Comisión de la Verdad, *De la locura a la esperanza; La Prensa Gráfica* (July 31, 1994, pp. 4A–5A; August 1, 1994, pp. 4A–5A; August 2, 1994, pp. 4A–5A; August 4, 1994, pp. 4A–5A); Williams and Walter, *Militarization and Demilitarization,* Chs. 7 and 8; and "Penal Laws Cause Controversy," *Central America Report,* May 7, 1998, p. 4.

Chapter 7

1. George Black et al., *Garrison Guatemala* (New York: Monthly Review Press, 1984), p. 13.

2. Jerry L. Weaver, "Guatemala: The Politics of a Frustrated Revolution," in Howard J. Wiarda and Harvey F. Kline, eds., *Latin American Politics and Development* (Boston: Houghton Mifflin, 1979), p. 337.

3. Richard H. Immerman, *The CIA in Guatemala: The Foreign Policy of Intervention* (Austin: University of Texas Press, 1982), Chs. 2–7.

4. Richard Newbold Adams, *Crucifixion by Power: Essays on Guatemalan National Social Structure, 1944–1966* (Austin: University of Texas Press, 1970), p. 195.

5. See John Sloan, "The Electoral Game in Guatemala," Ph.D. dissertation, University of Texas at Austin, 1968.

6. See Appendix Tables 1 and 2 in John A. Booth and Thomas W. Walker, *Understanding Central America,* 3rd ed. (Boulder: Westview Press, 1999).

7. Ibid., Appendix Tables 5 and 6.

8. Inforpress Centroamericana, *Guatemala: Elections 1985* (Guatemala City, 1985), p. 19.

9. Booth and Walker, *Understanding Central America,* 3rd ed., Appendix Table 8.

10. Ibid.; Thomas P. Anderson, *Politics in Central America: Guatemala, El Salvador, Honduras, and Nicaragua* (New York: Praeger, 1982), pp. 19–62; "Guatemala," *Mesoamérica,* May 1982; Consejo Superior Universitaria Centroamericana (CSUCA), *Estructura agrária, dinámica de población, y desarrollo capitalista en Centroamérica* (San José, Costa Rica: Editorial Universitaria Centroamericana, 1978), pp. 77–132; Technical Commission of the Great National Dialogue, *Economic and Social Policy Recommendations to the Head of State* (Guatemala City, 1985); Lars Schoultz, "Guatemala: Social Change and Political Conflict," in Martin Diskin, ed., *Trouble in Our Backyard* (New York: Pantheon, 1983), pp. 178–183; Brockett, *Land, Power, and Poverty,* pp. 99–123; and Jonas, *The Battle for Guatemala,* Ch. 5.

11. Julio Castellano Cambranes, "Origins of the Crisis of the Established Order in Guatemala," in Ropp and Morris, eds., *Central America: Crisis,* Table 4.2.

12. Mitchell A. Seligson et al., *Land and Labor in Guatemala: An Assessment* (Washington, DC: Agency for International Development-Development Associates, 1982), pp. 1–18.

13. Black et al., *Garrison Guatemala,* pp. 34–37; Schoultz, "Guatemala," p. 181; Seligson et al., *Land and Labor.*

14. Gustavo A. Noyola, "Integración centroamericana y absorción de mano de obra: Guatemala," in Camacho et al., *El fracaso.*

15. Richard Newbold Adams, *Crucifixion by Power: Essays on Guatemalan National Social Structure, 1944–1966* (Austin: University of Texas Press, 1970); Black et al., *Garrison Guatemala,* pp. 48–51.

16. John A. Booth, "A Guatemalan Nightmare: Levels of Political Violence, 1966–1972," *Journal of Interamerican Studies and World Affairs* 22 (May 1980), pp. 195–225.

17. Gabriel Aguilera Peralta, Romero Imery, et al., *Dialéctica del terror en Guatemala* (San José, Costa Rica: Editorial Universitaria Centroamericana, 1981); Americas Watch, *Human Rights in Guatemala: No Neutrals Allowed* (New York, 1982), and *Little Hope: Human Rights in Guatemala, January 1984–1985* (New York, 1985);

John A. Booth et al., *The 1985 Guatemalan Elections: Will the Military Relinquish Power?* (Washington, DC: International Human Rights Law Group-Washington Office on Latin America, 1985); see also Gordon L. Bowen, "The Origins and Development of State Terrorism," in Donald E. Schulz and Douglas H. Graham, eds., *Revolution and Counterrevolution in Central America and the Caribbean* (Boulder: Westview Press, 1984); and "Guatemala," *Mesoamérica,* July-August 1982, pp. 2–4; Jonas, *The Battle for Guatemala,* pp. 145–177; Brockett, *Land, Power, and Poverty,* pp. 112–119; Black et al., *Garrison Guatemala,* pp. 61–107; Anderson, *Politics,* pp. 19–60; Inforpress Centroamericana, *Guatemala: Elections 1985,* pp. 8–11; Jonathan Fried et al., *Guatemala in Rebellion: Unfinished History* (New York: Grove, 1983), pp. 151–316; Jonas, *The Battle for Guatemala,* Chapters 5–7.

18. Héctor Rosado Granados, *Guatemala 1984: Elecciones para Asamblea Nacional Constituyente* (San José, Costa Rica: Instituto Centroamericano de Derechos Humanos-Centro de Asesoría y Promoción Electoral, 1985), p. 41; "Guatemala," *Mesoamérica,* March 1982, pp. 2–4; Margaret E. Roggensack and John A. Booth, *Report of the International Human Rights Law Group and the Washington Office on Latin America Advance Election Observer Mission to Guatemala* (Washington, DC, 1985), Appendix B; Robert Trudeau, "Guatemalan Elections: The Illusion of Democracy," paper presented to the National Conference on Guatemala, Washington, DC, June 15, 1984.

19. Data for selected periods drawn from U.S. Embassy—Guatemala reports from 1966 through 1984, reported in Booth, "A Guatemalan Nightmare," and U.S. Department of State, *Country Report on Human Rights Practices* (Washington, DC: U.S. Government Printing Office, February 2, 1981), p. 441; later data came from Inforpress Centroamericana, *Central America Report,* February 1, 1985, p. 31; November 22, 1985, p. 357; January 21, 1988, p. 12.

20. For 1982 and after see U.S. Embassy—Guatemala, "A Statistical Comparison of Violence (1982–1985)," Guatemala City, xerox, 1985. Recent investigations have confirmed the extent of the violence; see for instance, Francisco Mauricio Martínez, "Guatemala, Never More: 55,000 Human Rights Violations," and "URNG Committed 44 Massacres," both from *La Prensa Libre* (Guatemala City), April 14, 1998, translated into English in Human Rights News Clips, Foundation for Human Rights in Guatemala, http://www._fhrg.org/042098.htm//G, July 13, 1998, pp. 1–3.

21. Lars Schoultz, "Guatemala: Social Change and Political Conflict," in Diskin, ed., *Trouble in Our Backyard,* pp. 188–189.

22. Historical Clarification Commission (CEH), *Guatemala: Memory of Silence* (Guatemala City, 1999), Ch. 1, section 27.

23. Quoted by Allan Nairn in "Guatemala Can't Take 2 Roads," *New York Times,* July 20, 1982, p. 23A. Material on the reformist military regime drawn in part from U.S. Department of State, *Background Notes: Guatemala,* Bureau of Inter-American

Affairs, March 1998, http://www.state.gov/www/background_notes/guatemala_0398_bgn.html, pp. 3–4.

24. Booth's conversation with U.S. Embassy personnel, Guatemala City, September 1985; see also Roggensack and Booth, *Report.*

25. Material based on Booth's field observations in Guatemala in 1985, plus Americas Watch, *Human Rights in Guatemala* and *Little Hope;* Booth et al., *The 1985 Guatemalan Elections;* Inforpress Centroamericana, *Guatemala: Elections 1985;* British Parliamentary Human Rights Group, *"Bitter and Cruel . . . ": Report of a Mission to Guatemala by the British Parliamentary Human Rights Group* (London: House of Commons, 1985); and Black et al., *Garrison Guatemala,* pp. 61–113. Much of the volume (55,000 deaths) and responsibility (80 percent military, 20 percent URNG) for human rights abuses in this period alleged in early reports have been confirmed and fleshed out in a preliminary report to a national truth commission compiled by the human rights office of the Archdiocese of Guatemala; see Martínez, "Guatemala, Never More," and "URNG Committed."

26. William I. Robinson, *Transnational Conflicts: Central America, Social Change, and Globalization* (London: Verso, 2003), pp. 106–108.

27. Black et al., *Garrison Guatemala,* pp. 107–109.

28. Interviews with Guatemalan labor sources, September–October 1985 and April–May 1987, Guatemala City; see Booth et al., *The 1985 Guatemalan Elections,* pp. 39–40, and David Carliner et al., *Political Transition and the Rule of Law in Guatemala* (Washington, DC: International Human Rights Law Group—Washington Office on Latin America, January 1988), pp. 7–8. For confirmation see also Jonas, *The Battle for Guatemala.*

29. Booth et al., *The 1985 Guatemalan Elections.*

30. Interviews with spokesmen for various parties, September–October 1985, Guatemala.

31. Robinson, *Transnational Conflicts,* quote pp. 111–112, and see pp. 110–113.

32. See Latin American Studies Association (LASA), *Extraordinary Opportunities . . . and New Risks: Final Report of the LASA Commission on Compliance with the Central America Peace Accord* (Pittsburgh: LASA, 1988), pp. 15–20; Booth's interviews with various Guatemalan political figures and expert observers, September 1988; "Año de tumulto en Guatemala," *Excelsior* (Mexico City), December 30, 1988, p. 4A; *Christian Science Monitor,* February 14, 1989, p. 3.

33. U.S. Department of State, *Background Notes: Guatemala,* Bureau of Inter-American Affairs, March 1998. http://www.state.gov/www/backqround_notes/guatemala_0398__bgn.html. *Amparo* and *habeas corpus* are court orders for the government to cease violating constitutional rights, helpful in protecting citizens from wrongful detention and other abuses of power.

34. Killed were U.S. citizens Diana Ortiz, a nun, and businessman Michael Devine, and Salvadoran Social Democratic Party leader Héctor Oqueli. On

counterinsurgency and indigenous, see Washington Office on Latin America, *Who Pays the Price? The Cost of War in the Guatemalan Highlands* (Washington, DC, April 1988). See also Carliner et al., *Political Transition;* LASA, *Extraordinary Opportunities . . . and New Risks,* pp. 15–20; "Guatemala," *Mesoamérica,* April 1990, pp. 4–5; "Guatemala," *Mesoamérica,* May 1990, p. 6; "Guatemala," *Mesoamérica,* June 1990, pp. 4–5; "Guatemala," *Mesoamérica,* July 1990, p. 2; "Guatemala," *Mesoamérica,* August 1990, pp. 5–6; "Guatemala," *Mesoamérica,* October 1990, pp. 2–3; "Guatemala," *Mesoamérica,* November 1990, pp. 2–3; "Guatemala," *Mesoamérica,* January 1991, pp. 1–2; "Four Guatemalan Troops Charged in Killings," *Boston Globe,* September 30, 1990, pp. 1–2; "Amnesty International Reports Guatemalan Police and Private Sector Forces Torture and Murder Street Children," *Excelsior* (Mexico City), November 10, 1990, p. 2A.

35. Robinson, *Transnational Conflicts,* p. 112.

36. Ibid., p. 113; "Guatemala," *Mesoamérica,* April 1991, pp. 3–4; "Guatemala," *Mesoamérica,* May 1991, pp. 10–11; "Guatemala," *Mesoamérica,* June 1991, pp. 4–5; "Guatemala," *Mesoamérica,* August 1991, pp. 11–12; "Guatemala," *Mesoamérica,* September 1991, pp. 1–2; Katherine Ellison, "Celebrity of Guatemalan Rights Activists Could Save His Life," *Miami Herald,* November 22, 1990, p. 20B; "Guatemalan Troops Said to Kill 11 Protesting Raid," *New York Times,* December 3, 1990, p. 8A; "Government Accuses Death Squads of Wave of Killings, Denies Connections to Armed Forces," *Excelsior,* August 5, 1991, p. 2A; Haroldo Shetemul, "National Blackout in Guatemala: Police Chief Assassinated," *Excelsior,* August 6, 1991, p. 2A; "Attacks on Journalists Condemned by President Serrano Elias," *Excelsior,* September 1, 1991, p. 2A.

37. Susanne Jonas, "Electoral Problems and the Democratic Prospect in Guatemala," and John A. Booth, "Introduction: Elections and Democracy in Central America: A Framework for Analysis," both in Mitchell A. Seligson and John A. Booth, eds., *Elections and Democracy in Central America, Revisited* (Chapel Hill: University of North Carolina Press, 1995), pp. 35–36, p. 1.

38. Susanne Jonas, "The Democratization of Guatemala Through the Peace Process," in Christopher Chase-Dunn, Susanne Jonas, and Nelson Amaro, eds., *Globalization on the Ground: Postbellum Guatemalan Democracy and Development* (Rowman and Littlefield, 2001); and U.S. Department of State, *Background Notes: Guatemala,* pp. 4–5.

39. This section is drawn mainly from Susanne Jonas's *Of Centaurs and Doves: Guatenmala's Peace Process* (Boulder: Westview Press, 2000) and Jonas's "The Democratization of Guatemala."

40. The indigenous rights accord, a landmark in this country profoundly marked by anti-indigenous racism, stated that Guatemala is a multiethnic, multicultural, and multilingual society and provided for education reform and indigenous representation in governmental structures; see Kay B. Warren, "Pan-Mayanism and Mul-

ticulturalism in Guatemala," a paper presented at the Symposium on Development and Democratization in Guatemala: Proactive Responses to Globalization, Universidad del Valle, Guatemala City, March 18, 1998, pp. 1–5.

41. Ibid., pp. 4–5; and U.S. Department of State, *Guatemala: Background Notes,* p. 5; "Mayans Win Local Representation," *Cerigua* (Peace Net), Weekly Briefs, No. 3, January 18, 1996; Tim Johnson, "Maya Mayor Triumphs over Entrenched Racism," *Miami Herald,* January 15, 1996, p. 1A; Robinson, *Transnational Conflicts,* p. 112.

42. "FDNG Activists Assassinated," *Cerigua* (Peace Net), Weekly Briefs, No. 2, January 11, 1996; "Human Rights Violations Continue to Rise," *Cerigua* (PeaceNet), Weekly Briefs, No. 5, February 1, 1996; Michael Riley, "Refugees Outside Looking In," *Christian Science Monitor,* January 10, 1996, p. 5; Larry Rohter, "Specter in Guatemala: Iron-Fisted General Looms Large Again," *New York Times,* January 10, 1996, p. 4A; "Arzú Greeted by Strikes and Protests," *Central America Report* (Guatemala City), January 19, 1996, p. 3.

43. Jonas, *Of Centaurs and Doves*; U.S. Department of State, *Background Notes: Guatemala,* pp. 10–11; J. Mark Ruhl, "Curbing Central America's Militaries," *Journal of Democracy* 15: 3 (July 2004).

44. See Chapter 1, Table 1.1, and Chapter 2, Table 2.2. See also U.S. Department of State, *Background Notes: Guatemala,* pp. 5–8; Jonas, *Of Centaurs and Doves*; "Uncertain Future: Social Watch Evaluates Guatemala," *Cerigua,* Weekly Briefs, June 4, 1998; "President Accused of 'Killing the Media,'" *Central America Report,* March 26, 1998, p. 1; Celina Zubieta, "Victims of Death Squads or Gang Warfare?" *InterPress Service* (Peace Net), March 31, 1998; Mike Lanchin, "Death Squad Claims Responsibility for Bishop's Death," *National Catholic Reporter,* May 22, 1998, p. 2; Francisco Mauricio Martínez, "Progress Towards Peace Evaluated," *La Prensa Libre,* www.prensalibre.com, December 28, 1998; and Michael Riley, "Stealing Guatemala's Peace Dividend."

45. "CEH Pressured to Denounce Genocide," *Central America Report,* May 21, 1998, p. 5; Lanchin, "Death Squad Claims," p. 12.

46. The three military officers received sentences of 30 years and Father Orantes, who had been Gerardi's cook, received a 20-year sentence for assisting in the crime.

47. Another closely watched trial was that of Colonel Juan Valencia Osorio for the murder of anthropologist Myrna Mack in 1990. Convicted by a trial court in 2002, his conviction was also overturned by the Fourth Appeals Court. In January 2004 the Guatemalan Supreme Court reinstated the conviction and sentence, making his the first conviction of a high-ranking officer for human rights abuses.

48. CEH, *Guatemala, Memoria del silencio,* Ch. 2, Section 82.

49. See Victoria Sanford, *Buried Secrets: Truth and Human Rights in Guatemala* (New York: Palgrave Macmillan, 2003) for a complete discussion of this issue.

50. CEH, Ch. 2, Section 86.

51. CEH, Ch. 1, Section 13.

52. Charles Babington, "Clinton: Support for Guatemala Was Wrong," *Washington Post,* March 11, 1999.

53. The PAN won 37 seats.

54. Ruhl, "Curbing Central America's Militaries," p. 144; see pp. 144–146.

55. In early 2004 Guatemala's Constitutional Court stripped ex-President Portillo and his Vice President Francisco Reyes Lopez of their immunity, which they enjoyed as members of the Central American Parliament. Portillo immediately fled to Mexico, while Reyes Lopez was arrested months later on corruption charges. See "Accused in Corruption case, ex-president leaves country," The *Miami Herald*, February 20, 2004; "Guatemala Former Vice President Arrested for Graft," Reuters, July 28, 2004.

56. Decertification as a cooperating nation would mean the loss of some U.S. aid.

57. According to the DEA, cocaine seizures fell from 9.2 and 10.05 metric tons in 1998 and 1999 to 1.4, 4.1, and 2.8 metric tons in subsequent years. U.S. Drug Enforcement Administration, *Drug Intelligence Brief, Country Brief: Guatemala,* www.dea.gov/pubs/intel/03002/03002.htm, April 2003.

58. Ibid., p. 5.

59. The paid protesters were apparently bused in from the countryside accompanied by hooded guards. One reporter died of a heart attack while covering the story.

60. URNG candidate Rodrigo Asturias won less than 3 percent of the vote.

61. The remaining 19 seats were split among six parties.

62. Berger also offered Colom a position in his administration, which Colom rejected.

63. "Guatemalan President Apologizes for Civil War," U.N. Wire, February 27, 2004 at www.unwire.org/UNWire/20040227/449_13525.asp.

64. Latin American Database, "Guatemala: Government Backs Away from Truth Commission Recommendations," *NotiCen*, April 15, 1999.

65. Frank Jack Daniel, "Guatemala Call in Troops to Fight Crime Wave," Reuters, July 26, 2004.

66. The 1996 Guatemalan Peace Accords forbid the use of the military for policing duties.

67. Jo Tuckman, "Land Where Women Are Killers' Prey," *The Observer,* June 6, 2004 at www.guardian.co.uk/gender/story/0%2C11812%2C1232430%2C00.html; and Marion Lloyd, "Guatemala Activists Seek Justice As Women Die," *Boston Globe*, June 14, 2004 at www.boston.com/news/world/latinamerica/articles/2004/06/14/guatemala_activists_seek_justice_as_women_die/?rss_id=Boston.com+/+News.

68. See the United Nations Economic and Social Council, "Integration of the Human Rights of Women and the Gender Perspective: Preliminary Note on the Mission to El Salvador and Guatemala," submitted by Special Rapporteur on Vio-

lence Against Women, Yakin Erturk, United Nations document number E/CN.4/2004/66/Add.2.

Chapter 8

1. Thanks to José García of New Mexico State University for his insight on these matters. See James A. Morris, "Honduras: The Burden of Survival in Central America," in Steve C. Ropp and James A. Morris, eds., *Central America: Crisis and Adaptation* (Albuquerque: University of New Mexico Press, 1984), pp. 189–223.

2. James A. Morris, "Honduras: A Unique Case," in Howard J. Wiarda and Harvey F. Kline, eds., *Latin American Politics and Development* (Boston: Houghton Mifflin, 1979), p. 349.

3. As quoted in "Commentary: The Region," *Mesoamérica,* September 1982, p. 1.

4. See Eva Gold, "Military Encirclement," in Thomas W. Walker, ed., *Reagan Versus the Sandinistas: The Undeclared War on Nicaragua* (Boulder: Westview Press, 1987), pp. 39–56.

5. Data from John A. Booth and Thomas W. Walker, *Understanding Central America* (Boulder: Westview Press, 1993), 3rd ed., Appendix Tables 1 and 2.

6. Alan Heston, Robert Summers, and Bettina Aten, *Penn World Table Version 6.1*, Center for International Comparisons at the University of Pennsylvania (CICUP), October 2002.

7. This theory is explained in detail in Chapter 2 of this volume.

8. Booth and Walker, *Understanding Central America,* 3rd ed., Appendix Table 6; see also Victor Bulmer-Thomas, *The Political Economy of Central America Since 1920* (New York: Cambridge University Press, 1987), Table 10.7, p. 219.

9. Booth and Walker, *Understanding Central America,* 3rd ed., Appendix Table 7.

10. Thomas P. Anderson, *Politics in Central America: Guatemala, El Salvador, Honduras, and Nicaragua* (New York: Praeger, 1982), pp. 109–147.

11. Discussion of Honduras drawn from Victor Meza, *Honduras: La evolución de la crisis* (Tegucigalpa: Editorial Universitaria, 1980); Victor Meza, *Historia del movimiento obrero hondureño* (Tegucigalpa: Editorial Guaymuras, 1980), pp. 123–167, Anderson, *Politics,* pp. 109–121; Mario Posas, *El movimiento campesino* (Tegucigalpa: Editorial Guaymuras, 1981); James A. Morris, "Government and Politics," in James D. Rudolph, ed., *Honduras: A Country Study* (Washington, DC: American University Foreign Area Studies series, U.S. Government Printing Office, 1984), pp. 168–193; Rosa María Pochet Coronado, "El reformismo estatal y la Iglesia en Honduras 1949–1982," *Estudios Sociales Centroamericanos* 33 (September–December 1982), pp. 155–188; J. Mark Ruhl, "Agrarian Structure and Political

Stability in Honduras," *Journal of Inter-American Studies and World Affairs* 26 (February 1984), pp. 33–68.

12. Castillo Rivas, "Modelos," pp. 199–201; Mario Posas, *El movimiento campesino hondureño* (Tegucigalpa: Editorial Guaymuras, 1981), pp. 34–42.

13. Author Booth's conversation with Lucas Aguilera, member of the executive committee of the Union Nacional Campesina, Tegucigalpa, and members of the Unión Maraíta cooperative farm, Departamento Francisco Morazán, August 21, 1985.

14. Discussion of Honduras based on Victor Meza, *Historia del movimiento obrero hondureño* (Tegucigalpa: Editorial Guaymuras, 1980), pp. 123–167, and Meza, *Honduras: La evolución,* pp. 14–41; Anderson, *Politics,* pp. 109–121; Posas, *El movimiento campesino.*

15. James A. Morris, "Government and Politics," in James D. Rudolph, ed., *Honduras: A Country Study* (Washington, DC: American University Foreign Area Studies series, U.S. Government Printing Office, 1984), pp. 168–193; Rosa María Pochet Coronado, "El reformismo estatal y la Iglesia en Honduras 1949–1982," *Estudios Sociales Centroamericanos* 33 (September–December 1982), pp. 155–188.

16. William I. Robinson, *Transnational Conflicts: Central America, Social Change, and Globalization* (London: Verso, 2003), p. 128.

17. Steve C. Ropp, "National Security," in Rudolph, ed., *Honduras: A Country Study,* pp. 391–396.

18. "Honduras," *Mesoamérica,* April 1990, p. 9; "Honduras," *Mesoamérica,* February 1991, pp. 10–11; "Honduras," *Mesoamérica,* May 1991, p. 12; "Honduras," *Mesoamérica,* June 1991, p. 2; *Excelsior,* January 13, 1991, p. 2A.

19. Richard L. Millett, "Historical Setting," in Rudolph, ed., *Honduras: A Country Study,* p. 47.

20. *Washington Report on the Hemisphere,* October 28, 1987, pp. 1, 60.

21. Ramón Custodio, "The Human Rights Crisis in Honduras," in Mark Rosenberg and Phillip Shepherd, eds., *Honduras Confronts Its Future* (Boulder: Lynne Reinner Publishers, 1986), pp. 69–71.

22. U.S. Department of State, *Country Reports on Human Rights,* p. 46; Morris, "Government and Politics," pp. 192–193; and James A. Morris, "Honduras: The Burden of Survival in Central America," in Ropp and Morris, eds., *Central America,* pp. 217–219; Charles W. Anderson, *Politics and Economic Change in Latin America: The Governing of Restless Nations* (New York: Van Nostrand Reinhold, 1967), pp. 116–132.

23. Americas Watch, *Review of the Department of State's Country Reports on Human Rights Practices for 1982: An Assessment* (New York, February 1983), p. 55. The discrepancy between this figure and the number of 40 cited earlier probably stems from a combination of two factors: Different reporting agencies are involved, and

they are reporting on somewhat different phenomena. The two figures may not, in fact, be incongruent.

24. James A. Morris, "Honduras: The Burden of Survival in Central America" in Ropp and Morris, *Central America,* pp. 201–204.

25. Economic data from Booth and Walker, *Understanding Central America,* 3rd ed., Appendix Tables 1, 4, 5, and 6. See also Mark Rosenberg, "Can Democracy Survive the Democrats? From Transition to Consolidation in Honduras," in John A. Booth and Mitchell A. Seligson, eds., *Elections and Democracy in Central America* (Chapel Hill: University of North Carolina Press, 1989); Latin American Studies Association (LASA), *Extraordinary Opportunities . . . and New Risks: Final Report of the LASA Commission on Compliance with the Central American Peace Accord* (Pittsburgh: LASA, 1988), pp. 20–26.

26. Robinson, *Transnational Conflicts,* p. 129.

27. "Honduras," *Mesoamérica,* April 1990, pp. 8–9; "Honduras," *Mesoamérica,* January 1991, pp. 9–10; "Honduras," *Mesoamérica,* February 1991, p. 10; "Honduras," *Mesoamérica,* May 1991, p. 12; "Honduras," *Mesoamérica,* June 1991, p. 2; "Honduras," *Mesoamérica,* September 1991, pp. 8–9; *Excelsior,* December 12, 1990, p. 2A; *Miami Herald,* December 15, 1990, p. 24A; and *Miami Herald,* December 2, 1990, p. 22A; Robinson, *Transnational Conflicts,* p. 129.

28. J. Mark Ruhl, "Honduras: Militarism and Democratization in Troubled Waters," a paper presented at the 21st Congress of the Latin American Studies Association, Chicago, September 25, 1998.

29. Jeff Boyer and Aaron Pell, "Mitch in Honduras: A Disaster Waiting to Happen," *NACLA Report on the Americas,* September/October 1999, pp. 36–43.

30. Latin American Database, "Hurricane Mitch Recovery Moving Slowly After One Year," *Noticen,* November 4, 1999.

31. J. Mark Ruhl, "Curbing Central America's Militaries," *Journal of Democracy* 15, No. 3 (July 2004), p. 143.

32. Edward Orlebar, "Honduran President Faces Battle with His Own Military," *Los Angeles Times,* December 18, 1993, p. 2A; "Demilitarization Runs into Problems," *Central America Report,* November 21, 1996, p. 1; "Transfer of Police from Military to Civil Power Ratified," *Central America Report,* January 10, 1997, p. 6; "Honduras," *Mesoamérica,* June 6, 1997, p. 4; Thelma Mejía, "Vice President Implicated in Disappearances," *Interpress Service*/Spanish (PeaceNet), January 23, 1998; "Military Files Confiscated," *Central American Report,* February 12, 1998, p. 3; "New Government Seeks to Broaden Support," *Central America Report,* January 29, 1998, p. 7; Thelma Mejía, "Extra-Judicial Executions on the Rise," *Interpress Service*/Spanish (PeaceNet), February 4, 1998; "Death Squads Assassinate Human Rights Leader," *Interpress Service*/Spanish (PeaceNet), February 11, 1998; Thelma Mejía, "The Army Wants You!" *InterPress Service*/Spanish (PeaceNet),

January 21, 1997; "Honduran Death Squads Active Again, Report Says," *Houston Chronicle,* January 15, 1998, p. 19A.

33. Latin American Database, "Honduras: Security Minister Guatama Fonseca Under Fire as Crime Rates Soar," *Noticen,* June 14, 2001.

34. Ismael Moreno, S.J., "A New President and Cracks in the Two-Party Structure," *Envío* (January–February 2002), pp. 37–43.

35. Latin American Database, "Honduras: President Ricardo Maduro Promises Action on Killings of Children," *Noticen,* October 10, 2002.

36. United Nations Report of the Special Rapporteur, *Civil and Political Rights, Including the Question of Disappearances and Summary Executions* (United Nations Economic and Social Council Commission on Human Rights, 2003).

37. Ismael Moreno, S.J., "The March on Tegucigalpa: 'It's Our Water,'" *Envío* (September 2003), pp. 46–51.

Chapter 9

1. Aristotle, *Politics (Aristotle's Politics)*, Richard Robinson, translator (Oxford: Clarendon Press, 1962); Carl Cohen, *Democracy* (New York: Free Press, 1971); Robert A. Dahl, *On Democracy* (New Haven: Yale University Press, 1998); John Stuart Mill, *Considerations on Representative Government* (Indianapolis: Bobbs-Merrill, 1958); Carole Pateman, *Participation and Democratic Theory* (Cambridge: Cambridge University Press, 1970); with special emphasis on Latin America see John A. Booth, "Introduction. Elections and Democracy in Central America: A Framework for Analysis," in Mitchell A. Seligson and John A. Booth, eds., *Elections and Democracy in Central America, Revisited* (Chapel Hill: University of North Carolina Press, 1995); John A. Peeler, *Building Democracy in Latin America* (Boulder: Lynne Rienner Publishers, 2004); and Larry Diamond, Juan Linz, Jonathan Hartlyn, and Seymour Martin Lipset, eds., *Democracy in Developing Countries: Latin America* (Boulder: Lynne Rienner Publishers, 1999).

2. Other key factors affecting democratic consolidation are the attitudes and behaviors of elites and of powerful foreign actors. When elites, who hold powerful political and economic positions in a society, share a broad consensus on democratic rules of the political game it strengthens democracy by reducing risks of disruptive challenges to the system. Influential foreign actors (hegemonic powers, neighboring countries significant donors of foreign aid, and international organizations) who prefer democratic rules of the game can impose costs that make it harder for local actors to abandon democratic institutions. (Of course, influential foreign actors may also pressure local actors to make decisions that might work against the survival of democracy.) On democratic consolidation see Samuel

Huntington, *The Third Wave: Democratization in the Late Twentieth Century* (Norman: University of Oklahoma Press, 1991); Larry Jay Diamond, *Developing Democracy: Toward Consolidation* (Baltimore: Johns Hopkins University Press, 1999).

3. Mitchell A. Seligson and John A. Booth, "Political Culture and Regime Type: Evidence from Nicaragua and Costa Rica," *Journal of Politics* 55 (August 1993), pp. 777–792.

4. John A. Booth and Patricia Bayer Richard: "Civil Society, Political Capital, and Democratization in Central America," *Journal of Politics* 60 (August 1998), pp. 780–800; "Civil Society and Political Context in Central America," *American Behavioral Scientist* 42 (September 1998), pp. 33–46; and "Repression, Participation, and Democratic Norms in Urban Central America," *American Journal of Political Science* 40:4 (November 1996), pp. 1205–1232; Seligson and Booth, "Political Culture and Regime Type."

5. The 2004 survey data were collected by research teams from our five Central American countries plus Panama, Colombia, and Mexico in April 2004. The survey was funded by the U.S. Agency for International Development and conducted under the leadership of Mitchell A. Seligson, then of the University of Pittsburgh and presently of Vanderbilt University. We report here only on the five Central American nations. Each nation was surveyed, using a large core of identical survey items. National probability samples of approximately 1,500 respondents were interviewed from each nation. Respondents were chosen using stratified national sample frames, with respondent clusters within sampling units chosen with the probability of selection proportionate to size. In the results reported here each national sample size is weighted to 1,500 respondents, for a regional sample of 7,500. Respondents were of voting age and citizens of the country in which the interviews were conducted. (The authors sincerely thank USAID and Professor Seligson for providing these public-domain data.)

6. The early 1990s surveys consisted of an urban sample only. Our comparisons between the 1990s and 2004 data here and elsewhere in the chapter are for the urban populations only. That is, we isolate the urban sample from 2004 to compare it to the urban-only early 1990s data. In general the sampling methodology from the early 1990s resembles that of the 2004 surveys. Items compared between the earlier and later surveys are identical in wording. The early 1990s data were collected by a team led by Mitchell A. Seligson and John Booth; for a full description and acknowledgments see Booth and Richard, "Repression, Participation, and Democratic Norms in Urban Central America."

7. Results of a multiple regression analysis using voter registration as the dependent variable, and with sex, age, educational attainment, standard of living, level of national economic development, and system-level repression as independent variables; results not shown to conserve space.

8. The early 1990s surveys consisted of an urban sample only. Our comparisons between the 1990s and 2004 data in this paragraph are for the urban populations only.

9. Booth, "Political Parties in Costa Rica," in P. Webb, S. White, and D. Stansfield, eds., *Political Parties in Transitional Democracies* (Oxford: Oxford University Press, forthcoming, 2005); Mitchell A. Seligson, "Trouble in Paradise: The Impact of the Erosion of System Support in Costa Rica, 1978–1999," *Latin America Research Review* 37, no. 1 (2002), pp. 160–185.

10. Results of a multiple regression analysis using reported voting in the most recent presidential election as the dependent variable, and with sex, age, educational attainment, standard of living, level of national economic development, and system-level repression as independent variables; results not shown to conserve space.

11. Booth, "Political Parties in Costa Rica."

12. While surveys from the 1990s revealed that Central Americans had generally low confidence in parties, that situation seems to have changed somewhat, especially for El Salvador. On a 1.0 (very low) to 7.0 (very high) self-evaluation of one's "trust in parties," the following mean scores were obtained by country from our 2004 survey: Costa Rica 3.1, El Salvador 3.4, Guatemala 2.8, Honduras 2.9, and Nicaragua 2.7. Costa Rica's parties, arguably in crisis at this writing, were lower than one might have expected a decade before. El Salvador's parties, given their links to past political violence, scored surprisingly well at 3.4 out of 7.0—the highest self-reported level of trust in parties in the region.

13. Results of a multiple regression analysis using party meeting involvement as the dependent variable, and with sex, age, educational attainment, standard of living, level of national economic development, and system-level repression as independent variables; results not shown to conserve space.

14. Results of a multiple regression analysis using campaign activism as the dependent variable, and with sex, age, educational attainment, standard of living, level of national economic development, and system-level repression as independent variables; results not shown to conserve space.

15. Booth and Richard, "Civil Society and Political Context in Central America"; "Repression, Participation, and Democratic Norms in Urban Central America"; and "Civil Society and Social Capital Formation in the Central American Context," a paper presented at the Midwest Political Science Association meeting, Chicago (April 15, 2004); and John A. Booth, "A Replication: Modes of Political Participation in Costa Rica," *Western Political Quarterly* 29 (December 1976), pp. 627–633.

16. The early 1990s surveys consisted of an urban sample only. Our comparisons between the 1990s and 2004 data in this paragraph are for the urban populations only.

17. The early 1990s surveys consisted of an urban sample only. Our comparisons between the 1990s and 2004 data in this paragraph are for the urban populations only.

18. Results of a multiple regression analysis using civil society engagement as the dependent variable, and with sex, age, educational attainment, standard of living, level of national economic development, national level of economic risk, national level of political risk, and system-level repression as independent variables; results not shown to conserve space. Somewhat paradoxically, other factors held equal by this regression analysis, civil society activism was also greater where political stability and economic development were higher. This suggested that, repression levels held constant, both greater economic activity and political stability generated more civil society activism in Central America in the early 2000s.

19. Booth and Richard, "Repression, Participation, and Democratic Norms in Urban Central America."

20. Results of a multiple regression analysis using contacting public officials as the dependent variable, and with sex, age, educational attainment, standard of living, level of national economic development, and system-level repression as independent variables; results not shown to conserve space.

21. John A. Booth, *Costa Rica: Quest for Democracy* (Boulder: Westview Press, 1998).

22. Results of a multiple regression analysis using reported protest participation as the dependent variable, and with sex, age, educational attainment, standard of living, level of national economic development, and system-level repression as independent variables; results not shown to conserve space.

23. Results of a multiple regression analysis using overall participation as the dependent variable, and with sex, age, educational attainment, standard of living, crime victimization, perceived freedom to participate in politics, perceived level of civil liberties, level of national economic development, and system-level repression as independent variables; results not shown to conserve space.

24. Seligson and Booth, "Political Culture and Regime Type."

25. Booth and Richard, "Repression, Participation, and Democratic Norms in Urban Central America."

26. Results of a multiple regression analysis using the support-for-a-strong-leader item quoted in the text as the dependent variable, and with sex, age, educational attainment, standard of living, level of national economic development, and system-level repression as independent variables; results not shown to conserve space.

27. We regard this datum for Nicaragua with some skepticism because in the 2004 survey on another measure of coup justification constructed from multiple items citing specific possible causes, an average of 87 percent of Nicaraguan

respondents agreed that coups could be justified. Nevertheless, almost three quarters of the Nicaraguan sample refused to answer these questions.

28. Results of a multiple regression analysis using respondent acceptance that certain circumstances could justify a coup d'état as the dependent variable, and with sex, age, educational attainment, standard of living, level of national economic development, and system-level repression as independent variables; results not shown to conserve space.

29. The samples compared between the early 1990s and 2004 are urban samples only.

30. Results of a multiple regression analysis using a measure of tolerance of political rights for regime critics as the dependent variable, and with sex, age, educational attainment, standard of living, level of national economic development, and system-level repression as independent variables; results not shown to conserve space.

31. The samples compared between the early 1990s and 2004 are urban samples only.

32. Michael W. Foley, "Laying the Groundwork: The Struggle for Civil Society in El Salvador," *Journal of Interamerican Studies and World Affairs* 38 (1996), pp. 67–104.

33. Again, the data compared between the early 1990s and 2004 are for urban samples only.

34. Results of a multiple regression analysis using the support for confrontational tactics (i.e., civil disobedience, protest) as the dependent variable, and with sex, age, educational attainment, standard of living, level of national economic development, and system-level repression as independent variables; results not shown to conserve space.

35. Booth and Richard, "Repression, Participation, and Democratic Norms in Urban Central America."

36. These apparently contradictory findings raise the possibility of inconsistency between held attitudes and reported behaviors. Such inconsistencies bedevil social analysts yet are relatively common among survey respondents.

37. The samples compared between the early 1990s and 2004 are urban samples only.

38. Seligson, "Trouble in Paradise."

39. The analysis was multiple regression analysis with system support as the dependent variable and the listed variables as independent variables plus urban vs. rural residence, sex, standard of living, age, and education. The model accounted for 13 percent of the variation in general system support.

40. The multiple regression model accounted for 13 percent of the variation in specific institutional support. Interestingly, specific institutional support is somewhat higher in countries with lower GDP/capita.

Chapter 10

1. Charles W. Anderson, "The Latin American Political System," in his *Politics and Economic Change in Latin America: The Governing of Restless Nations* (New York: Van Nostrand Reinhold Co., 1967), pp. 87–114.

2. See Robert A. Dahl, A *Preface to Democratic Theory* (Chicago: University of Chicago Press, 1956); E. E. Schattschneider, *The Semisovereign People: A Realist's View of Democracy in America* (New York: Holt, Rinehart, and Winston, 1960).

3. See, for instance, John A. Booth and Mitchell A. Seligson, eds., *Elections and Democracy in Central America* (Chapel Hill: University of North Carolina Press, 1989), passim.

4. National Bipartisan Commission on Central America, *Report of the National Bipartisan Commission on Central America* (Washington, DC, 1984), p. 30.

5. William I. Robinson, *Promoting Polyarchy: Globalization, U.S. Intervention, and Hegemony* (Cambridge: Cambridge University Press, 1996); and *Transnational Conflicts: Central America, Social Change, and Globalization* (London: Verso, 2003).

6. Paulo Freire, *The Pedagogy of the Oppressed* (New York: Herder and Herder, 1968).

7. Second General Conference of Latin American Bishops, *The Church and the Present-Day Transformation of Latin America in the Light of the Council* (Washington, DC: United States Catholic Conference, 1973).

8. For more information about the changing Catholic church in the past three decades, see Edward L. Cleary, O.P., *Crisis and Change: The Church in Latin America Today* (Maryknoll, NY: Orbis Books, 1985).

9. After the victory, the women's organization became the Luisa Amanda Espinosa Nicaraguan Women's Association (Asociación de Mujeres Nicaragüenses Luisa Amanda Espinosa—AMNLAE) and the CDCs became the Sandinista Defense Committees (Comités de Defensa Sandinista—CDS); otherwise all five movements remained essentially the same.

10. Estimate of U.S. Embassy Managua, June 25, 1985, to coauthor Thomas Walker.

11. For more information about mobilization in Nicaragua, see Luis Serra, "The Grass-Roots Organizations," in Thomas W. Walker, ed., *Nicaragua: The First Five Years* (New York: Praeger, 1985), pp. 65–89, or Gary Ruchwarger, *People in Power: Forging a Grassroots Democracy in Nicaragua* (Granby, MA: Bergin and Garvey Publishers, 1987).

12. See Deborah Barndt, "Popular Education," in Walker, ed., *Nicaragua: The First Five Years,* pp. 317–345.

13. The only Central American country in which some popular mobilization and socioeconomic reform has succeeded with U.S. support is Costa Rica, where

the social-democratic reformers of the National Liberation Party were associated with a political movement that ousted Communists from power in 1948.

14. For an illuminating discussion of the nature of the U.S. policymaker's perception of a Communist threat in Latin America, see Lars Schoultz, "Communism," in his *National Security and United States Policy Toward Latin America* (Princeton: Princeton University Press, 1987), pp. 106–139.

15. Tayacán, *Psychological Operations in Guerrilla Warfare: The CIA's Nicaragua Manual,* prepared by the Central Intelligence Agency (New York: Vintage Books, 1985); U.S. Department of Defense, "Fact Sheet Concerning Training Manuals Containing Materials Inconsistent with U.S. Policy" (Washington, DC: September 1996).

16. Michael McClintock, *The American Connection,* Volume 1, *State Terror and Popular Resistance in El Salvador* (London: Zed Books, 1985), p. 47.

17. See Michael Klare, *War Without End* (New York: Alfred A. Knopf, 1972), Ch. 9.

18. Americas Watch, *Review of the Department of State's Country Reports on Human Rights Practices for 1982: An Assessment* (New York: February 1983), pp. 1–9, 37–46, 55–61, 63–70. The report stated, for instance, that "a special effort appears to have been made to exculpate current leaders considered friends of the United States—such as . . . President Ríos Montt of Guatemala" (p. 5).

19. Latin American Studies Association, *The Electoral Process in Nicaragua: Domestic and International Influences* (Austin, TX: LASA, 1984), p. 17.

20. For detailed discussion and documentation, see Thomas W. Walker, "The Armed Forces," in Walker, ed., *Revolution and Counterrevolution in Nicaragua* (Boulder: Westview Press, 1991).

21. John A. Booth and Thomas W. Walker, *Understanding Central America,* 3rd ed. (Boulder: Westview Press, 1999), Appendix Table 9.

22. Mary B. Vanderlaan, *Revolution and Foreign Policy in Nicaragua* (Boulder: Westview Press, 1986), p. 322.

23. Excerpts from State Department and Pentagon, *Congressional Presentation Document,* Security Assistance Programs, FY 1981, as reproduced in Robert Matthews, "The Limits of Friendship: Nicaragua and the West," *NACLA Report on the Americas* 19, No. 3 (May–June 1985), p. 24.

24. Michael McClintock, *The American Connection,* Volume 2, *State Terror and Popular Resistance in Guatemala* (London: Zed Books, 1985), pp. 32–33. This volume is also a source of documentation for the general observations in the next two paragraphs. For additional information about demobilization in Guatemala see Tom Barry and Deb Preusch, *The Soft War: The Uses and Abuses of U.S. Economic Aid in Central America* (New York: Grove Press, 1988).

25. Andrew and Leslie Cockburn, *Dangerous Liaisons: The Inside Story of the U.S. Israeli Covert Relationship* (New York: HarperCollins, 1991), p. 218; Leslie H.

Gelb, "Israelis Said to Step Up Role as Arms Suppliers to Latins," *New York Times,* December 17, 1982, p. A.11; George Black, "Israeli Connection: Not Just Guns for Guatemala," *NACLA Report on the Americas* 17, No. 3 (May–June 1983), pp. 43–44; Benjamin Beit-Hallahmi, *The Israeli Connection: Who Israel Arms and Why* (New York: Pantheon Books, 1987), p. 78; Philip Taubman, "Israel Said to Aid Latin Aims of U.S.," *New York Times,* July 21, 1983, p. A4. The authors thank Richard E. Clinton, Jr. for his research in this matter.

26. Lindsey Gruson, "Terror's Toll Builds Again in El Salvador," *New York Times,* December 20, 1988, p. 1.

27. On August 2, 1979, less than two weeks after the Sandinista victory in Nicaragua, co-author Walker was one of three academics to deliver short presentations on "Central America After the Sandinista Victory" at a dinner seminar hosted by CIA director Stansfield Turner in his executive dining room. Walker agreed to participate only on the understanding that he would deliver a sharp criticism of prior U.S. policy in the region. Turner's first six words to the group were "There can be now more Nicaraguas." After the academic presentations, the assembled CIA, Pentagon, and Department of State personnel lapsed into a remarkably uninhibited discussion in which they identified El Salvador as the next possible "Nicaragua" and came to a consensus as to what type of regime could obviate such a, for them, worst-case scenario.

28. See McClintock, *The American Connection,* Vol. 1.

29. For a good description and documentation of the role of James Cheek, see Tommie Sue Montgomery, *Revolution in El Salvador: Origins and Evolution,* 2nd ed. (Boulder: Westview Press 1995), Ch. 7.

30. For material on U.S. officials' efforts to persuade El Salvador to improve its human rights performance, see "El Salvador," *Mesoamérica,* November 1982, p. 6; "El Salvador," *Mesoamérica,* October 1983, p. 6; "El Salvador," *Mesoamérica,* November 1983, p. 6; "El Salvador," *Mesoamérica,* December 1983, pp. 5–6; and the *Miami Herald,* December 19, 1983, p. 1.

31. Organization of American States, *Report on the Situation of Human Rights in Nicaragua: Findings of the "On-site" Observation in the Republic of Nicaragua, October 3–12, 1978* (Washington, DC: General Secretariat of the OAS, 1978).

32. Richard L. Millett, *Guardians of the Dynasty: A History of the U.S.-Created Guardia Nacional de Nicaragua and the Somoza Family* (Maryknoll, NY: Orbis Press, 1977), p. 252.

33. Arms Control and Foreign Policy Caucus, the U.S. House of Representatives, "Who Are the Contras?" *Congressional Record* 131, 48 (Daily Edition, April 23, 1985, H2335). The head of the Contras was a former guard officer, Enrique Bermúdez.

34. Booth's interview with Dora María Tellez, former FSLN guerrilla and former minister of health in the revolutionary government, Managua, June 30, 1998.

35. Tayacán [the CIA], *Operaciones sicológicas en guerra de guerrillas,* [1983]. This was later translated and published commercially as *Psychological Operations in Guerrilla Warfare: The CIA's Nicaragua Manual* (New York: Vintage Books, 1985).

36. The documentation of Contra brutality is massive. The numerous reports of Americas Watch are good sources. Others are Reed Brody, *Contra Terror in Nicaragua, Report of a Fact-Finding Mission: September 1984-January 1985* (Boston: South End Press, 1985); and Christopher Dickey, *With the Contras: A Reporter in the Wilds of Nicaragua* (New York: Simon and Schuster, 1985).

37. Data from the Nicaraguan Ministry of the Presidency, January 1990.

38. From an argument overheard by members of the Latin American Studies Association Commission to Observe the 1990 Election on February 26, 1990, in Managua.

39. As quoted in Thomas W. Walker, "The 1994 Research Seminar in Nicaragua," *LASA Forum* 25, No. 3 (Fall 1994), p. 14.

40. Among key Reagan-era Central America policy team players rehabilitated by George W. Bush was John D. Negroponte, former ambassador to Honduras (1981–1985) who worked as U.S. liaison to Nicaragua's contras. Bush appointed him ambassador to the United Nations, then ambassador to Iraq, and in early 2005, as national intelligence director. Elliott Abrams was Reagan-era assistant secretary of state for Inter-American Affairs who worked with the illegal Iran-Contra scheme and in 1991 pleaded guilty to two counts of illegally withholding information from Congress. Pardoned in 1992 by outgoing President George H. W. Bush, Abrams was appointed senior director for democracy, human rights and international operations of President George W. Bush's National Security Council. Cuban-American Otto Reich headed the Reagan-era State Department's Office of Public Diplomacy that manufactured anti-Sandinista and pro-Contra propaganda. George W. Bush named Reich the Department of State's assistant secretary of state for Western Hemisphere Affairs on a recess appointment after Congress refused to confirm him for a regular appointment. See *Central America and Mexico Report,* "Elliott Abrams Appointed to NSC," 2001, Vol. 3, accessed on January 5, 2005 at rtfcam.org/report/volume_21/No_3/article_3.htm; *CNN.com Inside Politics,* January 11, 2002, Accessed January 5, 2005 at archives.cnn.com/2002/ALLPOLITICS/01/11/recess.appointments/.

41. William I. Robinson, "Polyarchy: Coercion's New Face in Latin America," *NACLA Report on the Americas,* November/December 2000, pp. 42–48.

42. The CBI, a trade liberalization policy of the United States for nations of the Caribbean area, was initially established by the United States in 1983 to assist economies with duty-free access for most of their goods to the U.S. market. It sought to promote economic development and, consistent with neoliberalism, export diversification.

43. See the full text of the agreement at ustr.gov/Trade_Agreements/Bilateral/DR-CAFTA/DR-CAFTA_Final_Texts/Section_Index.html, accessed January 5, 2005.

44. Beatrice Edwards, "IDB Plan to Sell the Public Sector: The Cure or the Ill?" *NACLA Report on the Americas,* January/February 2003, pp. 13–19.

45. Ibid. See Article 20 and relevant subsections.

46. On generic drugs see Latin American Database, "Congress, Kerry, Could Kill CAFTA," *Noticen* 9, No. 21 (June 3, 2004); Latin American Database, "El Salvador First to Ratify CAFTA, But Followers May be Few," *Noticen* 10 No. 1 (January 6, 2004).

47. El Salvador's legislature ratified the treaty in December 2004.

48. See Robinson, *Transnational Conflicts,* pp. 203–209.

49. Inter-American Dialogue, "All in the Family: Latin America's Most Important International Flow," *Report of the Inter-American Dialogue Task Force on Remittances* (Washington, DC, January 2004), pp. 3–4.

50. Ibid., p. 4.

51. Ibid., derived from Tables 2 and 2a, p. 7.

52. TPS was extended until September 2006 for Salvadorans on January 6, 2005. Approximately 248,282 Salvadorans were eligible. U.S. Department of Homeland Security, U.S. Citizenship and Immigration Services Press Release, "DHS Announces 18-Month Extension of Temporary Protected Status (TPS) for Nationals of El Salvador," accessed January 8, 2005 at http://uscigov/graphics/publicaffairs/newsrels/elsal_2005_01_06.pdf. Nearly 82,000 Hondurans and 4,300 Nicaraguans were also granted extensions until July 2006. U.S. Department of Homeland Security, U.S. Citizenship and Immigration Services Press Release, "DHS Announces 18-Month Extension of Temporary Protected Status (TPS) for Nationals of Honduras and Nicaragua," October 29, 2004 (rev.11/2/04) at uscis.gov/graphics/publicaffairs/newsrels/Hon_Nica_TPS_04_11_01.pdf, accessed January 8, 2005.

53. Mary Beth Sheridan, "Salvadoran President Hails U.S. Work Plan: Immigrants Urged to Renew Benefits," *Washington Post,* January 9, 2005, page C01.

54. This section is derived from a paper by author Wade, "Play It Again Uncle Sam: The Role of the United States in Latin American Elections," presented at the 2004 Meeting of the Latin American Studies Association, Las Vegas, October 7–9, 2004.

55. In particular see "Disturbing Statement Out of El Salvador," *Congressional Record,* March 17, 2004, pp. E394-E395; "El Salvador," *Congressional Record,* March 17, 2004, p. E402; and "Election in El Salvador," *Congressional Record,* March 17, 2004, p. E389.

56. The troops were a part of the Spanish-led Plus Ultra brigade. When Spanish troops withdrew in the summer of 2004, Honduras and Nicaragua followed suit.

57. See Adam Isacson, Joy Olson, and Lisa Haugaard, "Blurring the Lines: Trends in U.S. Military Programs with Latin America." A joint publication by Latin American Working Group Education Fund, the Center for International Policy and the Washington Office on Latin America, Washington, DC, 2004. Available at http://wola.org/military/blurringthelinesfinal.pdf.

58. Dean Brackley, "Yanquis Return to El Salvador," *NACLA Report on the Americas* 34, No. 3 (November/December 2000), pp. 20–21.

59. Jerry Seper, "Al Qaeda Seek Ties to Local Gangs," *Washington Times*, September 28, 2004.

60. Latin American Database, "Strangely Circular Saga of Terrorism Disproved," *Noticen* 9, No. 39 (October 14, 2004).

Chapter 11

1. National Bipartisan Commission on Central America, *Report of the National Bipartisan Commission on Central America* (Washington, DC, 1984).

2. Rubén Zamora in an interview with the Presbyterian Task Force on Central America (UPCUSA) in Managua, in November 1982. Official spokespersons for the FMLN whom the Task Force also interviewed in Managua at that time agreed and went into detail about their intent to fight only until a negotiated settlement could be achieved. Thomas Walker, a member of the Task Force, was present at those meetings.

3. For more detail see "Epilogue: The 1996 National Elections," *Nicaragua Without Illusions: Regime Transition and Structural Adjustment in the 1990s*, Thomas W. Walker, ed. (Wilmington, DE: Scholarly Resources, 1997), pp. 306–307.

4. For an interesting attempt to interpret U.S. policy making in regard to the first Somoza in this way, see Paul Coe Clarke, Jr., *The United States and Somoza, 1933–1956: A Revisionist Look* (Westport, CT: Praeger Publishers, 1992).

5. The most articulate defense of the "practical" approach to regime types was made by Jeane J. Kirkpatrick in her article "Dictatorships and Double Standards," *Commentary* 68 (November 1979), pp. 34–45. In it Kirkpatrick, who soon became President Reagan's first ambassador to the United Nations and major adviser on Latin American affairs, argued that it was better to support "traditional autocracies" than run the risk of Communist totalitarian regimes.

6. The literature on democratization in Central America includes John A. Booth and Mitchell A. Seligson, eds., *Elections and Democracy in Central America* (Chapel Hill: University of North Carolina Press, 1989); Mitchell A. Seligson and John A. Booth, eds., *Elections and Democracy in Central America, Revisited* (Chapel Hill: University of North Carolina Press, 1995); Deborah J. Yashar, *Demanding Democracy: Reform and Reaction in Costa Rica and Guatemala, 1870s–1950s* (Stanford:

Stanford University Press, 1997); John A. Booth, *Costa Rica: Quest for Democracy* (Boulder: Westview Press, 1998); and Philip J. Williams and Knut Walter, *Militarization and Demilitarization in El Salvador's Transition to Democracy* (Pittsburgh: University of Pittsburgh Press, 1997). Among the major sources on democratization in Latin America that also include studies or discussion of Central America are John Peeler, *Latin American Democracies* (Chapel Hill: University of North Carolina Press, 1985); Larry Diamond, Juan Linz, and Seymour Martin Lipset, eds., *Democracy in Developing Countries,* Volume 4: *Latin America* (Boulder: Lynne Rienner Publishers, 1989); Guillermo O'Donnell, Philippe C. Schmitter, and Laurence Whitehead, eds. *Transitions from Authoritarian Rule: Latin America* (Baltimore: Johns Hopkins University Press, 1986); James M. Malloy and Mitchell A. Seligson, eds., *Authoritarians and Democrats: Regime Transition in Latin America* (Pittsburgh: University of Pittsburgh Press, 1987); Paul Drake and Eduardo Silva, eds., *Elections and Democratization in Latin America* (La Jolla, CA: Center for Iberian and Latin American Studies-Center for U.S.-Mexican Studies, University of California San Diego, 1986); and Dietrich Reuschemeyer, Evelyne Huber Stephens, and John D. Stephens, *Capitalist Development and Democracy* (Chicago: University of Chicago Press, 1992).

7. Michael Burton, Richard Gunther, and John Higley, "Introduction: Elite Transformations and Democratic Regimes," in John Higley and Richard Gunther, eds., *Elites and Democratic Consolidation in Latin America and Southern Europe* (Cambridge: Cambridge University Press, 1992, pp. 3–4) treat democratic consolidation somewhat differently than this—that is as equivalent to, rather than merely including, an elite settlement: "A *consolidated democracy* is a regime that meets all the procedural criteria of democracy and also in which all politically significant groups accept established political institutions and adhere to democratic rules of the game," p. 3.

8. See Peeler, *Latin American Democracies;* Burton et al., "Introduction: Elite Transformations . . . "; John A. Booth, "Elections and Democracy in Central America: A Framework for Analysis," in Booth and Seligson, *Elections and Democracy,* pp. 19–21; and Mitchell A. Seligson and John A. Booth, "Political Culture and Regime Type: Evidence from Nicaragua and Costa Rica," *Journal of Politics* 55 (August 1993), pp. 777–792.

9. Larry Diamond and Juan J. Linz, "Introduction: Politics, Society and Democracy in Latin America," in Diamond, Linz, and Lipset, *Democracy in Developing Countries,* Volume 4: *Latin America,* p. 15.

10. John A. Booth, "Toward Reconciliation and Democracy in Central America: Possible Roles for External Assistance," in Joaquín Roy, ed., *The Reconstruction of Central America: The Role of the European Community* (Coral Gables, FL: Iberian Studies Institute, University of Miami-European Community Research Institute, 1992), pp. 331–352; Diamond and Linz, "Introduction," pp. 10–17.

11. Diamond and Linz, "Introduction"; Samuel Huntington, *The Third Wave: Democratization in the Late Twentieth Century* (Norman: University of Oklahoma Press, 1991), pp. 208–316; Booth, "Elections and Democracy in Central America," pp. 16–21.

12. Peeler, *Latin American Democracies;* John Peeler, "Elites and Democracy in Central America," in John A. Booth and Mitchell A. Seligson, eds., *Elections and Democracy in Central America* (Chapel Hill: University of North Carolina Press, 1989); and John Peeler, "Autumn of the Oligarchs?" in Mitchell A. Seligson and John A. Booth, eds., *Elections and Democracy in Central America* (Chapel Hill: University of North Carolina Press, 1995).

13. Guatemala and Honduras have had at least two peaceful presidential turnovers to opposition parties, but Peeler sees lingering threats to democratic institutions in both. El Salvador and Nicaragua have, Peeler contends, both eliminated significant threats to democracy but neither had yet had two transitions to the opposition, by which he means to the former revolutionaries of the FSLN and FMLN. John Peeler, *Building Democracy in Latin America* (Boulder: Lynne Rienner, 2004), pp. 126–127.

14. John A. Booth and Patricia Bayer Richard, "Repression, Participation, and Democratic Norms in Urban Central America," *American Journal of Political Science* 40 (1996), pp. 1205–1232; and John A. Booth and Patricia Bayer Richard, "Civil Society, Political Capital, and Democratization in Central America," *Journal of Politics* 60 (August 1998), pp. 780–800.

15. See John A. Booth and Patricia Bayer Richard, "Revolution's Legacy: Residual Effects on Nicaraguan Participation and Attitudes in Comparative Context," *Latin American Politics and Society* (forthcoming Summer 2006).

16. Mark Ruhl, "Curbing Central America's Militaries," *Journal of Democracy* 15 (July 2004), pp. 137–151.

17. Ruhl, p. 148.

About the Book and Authors

Since the 1960s, political violence and war in Nicaragua, El Salvador, and Guatemala have taken 300,000 lives, displaced millions, and reversed decades of economic gains. Regional and international efforts to promote peace eventually brought negotiated ends to the region's wars. The politico-economic turmoil within the region and evolving policy in Washington also drove a process of regime change that by the late 1990s left all five Central American nations formally democratic. In this new, third edition of a widely praised book, two of the most respected writers on Central American politics examine the origins and development of the region's political conflicts, efforts to resolve them, and regional democratization. Highlights of the new edition include analyses of the peace processes and accords that ended the region's wars, the end of the Nicaraguan revolution and the Sandinistas' exit from power, recent elections, and the politics of the new civilian democratic regimes throughout the region.

The authors trace the roots of underdevelopment and crisis in the region by examining the shared and individual histories of the Central American nations. They offer a theory about regime change in Central America that explains both the rebellions of the 1970s and 1980s and the eventual development of civilian democratic regimes in all five nations. This theory accounts for the striking contrast between war-torn Guatemala, El Salvador, and Nicaragua and the stability of Costa Rica and Honduras. Booth and Walker examine the forces driving popular mobilization—economic change, liberation theology, and Marxism—and evaluate the dramatic changes in U.S. policy toward Central America since the early 1990s, and especially since the end of the cold war, as well as the implications of those changes for the future of the region.

John A. Booth is Regents Professor of Political Science at the University of North Texas. He is author of *The End and the Beginning: The Nicaraguan Revolution* and *Costa Rica: Quest for Democracy,* and has written widely on political conflict and democracy in Latin America.

Christine J. Wade is assistant professor of political science and international studies at Washington College. She is coauthor (with Tom Walker) of "Central America: From Revolution to Neoliberal Reform" in *Latin America: Its Problems and Its Promise*, edited by Jan Knippers Black.

Thomas W. Walker is professor of political science and director of Latin American Studies Program at Ohio University. He is author of *Nicaragua: Living in the Shadow of the Eagle* and *Nicaragua: The Land of Sandino,* and the editor/coauthor of *Reagan Versus the Sandinistas: The Undeclared War on Nicaragua* and *Nicaragua Without Illusions: Regime Transition and Structural Adjustment in the 1990s.*

Index